VIENNA TO SALZBURG

2nd Edition

Where to Stay and Eat
for All Budgets

Must-See Sights
and Local Secrets

Ratings You Can Trust

Excerpted from *Fodor's Austria*

Fodor's Travel Publications   New York, Toronto, London, Sydney, Auckland

www.fodors.com

FODOR'S VIENNA TO SALZBURG

Editor: Mary Beth Bohman, Christina Knight

Editorial Production: Tom Holton
Editorial Contributors: Mark Baker, Diane Naar-Elphee, Horst Ernst Reisenböck, Matthew Savage
Maps: David Lindroth, *cartographer;* Rebecca Baer and Bob Blake, *map editors*
Design: Fabrizio La Rocca, *creative director;* Guido Caroti, *art director;* Moon Sun Kim, *cover designer;* Melanie Marin, *senior picture editor*
Production/Manufacturing: Angela L. McLean
Cover Photo (Mozart Boys' Choir): Wiesenhofer/Austrian Views

SPECIAL SALES

This book is available for special discounts for bulk purchases for sales promotions or premiums. Special editions, including personalized covers, excerpts of existing books, and corporate imprints, can be created in large quantities for special needs. For more information, write to Special Markets/Premium Sales, 1745 Broadway, MD 6-2, New York, New York 10019, or e-mail specialmarkets@randomhouse.com.

AN IMPORTANT TIP & AN INVITATION

Although all prices, opening times, and other details in this book are based on information supplied to us at press time, changes occur all the time in the travel world, and Fodor's cannot accept responsibility for facts that become outdated or for inadvertent errors or omissions. So **always confirm information when it matters,** especially if you're making a detour to visit a specific place. Your experiences—positive and negative—matter to us. If we have missed or misstated something, **please write to us.** We follow up on all suggestions. Contact the Vienna to Salzburg editor at editors@fodors.com or c/o Fodor's at 1745 Broadway, New York, New York 10019.

Be a Fodor's Correspondent

Your opinion matters. It matters to us. It matters to your fellow Fodor's travelers, too. And we'd like to hear it. In fact, we *need* to hear it.

When you share your experiences and opinions, you become an active member of the Fodor's community. That means we'll not only use your feedback to make our books better, but we'll publish your names and comments whenever possible. Throughout our guides, look for "Word of Mouth," excerpts of your unvarnished feedback.

Here's how you can help improve Fodor's for all of us.

Tell us when we're right. We rely on local writers to give you an insider's perspective. But our writers and staff editors—who are the best in the business—depend on you. Your positive feedback is a vote to renew our recommendations for the next edition.

Tell us when we're wrong. We're proud that we update most of our guides every year. But we're not perfect. Things change. Hotels cut services. Museums change hours. Charming cafés lose charm. If our writer didn't quite capture the essence of a place, tell us how you'd do it differently. If any of our descriptions are inaccurate or inadequate, we'll incorporate your changes in the next edition and will correct factual errors at fodors.com *immediately.*

Tell us what to include. You probably have had fantastic travel experiences that aren't yet in Fodor's. Why not share them with a community of like-minded travelers? Maybe you chanced upon a coffeehouse or bed-and-breakfast that you don't want to keep to yourself. Tell us why we should include it. And share your discoveries and experiences with everyone directly at fodors.com. Your input may lead us to add a new listing or highlight a place we cover with a "Highly Recommended" star or with our highest rating, "Fodor's Choice."

Give us your opinion instantly at our feedback center at www.fodors.com/feedback. You may also e-mail editors@fodors.com with the subject line "Vienna to Salzburg Editor." Or send your nominations, comments, and complaints by mail to Vienna to Salzburg Editor, Fodor's, 1745 Broadway, New York, NY 10019.

You and travelers like you are the heart of the Fodor's community. Make our community richer by sharing your experiences. Be a Fodor's correspondent.

Tim Jarrell, Publisher

CONTENTS

MAPS

ABOUT THIS BOOK

Our Ratings

Sometimes you find terrific travel experiences and sometimes they just find you. But usually the burden is on you to select the right combination of experiences. That's where our ratings come in.

As travelers we've all discovered a place so wonderful that its worthiness is obvious. And sometimes that place is so unique that superlatives don't do it justice: you just have to be there to know. These sights, properties, and experiences get our highest rating, **Fodor's Choice**, indicated by orange stars throughout this book.

Black stars highlight sights and properties we deem **Highly Recommended**, places that our writers, editors, and readers praise again and again for consistency and excellence.

By default, there's another category: any place we include in this book is by definition worth your time, unless we say otherwise. And we will.

Disagree with any of our choices? Care to nominate a place or suggest that we rate one higher? Visit our feedback center at www. fodors.com/feedback.

Budget Well

Hotel and restaurant price categories from ¢ to $$$$ are defined in the opening pages of each chapter. For attractions, we always give standard adult admission fees; reductions are usually available for children, students, and senior citizens. Want to pay with plastic? **AE, D, DC, MC, V** following restaurant and hotel listings indicate whether American Express, Discover, Diner's Club, MasterCard, and Visa are accepted.

Restaurants

Unless we state otherwise, restaurants are open for lunch and dinner daily. We mention dress only when there's a specific requirement and reservations only when they're essential or not accepted—it's always best to book ahead.

Hotels

Hotels have private bath, phone, TV, and air-conditioning and operate on the European Plan (aka EP, meaning without meals), unless we specify that they use the Continental Plan (CP, with a Continental breakfast), Breakfast Plan (BP, with a full breakfast), or Modified American Plan (MAP, with breakfast and dinner) or are all-inclusive (AI, including all meals and most activities). We always

list facilities but not whether you'll be charged an extra fee to use them, so when pricing accommodations, find out what's included.

Many Listings

★	Fodor's Choice
★	Highly recommended
⊠	Physical address
⊹	Directions
⊄	Mailing address
☎	Telephone
🖷	Fax
⊕	On the Web
✆	E-mail
🖃	Admission fee
⊙	Open/closed times
►	Start of walk/itinerary
Ⓜ	Metro stations
🖃	Credit cards

Hotels & Restaurants

🏨	Hotel
⇪	Number of rooms
⚲	Facilities
ⅼⓄⅼ	Meal plans
✕	Restaurant
🖘	Reservations
🏛	Dress code
⚲	Smoking
⚱	BYOB
✕🏨	Hotel with restaurant that warrants a visit

Outdoors

🏌	Golf
⚑	Camping

Other

☺	Family-friendly
🛈	Contact information
⇨	See also
⊠	Branch address
☞	Take note

WHEN TO GO

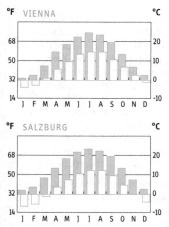

°F VIENNA °C

68 — — 20
50 — — 10
32 — — 0
14 — — -10
J F M A M J J A S O N D

°F SALZBURG °C

68 — — 20
50 — — 10
32 — — 0
14 — — -10
J F M A M J J A S O N D

Austria has two main tourist seasons. The weather usually turns glorious around Easter and holds until about mid-October, sometimes later. Because much of the country remains "undiscovered," you will usually find crowds only in the major cities and resorts. May and early June, September, and October are the most pleasant months for travel; there is less demand for restaurant tables, and hotel prices tend to be lower. A foreign invasion takes place between Christmas and New Year's Day and over the long Easter weekend, and hotel rooms in Vienna then are at a premium.

Climate

Austria has four distinct seasons, all fairly mild. But because of altitudes and the Alpine divide, temperatures and dampness vary considerably from one part of the country to another; for example, northern Austria's winter is often overcast and dreary, while the southern half of the country basks in sunshine. The eastern part of the country, especially Vienna and the areas near the Czech border, can become bitterly cold in winter. The *Föhn* is a wind that makes the country as a whole go haywire. It comes from the south, is warm, and announces itself by very clear air, blue skies, and long wisps of cloud. Whatever the reason, the Alpine people (all the way to Vienna) begin acting up: some become obnoxiously aggressive, others depressive; many people have headaches; and (allegedly) accident rates rise. The Föhn breaks with clouds and rain.

▶ Forecasts **Weather Channel Connection** (☎ 900/932-8437 95¢ a min ⊕ www.weather.com).

WHAT'S WHERE

VIENNA

Vienna is a white-glove yet modern metropolis. Its old-world charm is undeniable—a fact that the natives are ready to acknowledge and yet hate being reminded of. A walk through the city's neighborhoods—many dotted with masterpieces of Gothic, Baroque, and Secession architecture—offers a fascinating journey thick with history and peopled by the spirits of Empress Maria Theresa, Haydn, Beethoven, Metternich, Mozart, and Klimt. But there is also space and renown for an outrageous, antitraditional structure like Friedensreich Hundertwasser's modernist Hundertwasserhaus. The city's famous coffeehouses are havens for an age-old coffee-drinking ritual, but it's a ritual that every dutiful Viennese observes daily.

The city's vast holdings range from the Brueghels, Rembrandts, and Vermeers in the Kunsthistorisches Museum to the fabled modern-art collections in the gigantic Museums-Quartier complex, itself a Baroque landmark now fitted out with strikingly contemporary architectural additions. The Vienna of the past has inspired some of the world's most beautiful music, from Beethoven's *Pastoral Symphony* to Johann Strauss the Younger's "Blue Danube Waltz." These and other ineffable strains are heard nonstop in the Vienna of the present as well; the city is, after all, home to two of the world's greatest symphony orchestras and is graced with a top opera house as well as a world-renowned concert hall. And Vienna comes alive during the "Merry Season"—the first two months of the year—when raised trumpets and opera capes adorn its great Fasching balls; then more than ever, Vienna moves in three-quarter time.

THE DANUBE VALLEY

The famously blue Danube courses through Austria on its way from the Black Forest to the Black Sea, past medieval abbeys, fanciful Baroque monasteries, verdant pastures, and compact riverside villages. Though the river's hue is now somewhat less than pristine, this is still one of Europe's most important waterways, and to traverse its scenic length is to immerse yourself in history and culture. In enchantingly picturesque Dürnstein, Richard the Lion-Hearted spent a spell locked in a dungeon. Not far away, the Nibelungs—immortalized by Wagner—caroused at the top of their lungs in battlemented forts. For nonpareil splendor, head to Melk Abbey, best appreciated in the late afternoon when the setting sun lights the twin towers cradling its Baroque dome. In addition to Melk,

the Wachau Valley—"crown jewel of the Austrian landscape"—includes the castle of Burg Kreuzenstein.

SALZKAMMERGUT

The Salzkammergut stretches across three states—from Salzburg through Styria to Upper Austria. The region's name means "salt estates," and indeed the entire economy has been based on salt mining for millennia, but this unappealing moniker doesn't begin to do justice to the gorgeous scenery in Austria's Lake District. Think of *The Sound of Music,* filmed here on the home turf of the Trapp family, and you will easily envision the region's scenic pleasures. It would be hard to choose the region's prettiest lake. The clear blue Wolfgangsee, with the popular vacation village of St. Wolfgang on its shores, or the Traunsee, reflecting Schloss Orth in its breeze-rippled surface? Whichever you choose, you will be inspired.

SALZBURG

Depending on who is describing this elegant city filled with gilded salons, palatial mansions, and Italianate churches, Salzburg is alternately known as the "Golden City of the High Baroque," the "Austrian Rome," or, thanks to its position astride the River Salzach, the "Florence of the North." What you choose to call this beloved city will depend on what brings you here. It may well be music, of course, as Mozart was born here in 1756. His operas and symphonies ripple through the city constantly, most particularly during its acclaimed, celebrity-packed, summer music festival. Art lovers, on the other hand, will pounce on the city's heritage of Baroque churches, cloistered abbeys, and Rococo palaces, and, inevitably, climb the hill to Hohensalzburg, the brooding medieval fortress whose lavish state rooms are belied by its grim exterior. Many come here to follow in the footsteps of the Trapp family, or, at least, their Hollywood counterparts, as many of the city's most celebrated sights were used as ageless backdrops for that beloved Oscar-winner, *The Sound of Music.* Music may top the bill for some, but everyone will enjoy the stupendous panoply of churches and museums, old-fashioned cafés, narrow medieval streets, and glorious fountains.

QUINTESSENTIAL AUSTRIA

The Viennese Coffeehouse

Twice the Ottoman armies stood at the gates of Vienna (in the 16th and 17th centuries), and twice they were turned back after long, bitter sieges. Although the Turks never captured the city, they left a lasting legacy: the art of preparing and consuming coffee. Emotions about coffee tend to run high throughout Austria: Ask anyone on the street where you can get a good cup of coffee or homemade *Apfelstrudel,* and you're likely to get a lengthy and passionate exposition on why you must try a certain coffeehouse. Many Austrians spend a good part of the day sitting over a single cup of coffee in their favorite coffeehouse while reading the newspaper, discussing business or politics, or just catching up on the local gossip. As any Austrian will tell you, many of the world's great cultural moments had their genesis in coffeehouse discussions in Vienna. You'll hear about where Leo Trotsky regularly played chess while working out the subtleties of Communist theory (at Café Central), where Gustav Klimt and Egon Schiele worked out their ideas for modern art (Café Museum), and where Sigmund Freud spent Wednesday evenings laying the foundation for modern psychoanalytic theory (Kaffeehaus Korb). Although more and more generic Italian espresso bars and even Starbuck's coffee shops (gasp!) are cropping up in urban areas, these fulfill another purpose entirely and cannot begin to compete with the role the traditional Viennese coffeehouse has in defining Austrian identity.

The Outdoors

"Land der Berge, Land am Strome" ("Land of mountains, land on the river") is the first verse of the Austrian national anthem, and it sums up what Austrians treasure most about their country: the breathtaking and diverse landscapes. Austrians take every opportunity they can to get out and enjoy their nat-

If you want to get a sense of contemporary Austrian culture and indulge in some of its pleasure, start by familiarizing yourself with the rituals of daily life. These are a few highlights—things you can take part in with relative ease.

ural surroundings. A few hours during the workday is time enough to head for the hiking path. On weekends, the autobahn is clogged with Mercedes and BMWs with skis or bikes strapped to their tops. The mania for the outdoors transcends all age groups. Ten-year-olds, determined to follow in the footsteps of great Austrian skiers like Hermann Maier, will overtake you on the ski slope. And on a warm summer day when you finally reach that mountain hut in an Alpine meadow near the peak, out of breath after a five-hour hike, you'll find a score of seventy-year-olds who beat you there, occupying the best spots and enjoying glasses of schnapps and beer on the sunny terrace.

Music

Austrians are serious about their music. Cities and towns vie to put their special venue or music festival in the limelight. Top of the bill is of course Vienna, with such world-renowned institutions as the Vienna State Opera and the Vienna Philharmonic Orchestra. But even the Viennese are prepared to make the seven-hour journey to Bregenz, where elaborate opera productions on a giant stage overlooking Lake Constance occur every summer. Summer evenings in the Alps can often be quite chilly and wet, but music-hungry Austrians will brave even a downpour, sitting on heavy blankets and wearing parkas. Other events, such as the annual Salzburg festival, provide the perfect backdrop for society-conscious Austrians who gather in their most opulent evening attire to admire each other (and to hear good music, too). Such spectacles, however, are more the exception than the rule. Many Viennese, dressed only in jeans and a pullover, will go several times a week to the opera. They won't pay the high price for a seat but instead pay a few euros for a spot in the standing room (where they know the acoustics are better anyway).

IF YOU LIKE

Wine

Vienna is famous for: coffee houses, of course; music, of course. But wines? It might come as a surprise to hear that Vienna has quietly become a sensation in viticulture, especially in the last ten years. Local, home-grown wines have started to gather top awards and accolades from around the world. And although traditionally Vienna is a white wine area, many reds are making their mark, too. To be fair, it should be said that in all of Austria there are 16 different wine growing regions, with a total of 32,000 farms with vineyards; the Weinviertel being the largest area, Vienna the smallest. Nevertheless, in Vienna alone there are 22 wine growers. A *Heuriger*, or Buschenschank, is a rustic inn owned by a local wine producer serving exclusively his or her own wine, and it is the best place to start a discovery tour. Remember, too, that the name "Heuriger" also indicates the wine of this year's harvest. Cheers!

- **Wieninger, Stammersdorf.** You can taste by the glass and buy by the bottle in a friendly and relaxed atmosphere here at one of Vienna's top wine taverns. Fritz Wieninger creates a dry and fruity veltliner, tasty riesling, full-bodied chardonnay, and robust red wines, such as Blauburgunder and Danubis.

- **Vienna Heurigen Express.** Take a ride on the Vienna Heurigen Express, passing through picturesque wine-growing villages and past old winegrowers' homes via Kahlenberg and Grinzing.

- **Wein & Co.** If you don't have time for a tavern trip, don't worry. Head straight to an outlet of this specialty shop in Vienna for tasting and purchasing.

Castles, Palaces & Abbeys

It seems hard to travel a few miles in any direction in Austria and not be confronted with a fairy-tale castle, an ostentatious palace, or an ornate Baroque abbey. And for this very reason, it's easy to become overwhelmed by all the architectural splendor, the fanciful decorations, and the often impossibly intricate mythical lore attached to these sites. The secret to overcoming the "not-another-castle" syndrome is to take your time at each site, and not to limit yourself to the site alone.

Discover how rewarding it can be to leave the palace grounds or ancient castle walls and explore the surroundings, whether a city, small village, or mountainside. Around the corner might be a lovely chapel, a spectacular view, or an excellent local restaurant that, because it is somewhat off the beaten path and perhaps not (yet) in any guidebook, is yours alone to appreciate.

- **Schönbrunn Palace, Vienna.** You could spend an entire day here (and still not see all the rooms in the palace), or choose from several shorter tours of one of Austria's premier attractions, built by Empress Maria Theresa.

- **Melk, Lower Austria.** Perched on a hill overlooking the Danube and the Wachau, about 40 minutes outside Vienna, the giant abbey of Melk features imposing architecture, lovely gardens, and one of Europe's most resplendent Baroque libraries.

- **Fortress Hohensalzburg, Salzburg.** The medieval fortress, central Europe's largest, towers over the city of Salzburg and offers lavish state rooms, a collection of medieval art, a late-Gothic chapel, and magnificent views over the entire region.

Biking

Over the last decade or so, Austria has invested a lot in the construction and maintenance of thousands of kilometers of cycle routes along its rivers and through its lush valleys. The close proximity of many sites of interest means that cycling is often the best means of leisurely exploration. Many hotels now provide bikes to their guests for a nominal fee, or your hotel can direct you to a nearby bike rental shop. You will need a Radkarte (a map with the local bike routes), available also at hotels or at the local tourist office. Here are some of the best routes that combine cultural attractions with stimulating landscapes:

- **The Wachau, Lower Austria.** The Donauradweg–or Danube bike route–follows the Danube all the way from Passau to Vienna. The Wachau is not far from Vienna, and it offers one of the most spectacular landscapes along Austria's stretch of the Danube. Very-well-kept bike paths take you past the Baroque abbey of Melk and through the charming wine-making towns. The best time to go is spring, when the apricot trees are in glorious blossom, or in early fall, when grapes hang ripe and heavy on the vines of the terraced slopes.

- **Mozart Radweg, Salzburg.** The Mozart Route is a circuit around Salzburg, the city where the great musician was born. Leaving Salzburg the route passes through stations associated with Mozart's life and work, and continues on through the Salzburger Seenland, an arrestingly beautiful landscape of mountain lakes, castles, and small villages.

Museums

The museum landscape in Vienna today leaves nothing to be desired. Whether it's the ancient or the unfamiliar, the eccentric or the avant-garde—you're sure to find it in Austria's capital city. Salzburg too aims to impress, honoring composers, treasuring Hallstatt-era relics, and celebrating contemporary art with it own collection of collections. As there are over 100 museums in Vienna, plus Salzburg's offerings, choosing what to make time for can be hard. Some ideas:

- **Kunsthistorisches Museum, Vienna.** With its glory and grandeur, the Museum of Fine Art warrants first place on the list. The picture gallery contains the greatest works that the Venetian Renaissance (Titian, Veronese, Tintoretto) brought forth but also includes major works of the Flemish masters (van Eyck, Rubens, van Dyck).

- **Belvedere (Austrian Picture Gallery), Vienna.** Take your pick of the period around 1900. Gustav Klimt's "Kiss" is the highlight of the collection, followed by works from Oskar Kokoschka and Egon Schiele representing Austrian Early Expressionism.

- **Schatzkammer (Treasury), Vienna.** The crown of the Holy Roman Empire and the liturgical vestments of the order of the golden fleece alone make a trip to the Hofburg worthwhile.

- **Museum der Moderne, Salzburg.** Enjoy the classic view from Salzburg's traditional scenic overlook (even Maria and the kids made a stop here in *Sound of Music*), then head inside this strikingly modern structure for a glimpse of the most cutting-edge contemporary art.

ON THE
CALENDAR

Hundreds of festivals and events are held annually in Austria. Here are some of the better known and better attended in and around Vienna and Salzburg. If you plan to visit during one of them, book well in advance.

WINTER
December

The world-famous Christkindlmärkte set up shop in various locales in major cities in Austria. In Vienna the biggest Christmas Market goes up in late November in the plaza in front of the city's Rathaus (town hall); there are smaller ones in the Spittelberg Quarter and on the Freyung square, as well as famous markets that open during the Advent season in both Salzburg and Graz. The Christmas Eve service in the tiny memorial chapel at Oberndorf, north of Salzburg, features the singing of "Silent Night," written by Franz Gruber when he was organist here in the early 19th century. The New Year opens in Vienna with the world-famous concert by the Wiener Philharmoniker Orchestra (☎ 01/505–6525 ⊕ www.musikverein.at); write a year—or more—in advance. Those who can't get into the philharmonic concert can try for one of the performances of the Johann Strauss operetta *Die Fledermaus* or another light delight in the Volksoper (☎ 01/513–1513 ⊕ www.volksoper.at) or at the intimate Kammeroper (☎ 01/513–1513). The New Year is marked by an array of balls, such as the Kaiserball (☎ 01/587–3666–14), held in the elegant rooms of the Hofburg.

January

On January 6 children disguised as the Magi walk the streets, especially out in the country, knock at doors, sing a song and recite poems about coming from afar, and ask for a small donation. They then chalk a "C+M+B" and the year on entrance-door frames to bless the house for a year. Also special at this time is the ancient pre-Christian custom of the *Perchtenlauf,* masked figures that go on a rampage, mostly found in Salzburg Province, in Bad Gastein, for example.

Week of January 27

Mozart's Birthday (☎ 0662/889400 ⊕ www.mozarteum.at) is celebrated in Salzburg with Mozart Week, a festival organized by the city's Mozarteum, featuring operas, recitals, and theme concerts.

February

Fasching (or Fasnacht, as its called in the western part of the country), the Carnival period before Lent, can become very wild, with huge processions of disguised figures, occasional unwilling participation by spectators, who may even suffer (light) blows. The entire country starts going to dances—and the ball season begins. In Vienna, which is comparatively quiet at this time, the ball season opens on the Thursday before Fasching and lasts through Shrove

	Tuesday (Mardi Gras). The biggest gala is the Opernball (Opera Ball), held at the **Staatsoper** (☎ 01/514–44–2606 ⊕ www.staatsoper.at).
SPRING Late March–early April	Easter Festival (⊕ www.osterfestspiele-salzburg.at), Salzburg's "other" major music festival, offers opera and concerts of the highest quality, with ticket prices to match.
Mid-May–mid-June	The Wiener Festwochen (⊕ www.festwochen.at)—a festival of theater, music, films, and exhibitions—takes over Vienna.
Late May–early June	The religious holiday Corpus Christi is celebrated—on the second Thursday after Pentecost, falling in either late May or early—throughout Austria with colorful processions and parades. In the Lungau region of Salzburg Province, villagers dress up in local costumes. Equally colorful are the processions of gaily decorated boats and barges on the Traun and Hallstätter lakes.
SUMMER June 21	Midsummer Night is ablaze with bonfires throughout the country, the liveliest celebrations taking place in the Wachau region along the Danube in Lower Austria.
Last week of July–August	The Salzburger Festspiele (⊕ www.salzburgfestival.at) bring together the world's greatest musical artists for a citywide celebration, many events and performances revolving around the town's most famous native son, Mozart.
FALL September 1	This date marks the start of Vienna's theater and music season.

Vienna

WORD OF MOUTH

"Try for one of Vienna's top restaurants for lunch or dinner. There is SO much more to Austrian cuisine than Wiener schnitzel! Fortunately, you have many [restaurants] to choose from and, compared to the top restaurants in Paris and London, they're quite reasonably priced."

—BTilke

"The public transit in the city is fabulous. Buy a travel card and don't even consider a car. Even getting into the countryside can be done by streetcar."

—almcd

"To get out of the rain one day, we ended up at the Butterfly Museum and loved it . . . the butterflies tickle when they land on you."

—llopez

Updated by
Diane Naar-
Elphee

PROPER CITIZENS OF VIENNA, it has been said, waltz only from the waist down, holding their upper bodies ramrod straight while whirling around the crowded dance floor. The movement resulting from this correct posture is breathtaking in its sweep and splendor, and its elegant coupling of free-wheeling exuberance and rigid formality—of license and constraint—is quintessentially Viennese. The town palaces all over the inner city—built mostly during the 18th century—present in stone and stucco a similar artful synthesis. They make Vienna a Baroque city that is, at its best, an architectural waltz.

Those who tour Vienna today might feel they're keeping step in three-quarter time. As they explore churches filled with gilt statues of saints and cheeky cherubs, wander through treasure-packed museums, or take in the delights of a mecca of mocha (the ubiquitous cafés), they may feel destined to enjoy repeated helpings of the beloved *Schlagobers,* the rich, delicious whipped cream that garnishes the most famous Viennese pastry of all, the Sachertorte. The city's ambience is predominantly ornate: white horses dance to elegant music; snow frosts the opulent draperies of Empress Maria Theresa's monument, set in the formal patterns of "her" lovely square; a gilt Johann Strauss plays perpetually amid a grove of trees; town houses present a dignified face to the outside world while enclosing lavishly decorated interior courtyards; dark Greek legends are declawed by the voluptuous music of Richard Strauss; Klimt's paintings glitter with geometric impasto; a mechanical clock intones the hour with a stately pavane. All these will create in the visitor the sensation of a metropolis that likes to be visited and admired—and which indeed is well worth visiting and admiring.

For centuries this has been the case. One of the great capitals of Europe, Vienna was for centuries the main stamping grounds for the Habsburg rulers of the Austro-Hungarian Empire. The empire is long gone, but many reminders of the city's imperial heyday remain, carefully preserved by the tradition-loving Viennese. When it comes to the arts, the glories of the past are particularly evergreen, thanks to the cultural legacy created by the many artistic geniuses nourished here.

From the late 18th century on, Vienna's culture—particularly its music—was famous throughout Europe. Haydn, Mozart, Beethoven, Schubert, Brahms, Strauss, Mahler, and Bruckner all lived in the city, composing glorious music still played in concert halls all over the world. And at the tail end of the 19th century the city's artists and architects—Gustav Klimt, Egon Schiele, Oskar Kokoschka, Josef Hoffmann, Otto Wagner, and Adolf Loos ("Form follows function") among them—brought about an unprecedented artistic revolution, a revolution that swept away the past and set the stage for the radically experimental art of the 20th century. Innovation can still be seen in the city's contemporary arts-and-crafts galleries—even in the glinting, Space Needle–like object that hovers over the north end of Vienna—actually the city's waste incinerator, designed by the late, great artist Friedensreich Hundertwasser.

At the close of World War I the Austro-Hungarian Empire was dismembered, and Vienna lost its cherished status as the seat of imperial power.

GREAT ITINERARIES

Like a well-bred grande dame, Vienna doesn't rush about, and neither should you. Saunter through its stately streets—and rub elbows with its creative spirits—and marvel at its Baroque palaces. Then dream an afternoon away at a cozy *Kaffeehaus*.

IF YOU HAVE 3 DAYS

Begin with an organized sightseeing tour, which will describe the highlights. Plan to spend time at the **Stephansdom** ① and a full afternoon at **Schönbrunn Palace** (78). Reserve the second day for art, tackling the exciting **Kunsthistoriches Museum** (51) before lunch, and after you're refreshed, the dazzling **MuseumsQuartier** (52), which comprises several major modern art collections. If your tastes tend to the grand and royal, visit instead the magnificent collection of Old Master drawings at the **Albertina Museum** (67) and the impressive **Belvedere Palace** (75). Do as the Viennese do, and fill in any gaps with stops at cafés, reserving evenings for relaxing over music or wine. On the third day, head for the world-famous **Spanische Reitschule** ㉞ and watch the Lipizzaners prance through morning training. While you're in the neighborhood, view the sparkling court jewels in the Imperial Treasury, the **Schatzkammer** ㊸, and the glitzy **Silberkammer** ㊵, the museum of court silver and tableware, and take in one of Vienna's most spectacular Baroque settings, the glorious Grand Hall of the **Hofbibliothek** ㊲. For a total contrast, head out to the Prater amusement park in late afternoon for a ride on the giant Ferris wheel and end the day in a wine restaurant on the outskirts, perhaps in Sievering or Nussdorf.

IF YOU HAVE 5 DAYS

Spend your first three days as outlined above. On your fourth day, get better acquainted with the 1st District—the heart of the city. Treasures here range from Roman ruins to the residences of Mozart and Beethoven, the **Mozarthaus** (63) and the **Pasqualatihaus** ㉑; then, slightly afield, the **Freud Haus** (60) (in the 9th District) or the oddball **Hundertwasserhaus** (in the 3rd). Put it all in contemporary perspective with a backstage tour of the magnificent **Staatsoper** (68), the State Opera. On the fifth day, fill in some of the blanks with a stroll around the **Naschmarkt** (71) food-market district, taking in the nearby **Secession Building** (70) with Gustav Klimt's famous *Beethoven Frieze*. Don't overlook the superb Jugendstil buildings on the north side of the market. If you're still game for museums, head for any one of the less usual offerings, such as the Jewish Museum, the Haus der Musik, or the Ephesus Museum in the **Hofburg**, or visit the city's historical museum, **Wien Museum Karlsplatz** (74); by now, you'll have acquired a good concept of the city and its background, so the exhibits will make more sense. Cap the day by visiting the **Kaisergruft** (66) in the Kapuzinerkirche to view the tombs of the Habsburgs responsible for so much of Vienna.

Its influence was much reduced, and its population began to decline (unlike that of Europe's other great cities), falling from around 2 million to the current 1.8 million. Today, however, the city's future looks brighter, for with the collapse of the Iron Curtain, Vienna regained its traditional status as one of the main hubs of Central Europe.

For many first-time visitors the city's one major disappointment concerns the Danube River. The inner city, it turns out, does not lie on the river's main course but on one of its narrow offshoots, known as the Danube Canal. As a result, the expected sweeping river views fail to materialize.

For this the Romans are to blame, for when Vienna was founded as a Roman military encampment around AD 100, the walled garrison was not built not on the Danube's main stream. The wide, present-day Danube did not take shape until the late 19th century, when, to prevent flooding, its various branches were rerouted and merged.

The Romans maintained their camp for some 300 years (the emperor Marcus Aurelius is thought to have died in Vindobona, as it was called, in 180), not abandoning the site until around 400. The settlement survived the Roman withdrawal, however, and by the 13th century development was sufficient to require new city walls to the south. According to legend, the walls were financed by the English: in 1192 the local duke kidnapped England's King Richard I (the Lion-Hearted), en route home from the Third Crusade, and held him prisoner upriver in Dürnstein for several months then turned him over to the Austrian king after two years, until he was expensively ransomed by his mother, Eleanor of Aquitaine.

Vienna's third set of walls dates from 1544, when the existing walls were improved and extended. The new fortifications were built by the Habsburg dynasty, which ruled the Austro-Hungarian Empire for an astonishing 640 years, beginning with Rudolf I in 1273 and ending with Karl I in 1918. These walls stood until 1857, when Emperor Franz Josef decreed that they finally be demolished and replaced by the series of boulevards that make up the famous tree-lined Ringstrasse.

During medieval times the city's growth was relatively slow, and its heyday as a European capital did not begin until 1683, after a huge force of invading Turks laid siege to the city for a two-month period before being routed by an army of Habsburg allies. Among the supplies that the fleeing Turks left behind were sacks filled with coffee beans, and it was these beans, so the story goes, that gave a local entrepreneur the idea of opening the first public coffeehouse; they remain a Viennese institution to this day.

The passing of the Turkish threat encouraged a Viennese building boom in the Baroque style, the architectural choice of the day. Flamboyant, triumphant, joyous, and extravagantly ostentatious, the new art form—imported from Italy—transformed the city into a vast theater over the course of the 17th and 18th centuries. Life became a dream—the gorgeous dream of the Baroque, with its gilt madonnas and cherubs; its soaring, twisted columns; its painted heavens on ceilings; its graceful domes.

TOP REASONS TO GO

Ride the Ringstrasse. Hop on streetcar No. 1 or No. 2 and travel full circle along Vienna's best-known avenue. Those monumental buildings along it reflect the Imperial splendor of yesteryear.

World of Music. Delight your eyes and ears with a night out at the State Opera or Musikverein to experience what secured Vienna the title "heart of the music world."

Kunst Historisches Museum. Enjoy the classic collection of fine art, including the best of Breughel and Titian, at Austria's leading museum.

Schönbrunn Palace. Rococo romantics and Habsburg acolytes should step back in time and spend a half day experiencing the Habsburgs' former summer home.

An extended coffee break. Savor the true flavor of Vienna at some of its great café landmarks. Every afternoon at 4 the coffee-and-pastry ritual of *Kaffeejause* takes place from one end of the city to the other. For historical overtones, head for the Café Central or the opulent Café Landtmann, or elegant Café Sacher. Café Hawelka is seat of the smoky art scene.

In the early 19th century a reaction began to set in as middle-class industriousness and sober family values led the way to a new epoch characterized by the Biedermeier style. Then followed the Strauss era—that lighthearted period that conjures up imperial balls, "Wine, Women, and Song," heel clicking, and hand kissing. Today's visitors will find that each of these eras has left its mark on Vienna, making it a city filled with a special grace. It is this grace that gives Vienna the cohesive architectural character that sets the city so memorably apart from its great rivals—London, Paris, and Rome.

EXPLORING VIENNA

Most of Vienna lies roughly within an arc of a circle with the straight line of the Danube Canal as its chord. The most prestigious address of city's 23 *Bezirke,* or districts, is its heart, the **Innere Stadt** ("Inner City"), or 1st District, bounded by the Ringstrasse (Ring). The fabled 1st District holds the vast majority of sightseeing attractions and once encompassed the entire city. In 1857 Emperor Franz Josef decided to demolish the ancient wall surrounding the city to create the more cosmopolitan Ringstrasse, the multilane avenue that still encircles the expansive heart of Vienna. At that time several small villages bordering the inner city were given district numbers and incorporated into Vienna. Today the former villages go by their official district number, but they are sometimes referred to by their old village or neighborhood name, too.

The circular 1st District is bordered on its northeastern section by the Danube Canal and 2nd District, and clockwise from there along the Ringstrasse by the 3rd, 4th, 6th, 7th, 8th, and 9th districts. The 2nd District—Leopoldstadt—is home to the venerable Prater amusement park with its famous *Riesenrad* (Ferris wheel), as well as a huge park used for horseback riding and jogging. Along the southeastern edge of the 1st District is the 3rd District—Landstrasse—containing a number of embassies and the famed Belvedere Palace. Extending from its southern tip, the 4th District—Wieden—is fast becoming Vienna's new hip area, with trendy restaurants, art galleries, and shops, plus Vienna's biggest outdoor market, the Naschmarkt, which is lined with dazzling Jugendstil buildings.

The southwestern 6th District—Mariahilf—includes the biggest shopping street, Mariahilferstrasse, where small, old-fashioned shops compete with smart restaurants, movie theaters, bookstores, and department stores. Directly west of the 1st District is the 7th District—Neubau. Besides the celebrated Kunsthistorisches Museum and headline-making MuseumsQuartier, the 7th District also houses the charming Spittelberg quarter, its cobblestone streets lined with beautifully preserved 18th-century houses. Moving up the western side you come to the 8th District—Josefstadt—which is known for its theaters, good restaurants, and antiques shops. And completing the circle surrounding the Innere Stadt on its northwest side is the 9th District—Alsergrund—once Sigmund Freud's neighborhood and today a nice residential area with lots of outdoor restaurants, curio shops, and lovely early-20th-century apartment buildings.

The other districts—the 5th, and the 10th through the 23rd—form a concentric second circle around the 2nd through 9th districts. These are mainly suburbs and only a few hold sights of interest for tourists. The 11th District—Simmering—contains one of Vienna's architectural wonders, Gasometer, a former gas works that has been remodeled into a housing and shopping complex. The 13th District—Hietzing—whose centerpiece is the fabulous Schönbrunn Palace, is also a coveted residential area, including the neighborhood Hütteldorf. The 19th District—Döbling—is Vienna's poshest neighborhood and also bears the nickname the "Noble District" because of all the embassy residences on its chestnut-tree-lined streets. The 19th District also incorporates several other neighborhoods within its borders, in particular, the wine villages of Grinzing, Sievering, Nussdorf, and Neustift am Walde. The 22nd District—Donaustadt—now headlines Donau City, a modern business and shopping complex that has grown around the United Nations center. The 22nd also has several grassy spots for bathing and sailboat watching along the Alte Donau (Old Danube).

It may be helpful to know the neighborhood names of other residential districts. These are: the 5th/Margareten; 10th/Favoriten; 12th/Meidling; 14th/Penzing; 15th/Fünfhaus; 16th/Ottakring; 17th/Hernals; 18th/Währing; 20th/Brigittenau; 21st/Floridsdorf; and 23rd/Liesing. For neighborhood site listings below—*except* the 1st District—both the district and neighborhood name will be given.

■ TIP➔ For hard-core sightseers who wish to supplement the key attractions that follow, the tourist office has a booklet, "Vienna from A–Z" (€3.60), that gives short descriptions of some 250 sights around the city, all numbered and keyed to a fold-out map at the back, as well as to numbered wall plaques on the buildings themselves.

Vienna is a city to explore and discover on foot. The description of the city on the following pages is divided into eight areas: seven that explore the architectural riches of central Vienna and an eighth that describes Schönbrunn Palace and its gardens. Above all, *look up* as you tour Vienna: some of the most fascinating architectural and ornamental bits are on upper stories or atop the city's buildings.

Numbers in the text correspond to numbers in the margin and on the Exploring Vienna, Hofburg, and Schönbrunn Palace maps.

The Medieval Heart of the Inner City

For more than eight centuries, the enormous bulk of the Stephansdom has remained the nucleus around which the city has grown. Vienna of the Middle Ages is encapsulated behind the cathedral. You could easily spend half a day or more just prowling the narrow streets and passageways—Wollzeile, Bäckerstrasse, Blutgasse—typical remnants of an early era. Stephansplatz is the logical starting point from which to track down Vienna's past and present, as well as any acquaintance (natives believe that if you wait long enough at this intersection of eight streets you'll run into anyone you're searching for).

**A GOOD
WALK**

Within a largely pedestrian zone, the **Stephansdom** ❶, the mighty cathedral, marks the point from which distances to and from Vienna are measured. Take your first step here and then wander up the Wollzeile, cutting through the narrow Essiggasse and right into the Bäckerstrasse, to the **Universitätskirche** ❷ or Jesuitenkirche, a lovely Jesuit church. Note the contrasting Academy of Science diagonally opposite (Beethoven premiered his "Battle Symphony"—today more commonly known as "Wellington's Victory"—in its Ceremonial Hall). Follow the Sonnenfelsgasse, ducking through one of the tiny alleys on the right to reach the Bäckerstrasse; turn right at Gutenbergplatz into the Köllnerhofgasse, right again into tiny Grashofgasse, and go through the gate into the surprising **Heiligenkreuzerhof** ❸, a peaceful oasis (unless a handicrafts market is taking place). Through the square, enter the **Schönlaterngasse** (Beautiful Lantern Street) to admire the house fronts—film companies at times block this street to take shots of the picturesque atmosphere—on your way to the **Dominikanerkirche** ❹, the Dominican church with its marvelous Baroque interior. Head east two blocks to that repository of Jugendstil treasures, the **Museum für Angewandte Kunst (MAK)** ❺, then head north along the Stubenring to enjoy the architectural contrast of the **Postsparkasse** ❻ and former War Ministry, facing each other. Retrace your steps, following Postgasse into the Fleischmarkt to savor the famous inn **Griechenbeisl** ❼. The immediate neighborhood, dotted with cobbled lanes, is one of Vienna's most time-stained areas and a delight to explore. Nearby Hoher Markt, reached by taking Rotenturmstrasse west to Lichtensteg or Bauernmarkt, was part of the early Roman encampment, witness the Roman ruins under **Hoher Markt** ❽. The extension of Fleischmarkt ends in a set of stairs leading up past the eccentric Kornhäusel Tower. Up the

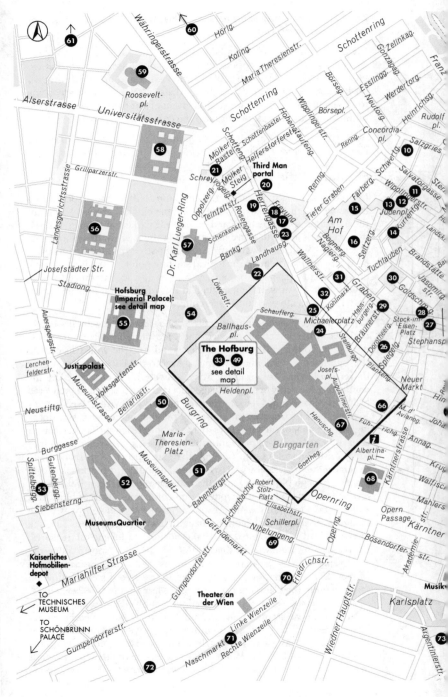

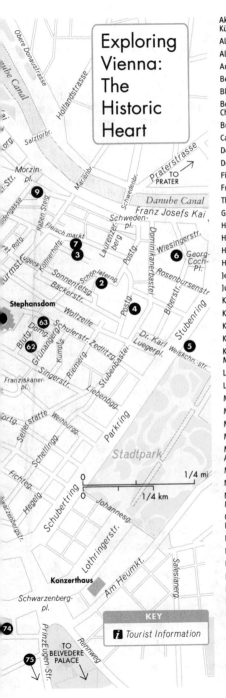

Exploring Vienna: The Historic Heart

KEY

ℹ *Tourist Information*

stairs to the right on Ruprechtsplatz is the **Ruprechtskirche** ⑨, St. Rupert's Church, allegedly the city's oldest. Take Sterngasse down the steps, turn left into Marc-Aurel-Strasse and right into Salvatorgasse to discover the lacework **Maria am Gestade** ⑩, which once sat above a small river, now underground.

TIMING   If you're pressed for time and happy with facades rather than what's behind them, this route could take half a day, but if you love to look inside and stop to ponder and explore the myriad narrow alleys, figure at least a day for this walk.

Main Attractions

★ ❼ **Griechenbeisl** (The "Greeks' Tavern"). If you want to find a Vienna nook-erie where time seems to be holding its breath, head to the intersection of the Fleischmarkt (Meat Market) street and the picturesque, hilly, cobble-stoned, and tiny Griechengasse. Part of the city's oldest core, this street has a medieval feel that is quite genuine, thanks to Vienna's only surviving 14th-century watchtower, houses bearing statues of the Virgin Mary, and the enchanting scene that presents you at the intersecting streets: an ivy-covered tavern, the Griechenbeisl, which has been in business for some 500 years, "*seit 1447.*" Half a millennium ago, this quarter was settled by Greek and Levantine traders (there are still many Near Eastern rug dealers here) and many of them made this tavern their "local." The wooden carving on the facade of the current restaurant commemorates Max Augustin—best known today from the song "Ach du lieber Augustin"—an itinerant musician who sang here during the plague of 1679. A favored Viennese figure, he managed to fall into a pit filled with plague victims but survived intact, presumably because he was so pickled in alcohol. In fact, this tavern introduced one of the great Pilsner brews of the 19th century and everyone—from Schubert to Mark Twain, Wagner to Johann Strauss—came here to partake. Be sure to dine here to savor its low-vaulted rooms adorned with engravings, mounted antlers, and bric-a-brac; the Mark Twain Zimmer has a ceiling covered with autographs of the rich and famous dating back two centuries. Adjacent to the tavern is a Greek Orthodox Church partly designed by the most fashionable Neo-classical designer in Vienna, Theophil Hansen. ⊠ *Fleischmarkt 11, 1st District* ☎ *01/533–1941* ⊕ *www.griechenbeisl.at/* Ⓤ *U1 or U4/Schwedenplatz.*

⑩ **Maria am Gestade** (St. Mary on the Banks). The middle-Gothic, seven-sided tower of Maria am Gestade, crowned by a delicate cupola, is a sheer joy to the eye and dispels the idea that Gothic must necessarily be austere. Built around 1400 (but much restored in the 17th and 19th centuries), the church incorporated part of the Roman city walls into its foundation; the north wall, as a result, takes a slight but noticeable dogleg to the right halfway down the nave. Like St. Stephen's, Maria am Gestade is rough-hewn Gothic, with a simple but forceful facade. The church is especially beloved, however, because of its unusual details—the pinnacled and saint-bedecked gable that tops the front facade, the stone canopy that hovers protectively over the front door, and (most appealing of all) the intricate openwork lantern atop the south-side bell tower. Appropriately enough in a city famous for its pastry, the lantern lends its tower an engaging suggestion of a sugar caster, while some see an allusion to hands intertwined in prayer. ⊠ *Passauer Platz/Salvator-gasse, 1st District* Ⓤ *U1 or U3/Stephansplatz.*

★ ❺ **Museum für Angewandte Kunst (MAK)** (Museum of Applied Arts). This fascinating museum contains a large collection of Austrian furniture, porcelain, art objects, and priceless Oriental carpets. The Jugendstil display devoted to Josef Hoffman and his Secessionist followers at the Wiener Werkstätte is particularly fine. The museum also showcases changing exhibitions of contemporary works, and the museum shop sells furniture and other objects (including great bar accessories) designed by young local artists. ■ TIP➔ **Consider lunch or dinner at the revamped restaurant, bar and lounge (Österreicher im MAK, open daily) here, which is run by one of Austria's best chefs, Helmut Österreicher.** Modern Austrian culinary creations include Österreicher's mayonnaise egg, spinach noodles with Austrian blue cheese, and mushroom meat loaf. ⊠ *Stubenring 5, 1st District* ☎ *01/711–36–0* ⊕ *www.mak.at* ⊠ *€7.90; free Sat.* ⊙ *Tues. 10 AM–midnight; Wed.–Sun. 10–6* Ⓤ *U3/Stubentor.*

❻ **Postsparkasse** (Post Office Savings Bank). The Post Office Savings Bank is one of modern architecture's greatest curiosities. It was designed in 1904 by Otto Wagner, whom many consider the father of 20th-century architecture. In his famous manifesto *Modern Architecture,* Wagner condemned 19th-century revivalist architecture and pleaded for a modern style that honestly expressed modern building methods. Accordingly, the exterior walls of the Post Office Savings Bank are mostly flat and undecorated; visual interest is supplied merely by varying the pattern of the bolts used to hold the marble slabs in place on the wall surface during construction. Later architects were to embrace Wagner's beliefs wholeheartedly, although they used different, truly modern building materials: glass and concrete rather than marble. The Post Office Savings Bank was indeed a bold leap into the future, but unfortunately the future took a different path, and today the whole appears a bit dated. Go inside for a look at the restored and functioning Kassa-Saal, or central cashier's hall, to see how Wagner carried his concepts over to interior design. ⊠ *Georg-Coch-Platz 2, 1st District* ☎ *01/51400* ⊙ *Lobby weekdays 8–3* Ⓤ *U1 or U4/Schwedenplatz, then Tram 1 or 2/Julius-Raab-Platz.*

OFF THE BEATEN PATH

PRATER – You have to head northeast from the historic city center, across the Danube Canal along Praterstrasse, to find the Prater, the city's foremost amusement park. In 1766, to the dismay of the aristocracy, Emperor Joseph II decreed that the vast expanse of imperial parklands known as the Prater would henceforth be open to the public. East of the inner city between the Danube Canal and the Danube proper, the Prater is a public park to this day, notable for its long promenade (the Hauptallee, more than 4½ km, or 3 mi, in length); its sports facilities (a golf course, a stadium, a racetrack, and a swimming pool, for starters); the landmark giant Ferris wheel (Riesenrad); the traditional, modern amusement-park rides; a number of less-innocent indoor, sex-oriented attractions; a planetarium; and a small but interesting museum devoted to the Prater's long history. If you look carefully, you can discover a handful of children's rides dating from the 1920s and '30s that survived the fire that consumed most of the Volksprater in 1945. The best-known attraction is the 200-foot Ferris wheel that figured so prominently in the 1949 film *The Third Man*. One of three built in Europe at the end of the last century (the others were in England and France but have long since been dismantled), the wheel was badly damaged during World War II but restored shortly thereafter. Its progress is slow and stately (a revolution takes 10 minutes), the views from its cars magnificent, particularly toward dusk. Try to eat at the famous **Schweizerhaus** (✉ Strasse des 1. Mai 116 ☎ 01/728–0152 ⊘ Closed Nov.–Feb.), which has been serving frosty mugs of beer, roast chicken, and *Stelze* (a huge hunk of crispy roast pork on the bone) for more than 100 years. Its informal setting with wood-plank tables indoors or in the garden in summer adds to the fun. Credit cards are not accepted. ✉ *2nd District/Leopoldstadt* 🎡 *Park free, Riesenrad €7.50* ⊘ *Mar., Apr., and Oct., daily 10–10; May–Sept., daily 9 AM–midnight; Nov.–Feb., daily 10–8* Ⓤ *U1/Praterstern.*

❾ Ruprechtskirche (St. Ruprecht's Church). Ruprechtsplatz, another of Vienna's time-warp backwaters, lies to the north of the Kornhäusel Tower. The church in the middle, Ruprechtskirche, is the city's oldest. According to legend it was founded in 740; the oldest part of the present structure (the lower half of the tower) dates from the 11th century. Set on the ancient ramparts overlooking the Danube Canal, it is serene and unpretentious. It is usually open afternoons and in evenings in summer for classical concerts. ✉ *Ruprechtsplatz, 1st District* Ⓤ *U1 or U4/Schwedenplatz.*

Schönlaterngasse (Street of the Beautiful Lantern). Once part of Vienna's medieval Latin Quarter, Schönlaterngasse is the main artery of a historic neighborhood that has reblossomed in recent years, thanks in part to government *Kulturschillinge*—or renovation loans. Streets are lined with beautiful Baroque town houses (often with colorfully painted facades), now distinctive showcases for art galleries, chic shops, and coffeehouses. At No. 5 you'll find a covered passage that leads to the historic **Heiligenkreuzerhof** courtyard. The quarter's most famous house is the **Basiliskenhaus** (House of the Basilisk; ✉ Schönlaterngasse 7, 1st District). According to legend, it was first built for a baker; on June 26, 1212, a foul-smelling basilisk (half-rooster, half-toad, with a glance that could kill) took up residence in the courtyard well, poisoning the water. An enterprising apprentice dealt with the problem by climbing down the well armed with a mirror; when the basilisk saw its own reflection it turned to stone. The petrified creature can still be seen in a niche on the building's facade. Modern science accounts for the contamination with a more prosaic explanation: natural-gas seepage. Be sure to take a look in the house's miniature courtyard for a trip back to medieval Vienna (the house itself is private). The picturesque street is named for the ornate wrought-iron wall lantern at Schönlaterngasse 6. Just a few steps from the Basiliskenhaus, note the Baroque courtyard at Schönlaterngasse 8—one of the city's prettiest. A blacksmith's workshop, **Alte Schmiede** (Old Smithy; ✉ Schönlaterngasse 9 Ⓤ U1 or U3/ Stephansplatz), is now a museum.

★ ❶ Stephansdom (St. Stephen's Cathedral). Vienna's soaring centerpiece, this beloved cathedral enshrines the heart of the city—although it is curious to note that when first built in 1144–47 it actually stood outside the

city walls. Vienna can thank a period of hard times for the Cathe
for the cathedral's distinctive silhouette. Originally the struct
have had matching 445-foot-high spires, a standard design
but funds ran out, and the north tower to this day remains a happy reminder of what gloriously is not. The lack of symmetry creates an im-
balance that makes the cathedral instantly identifiable from its profile
alone. The cathedral, like the Staatsoper and some other major buildings, was very heavily damaged in World War II. Since then it has risen
from the fires of destruction like a phoenix.

It is difficult now to tell what was original and what parts of the walls
and vaults were reconstructed. No matter: its history-rich atmosphere
is dear to all Viennese. That noted, St. Stephen's has a fierce presence
that is blatantly un-Viennese. It is a stylistic jumble ranging from 13th-
century Romanesque to 15th-century Gothic. Like the exterior, St.
Stephen's interior lacks the soaring unity of Europe's greatest Gothic
cathedrals, much of its decoration dating from the later Baroque era.

■ TIP→ **The wealth of decorative sculpture in St. Stephen's can be intimidat-
ing to the nonspecialist, so if you wish to explore the cathedral in detail, buy
the admirably complete English-language description sold in the small room
marked DOM SHOP.** One particularly masterly work should be seen by
everyone: the stone pulpit attached to the second freestanding pier on
the left of the central nave, carved by Anton Pilgram between 1510 and
1550. The delicacy of its decoration would in itself set the pulpit apart,
but even more intriguing are its five sculpted figures. Carved around the
outside of the pulpit proper are the four Church Fathers (from left to
right: St. Augustine, St. Gregory, St. Jerome, and St. Ambrose), and each

is given an individual personality so
sharply etched as to suggest satire,
perhaps of living models. There is
no satire suggested by the fifth figure, however; below the pulpit's
stairs Pilgram sculpted a fine self-
portrait, showing himself peering
out a half-open window. Note the
toads, lizards, and other creatures
climbing the spiral rail alongside
the steps up to the pulpit. As you
stroll through the aisles, remember
that many notable events occurred
here, including Mozart's marriage
in 1782 and his funeral in December 1791. The funeral service was
conducted to the left of the main entrance in a small chapel beneath
the Heidenturm, to the left of the
cathedral's main doorway. The funeral bier on which his casket was
placed stands in the Crucifix
Chapel, which marks the entrance

BIRD'S-EYE VIEW

A good way to break the ice on
your introduction to Vienna is from
high above it. There's the terrace
of the Upper Belvedere Palace or
the Prater's Ferris wheel—but the
city's preeminent panoramic lookout point is the observation platform of Vienna's mother cathedral,
the Stephansdom. The young and
agile will make it up the 343 steps
of the south tower in 8 to 10 minutes; the slower-paced will make
it in closer to 20. An elevator will
present much the same view from
the terrace of the north tower.
From atop, you can see that
St. Stephen's is the veritable hub
of the city's wheel.

to the crypt and can be reached from outside the church. His body rested at a spot not far from the famous open-air pulpit—near the apse, at the other end of the cathedral—named after the monk St. John Capistrano who, in 1450, preached from it to rouse the people to fight the invading Turks. Continuing around the cathedral exterior, at the apse you'll find a centuries-old sculpted torso of the Man of Sorrows, known irreverently as Our Lord of the Toothache because of its agonized expression. Inside, nearly every corner has something to savor: the Marienchor (Virgin's Choir) has the Tomb of Rudolph IV, the Wiener Neustadt altar is a masterpiece of woodcarving; and the Catacombs, where the internal organs of the Habsburgs rest.

The bird's-eye views from the cathedral's beloved **Alter Steffl** (Old Stephen Tower) will be a highlight for some. The south tower is 450 feet high and was built between 1359 and 1433. The climb up the 343 steps is rewarded with vistas that extend to the rising slopes of the Wienerwald, although until restoration is completed the view is somewhat limited. The north steeple houses the big Pummerin bell and a lookout terrace (access by elevator). ⊠ *Stephansplatz, 1st District* ☎ *01/515–5237–67* 🖃 *Guided tour €4; catacombs €4; stairs to south tower €3; elevator to Pummerin bell €4* ☉ *Daily 6 AM–10 PM. Guided tours in English daily Apr.–Oct. at 3:45; catacombs tour (minimum 5 people) Mon.–Sat. every half hr 10–11:30 and 1:30–4:30, Sun. every half hr 1:30–4:30; North Tower elevator to Pummerin bell, Apr.–Oct., daily 8:30–5:30; July and Aug., daily 8:30–6; Nov.–Mar., daily 8:30–5* Ⓤ *U1 or U3/Stephansplatz.*

NEED A BREAK?

Zanoni & Zanoni (⊠ Am Lugeck 7, 1st District ☎ 01/512–7979) near St. Stephen's, between Rotenturmstrasse and Bäckerstrasse, dishes up 25 or more flavors of smooth, Italian-style gelato, including mango, caramel, and chocolate chip. It's open 365 days a year and has tables for those who want to rest their feet and enjoy a sundae.

② **Universitätskirche** (Jesuit Church). The east end of Bäckerstrasse is punctuated by Dr.-Ignaz-Seipel-Platz, named for the theology professor who was chancellor of Austria during the 1920s. On the north side is the Universitätskirche, or Jesuitenkirche, built around 1630. Its flamboyant Baroque interior contains a fine trompe-l'oeil ceiling fresco by that master of visual trickery Andrea Pozzo, who was imported from Rome in 1702 for the job. You may hear a Mozart or Haydn mass sung here in Latin on many Sundays. ⊠ *Dr.-Ignaz-Seipl-Platz, 1st District* ☎ *01/512–5232–0* Ⓤ *U3 Stubentor/Dr.-Karl-Lueger-Platz.*

Also Worth Seeing

④ **Dominikanerkirche** (Dominican Church). The Postgasse, to the east of Schönlaterngasse, introduces an unexpected visitor from Rome: the Dominikanerkirche. Built in the 1630s, some 50 years before the Viennese Baroque building boom, its facade is modeled after any number of Roman churches of the 16th century. The interior illustrates why the Baroque style came to be considered the height of bad taste during the 19th century and still has many detractors today. "Sculpt 'til you drop" seems to have been the motto here, and the viewer's eye is given no respite.

This sort of Roman architectural orgy never really gained a foothold in Vienna, and when the great Viennese architects did pull out all the decorative stops—Hildebrandt's interior at the Belvedere Palace, for instance—they did it in a very different style and with far greater success. ⊠ *Postgasse 4, 1st District* ☎ *01/512–7460–0* Ⓤ *U3/Stubentor/Dr.-Karl-Lueger-Platz.*

❸ Heiligenkreuzerhof (Holy Cross Court). Amid the narrow streets and alleys behind the Stephansdom is this peaceful backwater, approximately a quarter-mile from the cathedral. This complex of buildings dates from the 17th century but got an 18th-century face-lift. Appropriately, the restraint of the architecture—with only here and there a small outburst of Baroque spirit—gives the courtyard the distinct feeling of a retreat. The square is a favorite site for seasonal markets at Easter and Christmas, and for occasional outdoor art shows. ⊠ *1st District* Ⓤ *U1 or U3/ Stephansplatz.*

❽ Hoher Markt. This square was badly damaged during World War II, but the famous Anker Clock at the east end survived the artillery fire. The huge mechanical timepiece took six years (1911–17) to build and still attracts crowds at noon when the full panoply of mechanical figures representing Austrian historical personages parades by. The figures are identified on a plaque to the bottom left of the clock. The graceless buildings erected around the square since 1945 do little to show off the square's lovely Baroque centerpiece, the St. Joseph Fountain (portraying the marriage of Joseph and Mary), designed in 1729 by Joseph Emanuel Fischer von Erlach, son of the great Johann Bernhard Fischer von Erlach. The Hoher Markt does harbor one wholly unexpected attraction, however: underground **Roman ruins** (⊠ *Hoher Markt 3* ⊙ *Tues.–Sun. 9–1 and 2–5* 💷 *€2*). ⊠ *1st District* Ⓤ *U1 or U4/Schwedenplatz.*

OFF THE BEATEN PATH

HUNDERTWASSERHAUS – To see one of Vienna's most amazing buildings, travel eastward from Schwedenplatz or Julius-Raab-Platz along Radetzkystrasse to the junction of Kegelgasse and Löwengasse. Here you'll find the Hundertwasserhaus, a 50-apartment public-housing complex designed by the late Austrian avant-garde artist Friedensreich Hundertwasser. The structure looks as though it was decorated by a crew of mischievous circus clowns wielding giant crayons. The building caused a sensation when it was erected in 1985 and still draws crowds of sightseers. ⊠ *Löwengasse and Kegelgasse, 3rd District/Landstrasse* Ⓤ *U1 or U4/Schwedenplatz, then Tram N to Hetzgasse.*

KUNSTHAUS WIEN – Near the Hundertwasserhaus you'll find another Hundertwasser project, an art museum that mounts outstanding international exhibits in addition to showings of the colorful Hundertwasser works. Like the apartment complex nearby, the building itself is pure Hundertwasser, with irregular floors, windows with trees growing out of them, and sudden architectural surprises, a wholly appropriate setting for modern art. ⊠ *Untere Weissgerberstrasse 13, 3rd District/Landstrasse* ☎ *01/ 712–0491–0* ⊕ *www.kunsthauswien.com* 💷 *€9* ⊙ *Daily 10–7* Ⓤ *U1 or U4/Schwedenplatz, then Tram N or O to Radetzkyplatz.*

Kriminal Museum (Criminal Museum). This might be the strangest museum in the city, and it is certainly the most macabre. The vast collection is entirely devoted to murder in Vienna of the most gruesome kind, with the most grisly displays situated, appropriately, in the cellar. Murderers and their victims are depicted in photos and newspaper clippings, and many of the actual instruments used in the killings are displayed, axes seeming to be the most popular. The Criminal Museum is across the Danube Canal from Schwedenplatz, about a 15-minute walk from the Ruprechtskirche, the Hoher Markt, or the Heiligenkreuzerhof. ⊠ *Grosse Sperlgasse 24, 2nd District/Leopoldstadt* ☎ *01/214–4678* ⊠ *€5* ☉ *Open Thurs.–Sun. 10–5* Ⓤ *Tram: From Schwedenplatz take Tram N along Taborstrasse to Obere Augartenstrasse.*

Baroque Gems & Cozy Cafés

As the city developed and expanded, new urban centers sprang up, to be ornamented by government buildings and elegant town residences. Since Vienna was the beating heart of a vast empire, nothing was spared to make the edifices as exuberant as possible, utility often a secondary consideration. The best architects of the day were commissioned to create impressions as well as buildings, and they did their job well. That so much has survived is a testimony to the solidity both of the designs and of the structures on which the ornamentation has been overlaid.

Those not fortunate enough to afford town palaces were relegated to housing that was often less than elegant and confining. Rather than suffer the discomfitures of a disruptive household environment, the city's literati and its philosophers and artists took refuge in cafés, which in effect became their combined salons and offices. To this day, cafés remain an important element of Viennese life. Many residents still have their *Stammtisch,* or regular table, at which they appear daily. Talk still prevails—but, increasingly, so do cell phones and even laptops.

A GOOD WALK

Start in the Wipplingerstrasse at the upper (west) end of Hoher Markt to find touches of both the imperial and the municipal Vienna. On the east side is the **Altes Rathaus** ⑪, which served as city hall until 1885; on the west is the **Bohemian Court Chancery** ⑫, once diplomatic headquarters for Bohemia's representation to the Habsburg court. Turn south into the short Fütterergasse to reach Judenplatz, in the Middle Ages the center of Judaism in Vienna and today site of the new **Judenplatz Museum** ⑬, landmarked by a memorial created by Rachel Whiteread, one of contemporary art's most important sculptors. Kurrentgasse leads south from the east end of Judenplatz; the beautifully restored 18th-century houses on its east side make this one of the most unpretentiously appealing streets in the city. At the end of Kurrentgasse is a clock-watcher's delight in the form of the **Uhrenmuseum** (Clock Museum) ⑭. Follow Parisergasse to Schulhof into the huge **Am Hof** ⑮ square, boasting the **Kirche am Hof** ⑯ and what must be the world's most elegant fire station. The square hosts an antiques and collectibles market on Thursday and Friday most of the year, plus other ad hoc events. Take the minuscule Irisgasse from Am Hof into Naglergasse, noting the mosaic Jugendstil facade on the pharmacy in Bognergasse, to your left. Around a bend in the narrow Naglergasse is the

Freyung, an irregular square bounded on the south side by two wonderfully stylish palaces, the **Palais Ferstel** ⓱, now a shopping arcade, and the elegantly restored **Palais Harrach** ⓲. The famous **Palais Daum-Kinsky** ⓳ at the beginning of Herrengasse is still partly a private residence. The north side of the Freyung is watched over by the **Schottenkirche** ⓴, established by Irish Benedictine monks; the complex also houses a small but worthwhile museum of the order's treasures. Follow Teinfaltstrasse from opposite the Schottenkirche, turning right into Schreyvogelgasse; at No. 8 is the famed **"Third Man" Portal.** Climb the ramp on your right past the so-called Dreimäderlhaus at Schreyvogelgasse 10—note the ornate facade of this pre-Biedermeier patrician house—to reach Molker Bastei, where Beethoven lived in the **Pasqualatihaus** ㉑, now housing a museum commemorating the composer. Follow the ring south to Löwelstrasse, turning left into Bankgasse; then turn right into Abraham-a-Sancta-Clara-Gasse (the tiny street that runs off the Bankgasse) to Minoritenplatz and the **Minoritenkirche** ㉒, with its strangely hatless tower. Inside is a kitschy mosaic of the *Last Supper.* Landhausgasse will bring you to Herrengasse, and diagonally across the street, in the back corner of the Palais Ferstel, is the **Café Central** ㉓, one of Vienna's hangouts for the famous. Across the street from it is the **Palais Mollard** and its collection of globes. As you go south on Herrengasse, on the left is the odd Hochhaus, a 20th-century building once renowned as Vienna's skyscraper. Opposite are elegant Baroque town palaces now used as museum and administration buildings by the province of Lower Austria.

TIMING   The actual distances in this walk are relatively short, and you could cover the route in 1½ hours or so. But if you take time to linger in the museums and sample a coffee with whipped cream in the Café Central, you'll develop a much better understanding of the contrasts between old and newer in the city. You could easily spend a day following this walk, if you were to take in all of the museums.

Main Attractions

⓯ **Am Hof.** Am Hof is one of the city's oldest squares. In the Middle Ages the ruling Babenberg family built their castle on the site of No. 2; hence the name of the square, which means simply "at court." The grand residence hosted such luminaries as Barbarossa and Walter von der Vogelweide, the famous Minnesinger who stars in Wagner's *Tannhäuser.* The Baroque **Column of Our Lady** in the center dates from 1667, marking the Catholic victory over the Swedish Protestants in the Thirty Years' War (1618–48). The onetime **Civic Armory** at the northwest corner has been used as a fire station since 1685 (the high-spirited facade, with its Habsburg eagle, was "Baroqued" in 1731) and today houses the headquarters of Vienna's fire department. The complex includes a firefighting museum (open only on Sunday mornings). Presiding over the east side of the square is the noted Kirche Am Hof. In Bognergasse to the right of the church, around the corner from the imposing Bank Austria headquarters, is the **Engel Apotheke** (pharmacy) at No. 9 with a Jugendstil mosaic depicting winged women collecting the elixir of life in outstretched chalices. At the turn of the 20th century the inner city was dotted with storefronts decorated in a similar manner; today this is the sole sur-

Mozart, Mozart, Mozart!

THE GREAT COMPOSER Wolfgang Amadeus Mozart (1756–91) crammed a prodigious number of compositions into his Vienna years (the last 10 of his life), along with the arrival of his six children and constantly changing Viennese addresses. It was in Vienna that many of his peaks were achieved, both personal and artistic. He wed his beloved Constanze Weber at St. Stephen's Cathedral in August 1782, and led the premieres of several of his greatest operas. But a knowledge of his troubled relations with his home city of Salzburg makes his Vienna soujourn an even more poignant one.

From the beginning of Wolfgang's precocious career, his father, frustrated in his own musical ambitions at the archbishopric in Salzburg, looked beyond the boundaries of the Austro-Hungarian empire to promote the boy's fame. At the age of six, his son caused a sensation in the royal courts of Europe with his skills as an instrumentalist and impromptu composer. As Mozart grew up, however, his virtuosity lost its power to amaze and he was forced to make his way as an "ordinary" musician, which then meant finding a position at court. Not much more successful in Salzburg than his father had been, he was never able to rise beyond the level of organist (allowing him, as he noted with sarcastic pride, to sit above the cooks at table), and, in disgust, he relocated to Vienna, where despite the popularity of his operas he was able to obtain only an unpaid appointment as assistant Kapellmeister at St. Stephen's mere months before his death. By then, patronage subscriptions had been taken up in Hungary and the Netherlands that would have paid him handsomely. But it was too late. Whatever the truth about the theories still swirling around his untimely death, the fact remains that not only was he not given the state funeral he deserved, but he was buried in an unmarked grave (although most Viennese at that time were) after a hasty, sparsely attended funeral.

Only the flint-hearted can stand in Vienna's Währingerstrasse and look at the windows behind which Mozart wrote those last three symphonies in the incredible short time of six weeks in the summer of 1788 and not be touched. For this was the time when the Mozart fortunes had slumped to their lowest. "If you, my best of friends, forsake me, I am unhappily and innocently lost with my poor sick wife and my child," he wrote. And if one is inclined to accuse Mozart's fellow countrymen of neglect, they would seem to have made up for it with a vengeance. The visitor to Vienna and Salzburg can hardly ignore the barrage of Mozart candies, wine, beer, coffee mugs, T-shirts, baseball caps—not to mention the gilt statues and all the other knickknacks. Mozart, always one to appreciate a joke, would surely see the irony in the belated veneration. Today the places he lived in or visited are all reverently marked by memorial plaques.

–Gary Dodson

vivor. Around the bend from the Naglergasse is the picturesque Freyung square. At No. 13 is the fairly stolid 17th-century **Palais Collalto**, famous as the setting for Mozart's first public engagement at the ripe age of six. This was but the first showing of the child prodigy in Vienna, for his father had him perform for three Viennese princes, four dukes, and five counts in the space of a few weeks. Having newly arrived from Salzburg, the child set Vienna on its ear, and he was showered with money and gifts, including some opulent children's clothes from the Empress Maria Theresa. Next door is the Jesuit church where Leopold Mozart directed his son's *Father Dominicus Mass* (K. 66) in August 1773. Some years later Mozart's first child, Raimund Leopold, was baptized here. Sadly, the child died two months later. ⊠ *1st District* Ⓤ *U3/Herrengasse.*

❷❸ **Café Central.** Part of the **Palais Ferstel** complex, the Café Central is one of Vienna's more famous cafés, its full authenticity blemished only by complete restoration in recent years. In its prime (before World War I), the café was "home" to some of the most famous literary figures of the day, who dined, socialized, worked, and even received mail here. The denizens of the Central favored political argument; indeed, their heated discussions became so well known that in October 1917, when Austria's foreign secretary was informed of the outbreak of the Russian Revolution, he dismissed the report with a facetious reference to a well-known local Marxist, the chess-loving (and presumably harmless) "Herr Bronstein from the Café Central." The remark was to become famous all over Austria, for Herr Bronstein had disappeared and was about to resurface in Russia bearing a new name: Leon Trotsky. Today things are a good deal more yuppified: the coffee now comes with a little chocolate biscuit and is overpriced, and the pianist is more likely to play Sinatra ballads than Strauss. But no matter how crowded the café may become, you can linger as long as you like over a single cup of coffee and a newspaper from the huge international selection provided. Across the street at Herrengasse 17 is the **Café Central Konditorei,** an excellent pastry and confectionery shop associated with the café. ⊠ *Herrengasse 14, 1st District* ☎ *01/533–3763–26* ⊕ *www.palaisevents.at* ▤ *AE, DC, MC, V* Ⓤ *U3/Herrengasse.*

The Freyung. Naglergasse, at its curved end, flows into Heidenschuss, which in turn leads down a slight incline from Am Hof to one of Vienna's most prominent squares, the Freyung, meaning "freeing." The square was so named because for many centuries the monks at the adjacent Schottenhof had the privilege of offering sanctuary for three days. In the center of the square stands the allegorical **Austria Fountain** (1845), notable because its Bavarian designer, one Ludwig Schwanthaler, had the statues cast in Munich and then supposedly filled them with cigars to be smuggled into Vienna for black-market sale. Around the sides of the square are some of Vienna's greatest patrician residences, including the Ferstel, Harrach, and Kinsky palaces. ⊠ *At intersection of Am Hof and Herrengasse, 1st District* Ⓤ *U3/Herrengasse.*

⓭ **Judenplatz Museum.** In what was once the old Jewish ghetto, construction workers discovered the remains of a 13th-century synagogue while digging for a new parking garage. Simon Wiesenthal (a former Vienna resident) helped to turn it into a museum dedicated to the Austrian Jews who died in World War II. Marking the outside is a concrete cube whose faces are casts of library shelves, signifying Jewish love of learning, designed by Rachel Whiteread. Downstairs are three exhibition rooms devoted to medieval Jewish life and the synagogue excavations. Also in Judenplatz is a statue of the 18th-century playwright Gotthold Ephraim Lessing, erected after World War II. ⊠ *Judenplatz 8, 1st District* ☎ *01/ 535–0431* ⊕ *www.jmw.at* ⊠ *€3; combination ticket with Jewish Museum €7* ☉ *Sun.–Fri. 10–6, Thurs. 10–8 PM.*

⑰ Palais Ferstel. At Freyung 2 stands the Palais Ferstel, which is not a palace at all but a commercial shop-and-office complex designed in 1856 and named for its architect, Heinrich Ferstel. The facade is Italianate in style, harking back in its 19th-century way to the Florentine palazzi of the early Renaissance. The interior is unashamedly eclectic: vaguely Romanesque in feel and Gothic in decoration, with here and there a bit of Renaissance or Baroque sculpted detail thrown in for good measure. Such eclecticism is sometimes dismissed as mindlessly derivative, but here the architectural details are so respectfully and inventively combined that the interior becomes a pleasure to explore. The 19th-century stock-exchange rooms upstairs are now gloriously restored and used for conferences, concerts, and balls. ⊠ *Freyung 2, 1st District* Ⓤ *U3/Herrengasse.*

Schottenhof. Found on the Freyung square and designed by Joseph Kornhäusel in a different style from his Fleischmarkt tower, the Schottenhof is a shaded courtyard. The facade typifies the change that came over Viennese architecture during the Biedermeier era (1815–48). The Viennese, according to the traditional view, were at the time so relieved to be rid of the upheavals of the Napoleonic Wars that they accepted without protest the iron-handed repression of Prince Metternich, chancellor of Austria, and retreated into a cozy and complacent domesticity. Restraint also ruled in architecture; Baroque license was rejected in favor of a new and historically "correct" style that was far more controlled and reserved. Kornhäusel led the way in establishing this trend in Vienna; his Schottenhof facade is all sober organization and frank repetition. But in its marriage of strong and delicate forces it still pulls off the great Viennese-waltz trick of successfully merging seemingly antithetical characteristics. ⊠ *1st District* Ⓤ *U2/Schottentor.*

NEED A BREAK?
In summer, **Wienerwald** restaurant, in the delightful tree-shaded courtyard of the Schottenhof at Freyung 6, is ideal for relaxing over lunch or dinner with a glass of wine or frosty beer. The specialty here is chicken, prepared just about every possible way. Especially good is the spit-roasted *Knoblauch* (garlic) chicken. It's open daily.

⑳ Schottenkirche. From 1758 to 1761 the noted Italian *vedutiste* (scene-painter) Bernardo Bellotto did paintings of the Freyung square looking north toward the Schottenkirche; the pictures hang in the Kunsthistorisches Museum, and the similarity to the view you see more than two centuries later is arresting. In fact, a church has stood on the site of the Schottenkirche since 1177, when the monastery was established by Benedictine monks from Ireland—Scotia Minor, in Latin, hence the name "Scots Church." The present edifice dates from the mid-1600s, when it replaced its predecessor, which had collapsed because the architects of the time had built on weakened foundations. The interior, with its ornate ceiling and a decided surplus of cherubs and angels' faces, is in stark contrast to the plain exterior. The adjacent small **Museum im Schottenstift** includes the best of the monastery's artworks, including the celebrated Late Gothic high altar dating from about 1470. The winged altar is fascinating for its portrayal of the Holy Family in flight into Egypt—with the city of Vienna clearly identifiable in the background. ✉ *Freyung 6, 1st District* ☎ *01/534–98–600* ⊕ *www.schottenstift.at* ✉ *Church free, museum €4* ☉ *Museum Thurs.–Sat. 11–5* Ⓤ *U2/Schottentor.*

⑭ Uhrenmuseum (Clock Museum). At the far end of Kurrentgasse, which is lined with appealing 18th-century houses, is one of Vienna's most appealing museums: the Uhrenmuseum (enter to the right on the Schulhof side of the building). The museum's three floors display a splendid parade of clocks and watches—more than 3,000 timepieces—dating from the 15th century to the present. The ruckus of bells and chimes pealing forth on any hour is impressive, but for the full cacophony try to be here at noon. ✉ *Schulhof 2, 1st District* ☎ *01/533–2265* ✉ *€4, Sun. free* ☉ *Tues.–Sun. 10–6* Ⓤ *U1 or U3/Stephansplatz.*

Also Worth Seeing

⑪ Altes Rathaus (Old City Hall). Opposite the Bohemian Chancery stands the Altes Rathaus, dating from the 14th century but displaying 18th-century Baroque motifs on its facade. The interior passageways and courtyards, which are open during the day, house a Gothic chapel (open at odd hours); a much-loved Baroque wall fountain (Georg Raphael Donner's **Andromeda Fountain** from 1741); and display cases exhibiting maps and photos illustrating the city's history. ✉ *Wipplingerstrasse/ Salvatorgasse 7, 1st District* Ⓤ *U1 or U4/Schwedenplatz.*

⑫ Böhmischehofkanzlei (Bohemian Court Chancery). This architectural jewel of the Inner City was built between 1708 and 1714 by Johann Bernhard Fischer von Erlach. Fischer von Erlach and his contemporary Johann Lukas von Hildebrandt were the reigning architectural geniuses of Baroque-era Vienna; they designed their churches and palaces during the building boom that followed the defeat of the Turks in 1683. Both had studied architecture in Rome, and both were deeply impressed by the work of the great Italian architect Francesco Borromini, who brought to his designs a wealth and freedom of invention that were looked upon with horror by most contemporary Romans. But for Fischer von Erlach and Hildebrandt, Borromini's ideas were a source of triumphant architectural inspiration, and when they returned to Vienna they produced between them many of the city's most beautiful buildings. Alas, narrow Wipplingerstrasse allows little more than a oblique view of this florid facade. The back side of the building, on Judenplatz, is less elaborate but gives a better idea of the design concept. The building first served as the offices of Bohemia's representatives to the Vienna-based monarchy, and still houses government offices today. ✉ *Wipplingerstrasse 7, 1st District* Ⓤ *U1 or U4/Schwedenplatz.*

⑯ Kirche Am Hof. On the east side of the Am Hof square, the Kirche Am Hof, or Church of the Nine Choirs of Angels, is identified by its sprawling Baroque facade designed by Carlo Carlone in 1662. The somber interior lacks appeal, but the checkerboard marble floor may remind you of Dutch churches. ⊠ *Am Hof 1, 1st District* Ⓤ *U3/Herrengasse.*

㉒ Minoritenkirche (Minorite Church). Minoritenplatz is named after its centerpiece, the Minoritenkirche, a Gothic affair with a strange stump of a tower, built mostly in the 14th century. The front is brutally ugly, but the back is a wonderful, if predominantly 19th-century, surprise. The interior contains the city's most imposing piece of kitsch: a large mosaic reproduction of Leonardo da Vinci's *Last Supper,* commissioned by Napoléon in 1806 and later purchased by Emperor Francis I. ⊠ *Minoritenplatz 2A, 1st District* ☎ *01/533–4162* Ⓤ *U3/Herrengasse.*

⑲ Palais Daum-Kinsky. Just one of the architectural treasures that comprise the urban set piece of the Freyung, the Palais Kinsky is the square's best-known palace, and is one of the most sophisticated pieces of Baroque architecture in the whole city. It was built between 1713 and 1716 by Hildebrandt, and its only real competition comes a few yards farther on: the Greek-temple facade of the Schottenhof, which is at right angles to the Schottenkirche, up the street from the Kinsky Palace. The palace now houses Wiener Kunst Auktionen, a public auction business offering artworks and antiques. If there is an auction viewing, try to see the palace's spectacular 18th-century staircase, all marble goddesses and crowned with a trompe-l'oeil ceiling painted by Marcantonio Chiarini. ⊠ *Freyung 4, 1st District* ☎ *01/532–4200* 🖷 *01/532–42009* ⊕ *www. imkinsky.com* ☉ *Weekdays 10–6* Ⓤ *U3/Herrengasse.*

⑱ Palais Harrach. Next door to the Palais Ferstel is the Palais Harrach. Mozart and his sister Nannerl performed here when children for Count Ferdinand during their first visit to Vienna in 1762. The palace was altered after 1845 and severely damaged during World War II. Many of the state rooms have lost their historical lustre, but the Marble Room, set with gilt boiseries, and the Red Gallery, topped with a spectacular ceiling painting, still provide grand settings for receptions. ⊠ *Freyung 3, 1st District* Ⓤ *U3/Herrengasse.*

Palais Mollard. Across the street from the Café Central, step into the beautifully renovated Palais Mollard to have a look at the rare collection of over 400 terrestrial and celestial globes on show on its second-floor museum—the only one of its kind in the world open to the public. The oldest globe is an earth globe dating from 1536, produced by Gemma Frisius, a Belgian doctor and cosmographer. On the ground floor there's a small but fascinating exhibition of the history of Esperanto, including a film. The library collection of the Esperanto Museum, the largest in the world, is accessible. ⊠ *Herrengasse 9, 1st District* ☎ *01/534–10* 🖻 *€5* ☉ *Mon.–Wed., Fri., and Sat. 10–2, Thurs. 3–7* Ⓤ *U3/Herrengasse.*

㉑ Pasqualatihaus. Beethoven lived in the Pasqualatihaus while he was composing his only opera, *Fidelio,* as well as his Seventh Symphony and Fourth Piano Concerto. Today his apartment houses a small commemorative museum (in distressingly modern style). After navigating the narrow and twisting stairway, you might well ask how he maintained the jubilant spirit of the works he wrote there. Some exhibits are fascinating: note particularly the prints that show what the window view out over the Mölker bastion was like when Beethoven lived here and the piano that dates from his era—one that was beefed-up to take the banging Beethoven made fashionable. This house is around the corner from the *Third Man* Portal. ⊠ *8 Mölker Bastei, 1st District* ☎ *01/535–8905* ⊕ *www.wienmuseum.at* ✉ *€2, Sun. free* ⊙ *Tues.–Sun. 10–1 and 2–6* Ⓤ *U2/Schottentor.*

Third Man Portal. The doorway at Schreyvogelgasse 8 (up the incline) was made famous in 1949 by the classic film *The Third Man* (*see* Close-up box, *below*). It was here that Orson Welles, as the malevolently knowing Harry Lime, stood hiding in the dark, only to have his smiling face illuminated by a sudden light from the upper-story windows of the house across the alley. To get to this apartment building from the nearby and noted Schottenkirche, follow Teinfaltstrasse one block west to Schreyvogelgasse on the right. ⊠ *1st District* Ⓤ *U2/Schottentor.*

Vienna's Shop Window: From Michaelerplatz to the Graben

The compact area bounded roughly by the back side of the Hofburg palace complex, the Kohlmarkt, the Graben, and Kärntnerstrasse belongs to the oldest core of the city. Remains of the Roman city are just below the present-day surface. This was and still is the city's commercial heart, dense with shops and markets for various commodities; today, the Kohlmarkt and Graben in particular offer the choicest luxury shops, overflowing into the Graben end of Kärntnerstrasse. The area is marvelous for its visual treats, ranging from the squares and varied architecture to shop windows. The evening view down Kohlmarkt from the Graben is an inspiring classic, with the night-lighted gilded dome of Michael's Gate into the palace complex as the glittering backdrop. Sights in this area range from the sacred—the Baroque Peterskirche—to the more profane pleasures of Demel, Vienna's beloved pastry shop, and the Modernist masterwork of the Looshaus.

A GOOD WALK

Start your walk through this fascinating quarter at **Michaelerplatz** ㉔, one of Vienna's most evocative squares, where the feel of the imperial city remains very strong; the buildings around the perimeter present a synopsis of the city's entire architectural history: medieval church spire, Renaissance church facade, Baroque palace facade, 19th-century apartment house, and 20th-century bank. Look in the Michaelerkirche (St. Michael's Church). Opposite the church is the once-controversial **Looshaus** ㉕, considered a breakthrough in modern architecture (visitors are welcome to view the restored lobby). From Michaelerplatz, take the small passageway to the right of the church; in it on your right is a relief dating from 1480 of Christ on the Mount of Olives. Follow the Stallburggasse through to Dorotheergasse, and turn right to discover the **Dorotheum,** the government-run auction house and Viennese equivalent of Christie's or Sotheby's. On your right in the Dorotheergasse (toward the Graben) is the **Jewish Museum** ㉖, which includes a bookstore and café. On the left is the famous Café Hawelka, haunt to the contemporary art and lit-

Tracking Down The Third Man

NOTHING HAS DONE MORE to create the myth of postwar Vienna than Carol Reed's classic 1949 film *The Third Man*. The bombed-out ruins of this proud, imperial city created an indelible image of devastation and corruption in the war's aftermath. Vienna was then divided into four sectors, each commanded by one of the victorious armies—American, Russian, French, and British. But their attempts at rigid control could not prevent a thriving black market.

Reed's film version of the Graham Greene thriller features Vienna as a leading player, from the top of its Ferris wheel to the depth of its lowest sewers—"which run right into the Blue Danube." It was the first British film to be shot entirely on location.

Joseph Cotten plays Holly Martins, a pulp-fiction writer who comes to Vienna in search of his friend Harry Lime (Orson Welles). He makes the mistake of delving too deeply into Lime's affairs, even falling in love with his girlfriend, Anna Schmidt (Alida Valli), with fatal consequences.

Many of the sites where the film was shot are easily visited. Harry Lime appears for the first time nearly one hour into the film in the doorway of Anna's apartment building at No. 8 Schreyvogelgasse, around the corner from the Mölker-Bastei (a remnant of the old city wall). He then runs to Am Hof, a lovely square lined with Baroque town houses and churches, which appears much closer to Anna's neighborhood than it actually is.

The famous scene between Lime and Martins on the Ferris wheel was filmed on the Riesenrad at the Prater, the huge amusement park across the Danube Canal. While the two friends talk in the enclosed compartment, the wheel slowly makes a revolution, with all Vienna spread out below them.

In the memorable chase at the end of the movie, Lime is seen running through the damp sewers of Vienna, hotly pursued by the authorities. In reality, he would not have been able to use the sewer system as an escape route because the tunnels were too low and didn't connect between the different centers of the city. A more feasible, if less cinematic, possibility of escape was offered by the labyrinth of cellars that still connected many buildings in the city.

Lime's funeral is held at the Zentralfriedhof (Central Cemetery), reachable by the 71 streetcar. This is the final scene of the movie, where Anna Schmidt walks down the stark, wide avenue (dividing sections 69 and 70), refusing to acknowledge the wistful presence of Holly Martins.

After touring sewers and cemeteries, treat yourself to a stop at the Hotel Sacher, used for a scene in the beginning of the movie when Holly Martins is using the telephone in the lobby. The bar in the Sacher was a favorite hangout of director Carol Reed, who left a signed note to the bartender, saying: "To the creator of the best Bloody Marys in the whole world."

The film is screened on Tuesday, Friday, and Sunday in the Burg Kino, and a memorabilia museum open on Saturday is near the Naschmarkt.

–Bonnie Dodson

erature crowd. Turn right in the Graben to come to **Stock-im-Eisen** ㉗; the famous nail-studded tree trunk is encased in the corner of the building. Opposite and impossible to overlook is the aggressive **Haas-Haus** ㉘, a new luxury hotel with an upmarket restaurant and ground floor shopping. Wander back through the **Graben** ㉙ for the full effect of this harmonious street and look up to see the ornamentation on the buildings. Pass the Pestsäule, or Plague Column, which shoots up from the middle of the Graben like a geyser of whipped cream. Just off to the north side is the **Peterskirche** ㉚, St. Peter's Church, a Baroque gem almost hidden by its surroundings. At the end of the Graben, turn left into the **Kohlmarkt** ㉛ for the classic view of the domed arch leading to the Hofburg, the imperial palace complex. Even if your feet aren't calling a sit-down strike, finish up at **Demel** ㉜, at Kohlmarkt 14, for some of the best *Gebäck* (pastries) in the world.

TIMING   Inveterate shoppers, window or otherwise, will want to take time to pause before or in many of the elegant shops during this walk, which then could easily take most of a day or even longer. If you're content with facades and general impressions, the exercise could be done in a bit over an hour, but it would be a shame to bypass the narrow side streets. In any case, look into St. Michael's and consider the fascinating Dorotheum, itself easily worth an hour or more.

Main Attractions

㉜ **Demel.** Vienna's best-known pastry shop, Demel offers a dizzying selection, so if you have a sweet tooth, a visit will be worth every euro. And
Fodor'sChoice   in a city famous for its tortes, their almond-chocolate Senegaltorte takes
★   the cake. Chocolate lovers will want to participate in the famous Viennese Sachertorte debate by sampling Demel's version and then comparing it with its rival at the **Café Sacher,** which is in the Hotel Sacher. Don't forget to press your nose against Demel's shop windows, whose displays are among the most mouthwatering and inventive in Austria. And during opening hours you can visit the Demel Museum in the basement. ⊠ *Kohlmarkt 14, 1st District* ☎ *01/535–1717–0* ⊠ *www.demel.at* Ⓤ *U1 or U3/Stephansplatz.*

Dorotheum. The narrow passageway just to the right of St. Michael's, with its large 15th-century relief depicting Christ on the Mount of Olives, leads into the Stallburggasse. The area is dotted with antiques stores, attracted by the presence of the Dorotheum, the famous Viennese auction house that began as a state-controlled pawnshop in 1707 (affectionately known as "Aunt Dorothy" to its patrons). Merchandise coming up for auction is on display at Dorotheergasse 17. The showrooms—packed with everything from carpets and pianos to cameras and jewelry and postage stamps—are well worth a visit. Some goods are not for auction but for immediate sale. ⊠ *Dorotheergasse 17, 1st District* ☎ *01/515–60–200* ⊕ *www.dorotheum.com* ☉ *Weekdays 10–6, Sat. 9–5* Ⓤ *U1 or U3/Stephansplatz.*

㉙ **The Graben.** One of Vienna's major crossroads, the Graben, leading west from Stock-im-Eisen-Platz, is a street whose unusual width gives it the presence and weight of a city square. Its shape is due to the Romans, who dug the city's southwestern moat here (Graben literally means "moat" or "ditch") adjacent to the original city walls. The Graben's centerpiece is the effulgently Baroque **Pestsäule,** or Plague Column. Erected by Emperor Leopold I between 1687 and 1693 as thanks to God for delivering the city from a particularly virulent plague, today the representation looks more like a host of cherubs doing their best to cope with the icing of a wedding cake wilting under a hot sun. The Catholic Church has triumphed over Protestantism in Austria, and Protestants may be disappointed to learn that the foul figure of the Pest also stands for the heretic plunging away from the "true faith" into the depths of hell. ⊠ *Between Kärntnerstrasse and Kohlmarkt, 1st District* Ⓤ *U1 or U3/Stephansplatz.*

㉖ Jewish Museum. The former Eskeles Palace, once an elegant private residence, now houses the Jüdisches Museum der Stadt Wien. Permanent exhibits tell of the momentous role that Vienna-born Jews have played in realms from music to medicine, art to philosophy, both in Vienna—until abruptly halted in 1938—and in the world at large. Changing exhibits add contemporary touches. The museum complex includes a café and bookstore. ⊠ *Dorotheergasse 11, 1st District* ☎ *01/535–0431* ▭ *€5 combination ticket with Judenplatz Museum €7* ⊙ *Sun.–Fri. 10–6, Thurs. 10–8* Ⓤ *U1 or U3/Stephansplatz.*

㉛ Kohlmarkt. The Kohlmarkt, aside from its classic view of the domed entryway to the imperial palace complex of the Hofburg, is best known as Vienna's most elegant shopping street. All the big brand names are represented here. The shops, not the buildings, are remarkable, although there is an entertaining odd-couple pairing: No. 11 (early 18th century) and No. 9 (early 20th century). The mixture of architectural styles is similar to that of the Graben, but the general atmosphere is low-key, as if the street were consciously deferring to the showstopper dome at the west end. The composers Haydn and Chopin lived in houses on the street, and indeed, the Kohlmarkt lingers in the memory when flashier streets have faded. ⊠ *Between Graben and Michaelerplatz, 1st District* Ⓤ *U3/Herrengasse.*

㉕ Looshaus. In 1911 Adolf Loos, one of the founding fathers of 20th-century modern architecture, built the Looshaus on imposing Michaelerplatz, facing the Imperial Palace entrance. It was considered nothing less than an architectural declaration of war. After 200 years of Baroque and neo-Baroque exuberance, the first generation of 20th-century architects had had enough. Loos led the revolt against architectural tradition; *Ornament and Crime* was the title of his famous manifesto, in which he inveighed against the conventional architectural wisdom of the 19th century. Instead, he advocated buildings that were plain, honest, and functional. When he built the Looshaus for Goldman and Salatsch (men's clothiers) in 1911, the city was scandalized. Archduke Franz Ferdinand, heir to the throne, was so offended that he vowed never again to use the Michaelerplatz entrance to the Imperial Palace. Today the Looshaus has lost its power to shock, and the facade seems quite innocuous. The interior remains a breathtaking surprise; the building now houses a bank, and you can go inside to see the stylish chambers and staircase. ■ TIP➔ **To really get up close and personal with Loos, head to**

the splendor of his Loos American Bar, five blocks or so to the east at No. 10 Kärntnerdurchgang. ⊠ *Michaelerplatz 3, 1st District* Ⓤ *U3/Herrengasse.*

㉔ Michaelerplatz. One of Vienna's most historic squares, this small plaza is now the site of an excavation revealing Roman plus 18th- and 19th-century layers of the past. The excavations are a latter-day distraction from the Michaelerplatz's most noted claim to fame—the eloquent entryway to the palace complex of the Hofburg.

Mozart's Requiem debuted in the **Michaelerkirche** on December 10, 1791. More people stop in today due a discovery American soldiers made in 1945, when they forced open the crypt doors, which had been sealed for 150 years. Found lying undisturbed, obviously for centuries, were the mummified remains of former wealthy parishioners of the church—even the finery and buckled shoes worn at their burial had been preserved by the perfect temperatures contained within the crypt.

Fascinatingly ghoulish tours are offered throughout the year (from Easter to November 1 at 11, 2, 3 and 4 weekdays, on Saturday at 3 and 4. For visits to the crypt during the rest of the year, phone 0650/533–80–03). The cost is €5. The tour is given first in German and then in English. Visitors are led down into the shadowy gloom and through a labyrinth of passageways, pausing at several tombs (many of which are open so one can view the remains) for a brief explanation of the cause of death. ⊠ *Between Hofburg Palace and Graben, 1st District* Ⓤ *U3/ Herrengasse.*

㉚ Peterskirche (St. Peter's Church). Considered the best example of church Baroque in Vienna—certainly the most theatrical—the Peterskirche was constructed between 1702 and 1708 by Lucas von Hildebrandt. According to legend, the original church on this site was founded in 792 by Charlemagne, a tale immortalized by the relief plaque on the right side of the church. The facade has angled towers, graceful turrets (said to have been inspired by the tents of the Turks during the siege of 1683), and an unusually fine entrance portal. Inside, the Baroque decoration is elaborate, with some fine touches (particularly the glass-crowned galleries high on the walls on either side of the altar and the amazing tableau of the martyrdom of St. John Nepomuk), but the lack of light and the years of accumulated dirt create a prevailing gloom, and the much-praised ceiling frescoes by J. M. Rottmayr are impossible to make out.

■ TIP→ Just before Christmastime each year the basement crypt is filled with a display of nativity scenes. The church is shoehorned into tiny Petersplatz, just off the Graben. ⊠ *Petersplatz, 1st District* Ⓤ *U1 or U3/ Stephansplatz.*

Also Worth Seeing

㉘ Haas-Haus. Designed by Hans Hollein, one of Austria's best-known living architects, the Haas-Haus is at once one of the trendiest

> **EURO TOUR**
>
> The more important churches, such as Stephansdom, Peterskirche, Minoritenkirche, and Michaelerkirche, have coin-operated (€1–€2) tape machines that give an excellent commentary in English on the structure's history and architecture.

places to stay in the heart of Vienna and the closest hotel to the venerable walls of St. Stephen's. The clear-cut line of the glass exterior is continued into the lobby and hotel. On the ground floor you can shop for the latest in ladies fashion. ⊠ *Stephansplatz 12, 1st District* Ⓤ *U1 or U3/Stephansplatz.*

㉗ **Stock-im-Eisen.** In the southwest corner of Stock-im-Eisen-Platz, set into the building on the west side of Kärntnerstrasse, is one of the city's odder relics: the Stock-im-Eisen, or the "nail-studded stump." Chronicles first mention the Stock-im-Eisen in 1533, but it is probably far older, and for hundreds of years any apprentice metalsmith who came to Vienna to learn his trade hammered a nail into the tree trunk for good luck. During World War II, when there was talk of moving the relic to a museum in Munich, it mysteriously disappeared; it reappeared, perfectly preserved, after the threat of removal had passed. ⊠ *Intersection of Kärtnerstrasse and Singerstrasse 1st District* Ⓤ *U1 or U3/Stephansplatz.*

An Imperial City: The Hofburg

A walk through the Imperial Palace, called the Hofburg, brings you back to the days when Vienna was the capital of a mighty empire. You can still find in Viennese shops vintage postcards and prints that show the revered and bewhiskered Emperor Franz Josef leaving his Hofburg palace for a drive in his carriage. Today you can walk in his very footsteps, gaze at the old tin bath the emperor kept under his simple iron bedstead, marvel at his bejeweled christening robe, and, along the way, feast your eyes on great works of art, impressive armor, and some of the finest Baroque interiors in Europe.

Until 1918 the Hofburg was the home of the Habsburgs, rulers of the Austro-Hungarian Empire. As a modern tourist lure, it has become a vast smorgasbord of sightseeing attractions: the Imperial Apartments, two imperial treasuries, six museums, the National Library, and the famous Winter Riding School all vie for attention. One of the latest Hofburg attractions is a museum devoted to "Sisi," the beloved Empress Elisabeth, wife of Franz Josef, whose beauty was the talk of Europe and whose tragic assassination (the recently purchased murder weapon is one of the various exhibits) was mourned by all. The entire complex takes a minimum of a full day to explore in detail. ■ TIP→ **If your time is limited (or if you want to save most of the interior sightseeing for a rainy day), you should omit the Imperial Apartments and all the museums mentioned below except the new museum of court silver and tableware, the Silberkammer, and probably the Schatzkammer.** An excellent multilingual, full-color booklet describing the palace in detail is for sale at most ticket counters within the complex; it gives a complete list of attractions and maps out the palace's complicated ground plan and building history wing by wing.

Vienna took its imperial role seriously, as evidenced by the sprawling Hofburg complex, which is still today, as then, the seat of government. But this is generally understated power; while the buildings cover a considerable area, the treasures lie within, not to be flamboyantly flaunted. Certainly under Franz Josef the reign was beneficent—witness the broad

Ringstrasse he ordained and the panoply of museums and public buildings it hosts. With few exceptions (Vienna City Hall and the Votive Church), rooflines are kept to an even level, creating an ensemble effect that helps integrate the palace complex and its parks into the urban landscape without making a domineering statement. Diplomats still bustle in and out of high-level international meetings along the elegant halls. Horse-drawn carriages still traverse the Ring and the roadway that cuts through the complex. Ignore the cars and tour buses, and you can easily imagine yourself in a Vienna of a hundred or more years ago.

Architecturally, the Hofburg—like St. Stephen's—is far from refined. It grew up over a period of 700 years (its earliest mention in court documents is from 1279, at the very beginning of Habsburg rule), and its spasmodic, haphazard growth kept it from attaining any sort of unified identity. But many of the bits and pieces are fine, and one interior (the National Library) is a tour de force.

A GOOD WALK

When you begin to explore the Hofburg you realize that the palace complex is like a nest of boxes, courtyards opening off courtyards and wings (*Trakte*) spreading far and wide. First tackle **Josefsplatz** ㉝, the remarkable square that interrupts Augustinerstrasse, ornamented by the equestrian statue of Josef II. On your right to the north is the **Spanische Reitschule** ㉞, the Spanish Riding School—one emblem of Vienna known throughout the world—where the famous white horses reign. Across Reitschulgasse under the arches are the **Lipizzaner Museum** ㉟ and the Imperial Stables. To the south stands the **Augustinerkirche** ㊱, St. Augustine's Church, where the Habsburg rulers' hearts are preserved in urns. The grand main hall (Prunksaal) of the **Hofbibliothek** ㊲, the National Library, is one of the great Baroque treasures of Europe, a site not to be missed (enter from the southwest corner of Josefsplatz).

Under the Michaelerplatz dome is the entrance to the **Kaiserappartements** ㊳, hardly the elegance you would normally associate with royalty, but Franz Josef, the residing emperor from 1848 to 1916, was anything but ostentatious in his personal life. For the representational side, however, go through into the **In der Burg** ㊴ courtyard and look in at the elegant **Silberkammer** ㊵ museum of court silver and tableware. Go through the **Schweizertor** ㊶, the Swiss Gate, to the south off In der Burg, to reach the small Schweizer Hof courtyard with stairs leading to the **Hofburgkapelle** ㊷, the Imperial Chapel where the Vienna Boys Choir makes its regular Sunday appearances. In a back corner of the courtyard is the entrance to the **Schatzkammer** ㊸, the Imperial Treasury, overflowing with jewels, robes, and royal trappings. From In der Burg, the roadway leads under the Leopold Wing of the complex into the vast park known as **Heldenplatz** ㊹, or Hero's Square. The immediately obvious heroes are the equestrian statues of Archduke Karl and Prince Eugene of Savoy. The Hofburg wing to the south with its concave facade is the **Neue Burg** ㊺, the "new" section of the complex, now housing four specialized museums. Depending on your interests, consider the **Ephesus Museum** ㊻, with Roman antiquities; the **Musical Instrument Collection** ㊼, where you also hear what you see; and the impressive **Weapons Collection** ㊽, with tons of steel armor. Ahead, the Burgtor gate separates the Hofburg

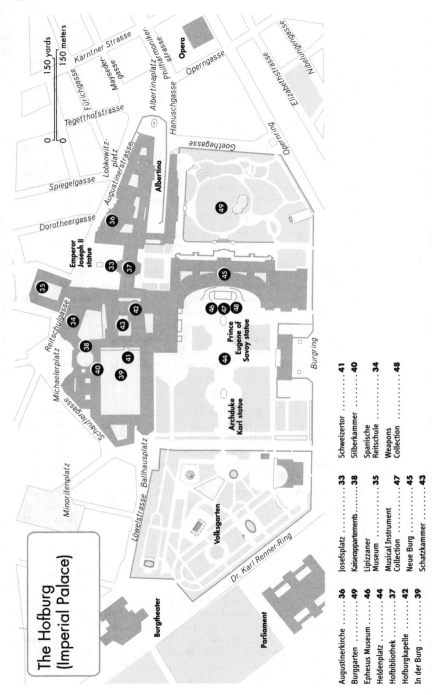

The Hofburg (Imperial Palace)

complex from the Ringstrasse. The quiet oasis in back of the Neue Burg is the **Burggarten** ㊾, home to the magical **Schmetterlinghaus** (Butterfly House). Catch your breath and marvel that you've seen only a small part of the Hofburg—a large part of it still houses the offices of the Austrian government and is not open to the public.

TIMING   You could spend a day in the Hofburg complex. For most of the smaller museums, figure on anything from an hour upward.

Main Attractions

㊱ **Augustinerkirche** (Augustinian Church). Built during the 14th century and presenting the most unified Gothic interior in the city, the church is something of a fraud; the interior, it turns out, dates from the late 18th century, not the early 14th. A historical fraud the church may be, but a spiritual fraud it is not. The view from the entrance doorway is stunning: a soaring harmony of vertical piers, ribbed vaults, and hanging chandeliers that makes Vienna's other Gothic interiors look earthbound by comparison. Note the magnificent **Tomb of the Archduchess Maria-Christina**, sculpted by the great Antonio Canova in 1805, with mournful figures of her and her family (her husband founded the Albertina) trooping into a temple. ■ TIP➔ **The imposing Baroque organ sounds as heavenly as it looks, and the Sunday-morning high mass (frequently by Mozart or Haydn) sung here at 11 AM can be the highlight of a trip.** To the right of the main altar in the small Loreto Chapel stand silver urns containing the hearts of Habsburg rulers. This rather morbid sight is viewable after early mass on Sunday, Monday, or by appointment. ✉ *Josefsplatz, 1st District* ☎ *01/533–7099–0* Ⓤ *U3/Herrengasse.*

㊾ **Burggarten.** The intimate Burggarten in back of the Neue Burg is a quiet oasis that includes a statue of a contemplative Franz Josef and an elegant statue of Mozart, moved here from the Albertinaplatz after the war, when the city's charred ruins were being rebuilt. Today the park is one of the most favored time-out spots for the Viennese; the alluring backdrop is formed by the striking former greenhouses that are now the gorgeous Palmenhaus restaurant and the **Schmetterlinghaus**. Total enchantment awaits you here at Vienna's unique Butterfly House. Inside are towering tropical trees, waterfalls, a butterfly nursery, and more than 150 species on display (usually 400 winged jewels are in residence). ✉ *Access from Opernring and Hanuschgasse/Goethegasse, 1st District* 🎫 *€5* ◷ *Apr.–Oct., weekdays 10–4:45, weekends 10–6:15; Nov.–Mar., daily 10–3:45* ⊕ *www.schmetterlinghaus.at* Ⓤ *U2/Museums-Quartier; Tram: 1, 2, and D/Burgring.*

㊲ **Hofbibliothek** (formerly Court, now National, Library). This is one of the grandest Baroque libraries in the world, in every sense a cathedral of books. Its centerpiece is the spectacular Prunksaal—the Grand Hall of the National Library—which probably contains more book treasures than any comparable collection outside the Vatican. The main entrance to the ornate reading room is in the left corner of Josefsplatz. Designed by Fischer von Erlach the Elder just before his death in 1723 and completed by his son, the Grand Hall is full-blown High Baroque, with trompe-l'oeil ceiling frescoes by Daniel Gran. Usually twice a year, lasting three to six

Fodor'sChoice
★

months, special exhibits highlight some of the finest and rarest tomes, well documented in German and English. From 1782 Mozart performed here regularly at the Sunday matinees of Baron Gottfried van Swieten, who lived in a suite of rooms in the grand, palacelike library. Four years later the baron founded the Society of Associated Cavaliers, which set up oratorio performances with Mozart acting as conductor. Across the street at Palais Palffy Mozart reportedly first performed *The Marriage of Figaro* before a select, private audience to see if it would pass the court censor. ⊠ *Josefsplatz 1, 1st District* ☎ *01/534–100* ⊕ *www.onb.ac.at* 🖭 *€5* ⊙ *Tues.–Sun. 10–6, Thurs. 10–9* Ⓤ *U3/Herrengasse.*

㊷ Hofburgkapelle (Chapel of the Imperial Palace). Fittingly, this is the main venue for the beloved Vienna Boys' Choir (Wiener Sängerknaben), since they actually have their earliest roots in the Hofmusikkapelle choir founded by Emperor Maximilian I five centuries ago (Haydn and Schubert were both participants as young boys). Today the choir sings mass here at 9:15 on Sunday from mid-September to June (even though this is a mass, tickets are sold to hear the choir, ranging from €5 to €35). Alas, the arrangement is such that you *hear* the choirboys but don't see them; their soprano and alto voices peal forth from a gallery behind the seating area. But the choir can be seen in all their apple-cheeked splendor at other places around town, notably the Musikverein and Schönbrunn Palace; see their Web site for their concert schedule. In case you miss out on tickets to the Sunday performance, note that just to the right of the chapel entrance a door leads into a small foyer. Here a television screen shows the whole mass for free. ▪ TIP→ **Most often, the choirboys leave the chapel via this exit, so you may have the chance to get some good pictures of these cute little lads in their sailor uniforms.** For ticket information, *see* Nightlife and the Arts, *below*. ⊠ *Hofburg, Schweizer Hof, 1st District* ☎ *01/533–9927* ⊕ *www.wsk. at* 🖷 *01/533–9927–75* Ⓤ *U3/Herrengasse.*

㊴ In der Burg. This prominent courtyard of the Hofburg complex is centered by a statue of Francis II and the noted **Schweizertor** gateway. Note the **clock** on the far upper wall at the north end of the courtyard: it tells time by a sundial, also gives the time mechanically, and even, above the clock face, indicates the phase of the moon. ⊠ *Hofburg, 1st District* Ⓤ *U3/Herrengasse.*

㉝ Josefsplatz. Many consider this Vienna's loveliest courtyard. Indeed, the beautifully restored imperial decor adorning the roof of the buildings forming Josefsplatz is one of the few visual demonstrations of Austria's onetime widespread power and influence. The square's namesake is represented in the equestrian **statue of Emperor Joseph II** (1807) in the center. ⊠ *Herrengasse, 1st District* Ⓤ *U3/Herrengasse.*

㊳ Kaiserappartements (Imperial Apartments). From the spectacular portal gate of the Michaelertor—you can't miss the four gigantic statues of Hercules and his Labors—you enter and climb the marble Kaiserstiege (Emperor's Staircase) to begin a tour of a long, repetitive suite of 18 conventionally luxurious state rooms. The red-and-gold decoration (19th-century imitation of 18th-century Rococo) tries to look regal, but much like the empire itself in its latter days it is only going through the motions and ends up looking merely official. Still, these are the rooms where the ruling family of the Habsburg empire ate, slept, and dealt with family tragedy—in the emperor's study on January 30, 1889, Emperor Franz Josef was told about the tragic death of his only son, Crown Prince Rudolf, who had shot himself and his soulmate, 17-year-old Baroness Vetsera, at the hunting lodge at Mayerling. Among the few signs of genuine life are Emperor Franz Josef's spartan, iron field bed, on which he slept every night, and his empress Elisabeth's wooden gymnastics equipment (obsessed with her looks, "Sisi" suffered from anorexia and was fanatically devoted to exercise). To commemorate the 150th wedding anniversary of this mismatched pair in 2004, a Sisi Museum was inaugurated, which is actually part of the regular tour. Five rooms are given over to the myths and realities of this Princess Diana of the 19th century; exhibits are displayed in high-style fashion, with colored spotlights, painted murals, and many of her treasured possessions, including her jewels, the gown she wore the night before her marriage, her dressing gown, and the reconstructed, opulent Court Salon railroad car she used. There is also a death mask made after her assassination by an anarchist in Geneva in 1898. ⊠ *Hofburg, Schweizer Hof, 1st District* ⊕ *www. hofburg-wien.at* ☏ *01/533–7570* 🎟 *€8.90* ☉ *Daily 9–5; July and Aug., daily 9–5:30* Ⓤ *U3/Herrengasse.*

43 **Schatzkammer** (Imperial Treasury). The entrance to the Schatzkammer, with its 1,000 years of treasures, is tucked away at ground level behind the staircase to the Hofburgkapelle. The elegant display is a welcome antidote to the monotony of the Imperial Apartments, for the entire Treasury was completely renovated in 1983–87, and the crowns and relics and vestments fairly glow in their surroundings. Here you'll find such marvels as the Holy Lance—reputedly the lance that pierced Jesus's side—the Imperial Crown (a sacred symbol of sovereignty once stolen on Hitler's orders), and the Saber of Charlemagne. Don't miss the Burgundian Treasure, connected with that most romantic of medieval orders of chivalry, the Order of the Golden Fleece. ⊠ *Schweizer Hof, 1st District* ☏ *01/525240* 🎟 *€8* ☉ *Wed.–Mon. 10–6* Ⓤ *U3/Herrengasse.*

FodorśChoice
★

40 **Silberkammer** (Museum of Court Silver and Tableware). The large courtyard on the far side of the Michaelertor rotunda is known as In der Burg; here on the west side is the entrance to the sparkling new Silberkammer. Fascinating for its "behind-the-scenes" views of state banquets and other elegant representational affairs, there's far more than forks and finger bowls here; stunning decorative pieces vie with glittering silver and gold for attention. Highlights include Emperor Franz Josef's vermeil banqueting service, the jardinière given to Empress Elisabeth by Queen Victoria, and gifts from Marie-Antoinette to her brother Josef II. The presentation of full table settings gives an idea of court life both as lived daily and on festive occasions. ⊠ *Hofburg, Michaelertrakt, 1st District* ☏ *01/533–7570* 🎟 *€8.90 including Kaiserappartements* ☉ *Daily 9–5; July and Aug., daily 9–5:30* Ⓤ *U3/Herrengasse.*

★ **34** **Spanische Reitschule** (Spanish Riding School). Between Augustinerstrasse and the Josefsplatz is the world-famous Spanish Riding School, a favorite for centuries, and no wonder: who can resist the sight of the stark-white

Lipizzaner horses going through their masterful paces? For the last 300 years they have been perfecting their *haute école* riding demonstrations to the sound of Baroque music in a ballroom that seems to be a crystal-chandeliered stable. The interior of the riding school, the 1735 work of Fischer von Erlach the Younger, is itself an attraction—surely Europe's most elegant sports arena—and if the prancing horses begin to pall, move up to the top balcony and examine the ceiling. ■ TIP➔ **The school's popularity is hardly surprising, and tickets to some performances must be ordered in writing many weeks in advance, or through their Web site.** Information offices have a brochure with the detailed schedule (performances are usually March–December, with the school on vacation in July and August). Generally the full, 80-minute show takes place Sunday at 11 AM plus selected Fridays at 6 PM. There are two yearly classical dressage final rehearsals with music, at the end of August and the end of December. Check the Web site for details.

Morning training sessions with music are held Tuesday–Saturday 10–noon. Tickets are available at the visitor center, Michaelerplatz 1, Tuesday to Saturday (except holidays) 9–5, and at Josefsplatz, Gate 2 on the day of the morning exercise 9–12:30. It's best to get there early to get a place in line. Note that if you purchase your tickets through a ticket agency for an actual performance, they can legally add a commission of 22%–25% to the face price of the ticket. For performance ticket orders, write to **Spanische Reitschule** (✉ Hofburg, A-1010 Vienna). Pick up reserved tickets at the office under the Michaelerplatz rotunda dome. ✉ *Michaelerplatz 1, Hofburg, A-1010, 1st District* ☎ *01/533-9031-0* 🖷 *01/535-0186* ⊕ *www.srs.com* 🎫 *€35–€160; standing room €22–€28, morning training sessions €12. Sat. classical dressage final rehearsal, €20* ⊘ *Mar.–June and late Aug.–mid-Dec. Closed tour wks* Ⓤ *U3/Herrengasse.*

Also Worth Seeing

㊻ Ephesus Museum. One of the museums in the Neue Burg, the Ephesus Museum contains exceptional Roman antiquities unearthed by Austrian archaeologists in Turkey at the turn of the century. ✉ *Hofburg, 1st District* 🎫 *Combined ticket with Musical Instrument Collection and Weapons Collection €8* ⊘ *Wed.–Mon. 10–6* Ⓤ *Tram: 1, 2, and D/ Burgring.*

㊹ Heldenplatz. The long wing with the concave bay on the south side of the square is the youngest section of the palace, called the Neue Burg. Although the Neue Burg building plans were not completed and the Heldenplatz was left without a discernible shape, the space is nevertheless punctuated by two superb equestrian statues depicting Archduke Karl and Prince Eugene of Savoy. The older section on the north includes the offices of the federal president. ✉ *Hofburg, 1st District* Ⓤ *Tram: 1, 2, and D/Burgring.*

㉟ Lipizzaner Museum. If you're interested in learning more about the Lipizzaner horses, visit this museum in what used to be the old imperial pharmacy. Exhibitions document the history of the Lipizzaners, including paintings, photographs, and videos giving an overview from the 16th century to the present. The breed was started in 1580, and the horses proved themselves in battle as well as in the complicated "dances" for which they are famous. A highlight is a visit to the stables, where you can see the horses up close, through a glass window. ⊠ *Reitschulgasse 2, 1st District* ☎ *01/525 24-583* ⊕ *www.lipizzaner.at* ⊠ *€5; combined ticket with morning training session €15* ⊙ *Daily 9–6* Ⓤ *U3/Herrengasse.*

47 **Musical Instrument Collection.** This Neue Burg museum houses pianos that belonged to Brahms, Schumann, and Mahler. An acoustic guided tour allows you to actually hear the various instruments on headphones as you move from room to room. ⊠ *Hofburg, 1st District* ⊠ *Combined ticket with Ephesus Museum and Weapons Collection €8, more for special exhibits* ⊙ *Wed.–Mon. 10–6* Ⓤ *U2/MuseumsQuartier.*

45 **Neue Burg.** The Neue Burg stands today as a symbol of architectural overconfidence. Designed for Emperor Franz Josef in 1869, this "new château" was part of a much larger scheme that was meant to make the Hofburg rival the Louvre, if not Versailles. The German architect Gottfried Semper planned a twin of the present Neue Burg on the opposite side of the Heldenplatz, with arches connecting the Neue Burg and its twin with the other pair of twins on the Ringstrasse, the Kunsthistorisches Museum (Museum of Art History), and the Naturhistorisches Museum (Museum of Natural History). But World War I intervened, and with the empire's collapse the Neue Burg became merely the last in a long series of failed attempts to bring architectural order to the Hofburg. (From its main balcony, in March 1938, Adolf Hitler told a huge cheering crowd below of his plan for the new German empire, declaring that Vienna "is a pearl! I am going to put it into a setting of which it is worthy!") Today the Neue Burg houses no fewer than four specialty museums: the **Ephesus Museum, Musical Instruments Collection, Ethnological Museum,** and **Weapons Collection.** For details on these museums, see separate listings. ⊠ *Heldenplatz, 1st District* ☎ *01/525240* Ⓤ *U2/MuseumsQuartier.*

41 **Schweizertor** (Swiss Gate). Dating from 1552 and decorated with some of the earliest classical motifs in the city, the Schweizertor leads from In der Burg through to the oldest section of the palace, a small courtyard known as the Schweizer Hof. The gateway is painted maroon, black, and gold; it gives a fine Renaissance flourish to its building facade. ⊠ *Hofburg, Schweizertor, 1st District* Ⓤ *U3/Herrengasse.*

48 **Weapons Collection.** Rivaling the armory in Graz as one of the most extensive arms and armor collections in the world is this Neue Burg museum. Enter at the triumphal arch set into the middle of the curved portion of the facade. ⊠ *Heldenplatz, 1st District* ⊠ *Combined ticket with Ephesus Museum and Musical Instrument Collection €8, more for special exhibits* ⊙ *Wed.–Mon. 10–6* Ⓤ *U2/MuseumsQuartier.*

The Ringstrasse: Gems of the "Ring"

Late in 1857 Emperor Franz Josef issued a decree announcing the most ambitious piece of urban redevelopment Vienna had ever seen. The inner city's centuries-old walls were to be torn down, and the *glacis*—

the wide expanse of open field that acted as a protective buffer between inner city and outer suburbs—was to be filled in. In their place was to rise a wide, tree-lined, circular boulevard, upon which would stand an imposing collection of new buildings reflecting Vienna's special status as the political, economic, and cultural heart of the Austro-Hungarian Empire. During the 50 years of building that followed, many factors combined to produce the Ringstrasse as it now stands, but the most important was the gradual rise of liberalism after the failed Revolution of 1848. By the latter half of the Ringstrasse era, support for constitutional government, democracy, and equality—all the concepts that liberalism traditionally equates with progress—was steadily increasing. As the Ringstrasse went up, it became the definitive symbol of this liberal progress; as Carl E. Schorske put it in his *Fin-de-Siècle Vienna,* it celebrated "the triumph of constitutional *Recht* (right) over imperial *Macht* (might), of secular culture over religious faith. Not palaces, garrisons, and churches, but centers of constitutional government and higher culture dominated the Ring."

As an ensemble, the collection is astonishing in its architectural presumption: it is nothing less than an attempt to assimilate and summarize the entire architectural history of Europe. The highest concentration of public building is found in the area around the Volksgarten. In and around the Ring ribbon you'll find an array of other unmissable gems: the quaint-now-trendy Spittelberg Quarter, Freud's apartment, and Vienna's new/old dazzler, the Liechtenstein "garden palace," home to princely Old Masters, including a fabled collection of paintings by Peter Paul Rubens.

A GOOD WALK

Is there a best way to explore the Ring? You can walk it from one end to the other—from where it begins at the Danube Canal to where it returns to the canal after its curving flight. Or, you can explore it whenever you happen to cross it on other missions. Although it is a pleasant sequence of boulevards, seeing its succession of rather pompous buildings all in one walk can be overpowering. Or, you can obtain the best of both options by following this suggested itinerary, which leavens the bombast of the Ring with some of Vienna's most fascinating sights. If you just want to do the highlights, plan on spending the morning at the Kunsthistorisches Museum, then take in the MuseumsQuartier (and lunch in the complex), followed by a leisurely afternoon spent at the Freud Haus and the spectacular Liechtenstein Museum.

Your walk begins at the twin museums across the Ringstrasse from the Hofburg. To the west is the **Naturhistorisches Museum** 🟢; to the east, the **Kunsthistorisches Museum** 🟢, the art museum packed with world-famous treasures. Allow ample time for exploration here. Behind them is the **MuseumsQuartier** 🟢, a complex that includes several highly important modern art collections, including the Leopold Collection of Austrian Art and the Museum Moderner Kunst. Farther west of the MuseumsQuartier is the compact and hip **Spittelberg Quarter** 🟢 of tiny streets between Burggasse and Siebensterngasse, often the site of handicraft and seasonal fairs. For more, and superspectacular, evidence of handicraft of an earlier era, detour south to Mariahilferstrasse and the **Kaiserliches Hofmo-**

1

biliendepot, the repository of much of the sumptuous furnishings of the old Habsburg palaces.

Heading back to the Ring, the **Volksgarten** ⓸ directly west of the Hofburg includes a café and rose garden among its attractions; look also for the lovely memorial to Franz Josef's wife, Empress Elisabeth, in the rear corner. Tackle the Ringstrasse buildings by the **Parlament** ⓹, the **Rathaus** ⓺ (City Hall), the **Burgtheater** ⓻ on the inside of the Ring, then the **Universität** ⓼ (the main building of Vienna's university) beyond, again on the outside of the Ring. Next to the university stands the neo-Gothic **Votivkirche** ⓽. If you still have time and energy, walk farther along the Ring to discover the Börse at the corner of the Ring and Wipplingerstrasse. The outside end of Hohenstaufengasse leads into Liechtensteinstrasse, which will bring you to Berggasse. Turn right to reach No. 19, the **Freud Haus** ⓾, now a museum and research facility. Not far from Freud's apartment and just off the Liechtensteinstrasse on Fürstengasse, is the **Liechtenstein Museum** ㉑, home of the Prince of Liechtenstein's fabulous private art collection, housed in the family's summer palace.

TIMING   If you can, plan to visit Vienna's Louvre—the Kunsthistorisches Museum—early in the day before the crowds arrive, although the size of crowds depends greatly on whatever special shows the museum may be exhibiting. As for the main sights off the Ringstrasse, you could easily lump together visits to the Freud Apartment and the MuseumsQuartier, figuring on about a half day for the two combined. ■ TIP➔ **Tram 1 and 2 go clockwise and counter-clockwise around the Ring.**

Main Attractions

⓻ **Burgtheater** (National Theater). One of the most important theaters in the German-speaking world, the Burgtheater was built between 1874 and 1888 in the Italian Renaissance style, replacing the old court theater at Michaelerplatz. Emperor Franz Josef's mistress, Katherina Schratt, was once a star performer here, and famous Austrian and German actors still stride across this stage. The opulent interior, with its 60-foot relief *Worshippers of Bacchus* by Rudolf Wyer and foyer ceiling frescoes by Ernst and Gustav Klimt, makes it well worth a visit. For information about performances here, *see* Theater *in* Nightlife and the Arts, *below.* ✉ *Dr.-Karl-Lueger-Ring 2, 1st District* ☎ *01/514–4441–40* 💳 *€4.50* ☉ *Guided tours Mon.–Sat. at 3, Sun. at 11 and 3* Ⓤ *Tram: 1, 2, and D/Burgtheater, Rathaus.*

⓾ **Freud Haus.** Not far from the historic Hofburg district, beyond the Votivkirche at the Schottenring along the Ringstrasse, you can skip over several centuries and visit that outstanding symbol of 20th-century Vienna: Sigmund Freud's apartment at Berggasse 19 (Apartment 6, one flight up; ring the bell and push the door simultaneously); this was his residence from 1891 to 1938. The five-room collection of memorabilia is mostly a photographic record of Freud's life, with some documents, publications, and a portion of his collection of antiquities also on display. The waiting-room furniture is authentic, but the consulting room and study furniture (including the famous couch) can be seen only in photographs. ✉ *Berggasse 19, 9th District/Alsergrund* ☎ *01/319–1596*

⊕ *www.freud-museum.at* ✉ €8 ⊙ *Jan.–June and Oct.–Dec., daily 9–5; July–Sept., daily 9–6* Ⓤ *U2/Schottentor.*

Ⓢ Kunsthistorisches Museum (Museum of Fine Art). However short your stay in Vienna, you will surely want to pay a visit to one of the greatest art collections in the world, that of the Kunsthistorisches Museum. For this is no dry-as-dust museum illustrating the history of art, as its name implies. Rather its collections of Old Master paintings reveal the royal taste and style of many members of the mighty House of Habsburg, who during the 16th and 17th centuries ruled over the greater part of the Western world. Today you can enjoy what this great ruling house assiduously (and in most cases, selectively) brought together through the centuries. The collection stands in the same class with those of the Louvre, the Prado, and the Vatican. It is most famous for the largest collection of paintings under one roof by the Netherlandish 16th-century master Pieter Brueghel the Elder—just seeing his sublime *Hunters in the Snow* is worth a trip to Vienna, many art historians will tell you. Brueghel's depictions of peasant scenes, often set in magnificent landscapes, distill the poetry and magic of the 16th century as few other paintings do. Room RX is the Brueghel shrine—on its walls, in addition to *Hunters in the Snow,* hang *Children's Games,* the *Tower of Babel,* the *Peasant Wedding,* the *Nest-Robber,* and eight other priceless canvases. But there are also hundreds of other celebrated Old Master paintings here. Even a cursory description would run on for pages, but a brief selection of the museum's most important works will give you an idea of the riches to be enjoyed. The large-scale works concentrated in the main galleries shouldn't distract you from the equal share of masterworks in the more intimate side wings.

The Flemish wing also includes Rogier van der Weyden's *Crucifixion Triptych,* Holbein's *Portrait of Jane Seymour, Queen of England,* a fine series of Rembrandt portraits, and Vermeer's peerless *Allegory of the Art of Painting.* The grand style of the 17th century is represented by Rubens's towering altarpieces and his *Nude of Hélène Fourment.* In the Italian wing are works by Titian, including his *Portrait of Isabella d'Este,* whose fiercely intelligent eyes make you realize why she was the first lady of the Renaissance, and Giorgione's *The Three Philosophers,* an enigmatic composition in uniquely radiant Venetian coloring. A short list of other highlights includes Raphael's *Madonna in the Meadow,* Correggio's *Jupiter Embracing Io,* Parmigianino's *Cupid Cutting a Bow,*

PASS THE SALT

Benevenuto Cellini's legendary 16th-century salt cellar, valued at €50 million, was stolen in 2003 by a security-installations salesman. He climbed in through a first-floor window via some construction scaffolding outside. The thief turned himself in along with the table piece after police released a picture of a suspect, which led to his being recognized. He had kept the Saliera hidden under his bed for nearly three years, and supposedly wanted to prove the security measures in the museum were not up-to-date. The unique treasure was returned to its home in a very well-guarded case in 2006.

Guercino's *Return of the Prodigal Son,* and Caravaggio's *Madonna of the Rosary.* One level down is the remarkable, less-visited **Kunstkammer,** displaying priceless objects created for the Habsburg emperors. These include curiosities made of gold, silver, and crystal (including Cellini's famous salt cellar "La Saliera"), and more exotic materials, such as ivory, horn, and gemstones. In addition, there are rooms devoted to Egyptian antiquities, Greek and Roman art, sculpture (ranging from masterworks by Tilmann Riemenschneider to Italian Mannerist bronzes, which the Habsburgs collected by the roomful) and the decorative arts, and numerous other collections. When

---

ART ON THURSDAY

The best time to see the museum's art collections is Thursday, when the museum caterer Gerstner sets out a sumptuous buffet dinner in the cupola rotunda. Just across from the seating area, take a leisurely stroll through the almost empty gallery chambers. Seating starts at 6:30 PM, and there's plenty of time between courses to take your fill of the finest art available. The museum galleries close at 9 PM, so make sure you get your fill of art beforehand. The buffet remains open until 10 PM.

---

your feet are ready to call a sit-down strike, repair to a comfy armchair in the wonderful café on the museum's second floor. Set under a grand dome, adorned with paintings, sculpture, and framed by gilt-tipped black marble columns, this spot is run by Gerstner, the famed pastry-shop. ⊠ *Maria-Theresien-Platz, 7th District/Neubau* ☎ *01/525240* ⊕ *www. khm.at* ✉ *€10* ⊙ *Tues.–Sun. 10–6; extended hrs for picture galleries, Thurs. until 9 PM* Ⓤ *U2/MuseumsQuartier, U2, or U3/Volkstheater.*

★ ☾ ❷ **MuseumsQuartier** (Museum Quarter). New and old, past and present, Baroque and Modernism dazzlingly collide in this headline-making, vast culture center that opened in 2001. Claiming to be the largest of its kind in the world, the MuseumsQuartier—or **MQ** as many now call it—is housed in what was once the Imperial Court Stables, the 250-year-old Baroque complex designed by Fischer von Erlach, and is ideally situated between the great Old Master treasures of the Kunsthistorisches Museum and the Spittelberg neighborhood, today one of Vienna's hippest enclaves. Where once 900 Lipizzaner horses were housed, now thousands of artistic masterworks of the 20th century and beyond are exhibited, all in a complex that is architecturally an expert and subtle blending of historic and cutting-edge—the original structure (fetchingly adorned with pastry-white stuccoed ceilings and rococo flourishes) was retained, while ultramodern wings were added to house five museums, most of which showcase modern art at its best.

Once ensconced in the Palais Liechtenstein, the **Leopold Museum** (⊕ www.leopoldmuseum.org ✉ €9 ⊙ Wed.–Mon. 10–6)comprises the holdings amassed by Rudolf and Elizabeth Leopold and famously contains one of the greatest collections of Egon Schiele in the world, as well as impressive works by Gustav Klimt and Oskar Kokoschka. Other artists worth noting are Josef Dobrowsky, Anton Faistauer, and Richard Gerstl. Emil Jakob Schindler's landscapes are well-represented, as are those by Biedermeier artist Ferdinand Georg Waldmüller. Center stage is held by Schiele (1890–1918), who died young, along with his wife and young baby, in the Spanish flu pandemic of 1918. His colorful, appealing landscapes are here, but all eyes are invariably drawn to the artist's tortured and racked depictions of nude mistresses, orgiastic self-portraits, and provocatively sexual couples, all elbows and organs.

Adjacent, in a broodingly modernistic, dark stone edifice, is **MUMOK, Museum moderner Kunst Stiftung Ludwig** (Museum of Modern Art; ⊕ www.mumok.at ✉ €9 ☉ Tues.–Sun. 10–6), which houses the national collection of 20th-century art on eight floors, mainly a bequest of Herr Ludwig, a billionaire industrialist who collected the cream of the cream of 20th-century art. Top works here are of the American Pop Art school, but all the trends of the last century—Nouveau Réalisme, Radical Realism, and Hyperrealism of the '60s and '70s, Fluxus, Viennese Actionism, Conceptual Art and Minimal Art, Land Art and Arte Povera, as well as installation art vie for your attention. Names run from René Magritte and Max Ernst to Andy Warhol, Jackson Pollock, Cy Twombly, Nam June Paik, and the very latest superstars of contemporary art, such as Chris Burden (whose installation was of $1 million worth of gold ingots) and Kara Walker's daringly revisionist silhouettes. Kids will make a beeline for Claes Oldenburg's walk-in sculpture in the shape of Mickey Mouse.

Nearby, the **Kunsthalle** (⊕ www.kunsthallewien.at ✉ €6.50 ☉ Mon.–Wed., Fri.–Sun. 10–7) is used for temporary exhibitions—gigantic halls used for the installation of avant-avant-garde art. The **Architekturzentrum** (Architecture Center; ⊕ www.azw.at ✉ €5 ☉ Daily 10–7) displays new architecture models, with computers showing the latest techniques used in restoring old buildings.

A definite change of pace is offered by the **ZOOM Kinder Museum** (☎ 01/ 524–7908 ⊕ www.kindermuseum.at ✉ €3.50; child €5; Zoom Ozean, child with one adult €4 ☉ By reservation) which caters to children. In the ZOOM lab, kids age 7 and up can experience the fine line between the real and virtual worlds, making their imagined screenplays come to life by becoming directors, sound technicians, authors, and actors. For the little ones there's the ZOOM Ozean (ocean), where with their parents they can enter a play area inhabited by magical creatures from the underwater world, featuring a ship with a captain's quarters and lighthouse. Reserve tickets in advance for this museum.

The **Quartier21** showcase up-and-coming artists and musicians in the huge Fischer von Erlach wing facing the Museumsplatz. In the planning are artist studios that will be open to the public. After a two-year residency, the artists' output might be judged by a panel of visiting museum curators who will decide—*Survivor*-fashion?—if they should be invited to remain another two years. The annual Wiener Festwochen (theater-arts festival) and the International Tanzwochen (dance festival) are held every year in the former Winter Riding Hall, and a theater for the annual Viennale Film Festival is planned. All in all, modern-art lovers will find it easy to spend the entire day at MuseumsQuartier (even that may

CLOSE UP

The "Neue" City

1

ONE MORNING IN 1911, Emperor Franz Josef, starting out on a morning drive from the Hofburg, opened his eyes in amazement as he beheld the defiantly plain Looshaus, constructed just opposite the Michaelerplatz entrance to the imperial palace. Never again, it was said, did the royal carriage use the route, so offensive was this modernist building to His Imperial Highness. One can only imagine the Josefian reaction to the Haas-Haus, built in 1985 on Stephansplatz. Here, across from the Gothic cathedral of St. Stephen's, famed architect Hans Hollein designed a complex whose elegant curved surfaces and reflecting glass interact beautifully with its environment. The architecture proved an intelligent alternative to the demands of historicism on one hand and aggressive modernism on the other.

This balancing act has always been a particular challenge in Vienna. For a few critics, the Gaudíesque eccentricities of the late Friedensreich Hundertwasser (besides the Kunsthaus museum he is also responsible for the multicolor, golden globe-top central heating tower that has become almost as much a part of the skyline as St. Stephen's spire) did the trick. But for all their charm, they have now been overshadowed by the Viennese modernism of today. By far the most exciting urban undertaking has to be the Spittelau Viaducts, just across from the Hundertwasser power plant. This revitalization plan for the Wiener Gürtel, perhaps Vienna's busiest thoroughfare, includes public-housing apartments, offices, and artists' studios that interact with the arched bays of the viaduct, a landmarked structure built by Otto Wagner.

Responsible for the staggering three-part complex, partly perched on stilts, is star architect Zaha Hadid. A pedestrian and bicycle bridge will connect the whole project to the University of Business and the North Railway Station and the Danube Canal.

A discreet example of Vienna's new architecture is the vast MuseumsQuartier. Hidden behind the Baroque facade of the former imperial stables, the design by Laurids and Manfred Ortner uses its enclosed space to set up a counterpoint between Fischer von Erlach's riding school and the imposing new structures built to house the Leopold Museum and the Modern Art Museum. From the first, old and new collide: to enter the complex's Halle E + G, you pass below the Emperor's Loge, whose double-headed Imperial eagles now form a striking contrast to a silver-hue steel double staircase. Other important projects—notably the new underground Jewish history museum on Judenplatz (look for a stark cube memorial by English sculptor Rachel Whiteread); the Gasometer complex, a planned community recycled from the immense brick drums of 19th-century gasworks; the ellipse-shape Uniqa Tower on the Danube Canal designed by Heinz Neumann, and the ecologically responsible Donau City—are among the architectural highlights on tours now organized by the Architecture Center (AZW) of the MuseumsQuartier; their maps and brochures can be used for self-guided tours.

—Gary Dodson

not be enough), and with several cafés, restaurants, gift shops, and bookstores, they won't need to venture outside. ⊠ *Museumsplatz 1–5, 7th District/Neubau* ☎ *01/523–5881* ⊕ *www.mqw.at* ▣ *Combination ticket to all museums €16–€25, depending on the museums/ exhibitions included* ⊗ *Open daily 10–7* Ⓤ *U2 MuseumsQuartier/U2 or U3/Volkstheater.*

⑤⓪ Naturhistorisches Museum (Natural History Museum). The palatial, archetypally "Ringstrasse" 19th-century museum complex just outside the Ring has two elements—to the east is the celebrated Kunsthistorisches Museum, to the west is the Naturhistorisches Museum, or Natural History Museum. This is the home of, among other artifacts, the famous Venus of Willendorf, a tiny statuette (actually, replica—the original is in a vault) thought to be some 20,000 years old; this symbol of the Stone Age was originally unearthed in the Wachau Valley, not far from Melk. The reconstructed dinosaur skeletons understandably draw the greatest attention. ⊠ *Maria-Theresien-Platz, 7th District/Neubau* ☎ *01/521–77–0* ▣ *€8* ⊗ *Wed. 9–9, Thurs.–Mon. 9–6:30* Ⓤ *U2 or U3/Volkstheater.*

⑤⑤ Parlament. This sprawling building reminiscent of an ancient Greek temple is the seat of Austria's elected representative assembly. An embracing, heroic ramp on either side of the main structure is lined with carved marble figures of ancient Greek and Roman historians. Its centerpiece is the **Pallas-Athene-Brunnen** (fountain), designed by Theophil Hansen, which is crowned by the goddess of wisdom and surrounded by water nymphs symbolizing the executive and legislative powers governing the country. ⊠ *Dr. Karl-Renner-Ring 1, 1st District* ☎ *01/401– 110–2570* ⊕ *www.parlament.gv.at* ▣ *€4* ⊗ *Tours mid-Sept.–June, Mon., Wed. 10 and 11, Tues., Thurs. 2 and 3, Fri. 11, 1, 2, and 3 (except on days when Parliament is in session); July–mid-Sept., weekdays 9, 10, 11, 1, 2, and 3* Ⓤ *Tram: 1, 2, or D/Stadiongasse, Parlament.*

⑤⑥ Rathaus (City Hall). Designed by Friedrich Schmidt and resembling a Gothic fantasy castle with its many spires and turrets, the Rathaus was actually built between 1872 and 1883. The facade holds a lavish display of standard-bearers brandishing the coats of arms of the city of Vienna and the monarchy. Guided tours include the banqueting hall and various committee rooms. A regally landscaped park graces the front of the building, and is usually brimming with activity. In winter it is the scene of the *Christkindlmarkt,* the most famous Christmas market in Vienna; in summer concerts are performed here. ⊠ *Rathausplatz 1, 1st District* ☎ *01/5255–0* ▣ *Free* ⊗ *Guided tours Mon., Wed., Fri., at 1. 5 person minimum* Ⓤ *Tram: 1, 2, or D/Rathaus.*

Also Worth Seeing

OFF THE BEATEN PATH

KAISERLICHES HOFMOBILIENDEPOT (IMPERIAL FURNITURE MUSEUM) – In the days of the Habsburg empire, palaces remained practically empty if the ruling family was not in residence. Cavalcades laden with enough furniture to fill a palace would set out in anticipation of a change of scene, while another caravan accompanied the royal party, carrying everything from traveling thrones to velvet-lined portable toilets. Much of this furniture is now on display here, allowing you a fascinating glimpse into everyday court life. The upper floors contain re-created rooms from the Biedermeier to the Jugendstil periods, and document the tradition of furniture-making in Vienna. Explanations are in German and English. ✉ *Mariahilferstrasse 88 /entrance on Andreasgasse, 7th District/Neubau* ☎ *01/524–3357–0* ✆ *€6.90* ◷ *Tues.–Sun. 10–6* Ⓤ *U3 Zieglergasse/ follow signs to Otto-Bauer-Gasse/exit Andreasgasse.*

★ ⓺① **Liechtenstein Museum.** Palais Liechtenstein is home to the Prince of Liechtenstein's fabulous private art collection, an accumulation so vast only a tenth of it is on display. Prince Karl I of Liechtenstein began collecting art back in the 17th century, and each of his descendents added to the family treasure trove. The palace itself is a splendid example of Baroque architecture. While this was built up on the then-outskirts of the city, a mere "summer palace" was not grand enough for Prince Johann Adam Andreas I, who had already erected five other Liechtenstein palaces, including his family's gigantic Viennese "winter palace" on the Bankgasse. He instead commissioned a full-blown town palace from plans drawn up by Domenicio Martinelli. A Marble Hall, grand staircases, impressive stucco work by Santino Bussi (who was paid with 40 buckets of wine in addition to a tidy sum), and sumptuous ceiling frescoes by Marcantonio Franceschini and Andrea Pozzo made this a residence fitting for one of the J. Paul Gettys of his day. Surrounding the palace was a great swampland soon dubbed "Lichtenthal" when it was transformed into a magnificent Baroque-style garden; today, it has been restored along the lines of an English landscape park, but with Baroque statues and topiaries.

The pride of the museum is the Peter Paul Rubens Room, showcasing the tremendous Decius Mus cycle, which illustrates episodes from the life of the heroic ancient Roman consul who waged a war against the Latins. The grandest picture of the eight-painting cycle illustrates the death of the consul, and it is high drama, indeed: Decius Mus gazes up to heaven as he falls off his massive grey steed as a lance pierces his throat in the middle of a pitched battle. All these paintings were made as models for a tapestry series, which is why Rubens's panels are so enormous. There are other Rubens gems here, including one of his best children's portraits, that of his daughter, *Clara Serena Rubens*. It's easy to spend the greater part of a day here. Behind the palace is the exquisite landscaped park. ✉ *Fürstengasse 1, 9th District/Alsergrund* ☎ *01/319– 5767–0* ⊕ *www.liechtensteinmuseum.at* ✆ *€10* ◷ *Fri.–Mon. 10–5* Ⓤ *Bus: 40A/Bauernfeldplatz, Tram: D/Bauernfeldplatz.*

⓾③ **Spittelberg Quarter.** People like to come to the Spittelberg because it's a slice of Old Vienna, a perfectly preserved little enclave that allows you to experience the 18th century by strolling along cobblestone pedestrian streets lined with pretty Baroque town houses. As such, the quarter— one block northwest of Maria-Theresien-Platz off the Burggasse—offers a fair visual idea of the Vienna that existed outside the city walls a century ago. Most buildings have been replaced, but the engaging 18th-century survivors at Burggasse 11 and 13 are adorned with religious and secular decorative sculpture, the latter with a niche statue of St. Joseph, the former with cherubic work-and-play bas-reliefs. For several blocks around—walk down Gutenberggasse and back up Spittelberggasse—the 18th-century houses have been beautifully restored. The sequence from Spittelberggasse 5 to 19 is an especially fine array of Viennese plain and fancy. Around holiday times, particularly Easter and Christmas, the Spittelberg quarter, known for arts and handicrafts, hosts seasonal markets offering unusual and interesting wares. Promenaders will also be able to enjoy art galleries and loads of restaurants. ⊠ *Off Burggasse, 7th District/Spittelberg* Ⓤ *U2 or U3/Volkstheater.*

❺⓼ **Universität** (University of Vienna). After the one in Prague, Vienna's is the oldest university in the German-speaking world (founded in 1365, but this is not the original building). The main section of the university is a massive block in Italian Renaissance style designed by Heinrich Ferstel and built between 1873 and 1884. Thirty-eight statues representing important men of letters decorate the front of the building, while the rear, which encompasses the library (with nearly 2 million volumes), is adorned with *sgraffito.* ⊠ *Dr.-Karl-Lueger-Ring/Universitätstrasse, 1st District* Ⓤ *U2/Schottentor.*

❺❹ **Volksgarten.** Just opposite the Hofburg is a green oasis with a beautifully planted rose garden, a 19th-century Greek temple, and a rather wistful white marble monument to Empress Elisabeth—Franz Josef's Bavarian wife, who died of a dagger wound inflicted by an Italian anarchist in Geneva in 1898. If not overrun with latter-day hippies, these can offer appropriate spots to sit for a few minutes while contemplating Vienna's most ambitious piece of 19th-century city planning: the famous Ringstrasse. ⊠ *Volksgarten, 1st District* Ⓤ *Tram: 1, 2, or D/ Rathausplatz, Burgtheater.*

❺❾ **Votivkirche** (Votive Church). When Emperor Franz Josef was a young man, he was strolling along the Mölker Bastei, now one of the few remaining portions of the old wall that once surrounded the city, when he was taken unawares and stabbed in the neck by a Hungarian revolutionary. The assassination attempt was unsuccessful, and in gratitude for his survival Franz Josef ordered that a church be built exactly at the spot he was gazing at when he was struck down. The neo-Gothic church was built of gray limestone with two openwork turrets between 1856 and 1879. ⊠ *Rooseveltplatz, 9th District/Alsergrund* ☎ *01/406–1192* ⊙ *Tours by prior arrangement* Ⓤ *U2/Schottentor.*

From St. Stephen's to the Opera House

The cramped, ancient quarter behind St. Stephen's Cathedral offers a fascinating contrast to the luxurious expanses of the Ringstrasse and more recent parts of Vienna. This was—and still is—concentrated residential territory in the heart of the city. Mozart lived here; later, Prince Eugene and others built elegant town palaces as the smaller buildings were replaced. Streets—now mostly reserved for pedestrians—are narrow, and tiny alleyways abound. Facades open into courtyards that once housed carriages and horses. The magnificent State Opera shares with St. Stephen's the honor of being one of the city's most familiar and beloved landmarks.

A Hop Through Hip Vienna

PARIS HAS THE LATIN Quarter and London has Notting Hill, but until recently Vienna did not have the Bohemian district it always longed for. Now the **Freihaus** sector makes its claim as Vienna's trendiest neighborhood.

In the 17th century, this enclave, within what is now the 4th District (Wieden), provided free housing to the city's poor, hence its name "Freihaus" or Free House. Destroyed in the Turkish siege of 1683, the complex was rebuilt on a much larger scale, becoming arguably the largest housing project in Europe at the time. It was a city within a city, including shops and even the old Theater auf der Wieden, in which Mozart's *The Magic Flute* premiered. A slow decline followed, spanning Franz Josef's reign from the mid-19th century to the early 20th century, some of it being razed to the ground before World War I. During World War II, bombing raids practically finished it off.

But then in the late 1990s a group of savvy local merchants revitalized the area, opening funky art galleries, antiques shops, espresso bars, trendy restaurants, fashion boutiques, and the city's coolest video and DVD store, Alphaville. Freihaus is quite small, stretching from Karlsplatz to Kettenbrückengasse, which encompasses part of the Naschmarkt, the city's largest open-air market. Two of the most fascinating streets are Operngasse and Schleifmühlgasse. For a preview, check out ⊕ www. freihausviertel.at.

What do you do with four immense gasometers more than 100 years old? Turn them into a cool, urban complex combining living and shopping, that's what. Looming large on the Vienna horizon, the **Gasometer** (⊕ www. gasometer.org) has generated a lot of publicity. Just to give an idea of their size, Vienna's giant Ferris wheel (the Riesenrad) at the Prater Amusement Park would fit easily inside each one. Top architects were hired to accomplish the sleek and modern interior renovations, creating over 600 modern apartments and a huge shopping mall with movie theaters and restaurants. It's in Simmering, Vienna's 11th District, and is 8 minutes from the heart of the city on the U3 subway.

A visit to Vienna during the summer months would not be complete without a few hours spent on the Donauinsel (Danube Island), more popularly known as the **Copa Kagrana**. ("Kagrana" is taken from the name of the nearby local area known as Kagran.) It was originally built as a safeguard against flooding, but now this 13-square-mi island is where the Viennese head for bicycling, skateboarding, jogging, swimming, or just a leisurely stroll and dinner by the water. There are dozens of stalls and restaurants, offering grilled steaks, fried chicken, or freshly caught fish to go along with a mug of ice-cold draft beer or Austrian wine. Every year, 2 million visitors converge on the island for three days in June for an admission-free summer festival, the Donaufest (⊕ www.donauinselfest.at). The Copa Kagrana can be reached by subway: either the U1 to Donauinsel or the U6 to Handelskai.

A GOOD WALK

To pass through these streets is to take a short journey through history and art. In the process—as you visit former haunts of Mozart, kings, and emperors—you can be easily impressed with a clear sense of how Vienna's glittering Habsburg centuries unfolded. Start from St. Stephen's Cathedral by walking down Singerstrasse to Blutgasse and turn left into the **Blutgasse District** ⓺—a neighborhood redolent of the 18th century. At the north end, in Domgasse, is the **Mozarthaus** ⓻, now a memorial museum, the house in which Wolfgang Amadeus Mozart lived when he wrote the opera *The Marriage of Figaro*. Follow Domgasse east to Grünangergasse, which will bring you to Franziskanerplatz and the Gothic-Renaissance Franziskanerkirche (Franciscan Church). Follow the ancient Ballgasse to Rauhensteingasse, turning left onto **Himmelpfortgasse**—Gates of Heaven Street. Prince Eugene of Savoy had his town palace here at No. 8, now the **Finanzministerium** ⓼, living here when he wasn't enjoying his other residence, the Belvedere Palace. Continue down Himmelpfortgasse to Seilerstätte to visit a museum devoted to the wonders of music, the **Haus der Musik** ⓽. Then turn into Annagasse with its beautiful houses, which brings you back to the main shopping street, **Kärnterstrasse,** where you can find everything from Austrian jade to the latest Jill Sander fashion turnouts. Turn left, walking north two blocks, and take the short Donnergasse to reach **Neuer Markt** square and the Providence Fountain. At the southwest corner of the square is the **Kaisergruft** ⓾ in the Kapuzinerkirche (Capuchin Church), the burial vault for rows of Habsburgs. Tegetthofstrasse south will bring you to Albertinaplatz, the square noted for the obvious war memorial and even more for the **Albertina Museum** ⓺⓻, one of the world's great collections of Old Master drawings and prints. The southeast side of the square is bounded by the famous **Staatsoper** ⓺⓼, the State Opera House; check for tour possibilities or, better, book tickets for a great *Rosenkavalier*. Celebrate with a regal time-out at the famed **Café Sacher.**

TIMING A simple walk of this route could take you a full half day, assuming you stop occasionally to survey the scene and take it all in. The restyled Mozarthaus is worth a visit, and the Kaisergruft in the Kapuzinerkirche is impressive for its shadows of past glories, but there are crowds, and you may have to wait to get in; the best times are early morning and around lunchtime. Tours of the State Opera House take place in the afternoons; check the schedule posted outside one of the doors on the arcaded Kärntnerstrasse side. Figure about an hour each for the various visits and tours.

Main Attractions

★ ⓺⓻ **Albertina Museum.** An impressive collection not to be missed is home to some of the greatest Old Master drawings in Vienna—including Dürer's iconic *Praying Hands* and beloved *Alpine Hare*. The core collection of nearly 65,000 drawings and almost a million prints was begun by the 18th-century Duke Albert of Saxony-Teschen. All the legendary names are here, from Leonardo da Vinci, Michelangelo, Raphael, and Rembrandt on down. The mansion's glorious early-19th-century salons—all gilt-boiserie and mirrors—provide a jewelbox setting. DO & CO Albertina, the excellent in-house restaurant with an immense patio long enough for an empress's promenade, offers splendid vistas of the historical center and the Burggarten—the perfect place to take a break for a meal (⇨ *Where to Eat*). ✉ *Augustinerstrasse 1, 1st District* ☎ *01/534–830* ⊕ *www.albertina.at* ✆ *€10* ☉ *Daily 10–6, Wed. 10–9* Ⓤ *U3/ Herrengasse.*

☾ ⑥⑤ **Haus der Musik** (House of Music). It would be easy to spend an entire day at this ultra-high-tech museum housed on several floors of an early-19th-century palace near Schwarzenbergplatz. Pride of place goes to the special rooms dedicated to each of the great Viennese composers— Haydn, Mozart, Beethoven, Strauss, and Mahler—complete with music samples and manuscripts. Other exhibits trace the evolution of sound (from primitive noises to the music of the masters) and illustrate the mechanics of the human ear (measure your own frequency threshold). There are also dozens of interactive computer games. You can even take a turn as conductor of the Vienna Philharmonic—the conductor's baton is hooked to a computer, which allows you to have full control over the computer-simulated orchestra. Cantino is the wonderful in-house restaurant with fabulous views of the city (⇨ *Where to Eat*). ✉ *Seilerstätte 30, 1st District* ☎ *01/51648–51* ✆ *€10* ☉ *Daily 10–10* ☖ *Restaurant, café* Ⓤ *U1, U2, or U4/Karlsplatz, then Tram D/Schwarzenbergplatz.*

NEED A BREAK? Take a break at a landmark café in one of the most charming squares in Vienna, between Himmelpfortgasse and Singerstrasse. The **Kleines Cafe** (✉ Franziskanerplatz 3, 1st District), open daily, is more for coffee, cocktails, and light snacks than for pastries, and few places are more delightful to sit in and relax on a warm afternoon or evening. In summer, tables are set outside on the intimate cobblestone square where the only sounds are the tinkling fountain and the occasional chiming of bells from the ancient Franciscan monastery next door. Before heading on, be sure to take a short stroll up Ballgasse, the tiny 18th-century street opposite the café.

Himmelpfortgasse. The maze of tiny streets including Ballgasse, Rauhensteingasse, and Himmelpfortgasse (literally, "Gates of Heaven Street") masterfully conjures up the Vienna of the 19th century. The most impressive house on the street is the Ministry of Finance. The back side of the Steffl department store on Rauhensteingasse now marks the site of the house in which Mozart died in 1791. There's a commemorative plaque that once identified the streetside site together with a small memorial corner devoted to Mozart memorabilia that can be found on the sixth floor of the store. ✉ *1st District* Ⓤ *U1 or U3/Stephansplatz.*

Kärntnerstrasse. Kärntnerstrasse remains Vienna's leading central shopping street, if much maligned. Too commercial, too crowded, too many tasteless signs, too much gaudy neon—the complaints go on and on. Nevertheless, when the daytime tourist crowds dissolve, the Viennese arrive regularly for their evening promenade, and it is easy to see why. Vulgar the street may be, but it is also alive and vital, with an energy that the more tasteful Graben and the impeccable Kohlmarkt lack. For the sightseer beginning to suffer from an excess of art history, classic buildings, and museums, a Kärntnerstrasse window-shopping respite will be welcome. ✉ *1st District* Ⓤ *U1, U4/Karlsplatz, or U1, U3/Stephansplatz.*

★ ⑥③ **Mozarthaus.** This is Mozart's only still existing abode in Vienna. Equipped with an excellent audio-guide starting out on the third floor of the building, you can hear about Mozart's time in Vienna: where he lived and performed, who his friends and supporters were, his relationship to the Freemasons, his passion for expensive attire and gambling—he spent more money on clothes than most royals at that time. The second floor deals with Mozart's operatic works. The first floor focuses on the 2½ years that Mozart lived here, when he wrote dozens of piano concertos, as well as *The Marriage of Figaro* and the six quartets dedicated to Joseph Haydn (who once called on Mozart here, saying to Leopold, Mozart's father, "your son is the greatest composer that I know in person or by name"). For two weeks in April 1787 Mozart taught a pupil who would become famous in his own right, the 16-year-old Beethoven.
■ TIP➜ **Save on the entrance fee by purchasing a combined ticket for Mozarthaus Vienna and Haus der Musik for €15.** ✉ *Domgasse 5, 1st District* ☎ *01/ 512–1791* ⊕ *www.mozarthausvienna.at* ✑ *€9* ◷ *Daily 10–8* Ⓤ *U1 or U3/Stephansplatz.*

★ ⑥⑧ **Staatsoper** (State Opera House). The famous Vienna Staatsoper on the Ring vies with the cathedral for the honor of marking the emotional heart of the city—it is a focus for Viennese life and one of the chief symbols of resurgence after the cataclysm of World War II. Its directorship is one of the top jobs in Austria, almost as important as that of president, and one that comes in for even more public attention. Since the huge salary comes out of taxes, Austrians feel they have every right to criticize, often and loudly. The first of the Ringstrasse projects to be completed (in 1869), the opera house suffered disastrous bomb damage in the last days of World War II (only the outer walls, the front facade, and the main staircase area behind it survived). The auditorium is plain when compared to the red and gold eruptions of London's Covent Garden or some of the Italian opera houses, but it has an elegant individuality that shows to best advantage when the stage and auditorium are turned into a ballroom for the great Opera Ball.

The construction of the Opera House is the stuff of legend. When the foundation was laid, the plans for the Opernring were not yet complete, and in the end the avenue turned out to be several feet higher than originally planned. As a result, the Opera House lacked the commanding prospect that its architects, Eduard van der Nüll and August Sicard von Sicardsburg, had intended, and even Emperor Franz Josef pronounced the building a bit low to the ground. For the sensitive van der Nüll (and here the story becomes a bit suspect), failing his beloved emperor was the last straw. In disgrace and despair, he committed suicide. Sicardsburg died of grief shortly thereafter. And the emperor, horrified at the deaths his innocuous remark had caused, limited all his future artistic pronouncements to a single immutable formula: *"Es war sehr schön, es hat mich sehr gefreut"* ("It was very nice, it pleased me very much").

Renovation could not avoid a postwar look, for the cost of fully restoring the 19th-century interior was prohibitive. The original basic design was followed in the 1945–55 reconstruction, meaning that sight lines from some of the front boxes are poor at best. These disappointments hardly detract from the fact that this is one of the world's half-dozen greatest opera houses, and experiencing a performance here can be the highlight of a trip to Vienna. Tours of the Opera House are given regularly, but starting times vary according to opera rehearsals; the current schedule is posted at the east-side entrance under the arcade on the Kärntnerstrasse marked GUIDED TOURS, where the tours begin. Alongside under the arcade is an information office that also sells tickets to the main opera and the Volksoper. ⊠ *Opernring 2, 1st District* ☎ *01/ 514–44–2613* ⊕ *www.staatsoper.at* ⊠ *€4* ☉ *Tours year-round when there are no rehearsals, but call for times* Ⓤ *U1, U2, or U4 Karlsplatz.*

Also Worth Seeing

62 **Blutgasse District.** The small block bounded by Singerstrasse, Grünangergasse, and Blutgasse is known as the Blutgasse District. Nobody knows for certain how the gruesome name—*Blut* is German for "blood"—originated, although one legend has it that Knights Templar were slaughtered here when their order was abolished in 1312, although in later years the narrow street was known in those unpaved days as Mud Lane. Today the block is a splendid example of city renovation and restoration, with cafés, small shops, and galleries tucked into the corners. You can look inside the courtyards to see the open galleries that connect various apartments on the upper floors, the finest example being at Blutgasse 3. At the corner of Singerstrasse sits the 18th-century **Neupauer-Breuner Palace,** with its monumental entranceway and inventively delicate windows. Opposite, at Singerstrasse 17, is the **Rottal Palace,** attributed to Hildebrandt, with its wealth of classical wall motifs. For contrast, turn up the narrow Blutgasse, with its simple 18th-century facades. ⊠ *1st District* Ⓤ *U1 or U3/Stephansplatz.*

64 **Finanzministerium** (Ministry of Finance). The architectural jewel of Himmelpfortgasse, this imposing abode—designed by Fischer von Erlach in 1697 and later expanded by Hildebrandt—was originally the town palace of Prince Eugene of Savoy. As you study the Finanzministerium, you'll realize its Baroque details are among the most inventively conceived and beautifully executed in the city; all the decorative motifs are so softly carved that they appear to have been freshly squeezed from a pastry tube. The Viennese are lovers of the Baroque in both their architecture and their pastry, and here the two passions seem visibly merged. Such Baroque elegance may seem inappropriate for a finance ministry, but the contrast between place and purpose could hardly be more Viennese. ⊠ *Himmelpfortgasse 8, 1st District* Ⓤ *U1 or U3/Stephansplatz.*

66 **Kaisergruft** (Imperial Burial Vault). In the basement of the Kapuzinerkirche, or Capuchin Church (on the southwest corner of the Neuer Markt), is one of the more intriguing sights in Vienna: the Kaisergruft, or Imperial Burial Vault. The crypts contain the partial remains of some 140 Habsburgs (the hearts are in the Augustinerkirche and the entrails in St. Stephen's) plus one non-Habsburg governess ("She was always with us in life," said Maria Theresa, "why not in death?"). Perhaps starting with their tombs is the wrong way to approach the Habsburgs in Vienna, but it does give you a chance to get their names in sequence as they lie in rows, their coffins ranging from the simplest explosions of funerary conceit—with decorations of skulls and other morbid symbols—to the lovely and distinguished tomb of Maria Theresa and her husband. Designed while the couple still lived, their monument shows the empress in bed with her husband—awaking to the Last Judgment as if it were just another weekday morning, while the remains of her son (the ascetic Josef II) lie in a simple casket at the foot of the bed as if he were the family dog. ☒ *Neuer Markt/Tegetthofstrasse 2, 1st District* ☎ *01/512–6853–12* ☒ *€4* ☉ *Daily 10–6* Ⓤ *U1, U3/Stephansplatz or U1, U4/Karlsplatz.*

South of the Ring to the Belvedere

City planning in the late 1800s and early 1900s clearly was essential to manage the growth of the burgeoning imperial capital. The elegant Ringstrasse alone was not a sufficient showcase, and anyway, it focused on public rather than private buildings. The city fathers as well as private individuals commissioned the architect Otto Wagner to plan and undertake a series of projects. The area around Karlsplatz and the fascinating open food market remains a classic example of unified design. Not all of Wagner's concept for Karlsplatz was realized, but enough remains to be convincing and to convey the impression of what might have been. The unity concept predates Wagner's time in the former garden of Belvedere Palace, one of Europe's greatest architectural triumphs.

⌐ A GOOD
WALK

The often overlooked **Akademie der bildenen Künste** ⓖ, or Academy of Fine Arts, is an appropriate starting point for this walk, as it puts into perspective the artistic arguments taking place around the turn of the century. While the Academy represented the conservative viewpoint, a group of modernist revolutionaries broke away and founded the Secessionist movement, with its culmination in the gold-crowned **Secession Building** ⓐ. Now housing changing exhibits and Gustav Klimt's provocative *Beethoven Frieze*, the museum stands appropriately close to the Academy; from the Academy, take Makartgasse south one block. The famous **Naschmarkt** ⓐ open food market starts diagonally south from the Secession; follow the rows of stalls southwest. Pay attention to the northwest side, the Linke Wienzeile, with the Theater an der Wien at the intersection with Millöckergasse (Mozart and Beethoven personally premiered some of their finest works at this opera house–theater) and the **Otto Wagner Houses** ⓐ. Head back north through the Naschmarkt; at the top end, cross Wiedner Hauptstrasse to your right into the park complex that forms Karlsplatz, creating a frame for the classic **Karlskirche** ⓐ. Around **Karlsplatz,** note the Technical University on the south side, and the Otto Wagner subway-station buildings on the north. Across Lothringer Strasse on the north side are the Künstlerhaus art exhibition hall and the Musikverein. The out-of-place and rather undistinguished modern building to the left of the Karlskirche houses the worthwhile **Wien Museum Karlsplatz** ⓐ. Cut through Symphonikerstrasse (a passageway through the modern complex) and take Brucknerstrasse to **Schwarzenbergplatz.** The Jugendstil edifice on your left is the French Embassy; ahead is the Russian War Memorial. On a rise behind the memorial sits Palais Schwarzenberg, a jewel of a onetime summer palace and now a luxury hotel. Follow Prinz-Eugen-Strasse up to the entrance of the **Belvedere Palace** ⑳ complex on your left. Besides the palace itself there are other structures and, off to the east side, a remarkable botanical garden. After viewing the palace and grounds you can exit the complex from the lower building, the Untere Belvedere, onto Rennweg, which will steer you back to Schwarzenbergplatz.

TIMING   The first part of this walk, taking in the Academy of Fine Arts and the Secession, plus the Naschmarkt and Karlsplatz, can be accomplished in an easy half day. The Wien Museum Karlsplatz is good for a couple of hours, more if you understand some German. Give the Belvedere Palace and grounds as much time as you can. Organized tours breeze in and out—without so much as a glance at the outstanding modern art museum—in a half hour or so, not even scratching the surface of this fascinating complex. If you can, budget up to a half day here, but plan to arrive fairly early in the morning or afternoon before the busloads descend. Bus tourists aren't taken to the Lower Belvedere, so you'll have that and the formal gardens to yourself.

Main Attractions

OFF THE
BEATEN
PATH

AM STEINHOF CHURCH – Otto Wagner's most exalted piece of Jugendstil architecture lies in the suburbs to the west: the Am Steinhof Church, designed in 1904 during his Secessionist phase. You can reach the church by taking the U4 subway line, which is adjacent to the Otto Wagner Houses. On the grounds of the Vienna City Psychiatric Hospital, Wagner's design unites mundane functional details (rounded edges on the pews to prevent injury to the patients and a slightly sloped tile floor to facilitate cleaning) with a soaring, airy dome and glittering Jugendstil decoration (stained glass by Koloman Moser). The church is open Saturdays at 3 for a guided tour (in German) for €4. English tours can be arranged in advance at €4 per person *if* it's a group of 10 people. If there are only two of you, then you still must pay the total price for 10. You may come during the week to walk around the church on your own, but you must call first for an appointment. ⌂ *Baumgartner Höhe 1, 13th District/Hütteldorf* ☎ *01/91060–11–204* ⍗ *Free* ⊙ *Sat. 3–4* Ⓤ *U4/Unter-St.-Veit, then Bus 47A to Psychiatrisches Krankenhaus; or U2/Volkstheater, then Bus 48A.*

⑳ **Belvedere Palace (including the Österreichische Galerie).** One of the most
Fodor'sChoice splendid pieces of Baroque architecture anywhere, the Belvedere Palace—
★   actually two imposing palaces separated by a 17th-century French-style garden parterre—is one of the masterpieces of architect Lucas von Hildebrandt. Built outside the city fortifications between 1714 and 1722, the complex originally served as the summer palace of Prince Eugene of Savoy; much later it became the home of Archduke Franz Ferdinand, whose assassination in 1914 precipitated World War I. Though the lower palace is impressive in its own right, it is the much larger upper palace, used for state receptions, banquets, and balls, that is acknowl-

edged as Hildebrandt's masterpiece. The usual tourist entrance for the Upper Belvedere is the gate on Prinz-Eugen-Strasse (No. 27); for the Lower Belvedere, use the Rennweg gate (No. 6a). But for the most impressive view of the upper palace, approach it from the south garden closest to the South Rail Station. The upper palace displays a remarkable wealth of architectural invention in its facade, avoiding the main design problem common to all palaces because of their excessive size: monotony on the one hand and pomposity on the other. Hildebrandt's decorative manner here approaches the Rococo, that final style of the Baroque era when traditional classical motifs all but disappeared in a whirlwind of seductive asymmetric fancy. The main interiors of the palace go even further: columns are transformed into muscle-bound giants, pilasters grow torsos, capitals sprout great piles of symbolic imperial paraphernalia, and the ceilings are set aswirl with ornately molded stucco. The result is the finest Rococo interior in the city. On the garden level you are greeted by the celebrated **Sala Terrena** whose massive Atlas figures shoulder the marble vaults of the ceiling and, it seems, the entire palace above. The next floor is centered around a gigantic Marble Hall covered with trompe l'oeil frescoes, while down in the Lower Belvedere palace, there are more 17th-century salons, including the Grotesque Room painted by Jonas Drentwett and another Marble Hall (which really lives up to its name).

Today both the upper and lower palaces of the Belvedere are noted museums devoted to Austrian painting. The **Österreichisches Barockmuseum** (Austrian Museum of Baroque Art) in the lower palace at Rennweg 6a displays Austrian art of the 18th century (including the original figures from Georg Raphael Donner's Providence Fountain in the Neuer Markt). Next door (outside the west end) is the converted Orangerie, devoted to works of the medieval period.

The main attraction in the upper palace's **Galerie des 19. und 20. Jahrhunders** (Gallery of the 19th and 20th Centuries) is the legendary collection of 19th- and 20th-century Austrian paintings, centering on the work of Vienna's three preeminent early-20th-century artists: Gustav Klimt, Egon Schiele, and Oskar Kokoschka. Klimt was the oldest, and by the time he helped found the Secession movement he had forged a highly idiosyncratic painting style that combined realistic and decorative elements in a way that was completely revolutionary. *The Kiss*—his greatest painting and one of the icons of modern art—is here on display. Schiele and Kokoschka went even further, rejecting the decorative appeal of Klimt's glittering abstract designs and producing works that completely ignored conventional ideas of beauty. Today they are considered the fathers of modern art in Vienna. Modern music, too, has roots in the Belvedere complex: the composer Anton Bruckner lived and died here in 1896 in a small garden house now marked by a commemorative plaque. ✉ *Prinz-Eugen-Strasse 27, 3rd District/Landstrasse* ☎ *01/795–57–134* ⊕ *www.belvedere.at* 🎫 €9 🕙 *Tues.–Sun. 10–6, Thurs. until 8* Ⓤ *U1, U2, or U4 Karlsplatz, then Tram D/Belvederegasse.*

★ ❼❸ **Karlskirche.** Dominating the Karlsplatz is one of Vienna's greatest buildings, the Karlskirche, dedicated to St. Charles Borromeo. At first glance the church seems like a fantastic vision—one blink and you half expect the building to vanish. For before you is a giant Baroque church framed by enormous freestanding columns, mates to Rome's famous Trajan's Column. These columns may be out of keeping with the building as a whole, but were conceived with at least two functions in mind: one was to portray scenes from the life of the patron saint, carved in imitation of Trajan's triumphs, and thus help to emphasize the imperial nature of the building; and the other was to symbolize the Pillars of Hercules, suggesting the right of the Habsburgs to their Spanish dominions, which the emperor had been forced to renounce. Whatever the reason, the end result is an architectural tour de force.

The Karlskirche was built in the early 18th century on what was then the bank of the River Wien and is now the southeast corner of the park complex. The church had its beginnings in a disaster. In 1713 Vienna was hit by a brutal outbreak of plague, and Emperor Charles VI made a vow: if the plague abated, he would build a church dedicated to his namesake, St. Charles Borromeo, the 16th-century Italian bishop who was famous for his ministrations to Milanese plague victims. In 1715 construction began, using an ambitious design by Johann Bernhard Fischer von Erlach that combined architectural elements from ancient Greece (the columned entrance porch), ancient Rome (the Trajanesque columns), contemporary Rome (the Baroque dome), and contemporary Vienna (the Baroque towers at either end). When it was finished, the church received a decidedly mixed press. History, incidentally, delivered a negative verdict: in its day the Karlskirche spawned no imitations, and it went on to become one of European architecture's most famous curiosities. Notwithstanding, seen lighted at night, the building is magical in its setting.

The main interior of the church utilizes only the area under the dome and is surprisingly conventional given the unorthodox facade. The space and architectural detailing are typical High Baroque; the fine vault frescoes, by J. M. Rottmayr, depict St. Charles Borromeo imploring the Holy Trinity to end the plague. ⊠ *Karlsplatz, 4th District/Wieden* ☎ *01/504–61–87* ⊙ *Daily 8–6* Ⓤ *U1, U2, or U4 Karlsplatz.*

Karlsplatz. Like the space now occupied by the Naschmarkt, Karlsplatz was formed when the River Wien was covered over at the turn of the 20th century. At the time, Wagner expressed his frustration with the result—too large a space for a formal square and too small a space for an informal park—and the awkwardness is felt to this day. The buildings surrounding the Karlsplatz, however, are quite sure of themselves: the area is dominated by the classic **Karlskirche,** made less dramatic by the unfortunate reflecting pool with its Henry Moore sculpture, wholly out of place, in front. On the south side of the Resselpark, that part of Karlsplatz named for the inventor of the screw propeller for ships, stands the **Technical University** (1816–18). In a house that occupied the space closest to the church, Italian composer Antonio Vivaldi died in 1741; a plaque marks the spot. On the north side, across the heavily traveled roadway, are the **Künstlerhaus** (the exhibition hall in which the Secessionists refused to exhibit, built in 1881 and still in use) and the famed

Musikverein. The latter, finished in 1869, is now home to the Vienna Philharmonic. The downstairs lobby and the two halls upstairs have been gloriously restored and glow with fresh gilding. The main hall has what may be the world's finest acoustics; this is the site of the annual, globally televised New Year's Day concert.

Some of Otto Wagner's finest Secessionist work can be seen two blocks east on the northern edge of Karlsplatz. In 1893 Wagner was appointed architectural supervisor of the new Vienna City Railway, and the matched pair of small pavilions he designed, the **Otto Wagner Stadtbahn Pavilions**, at No. 1 Karlsplatz, in 1898 are among the city's most ingratiating buildings. Their structural framework is frankly exposed (in keeping with Wagner's belief in architectural honesty), but they are also lovingly decorated (in keeping with the Viennese fondness for architectural finery). The result is Jugendstil at its very best, melding plain and fancy with grace and insouciance. The pavilion to the southwest is utilized as a small, specialized museum. In the course of redesigning Karlsplatz, it was Wagner, incidentally, who proposed moving the fruit and vegetable market to what is now the Naschmarkt. ⊠ *4th District/Wieden* Ⓤ *U1, U2, or U4/Karlsplatz.*

❼❶ Naschmarkt. The area between Linke and Rechte Wienzeile has for 80 years been home to the Naschmarkt, Vienna's main outdoor produce market, certainly one of Europe's—if not the world's—great open-air markets, where packed rows of polished and stacked fruits and vegetables compete for visual appeal with braces of fresh pheasant in season; the nostrils, meanwhile, are accosted by spice fragrances redolent of Asia or the Middle East. It's open Monday to Saturday 6:30–6:30 (many stalls close two hours earlier in winter months). ■ TIP→ **When making a purchase, be sure you get the correct change.** ⊠ *Between Linke and Rechte Wienzeile, 4th District/Wieden* Ⓤ *U1, U2, or U4 Karlsplatz (follow signs to Secession).*

■
NEED A BREAK?

Beginning in 2005, so many enticing snack stands opened up in the Naschmarkt that the city council put a stop to further eateries taking over where food stalls had once been. There are a host of Turkish stands that offer the juicy *Döner* sandwiches—thinly sliced, pressed lamb with onions and a yogurt sauce in a freshly baked roll. A number of Asian "noodle" and sushi stalls offer quick meals, and many snack bars offer Viennese dishes. At the Karlsplatz end of the Naschmarkt is the "Nordsee" glass-enclosed seafood hut.

❼❷ Otto Wagner Houses. The Ringstrasse-style apartment houses that line the Wienzeile are an attractive, if generally somewhat standard, lot, but two stand out: **Linke Wienzeile 38 and 40**—the latter better known as the "Majolica House"—designed (1898–99) by the grand old man of Viennese fin-de-siècle architecture, Otto Wagner. A good example of what Wagner was rebelling against can be seen next door, at **Linke Wienzeile 42,** where decorative enthusiasm has blossomed into Baroque Revival hysteria. Wagner banished classical decoration and introduced a new architectural simplicity, with flat exterior walls and plain, regular window treatments meant to reflect the orderly layout of the apartments

Jugendstil Jewels

FROM 1897 TO 1907, the Vienna Secession movement gave rise to one of the most spectacular manifestations of the pan-European style known as Art Nouveau. Viennese took to calling the look *Jugendstil,* or the "young style." In such dazzling edifices as Otto Wagner's Wienzeile majolica-adorned mansion, Jugendstil architects rebelled against the prevailing 19th-century historicism that had created so many imitation Renaissance town houses and faux Grecian temples. Josef Maria Olbrich, Josef Hoffman, and Otto Schönthal took William Morris's Arts and Crafts movement, added dashes of Charles Rennie Mackintosh and flat-surface Germanic geometry, and came up with a luxurious style that shocked turn-of-the-20th century Viennese traditionalists (and infuriated Emperor Franz Josef). Many artists united to form the Vienna Secession—whose most famous member was painter Gustav Klimt—and the Wiener Werkstätte, which transformed the objects of daily life with a sleek modern look. Today Jugendstil buildings are among the most fascinating structures in Vienna. The shrine of the movement is the world-famous Secession Building.

---

behind them. There the simplicity ended. For exterior decoration, he turned to his younger Secessionist cohorts Joseph Olbrich and Koloman Moser, who designed the ornate Jugendstil patterns of red majolica-tile roses (No. 40) and gold stucco medallions (No. 38) that gloriously brighten the facades of the adjacent houses—so much so that their Baroque-period neighbor is ignored. The houses are privately owned. ⊠ *4th District/Wieden* Ⓤ *U1, U2, or U4/Karlsplatz.*

Schwarzenbergplatz. The center of this square off the Ring is marked by an oversize equestrian sculpture of Prince Schwarzenberg—he was a 19th-century field marshal for the imperial forces. In this remarkable urban ensemble, see if you can guess which building is the newest; it's the one on the northeast corner (No. 3) at Lothringer Strasse, an exacting reproduction of a building destroyed by war damage in 1945 and dating only from the 1980s. The military monument occupying the south end of the square behind the fountain is the **Russian War Memorial,** set up at the end of World War II by the Soviets; the Viennese, remembering the Soviet occupation, call its unknown soldier the "unknown plunderer." South of the memorial is the stately **Schwarzenberg Palace,** designed as a summer residence by Johann Lukas von Hildebrandt in 1697 and completed by Fischer von Erlach father and son. ⊠ *Schwarzenbergplatz, 3rd District/Landstrasse* Ⓤ *Tram: Schwarzenbergplatz.*

❼⓪ Secession Building. If the Academy of Fine Arts represents the conservative attitude toward the arts in the late 1800s, then its antithesis can be found in the building immediately behind it to the southeast: the Secession Pavilion, one of Vienna's preeminent symbols of artistic rebellion. Rather than looking to the architecture of the past, like the revivalist Ringstrasse, it looked to a new antihistoricist future. It was, in its day, a riveting trumpet-blast of a building, and is today considered by many to be Europe's first example of full-blown 20th-century architecture.

The Secession began in 1897, when 20 dissatisfied Viennese artists, headed by Gustav Klimt, "seceded" from the Künstlerhausgenossenschaft, the conservative artists' society associated with the Academy of Fine Arts. The movement promoted the radically new kind of art known as Jugendstil, which found its inspiration in both the organic, fluid designs of Art Nouveau and the related but more geometric designs of the English Arts and Crafts movement. (The Secessionists founded an Arts and Crafts workshop of their own, the famous Wiener Werkstätte, in an effort to embrace the applied arts.) The Secession building, designed by the architect Joseph Olbrich and completed in 1898, was the movement's exhibition hall. The lower story, crowned by the entrance motto *Der Zeit Ihre Kunst, Der Kunst Ihre Freiheit* ("To Every Age Its Art, To Art Its Freedom"), is classic Jugendstil: the restrained but assured decoration (by Koloman Moser) beautifully complements the facade's pristine flat expanses of cream-color wall. Above the entrance motto sits the building's most famous feature, the gilded openwork dome that the Viennese were quick to christen "the golden cabbage" (Olbrich wanted it to be seen as a dome of laurel, a subtle classical reference meant to celebrate the triumph of art). The plain white interior—"shining and chaste," in Olbrich's words—was also revolutionary; its most unusual feature was movable walls, allowing the galleries to be reshaped and redesigned for every show. One early show, in 1902, was an exhibition devoted to art celebrating the genius of Beethoven; Gustav Klimt's *Beethoven Frieze*, painted for the occasion, has now been restored and is permanently installed in the building's basement. ⊠ *Friedrichstrasse 12, 4th District/ Wieden* ☎ *01/587–5307–0* ⊕ *www.secession.at* 🖙 *€4.50 exhibition, €6 exhibition with Beethoven Frieze, €1.50 guided tour* ☉ *Tues.–Sun. 10–6, Thurs. 10–8, guided tours Sat. at 3 and Sun. at 11.*

74 **Wien Museum Karlsplatz** (Museum of Viennese History). Housed in an incongruously modern building at the east end of the regal Karlsplatz, this museum possesses a dazzlement of Viennese historical artifacts and treasures: everything from 16th-century armor to great paintings by Schiele and Klimt and the preserved facade of Otto Wagner's *Die Zeit* offices. ⊠ *Karlsplatz, 4th District/Wieden* ☎ *01/505–8747–0* ⊕ *www. wienmuseum.at* 🖙 *€6* ☉ *Tues.–Sun. 9–6* Ⓤ *U1, U2, or U4 Karlsplatz.*

Also Worth Seeing

69 **Akademie der bildenen Künste** (Academy of Fine Arts). If the teachers here had admitted Adolf Hitler as an art student in 1907 and 1908 instead of rejecting him, history might have proved very different. The Academy was founded in 1692, but the present Renaissance Revival building dates from the late 19th century. The idea was conservatism and traditional values, even in the face of a growing movement that scorned formal rules. The Academy includes a museum focusing on Old Masters. The collection is mainly of interest to specialists, but Hieronymus Bosch's famous *Last Judgment* triptych hangs here—an imaginative, if gruesome, speculation on the hereafter. ⊠ *Schillerplatz 3, 1st District*

☎ *01/588–16–225* ⊕ *www.akademiegalerie.at* 🖼 *€7* ☉ *Tues.–Sun. 10–6* Ⓤ *U1, U2, or U4 Karlsplatz.*

Dritte Mann Museum (Third Man Museum). This shrine for film aficionados is close to the famous Naschmarkt and offers an extensive private collection of memorabilia dedicated to the classic film directed by Carol Reed and shot entirely on location in Vienna. Authentic exhibits include cinema programs, autographed cards, movie and sound recordings, and first editions of Graham Greene's novel, which was the basis of the screenplay. Also here is the original zither used by Anton Karas to record the famous film music, the tune that was to become an evergreen and started a tremendous zither boom in the '50s. Karas, born in Vienna in 1906 had his 100th birthday justly celebrated with commemorative performances of the music that made history: the "Harry Lime Theme." Listen to the original shellac that's played on an old music cabinet. In the reading corner, one can browse through historic newspaper articles about the film. ⊠ *Pressgasse 25, 4th District* ☎ *01/586–4872* ⊕ *www.3mpc.net* ☉ *Sat. 2–6* 🖼 *€6* Ⓜ *U4/Kettenbrückengasse.*

<table>
<tr><td>OFF THE
BEATEN
PATH</td><td>

ZENTRALFRIEDHOF – Taking a streetcar out of Schwarzenbergplatz, music lovers will want to make a pilgrimage to the **Zentralfriedhof** (Central Cemetery), which contains the graves of most of Vienna's great composers: Ludwig van Beethoven, Franz Schubert, Johannes Brahms, the Johann Strausses (father and son), and Arnold Schönberg, among others. The monument to Wolfgang Amadeus Mozart is a memorial only; the approximate location of his unmarked grave can be seen at the now deconsecrated St. Marx-Friedhof at Leberstrasse 6–8. ⊠ *Simmeringer Hauptstrasse, 11th District/Simmering* Ⓤ *Tram: 71 to St. Marxer Friedhof, or on to Zentralfriedhof Haupttor/2.*

</td></tr>
</table>

The Habsburgs' Schönbrunn Palace

The glories of imperial Austria are nowhere brought together more convincingly than in the Schönbrunn Palace (Schloss Schönbrunn) complex. Brilliant "Maria Theresa yellow"—she, in fact, caused Schöbrunn to be built—is everywhere in evidence. An impression of imperial elegance, interrupted only by tourist traffic, flows unbroken throughout the grounds. This is one of Austria's primary tourist sites, although sadly, few stay long enough to discover the real Schönbrunn (including the little maiden with the water jar, after whom the complex is named). Although the assorted outbuildings might seem eclectic, they served as centers of entertainment when the court moved to Schönbrunn in summer, accounting for the zoo, the priceless theater, the fake Roman ruins, the greenhouses, and the walkways. In Schönbrunn you step back 300 years into the heart of a powerful and growing empire and follow it through to defeat and demise in 1917.

<table>
<tr><td>A GOOD
WALK</td><td>

The usual start for exploring the Schönbrunn complex is the main palace. There's nothing wrong with that approach, but as a variation, consider first climbing to the **Gloriette** ⑳ on the hill overlooking the site for a bird's-eye view to put the rest in perspective (take the stairs to the Gloriette roof for the ultimate experience). While at the Gloriette, take a few steps west to discover the **Tiroler House** ㉗ and follow the zigzag path downhill to

</td></tr>
</table>

the palace; note the picture-book views of the main building through the woods. Try to take the full tour of **Schönbrunn Palace** rather than the shorter, truncated version. Check whether the ground-floor back rooms (Berglzimmer) are open for viewing. After the palace guided tour, take your own walk around the grounds. The Schöner Brunnen, the namesake fountain, is hidden in the woods to the southeast; continue along to discover the convincing (but fake) Roman ruins. At the other side of the complex to the west are the excellent **Tiergarten** (zoo), and **Palmenhaus** (tropical greenhouse). Closer to the main entrance, both the **Wagenburg** (carriage museum) and Schlosstheater (palace theater) are frequently overlooked treasures. Before heading back to the city center, visit the **Hofpavillon** , the private subway station built for Emperor Franz Josef, to the west across Schönbrunner Schlossstrasse.

TIMING If you're really pressed for time, the shorter guided tour will give you a fleeting impression of the palace itself, but try to allot at least half a day to take the full tour and include the extra rooms and grounds as well. The 20-minute hike up to the Gloriette is a bit strenuous but worthwhile, and there's a café as reward at the top. The zoo is worth as much time as you can spare, and figure on at least a half hour to an hour each for the other museums. Tour buses begin to unload for the main building about mid-morning; start early or utilize the noon lull to avoid the worst crowds. The other museums and buildings in the complex are far less crowded.

What to See

 Gloriette. At the crest of the hill, topping off the Schönbrunn Schlosspark, sits a Baroque masterstroke: Johann Ferdinand von Hohenberg's incomparable Gloriette, now restored to its original splendor. Perfectly scaled, the Gloriette—a palatial pavilion that once offered royal guests a place to rest and relax on their tours of the palace grounds and that now houses an equally welcome café—holds the whole vast garden composition together and at the same time crowns the ensemble with a brilliant architectural tiara. This was a favorite spot of Maria Theresa's, though in later years she grew so obese it took six men to carry her in her palanquin to the summit. ⊠ *13th District* Ⓤ *U4/Schönbrunn.*

 Hofpavillon. The most unusual interior of the Schönbrunn Palace complex, the restored imperial subway station known as the Hofpavillon is just outside the palace grounds (at the northwest corner, a few yards east of the Hietzing subway station). Designed by Otto Wagner in conjunction with Joseph Olbrich and Leopold Bauer, the Hofpavillon was built in 1899 for the exclusive use of Emperor Franz Josef and his entourage. Exclusive it was: the emperor used the station only once. The exterior, with its proud architectural crown, is Wagner at his best, and the lustrous interior is one of the finest examples of Jugendstil decoration in the city. ⊠ *Schönbrunner Schloss-Strasse, next to Hietzing subway station, 13th District/Hietzing* 🕾 *01/877–1571* 🎫 *€2* 🕓 *Sun. 11–12:30* Ⓤ *U4/Hietzing.*

 Palmenhaus. On the grounds to the west of Schönbrunn Palace is a huge greenhouse filled with exotic trees and plants. ⊠ *Nearest entrance Hi-*

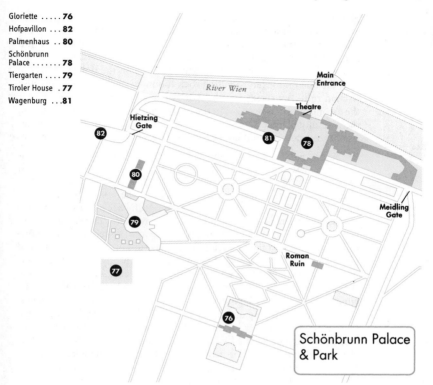

Schönbrunn Palace & Park

etzing, 13th District/Hietzing ☎ *01/877–5087* ✉ *€3.50* ☽ *May–Sept., daily 9:30–6; Oct.–Apr., daily 9:30–5.*

78 **Schönbrunn Palace.** Designed by Johann Bernhard Fischer von Erlach in
Fodor's Choice 1696, Schönbrunn Palace, the huge Habsburg summer residence, lies
★ well within the city limits, just a few subway stops west of Karlsplatz
on line U4. The vast and elegantly planted **gardens** are open daily from
dawn until dusk, and multilingual guided tours of the palace interior
are offered daily. A visit inside the palace is not included in most general city sightseeing tours, which offer either a mercilessly tempting drive
past or else an impossibly short half hour or so to explore. The four-
hour commercial sightseeing-bus tours of Schönbrunn offered by tour
operators cost several times what you'd pay if you tackled the easy excursion yourself; their advantage is that they get you there and back with
less effort. Go on your own if you want time to wander through the
magnificent grounds.

The most impressive approach to the palace and its gardens is through
the front gate, set on Schönbrunner Schloss-Strasse halfway between the
Schönbrunn and Hietzing subway stations. The vast main courtyard is
ruled by a formal design of impeccable order and rigorous symmetry:
wing nods at wing, facade mirrors facade, and every part stylistically com-

plements every other. The courtyard, however, turns out to be a mere appetizer; the feast lies beyond. The breathtaking view that unfolds on the other side of the palace is one of the finest set pieces in all Europe and one of the supreme achievements of Baroque planning. Formal *Allées* (garden promenades) shoot off diagonally, the one on the right toward the zoo, the one on the left toward a rock-mounted obelisk and a fine false Roman ruin. But these, and the woods beyond, are merely a frame for the astonishing composition in the center: the sculpted marble fountain; the carefully planted screen of trees behind; the sudden, almost vertical rise of the grass-covered hill beyond, with the **Gloriette** a fitting crown.

Within the palace, the magisterial state salons are quite up to the splendor of the gardens, but note the contrast between these chambers and the far more modest rooms in which the rulers—particularly Franz Josef—lived and spent most of their time. Of the 1,400 rooms, 40 are open to the public on the regular tour, of which two are of special note: the Hall of Mirrors, where the six-year-old Mozart performed for Empress Maria Theresa in 1762 (and where he met six-year-old Marie Antoinette for the first time, developing a little crush on her), and the Grand Gallery, where the Congress of Vienna (1815) danced at night after carving up Napoléon's collapsed empire during the day. Ask about viewing the ground-floor living quarters (Berglzimmer), where the walls are fascinatingly painted with palm trees, exotic animals, and tropical views. As you go through the palace, glance occasionally out the windows; you'll be rewarded by a better impression of the beautiful patterns of the formal gardens, punctuated by hedgerows and fountains. These window vistas were enjoyed by rulers from Maria Theresa and Napoléon to Franz Josef. ⊠ *Schönbrunner-Schloss-Strasse, 13th District/Hietzing* ☎ *01/81113–239* ⊕ *www.schoenbrunn.at* ✉ *Guided grand tour of palace interior (40 rooms) €14, self-guided tour €11.50* ⊘ *Apr.–June, Sept., and Oct., daily 8:30–5; July and Aug., daily 8:30–6; Nov.–Mar., daily 8:30–4:30. Park Apr.–Oct., daily 6 AM–dusk; Nov.–Mar., daily 6:30 AM–dusk* Ⓤ *U4/Schönbrunn.*

☺ ㊆ **Tiergarten.** Claimed to be the world's oldest, the Tiergarten zoo has retained its original Baroque decor, but new settings have been created for both animals and public. In one case, the public looks out into a new, natural display area from one of the Baroque former animal houses. The zoo is constantly adding new attractions and undergoing renovations, so there's plenty to see. ⊠ *Schönbrunner Schlosspark, 13th District/Hietzing* ☎ *01/877–9294–0* ⊕ *www.zoovienna.at* ✉ *€12; combination ticket with Palmenhaus €16* ⊘ *Nov.–Jan., daily 9–4:30; Feb., daily 9–5; Mar. and Oct., daily 9–5:30; Apr.–Sept., daily 9–6:30* Ⓤ *U4/Schönbrunn.*

㊆ **Tiroler House.** This charming Tyrolean-style building to the west of the Gloriette was a favorite retreat of Empress Elisabeth; it now includes a small restaurant (open according to season and weather). ⊠ *Schönbrunner Schlosspark, 13th District/Hietzing* Ⓤ *U4/Schönbrunn.*

☺ ㊁ **Wagenburg** (Carriage Museum). Most of the carriages are still roadworthy, and in fact Schönbrunn dusted off the gilt-and-black royal funeral carriage that you see here for the burial ceremony of Empress Zita in

1989. ⊠ *Schönbrunner Schlosspark, 13th District/Hietzing* ☎ *01/877–3244* ⊕ *www.khm.at/* ⊠ *€4.50* ☺ *Apr.–Oct., daily 9–6; Nov.–Mar., daily 10–4* Ⓤ *U4/Schönbrunn.*

OFF THE
BEATEN
PATH

⤶

TECHNISCHES MUSEUM – About a 10-minute walk from Schönbrunn Palace is the **Technical Museum,** which provides a fascinating learning experience by tracing the evolution of industrial development over the past two centuries. On four floors you'll find actual locomotives from the 19th century, a Tin Lizzie, airplanes from the early days of flying, as well as examples of factory life, how electric lighting took the place of gas lamps, and how mountain highway tunnels are constructed. And, appropriate for such a music-loving city, a whole section is devoted to the work involved in creating different musical instruments. ⊠ *Mariahilferstrasse 212, 14th District/Penzing* ☎ *01/899–9860–00* ⊕ *www.tmw.at* ⊠ *€8.50* ☺ *Weekdays 9–6, weekends 10–6* Ⓤ *U3 or U6/Westbahnhof, then Tram 52 or 58/Penzingerstrasse.*

WHERE TO EAT

To appreciate how far the restaurant scene in Vienna has come in recent years, it helps to recall the way things used to be. Up until five years ago, Austria was still dining in the 19th century. Most dinners were a *mittel-europäisch* sloshfest of *Schweinebraten, Knödeln,* and *Kraut* (pork, dumplings, and cabbage). No one denies that such courtly delights as *Tafelspitz*—the blush-pink boiled beef famed as Emperor Franz Josef's favorite dish—is delicious, but most traditional carb-loaded, nap-inducing meals left you stuck to your seat like a suction pad. If you consumed a plate-filling Schnitzel and were able to eat anything after it, you were looked upon as a phenomenon—or an Austrian. A lighter, more nouvelle take on cuisine had difficulty making incursions because many meals were centered around *Rehrücken* (venison), served up in wine-cellar recipes of considerable—nay, medieval—antiquity.

Today Vienna's dining scene is as lively, experimental, and as good as it is thanks in part to changing epicurean tastes and a rising generation of chefs dedicated to taking the culinary heritage of the nation to a new phase of *Neu Wiener Küche* (New Vienna Cuisine). No longer tucked away in anonymous kitchens, cooks now create signature dishes that rocket them to fame; they earn fan clubs and host television shows. The Austrian chef has become a star, a phenomenon that has also been seen in the United States, as witness New York's David Bouley and Hollywood's Wolfgang Puck. Back in Vienna, chefs want to delight an audience hungry for change. Schmaltzy schnitzels have been replaced by Styrian beef, while soggy *Nockerl* (small dumplings) are traded in for seasonal delights like Carinthian asparagus, Styrian wild garlic, or the common alpine-garden stinging nettle. The old goulash and bratwurst have given way to true gustatory excitement. You can always find the time-honored standards of Wiener Küche at the famous *Beisln,* Vienna's answer to Paris's bistros and London's gastro-pubs.

Be aware that the basket of bread put on your table is not free. Most of the older-style Viennese restaurants charge €0.80–€1.50 for each roll

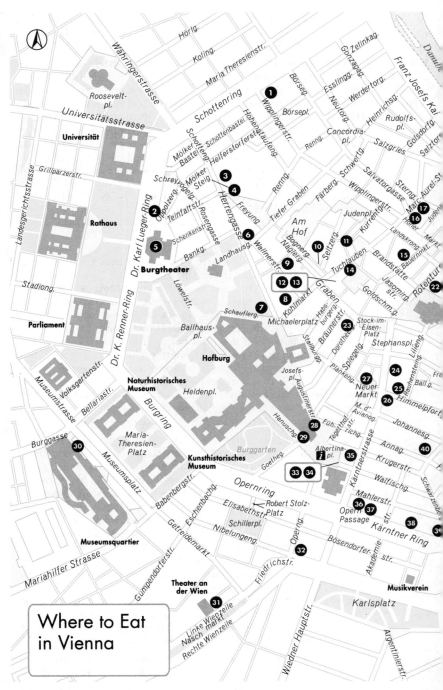

Where to Eat
in Vienna

Restaurants ▼

Munch-on-the-Run ▼

Wine Taverns ▼

Cafés

Pastry Shops ▼

...ut more and more establishments are beginning to charge cover charge—anywhere from €1.50 to €4—which includes ...ad you want, plus usually an herb spread and butter.

...HAT IT COSTS In euros				
,	$$$	$$	$	¢
...ver €28	€23–€28	€17–€22	€10–€16	under €10

Prices are per person for a main course at dinner.

Restaurants

$$$$
FodorsChoice
★
✕ **Julius Meinl am Graben.** A few doors down from the Hofburg Palace, Meinl opened as a caterer to the Habsburgs in 1862, and has remained Vienna's poshest grocery store and ranks among the city's best restaurants. Take a left at the door, walk through the coffee and tea sections, head upstairs past the cheese bar, and then, turning the corner, you'll find a cozy salon, all deep orange banquettes and dark wood. The window tables have stunning views over the pedestrian crossroads of Graben/Kohlmarkt. The maestro in command is Joachim Gradwohl, whose young sous-chef, Thomas Göls, is a past winner of the "Newcomer of the Year" award at the international Bocuse d'Or competition. The staff is tremendous with advice. The lobster terrine and its side of lobster bisque (adorably served in an espresso cup) is always a winner, and the sizzling duck, carved tableside and served with roasted chestnuts and apple-studded *Rotkraut* (red cabbage) is delicious. ✉ *Graben 19 (entrance after 7 PM from outdoor elevator on Naglergasse), 1st District* 🕾 *01/532–3334–99* ⏦ *Reservations essential* 🚌 *AE, DC, MC, V* ☉ *Closed Sun.* Ⓤ *U3/Herrengasse.*

$$$$
FodorsChoice
★
✕ **Steirereck.** Possibly the most raved-about restaurant in Austria is Steirereck, in the former Milchhauspavilion, a grand Jugendstil-vintage "drinking hall" overlooking the Wienfluss promenade in the Stadtpark, the main city park on the Ringstrasse. At the entrance is a 20-foot-long Rococo banqueting table topped by a video screen that allows a peek into the kitchen that achieves perfection in all its creations. Winners include delicate smoked catfish, turbot in an avocado crust, or char on a bed of white garlic sauce. At the end of the meal, an outstanding selection of more than 60 cheeses from Steirereck's own cheese cellar await the palate. If you don't want the gala Steirereck experience, opt for a bite in the lower-floor "Meierei," which is strikingly stylish with a hand-painted floor and furniture in shades of milky white. ✉ *Im Stadtpark, 3rd District/Landstrasse* 🕾 *01/713–3168* ⊕ *www.steirereck.at* ⏦ *Reservations essential* 🚌 *AE, DC, MC, V* Ⓤ *U4/Stadtpark.*

$$$–$$$$
✕ **Anna Sacher.** Complete renovation and a new foyer brought the Hotel Sacher into the 21st century. What remains traditional is the restaurant Anna Sacher, a name that has almost as many reverberations as Strauss's. The legendary Sachertorte cake is the crown of a family saga that began with Franz Sacher, Prince von Metternich's pastry chef. Franz's son and his wife Anna, Vienna's "hostess with the mostest," opened the famed 19th-century hotel. Near the entrance to the restaurant, pay your re-

spects to Anna's oil portrait—it reveals her formidable character and her weakness for cigars and bulldogs (shades of Churchill). A showcase for "internationale und typische Wiener Küche," it seeps the monarchical magic of former glory: wainscotted oak walls, beige silk fabrics, gilt-frame oil paintings, and sparkling chandeliers create a suitably aristo ambience. Sacher offers some of the city's best Tafelspitz (boiled beef), garnished with creamed spinach and hash-brown potatoes, with chive cream sauce and apple horseradish adding extra flavor to this favorite dish of Emperor Franz Josef. Angus beef served with chanterelles and quail eggs is

> ## A STRUDEL STEAL
>
> Take your afternoon coffee break in one of the very best restaurants in town, for less than you would pay in most Viennese cafés. Make your way around 2 PM weekdays to the Steirereck's "Meierei" in Stadtpark and savor the freshest *Apfelstrudel* in town. If you don't make it in time for the fruitiest and juiciest of Apfelstrudel arrivals, then at least try for the 3 PM creamy *Topfenstrudel* experience. Both are best served warm and accompanied by a smooth, aromatic coffee.

another good choice. ⊠ *Philharmonikerstrasse 4, 1st District* ☎ *01/5145–6840* ⊕ *www.sacher.com* ⌃ *Reservations essential* 🏛 *Jacket and tie* 🖃 *AE, DC, MC, V* ⊗ *No lunch* Ⓤ *U1, U2, or U4/Karlsplatz/Opera.*

\$\$\$–\$\$\$\$
FodorsChoice
★

✕ **Korso.** In the Bristol Hotel, just across from the Staatsoper (don't be surprised if you see Domingo at the next table), the Korso bei der Oper has always been one of the great favorites of Vienna's posherie. Chef Reinhard Gerer's specialty is fish, and he's known throughout Austria for his creative touch. Try the delicately fried *Rotbarsch* (rosefish) paired with tiny, crispy fried parsley and the smoothest of pureed polenta. Salzkammergut lake trout is grilled and drizzled with a sensational shallot sauce, and *Saibling* (char) caviar is enhanced with organic olive oil. Service can be a little stiff and formal, but it goes with the sparkling Riedel crystal and baronial fireplace. ⊠ *Mahlerstrasse 2, 1st District* ☎ *01/515–16–546* 🖶 *01/515–16–550* ⌃ *Reservations essential* 🏛 *Jacket and tie* 🖃 *AE, DC, MC, V* ⊗ *Closed 3 wks in Aug. No lunch Sat.* Ⓤ *U4/Karlsplatz.*

\$\$\$–\$\$\$\$
FodorsChoice
★

✕ **Zum Schwarzen Kameel.** The ladies who lunch love to shop and dine at "the Black Camel," a foodie landmark already 200 years ago, back when Beethoven used to send his manservant here to buy wine and ham. In timeless Viennese fashion, this provisioner split into both a *Delikatessen* and a restaurant. You can use the former if you're in a hurry—the fabulously fresh sandwiches are served at the counter. If time is not an issue, dine in the elegant Art Nouveau dining area. Let the head waiter do his number—he's the one with the Emperor Franz Josef beard who, in almost perfect English, will rattle off the specials of the day. He recently won the award "Best Waiter of the Year." ⊠ *Bognergasse 5, 1st District* ☎ *01/533–8125* ⌃ *Reservations essential* 🖃 *AE, DC, MC, V* ⊗ *Closed Sun.* Ⓤ *U3/Herrengasse.*

\$\$–\$\$\$

✕ **Cantino.** After a visit to the Haus der Musik, repair to its restaurant overlooking the towers, roofs, and steeples of the city. Chef Richard Rainer's lemon risotto is unbeatable, while his *Bonito del Norte* (white

Spanish tuna) on arugula salad with lemon-olive oil dressing is a delight. Wines are mainly home-grown Austrian, but there is also a fine array of Italian vintages. When you've tired of the view out of the enormous windows, study the historic prints and photos decorating the slanting ceiling to see if you can recognize any of the celebrated conductors and composers. ⊠ *Seilerstätte 30, 1st District* ☎ *01/512–54–46* ▤ *AE, DC, MC, V* ☉ *No dinner Sun.* Ⓤ *U1 or U3/Stephansplatz.*

★ **$$–$$$**   ✕ **Fabios.** The easiest way for Viennese to visit sleek, suave, power-dining New York—short of paying $800 for a round-trip ticket—is to book a table at this cool hot spot. If they can, that is. Exceedingly popular and wait-listed weeks in advance, this modernist extravaganza has brought a touch of big-city glamour to Alt Wien, and foodies to fashionistas love it. Chef Christoph Brunnhuber has a truly sophisticated touch, as you'll see with his octopus carpaccio with paprika, crispy pork with orange pesto on fennel, or duckling breast on kumquat-cassis-sauce with potato-olive puree. ⊠ *Tuchlauben 6, 1st District* ☎ *01/532–2222* ⊕ *www.fabios.at* ⚖ *Reservations essential* ▤ *AE, DC, MC, V* ☉ *Closed Sun.*

$$–$$$ ✕ **Theatercafe Wien.** A bright star of Vienna's culinary scene, Alexander Mayer, is at the helm of this sleek eatery with light pine furnishings, metal trim, and white walls. In addition to the weekday business lunch (a two-course classic Viennese meal including drinks all for €10.90), there's a great choice of Asian, Mediterranean and, for good measure, Viennese delights served here in the evening. ⊠ *Linke Wienzeile 6, 6th District/Mariahilf* ☎ *01/585–6262* ⊕ *www.theatercafe-wien.at/* ⚖ *Reservations essential* ▤ *AE, DC, MC, V* ☉ *Closed Sun.* Ⓤ *U4/Karlsplatz.*

★ **$$–$$$**   ✕ **Urania.** The year 1910 saw the inauguration of the Urania under the auspices of Emperor Franz Josef. Today this beautifully restored Jugendstil building is one of Vienna's trendiest locations. The interior design is cool, modern, and urban. Chef Norbert Fiedler's creations include fillet of trout on chanterelle risotto and tender duck served with ginger ravioli. You can sit inside to take in the crowd and some of the handsomest waiters in town (rumor has it they are mostly models). Or sit outside on the upper or lower terrace overlooking the Danube Canal. Friendly open times run from 9 AM until 2 AM, but the big event on Sunday is brunch. ⊠ *Uraniastrasse 1, 1st District* ☎ *01/7133066* ⚖ *Reservations essential* ▤ *AE, DC, MC, V* Ⓤ *U1 or U4/Schwedenplatz.*

★ **$$–$$$**   ✕ **Vestibül.** Attached to the Burgtheater, this was once the carriage vestibule of the emperor's court theater. The Marmorsaal dining room with marble Corinthian columns, coffered arcades, and lots of candlelight adds romance, but don't expect high drama: as an example of Ringstrasse architecture, the Burgtheater offers up splendor at its most staid. In fact, you might opt instead for a lighter meal in the adjoining bar salon that has views of the boulevard. The menu changes frequently, and may include veal goulash and Wiener Schnitzel as well as some classic *Beuschel* (a hash made of heart and lung, Viennese-style), plus a full array of nouvelle novelties. It's open late to accommodate theatergoers. In warm weather you can also choose a table on the Ringstrasse garden terrace. ⊠ *Burgtheater/Dr.-Karl-Lueger-Ring 2* ☎ *01/532–4999* 🖷 *01/532–4999–10* ⊕ *www.vestibuel.at* ▤ *AE, DC, MC, V* ☉ *Closed Sun. No lunch Sat.* Ⓤ *Tram: 1 or 2.*

$–$$$ ✕ **DO & CO Albertina.** When you're ready to drop from taking in all the
Fodor's Choice art treasures at the fabulous Albertina, then just fall into the museum
★ eatery's high-back, camel-color leather seating. For exotic, go for the
Thai wok dish with steamed rice, oysters, and sweet chili sauce that can
be served with vegetables, prawns, or beef. If you fancy just a snack, sit
at the bar and enjoy the Baguette Albertina, stuffed with juicy smoked
salmon, cream cheese, arugula, and sun-dried tomatoes. DO & CO is
open all day, every day, 10 AM to midnight. In warm weather you can
also sit outside on the terrace overlooking the Burggarten. ⊠ *Alberti-
naplatz 1, 1st District* ☎ *01/532–9669* ⚭ *Reservations essential* ⊕ *www.
doco.com* ▤ *V* Ⓤ *U1, U2, or U4/Karlsplatz/Opera.*

★ **$–$$$** ✕ **Griechenbeisl.** Mozart, Beethoven, and Schubert all dined here—so how
can you resist? Neatly tucked away in a quiet and quaint area of the
Old City, this ancient inn goes back half a millennium. You can hear its
age in the creaking floor boards when you walk through some of the
small dark wood–panel rooms. Yes, it's historic and touristy, yet the food,
including all the classic hearty dishes like goulash soup, Wiener Schnitzel,
and *Apfelstrudel,* is as good as in many other Beisln. The Mark Twain
room has walls and ceiling covered with signatures of the famed who
have been served here—ask the waiter to point out the most famous.
⊠ *Fleischmarkt 11, 1st District* ☎ *01/533–1941* ⊕ *www.griechenbeisl.
at* ▤ *AE, DC, MC, V* Ⓤ *U1 or U4/Schwedenplatz.*

$–$$ ✕ **Wrenkh.** Once Vienna's vegetarian pioneer extraordinaire, Christian
Wrenkh now prefers a mixed cuisine in his house (over in the 15th District his ex-wife keeps up with the healthy kitchen). Happily, those delightful dishes like the wild-rice risotto with mushrooms or the Greek
fried rice with vegetables, sheep's cheese, and olives, or the tofu and tomato
and basil-pesto tarts still carry his signature. Now, however, you can also
be tempted by steak, fish, and fowl. The minimalist-style café section
offers inexpensive lunch specials, while the more elegant adjacent dining room is perfect for a relaxed lunch or dinner. Fortunately, Christian hasn't changed the no-smoking policy in his restaurant.
⊠ *Bauernmarkt 10, 1st District* ☎ *01/533–1526* ⊕ *www.wrenkh.at*
▤ *AE, DC, MC, V* Ⓤ *U1 or U3/Stephansplatz.*

★ **$–$$** ✕ **Zum Finsteren Stern.** Paging all Mozart maniacs: this is the old Gothic
cellar of the one and only Palais Collalto, the site where six-year-old
Amadeus made his first public appearance. Not much has changed in
the *Keller* since 1762—the vaulted ceiling, cool white walls, and dark
plank floor are just as they have always been. It takes courage in Vienna to offer a choice of only two three-course menus, but the success
of Ella de Silva's establishment proves her right. If available, go for the
rabbit with sweet and sour lentils or the lamb steak with polenta tomato,
zucchini cakes, and red-wine shallot sauce. Opening hours are 5 PM until
1 AM, and there's a lovely seating area outside underneath an old blue-
bell tree. ⊠ *Schulhof 8 at Parisergasse, 1st District* ☎ *01/535–2100*
▤ *MC, V* ⊗ *Closed Sun.* Ⓤ *U3/Herrengasse.*

★ **¢–$$** ✕ **Hansen.** This fashionable establishment, housed in the basement of the
19th-century Vienna Stock Exchange, shares an enormous space with the
flower shop Lederleitner. In the air are the sweet perfume of tuberoses and
the tantalizing whiff of the truffle. While dining you can see shoppers brows-

ing for everything from a single rose to a $2,000 lemon tree. Although this eatery is named after Theophil Hansen—the ornament-crazy architect of the Börse—its decor is sleek and modern. Tables set a bit too close together are compensated by the fantastic Austrian-Mediterranean menu. Lunch is the main event here, though you can also come for breakfast or a pretheater dinner. ⊠ *Wipplingerstrasse 34, 1st District* ☎ *01/532–0542* ⍍ *Reservations essential* ═ *AE, DC, MC, V* ⊘ *Closed Sun. and after 9* PM *weekdays. No dinner Sat.* Ⓤ *U2/Schottenring.*

★ $　✕ **Figlmüller.** This Wiener Schnitzel institution is known for its gargantuan breaded veal and pork cutlets so large they overflow the plate, and is always packed. The cutlet is so large because it has been hammered into a two-fisted portion (you can hear the kitchen's pounding mallets from a block away). They wind up wafer-thin but delicious, because the quality, as well as the size, is unrivaled (a quarter kilo of quality meat for each schnitzel). As the Viennese are fond of saying, "A Schnitzel should swim," so don't forget the lemon juice. ⊠ *Wollzeile 5, 1st District* ☎ *01/512–6177* ═ *AE, DC, MC, V* ⊘ *Closed first 2 wks Aug.* Ⓤ *U1 or U3/Stephansplatz.*

★ ¢–$　✕ **Gmoa Keller.** One of the friendliest places in Vienna, this wonderful old vaulted spot—just across the street from the Konzert Haus offers some of the most *gutbürgerlich* (hearty) home cooking in town. Come here to enjoy dishes that hail from Carinthia, one of the best being the *Käsnudeln* (potatoes and spinach pasta filled with cheese and onion), served best with green leaf salad. Needless to say, a real favorite here is the *Tafelspitzsulz mit Kernoel und Zwiebeln* (cold cut of beef in aspic served with onions and lashings of dark green pumpkin seed oil)—like everyone else, you'll wind up using the *Semmel* (the white bread roll) to sop up that last drop of wonderful oil. ⊠ *Am Heumarkt 25, 3rd District/Landstrasse* ☎ *01/712–5310* ═ *AE, DC, MC, V* ⊘ *Closed Sun.* Ⓤ *U4/Stadtpark.*

¢–$　✕ **Gösser Bierklinik.** This engaging old-world house, which dates back four centuries, is in the heart of Old Vienna. One of the top addresses for beer connoisseurs in Austria, it serves up brews, both draft and bottled, *Dunkeles* (dark) and *Helles* (light), from the Gösser brewery in Styria. Of the four dining areas, many diners opt for the covered courtyard, where your beer will taste better no matter the weather. Besides the obligatory (but first-class) Wiener Schnitzel, there are substantial, dark whole-wheat sandwiches stuffed with ham, cheese, and different vegetables, along with *Kas'nocken* (little pasta dumplings topped with melted Tyrolean mountain cheese and crispy fried onions). ⊠ *Steindlgasse 4, 1st District* ☎ *01/ 533–7598* ═ *DC, MC, V* ⊘ *Closed Sun.* Ⓤ *U3/Herrengasse.*

¢–$　✕ **Una.** Part of Vienna's mammoth MuseumsQuartier, this spot has drawn crowds with its unpretentious air, knowing menu, and amazing vaulted tiled ceiling with a Turkish look. Under this white-and-turquoise fantasia of arabesques and Bosporus blues, an arty crowd ponders a menu that is varied, reasonably priced, and comes with plenty of vegetarian dishes. Try the couscous and herb salad with a sprinkling of mint or the tangy prawn and watercress sandwich. ⊠ *Museumsplatz 1, MuseumsQuartier, 7th District/Neubau* ☎ *1/523–6566* ═ *No credit cards* Ⓤ *U2/MuseumsQuartier.*

MUNCH ON THE RUN

If you don't have time for a leisurely lunch, or you'd rather save your money for a splurge at dinner, here's a sampling of the best places in the city center to grab a quick, inexpensive, and tasty bite to eat. In the lower level of the Ringstrasse Galerie shopping mall, the gourmet supermarket **Billa Corso** (⊠ Kärntner Ring 9–13, 1st District ☎ 01/512–6625 ⊗ Closed Sun.) has a good salad bar, and will prepare the sandwich of your choice at the deli counter. (The Ringstrasse Galerie is in two similar buildings, so make sure you're in the one on the Kärntner Ring.) The best pizza by the slice can be found near St. Stephen's at **Bizi Pizza** (⊠ Rotenturmstrasse 4, 1st District ☎ 01/513–3705). Next to the produce section on the ground floor of Vienna's premier gourmet grocery store, **Meinl am Graben** (⊠ Graben 19, 1st District ☎ 01/532–3334 ⊗ Closed Sun.) is a smart, stand-up café where you can choose from a selection of soups, sandwiches, or antipasti (don't confuse it with the full-service restaurant upstairs). Near the Freyung, the epicurean deli **Radatz** (⊠ Schottengasse 3a, 1st District ☎ 01/533–8163 ⊗ Closed Sun.) offers made-to-order sandwiches from a vast selection of mouthwatering meats and cheeses. Around the corner from Am Hof, **Zum Schwarzen Kameel** (⊠ Bognergasse 5, 1st District ☎ 01/533–8967 ⊗ Closed Sun.) serves elegant little open-faced sandwiches and baby quiches in their stand-up section. Directly beneath the Vienna State Opera House, discover the **"Karlsplatz" underground mall** (⊠ Opern Passage, 1st District), where you'll find a huge choice of quick-food alternatives within the space of a hundred yards. Take the escalator at the corner of the Opera across from Hotel Bristol and descend to the subway station "Karlsplatz" mall.

A sure way to spike a lively discussion among the Viennese is to ask which *Würstelstand* serves the most delicious grilled sausages. Here are three that are generally acknowledged to be the best: **Ehrenreich's** (⊠ Naschmarkt, on Linke Wienzeile across from Piccini, under clock, 1st District ⊗ Closed Sun.) serves scrumptious *Käsekrainer* (beef sausages oozing with melted cheese), alongside a *Semmel* (soft roll) and mild, sweet mustard. Considered by gourmets to be the best sausage stall in the city center—behind the Opera House, **Oper** (⊠ Corner of Philharmonikerstrasse/Hanuschgasse, 1st District) entices passersby with its plump, sizzling *Bratwurst*. **Würstelstand am Hoher Markt.** Hot on the trail of that "Best Sausage" appellation, this stall (⊠ Hoher Markt, corner of Marc-Aurel-Strasse, 1st District) serves the best *Bürenwurst* and American-style hot dogs, and is open daily from 7 AM to 5 AM.

Wine Taverns

In the city center, wine taverns are known as *Weinkeller*. Hundreds of years ago Vienna's vintners started taking advantage of the cavernous spaces found below ancient monasteries and old houses by converting them into underground wine cellars. The fact that these subterranean cellars were some of the coolest spots in summertime Vienna has always proved a big drawing card.

$–$$ ✗ **Augustinerkeller.** Built into the old brick vaults of the 16th-century historic fortifications surrounding the old city, this is one of the last monastic wine cellars in central Vienna. The atmosphere is very *gemütlich* (cozy)—vaulted brick ceiling, wooden "cow-stall" booths, street lanterns, Austrian bric-a-brac, and a troupe of roaming musicians (dig that accordion!) in the evening. The spit-roasted chicken is excellent, as is the filling *Stelze* (roast knuckle of pork). ⊠ *Augustinerstrasse 1, Albertinaplatz, 1st District* ☎ *01/533–1026* ⊟ *DC, MC, V* Ⓤ *U3/Herrengasse.*

$–$$ ✗ **Esterházykeller.** The roots here go way back to 1683, when this spot opened as one of the official *Stadtheuriger* (city wine taverns). Below the Esterházy palace, its atmosphere is like that of a cozy subterranean cave, with low-hanging vaults and Alpine wooden booths. The maze of rooms offers some of the best wines of any cellar in town, plus a typical Viennese menu noontime and evenings, as well as a hot and cold buffet. ⊠ *Haarhof 1, 1st District* ☎ *01/533–3482* ⊕ *www.esterhazykeller. at/* ⊟ *No credit cards* ⊙ *Closed weekends in summer. No lunch weekends* Ⓤ *U1 or U4/Stephansplatz.*

¢–$ ✗ **Melker Stiftskeller.** Down and down you go, into one of the friendliest cellars in town, where *Stelze* is a popular feature, along with outstanding wines by the glass or, rather, mug. Part of the fabled Melkerhof complex—dating from 1438 but rebuilt in the 18th century—this was originally the storehouse for wines from the great Melk Abbey in the Danube Valley. It is a complex of six cavernous rooms, the most atmospheric of them with low-arched vaults right out of a castle dungeon. ⊠ *Schottengasse 3, 1st District* ☎ *01/533–5530* ⊟ *AE, DC, MC, V* ⊙ *Closed Sun., Mon. No lunch* Ⓤ *U2/Schottentor.*

Heurigen

The city's light and slightly fizzy "new wine"—the *Heurige,* harvested every September and October in hills around the city—has been served up for centuries in suburban taverns known as "Heurigen." These are charmingly set in the picturesque wine villages that dot Vienna's outskirts: Stammersdorf, Grinzing, Sievering, Nussdorf, and Neustift (tram lines to take from the city center are listed under the reviews below). Grinzing is a particularly enchanting destination. Although colonized by faux-Heurigen and tour buses, it has enough winding streets, antique lanterns, stained-glass windows, and oh-so-cozy taverns that you may feel you're wandering through a stage set for an "Old Austria" operetta (don't forget to look for the town organ-grinder). The best times to visit the Heurigen are in summer and fall, when many of these places famously hang a pine branch over their doorway to show they are open, though

CLOSE UP

Wine·Wien·Wein·Vienna

1

IT MAKES FOR A memorable experience to sit at the edge of a vineyard on the Kahlenberg with a tankard of young white wine and listen to the *Schrammel* quartet playing sentimental Viennese songs. The wine taverns, called *Heurigen* (the singular is *Heurige*) after the new wine that they serve, sprang up in 1784 when Joseph II decreed that owners of vineyards could establish their own private wine taverns; soon the Viennese discovered it was cheaper to go out to the wine than to bring it inside the city walls, where taxes were levied. The Heurige owner is supposed to be licensed to serve only the produce of his own vineyard, a rule more honored in the breach than the observance. These taverns in the wine-growing districts on the outskirts of the city vary from the simple front room of a vintner's house to ornate settings. The true Heurige is open for only a few weeks a year to allow the vintner to sell a certain quantity of his production, tax-free, when consumed on his own premises. The choice is usually between a "new" and an "old" white (or red) wine, but you can also ask for a milder or sharper wine according to your taste. Most Heurigen are happy to let you sample the wines before you order. You can also order a *Gespritzter,* half wine and half soda water. The waitress brings the wine, usually in a ¼-liter mug or liter carafe, but you serve yourself from the food buffet. The wine tastes as mild as lemonade, but it packs a punch. If it isn't of good quality, you will know from your raging headache the next day.

often the more elegant and expensive establishments, called *Noble-Heurigen,* stay open year-round. Begin by ordering the classic *Viertel*— a quarter liter of wine—then check out the buffet. In the old days the *Salamutschi* (sausage seller) would trot his wares from one tavern to another. Today, increasingly, full dinners are available. If you go to a Heurige in the fall, be sure to order a glass of *Sturm,* a cloudy drink halfway between grape-juice and wine, with a delicious yeasty fizz.

$$–$$$ ✕ **Kronprinz Rudolfshof.** Named after the crown prince who died a tragic death at Mayerling, this Heurige has always been one of Grinzing's most famous. Sigmund Freud, C. G. Jung, and Albert Einstein sipped glasses of Viennese wine here. Although it might be hard to channel their spirits—a modern Hundertwasser pavilion has been added here—you might enjoy the kitschy blast of the "1st Grinzinger Heurigen Show," which features a troupe of costumed singers and musicians warbling the heart out of "Wiener Blut." The price is €40 a ticket. If not, if you're lucky, you might catch a *Natursänger* roaming the village streets. ⊠ *Cobenzlgasse 8, 19th District/Grinzing* ☎ *01/524-7478* ⊕ *www.heuriger. com/* ⊟ *AE, DC, MC, V* Ⓤ *U2/Schottentor; Tram: 38/Grinzing.*

★ **$$–$$$** ✕ **Mayer am Pfarrplatz.** Heiligenstadt is home to this legendary Heurige in one of Beethoven's former abodes. The composer lived in this house in the summer of 1817. At that time there was a spa in Heiligenstadt, where Beethoven hoped cure to his deafness. In this town he composed his Sixth (Pastoral) Symphony, and while staying here he also created parts of his famous Ninth Symphony ("Ode to Joy"). The atmosphere in the collection of rooms is genuine, with vaulted rooms filled with Tyrolean iron chandeliers, antique engravings, and mounted antlers. The à la carte offerings and buffet are more than abundant, and the house wines among the most excellent of all Heurigen nectars. You'll find lots of Viennese among the tourists here. ⊠ *Heiligenstädter Pfarrplatz 2, 19th District/Nussdorf* ☎ *01/370–1287* ⊕ *www.mayer. pfarrplatz.at/* ⊟ *DC, MC, V* ⊘ *No lunch weekdays or Sat.* Ⓤ *Tram: D/Nussdorf from the Ring.*

$$–$$$ ✕ **Weingut Reinprecht.** The grandest Heurige in Grinzing (the town has more than 30 of them), Reinprecht is *gemütlichkeit*-heaven: Tyrolean wood beams, 19th-century oil paintings, Austrian-eagle banners, portraits of army generals, globe lanterns, marble busts, trellised tables, and the greatest collection of corkscrews in Austria. The building—a former monastery—is impressive, as is the garden, which can hold up to 700 people (to give you an idea of how popular this place is). If you ignore the crowds, get a cozy corner table, and focus on the archetypal *Atmosphäre,* you might have a great time. ⊠ *Cobenzlgasse 20, 19th District/Grinzing* ☎ *01/320–1389* ⊕ *http://heuriger-reinprecht.at/* ⊟ *AE, DC, MC, V* ⊘ *Closed Dec.–Feb.* Ⓤ *U2/Schottentor; Tram: 38/ Grinzing.*

¢–$ ✕ **Passauerhof.** If you want live folk music (offered nightly) to accompany your meal, this is the place to go. But you may have to share the experience with the tour groups that descend on Grinzing. The food from the menu, such as roast chicken and Wiener Schnitzel, is tasty, while the buffet offers a limited selection. It's a pleasant five-minute walk up the hill from the town center. ⊠ *Cobenzlgasse 9, 19th District/Grinzing* ☎ *01/ 320–6345* ⊟ *AE, DC, MC, V* ⊘ *Closed Jan. and Feb. No lunch* Ⓤ *U2/ Schottentor; Tram: 38/Grinzing.*

¢–$ ✕ **Schreiberhaus.** In Neustift am Walde, the Schreiberhaus has one of the prettiest terraced gardens in the city, with picnic tables stretching straight up into the vineyards. The buffet offers delicious treats such as spit-roasted chicken, salmon pasta, and a huge selection of tempting grilled vegetables and salads. The golden traminer wine is excellent. ⊠ *Rathstrasse 54, 19th District/Neustift am Walde* ☎ *01/440–3844* ⊟ *AE, DC, MC, V* Ⓤ *U4, U6/Spittelau; Bus 35A/Neustift am Walde.*

¢–$ ✕ **Wieninger.** Heurige wine and food are both top-notch here, and the charming, tree-shaded inner courtyard and series of typical vintner's rooms are perfect for whiling away an evening. Wieninger's bottled wines are ranked among the country's best. It's across the Danube in Stammersdorf, one of Vienna's oldest Heurige areas. ⊠ *Stammersdorferstrasse 78, 21st District/Floridsdorf* ☎ *01/292–4106* ⊟ *V* ⊘ *Closed late Dec.–Feb. No lunch except Sun.* Ⓤ *U2, U4/Schottenring; Tram: 31/Stammersdorf.*

¢–$ ✕ **Zimmermann.** East of the Grinzing village center, the Zimmermann Heurige has excellent wines, an enchanting tree-shaded garden, and an endless series of small paneled rooms and vaulted cellars. You can order from the menu or choose from the tempting buffet. This well-known Heurige attracts the occasional celebrity, including fashion model Claudia Schiffer when she's in town. ✉ *Armbrustergasse 5/Grinzinger-strasse, 19th District/Grinzing* ☎ *01/370–2211* ▭ *AE, DC, MC, V* ⊗ *No lunch* Ⓤ *U2/Schottentor; Tram: 38/Grinzing.*

Cafés & Coffeehouses

Is it the coffee they come for or the coffeehouse? This question is one of the hot topics in town, as Vienna's café scene has become increasingly overpopulated with Starbucks branches and Italian outlets. The ruckus over whether the quality of the coffee or the *Atmosphäre* is more important is not new, but is becoming fiercer as competition from all sides increases. The result is that the legendary landmark Wiener Kaffeehäuser—the famous cafés known for centuries as "Vienna's parlors," where everyone from Mozart and Beethoven to Lenin and Andy Warhol were likely to hang out—are smarting from the new guys on the block. On the plus side, their ageless charms remain mostly intact: the sumptuous red-velvety padded booths, the marble-top tables, the rickety yet indestructible Thonet bentwood chairs, the waiter—still the *Herr Ober,* dressed in a Sunday-best outfit—pastries, cakes, strudels, and rich tortes, newspapers, magazines, and journals, and, last but not least, a sense that here time stands still. To savor the traditional coffeehouse experience, set aside a morning or an afternoon, or at least a couple of hours, and settle down in the one you've chosen. Read a while, or catch up on your letter writing, or plan tomorrow's itinerary: there is no need to worry about overstaying one's welcome, even over a single small cup of coffee, though don't expect refills. (Of course, in some of the more opulent coffeehouses your one cup of coffee may cost as much as a meal somewhere else.)

And remember that in Austria coffee is never merely coffee. It comes in countless forms and under many names. Ask a waiter for *ein Kaffee* and you'll get a vacant stare. If you want a black coffee, you must ask for a *kleiner* or *grosser Schwarzer* (small or large black coffee, small being the size of a demitasse cup). If you want it strong, add the word *gekürzt* (shortened); if you want it weaker, *verlängert* (stretched). If you want your coffee with cream, ask for a *Brauner* (again *gross* or *klein*); say *Kaffee Creme* if you wish to add the cream yourself (or *Kaffee mit Milch extra, bitte* if you want to add milk, not cream). Others opt for a *Melange,* a mild roast with steamed milk (which you can even get *mit Haut,* with skin, or *Verkehrter,* with more milk than coffee). The usual after-dinner drink is espresso. Most delightful are the coffee-and-whipped-cream concoctions, universally cherished as *Kaffee mit Schlag,* a taste that is easily acquired and a menace to all but the very thin. A customer who wants more whipped cream than coffee asks for a *Doppelschlag.* Hot black coffee in a glass with one knob of whipped cream is an *Einspänner* (literally, "one-horse coach"—as coachmen needed one hand free to hold the reins). Then you can go to town on a *Mazagran,* black coffee with ice and a tot of rum, or *Eiskaffee,* cold coffee with ice cream, whipped cream, and cookies. Or you can simply order *eine Portion Kaffee* and have an honest pot of coffee and jug of hot milk. And watch out: if you naively request a *Menu,* you'll wind up with a Schwarzer with a double shot of pear liqueur. As for the actual *Speisekarte* (menu), most places offer hot food, starting with breakfast, from early morning until around 11 AM, lunch menus in some, and many offer a great variety of meals until about an hour before closing time.

✓ ¢–$ ✕ **Café Central.** The coffeehouse *supreme*. Made famous by its illustrious guests, the Café Central is probably the world's most famous coffeehouse—outside of Florian's in Venice. Although recently somewhat over-restored (by its Donald Trump–like new owner), its old vibes remain attached to it as though by suction pad. Don't expect a cozy hole-in-the-wall Kaffeehaus. With soaring ceiling and gigantic columns giving it the look of an apse strayed from St. Stephen's cathedral, it provided a rather sumptuous home away from home for Leon Trotsky, who mapped out the Russian Revolution here beneath portraits of the imperial family. It's just across from the Spanish Riding School. Piano music fills the marble pillared hall in the afternoon and although it will never again be all that it used to be, Central should be on the "must see" list. ⊠ *Herrengasse 14, corner Strauchgasse 1st District* ☎ *01/5333–76424* ⊕ *www.palaisevents.at/* Ⓤ *U3/Herrengasse.*

¢–$ ✕ **Café Frauenhuber.** Repair here to find some peace and quiet away from the Himmelpfortgasse's busy shoppers. A visual treat is the original turn-of-the-20th-century interior with the obligatory red-velvet seating and somewhat tired upholstery (if you don't suffer from back problems you'll be fine). The breakfasts served here are legendary, having never lost that original "egg-in-a-glass" touch. You'll find fewer tourists here than in other typical Viennese cafés, so head here for real patina, which it has earned as this establishment first opened its doors in 1824. ⊠ *Himmelpfortgasse 6, 1st District* ☎ *01/512–4323* Ⓤ *U1 or U3/Stephansplatz.*

¢–$ ✕ **Café Griensteidl.** Once the site of one of Vienna's oldest coffeehouses and named after the pharmacist Heinrich Griensteidl—the original dated back to 1847 but was demolished in 1897—this café was resurrected in 1990. Here Karl Kraus, the sardonic critic, spent many hours writing his feared articles, and here Hugo von Hofmannsthal took time out from writing libretti for Richard Strauss. Although this establishment is still looking for the patina needed to give it back its real flair, locals are pleased by the attempt to re-create the former atmosphere that exuded history. The daily, reasonably priced midday menu is a winner. Numerous newspapers and magazines hang on the rack (a goodly number of them in English). ⊠ *Michaelerplatz 2, 1st District* ☎ *01/533–2692* Ⓤ *U3/Herrengasse.*

¢–$ ✕ **Café Hawelka.** Practically a shrine, nearly a museum, the beloved Hawelka has been presided over for more than 70 years by Leopold Hawelka, in person, day in, day out. Will this institution live forever? This was the hang-out of most of Vienna's modern artists, and the café has acquired quite an admirable art collection over the years. As you enter the rather dark interior, wait to be seated—unusual in Vienna—and then speak up and ask to have a look at the guest book, in itself a work of art, with entries including some very illustrious names (Elias Canetti, Andy Warhol, Tony Blair, et al.). Back in the 1960s, the young John Irving enjoyed the atmosphere here, too, as you can see when reading *The Hotel New Hampshire*. The Hawelka is most famous for its

Buchteln, a baked bun with a sweet filling that goes down well with a Melange. ⊠ *Dorotheergasse 6, 1st District* ☎ *01/512–8230* Ⓤ *U1 or U3/Stephansplatz.*

¢–$ ✕ **Café Landtmann.** A recent $500,000 government-sponsored renovation has brought new lustre to the chandeliers of Landtmann, a century-old favorite of politicians, theater stars (the Burg is next door), and celeb-watchers. Sigmund Freud, Burt Lancaster, Hillary Rodham Clinton, and Sir Paul McCartney are just a few of the famous folk who have patronized this vaguely Secession-ish-looking café, whose glass-and-brass doors have been open since 1873. If you want a great meal at almost any time of the day, there are few places that can beat this one. If you just want coffee and cake, then choose the right-hand seating area (just beyond the door). But if it is bustle and star-sightings, head for the elongated salon that runs parallel with the Ring avenue, just opposite the main university building. At night lots of theatergoers turn up after the Burg has turned out. ⊠ *Dr.-Karl-Lueger-Ring 4, 1st District* ☎ *01/ 532–0621* Ⓤ *U2/Schottenring.*

★ ¢–$ ✕ **Café Mozart.** Graham Greene, staying in the Hotel Sacher next door, loved having his coffee here while working on the script for *The Third Man* (in fact, Greene had the café featured in the film and Anton Karas, the zither player who did the famous Harry Lime theme, wrote a waltz for the place). The café was named after the monument to Mozart (now in the Burggarten) that once stood outside the building; reputedly, Wolfie came here to enjoy his coffee, but the decor is entirely changed from his era. Although the place is overrun with sightseers, the waiters are charming as all get out, and manage to remain calm even when customers run them ragged. Crystal chandeliers, a brass-and-oak interior, comfortable seating, and delicious food—the excellent Tafelspitz here has to be mentioned—add to its popularity. With the Opera just behind the café, this is a fine place for an after-performance snack. Be on the lookout for opera divas here for the same thing. ⊠ *Albertinaplatz 2, 1st District* ☎ *01/2410–0210* ⊕ *www.cafe-wien.at/* Ⓤ *U1, U2, or U4/ Karlsplatz/Opera.*

¢–$ ✕ **Café Museum.** The controversial architect Adolf Loos (famed for his pronouncement: "Ornament is a sin") laid the foundation stone for this "puristically" styled coffeehouse in 1899. Throughout the past century, this was a top rendezvous spot for Wien Secession artists, along with actors, students, and professors due to its proximity to the Secession Pavilion, the Academy of Fine Arts, the Theater an der Wien, and Vienna's Technical University. Gustav Klimt, Egon Schiele, and Josef Hoffmann all enjoyed sipping their Melange here. Today, after years of intensive and painstaking restoration (following Loos's detailed documents discovered in the Albertina), it once again lives up to its former glory. ⊠ *Operngasse 7, 1st District* ☎ *01/586–5202* Ⓤ *U1, U2, or U4/Karl-splatz/Opera.*

¢–$ ✕ **Café Sacher.** You'll see people wandering out of this legendary café in a whipped-cream stupor. This legend began life as a *Delikatessen* opened by Sacher, court confectioner to Prince von Metternich, the most powerful prime minister in early-19th-century Europe and fervent chocoholic. Back then, cookbooks of the day devoted more space to desserts

CLOSE UP

Vienna's Sweetest Vice

MANY THINK THAT THE CHIEF contribution of the people who created the Viennese waltz and the operetta naturally comes with the dessert course, in the appropriate form of rich and luscious pastries, and in the beloved and universal *Schlagobers* (whipped cream). There is even one place where you can stand and watch the confectioner at work. Watch the cakes being iced, marzipan figures shaped to form flower petals, strudels being rolled, or chocolate being poured over the dark sponge.

First stop for sweet lovers, pastry fans, and marzipan maniacs has to be **Demel** (✉ Kohlmarkt 14, 1st District ☎ 01/535–1717–0), a 200-year-old confectioner famous for its sweetmeats that make every heart beat faster (and eventually slower). The display cases are filled to the brim; all you have to do is point at what you want and then go and sit where you want. But don't forget to watch the pastry chef at work in the glassed-over, glassed-in courtyard. The cellar Marzipan Museum holds a strange display of famous heads— among others Bill Clinton, Barbara Cartland, and Kofi Annan—in colored marzipan. Beyond the shop proper are stairs that lead to dining salons where the decor is almost as sweet as the goods on sale.

Gerstner (✉ Kärntnerstrasse 13–15 ☎ 01/5124963) is in the heart of the bustling Kärntnerstrasse and is one of the best places for dark, moist, mouthwatering poppyseed cake (*Mohntorte*), carrot cake, and chocolate-dipped strawberries. Rumor has it that the best strudel in town is to be had here. Its decor is modern,

but the place has been here since the mid-18th century. **Heiner** (✉ Kärntnerstrasse 21–23 ☎ 01/512–6863 ✉ Wollzeile 9 ☎ 01/512-2343) is dazzling for its crystal chandeliers as well as for its pastries. The great favorite here has to be the almond-orange torte. **Oberlaa** (✉ Neuer Markt 16 ☎ 01/513-2936 ✉ Babenbergerstrasse 7, opposite Kunsthistoriches Museum ☎ 01/5867-2820 ✉ Landstrasser Hauptstrasse 1 ☎ 01/7152-7400) has irresistible confections such as the *Oberlaa Kurbad* cake, truffle cake, and chocolate mousse cake. Highly popular with the locals and great value for money, there are now six Oberlaa branches to choose from. Their good lunch menu includes vegetarian dishes. **Sperl** (✉ Gumpendorferstrasse 11, 6th District/Mariahilf ☎ 01/586-4158), founded in 1880, has an all-around Old Viennese ambience.

It doesn't really matter which of the many branches of **Aida** (✉ Neuer Markt 16 ☎ 01/513-2936 ✉ Opernring 7 ☎ 01/533-1933 ✉ Bognergasse 3 ☎ 01/533-9442 ✉ Stock-im-Eisen-Platz 2 ☎ 01/512-2977 ✉ Wollzeile 28 ☎ 01/512-3724 ✉ Praterstrasse 78 ☎ 01/216-2137 ✉ Rotenturmstrasse 24 ☎ 01/58-2585) you go to, as they are all quite similar. Aida is most famous for the cheapest cup of (excellent) coffee in town, but the incredibly inexpensive pastries are just fantastic.

1

than to main courses, and Sacher's creations were practically ranked on the order of painting and sculpture. When the populace at large was allowed to enjoy the prime minister's favorite chocolate cake—a sublime mixture of flour, eggs, butter, chocolate, and apricot preserves—the fashion for Sachertorte was created. War-weary Metternich must have been amused to see a battle break out between Sacher and Demel—a competing confectioner—as to who served the real Sachertorte, but the jury has now awarded the prize to Sacher, after a much-publicized trial, which came to a decision worthy of Solomon, that the original article should be spelled as one word whereas others using a similar recipe must use two words. Sacher puts its apricot jam in the cake middle, while Demel puts it just below the icing. Red flocks the drapes, walls, and floors here, mirrors and chandeliers add glitter, and there is live piano music every day from 4:30 until 7 PM. ⊠ *Philharmonikerstrasse 4, 1st District* ☎ *01/514560* Ⓤ *U1, U2, or U4/Karlsplatz/Opera.*

¢–$ ✕ **Café Schwarzenberg.** A bright yellow facade and a large terrace welcome all to this café across from the Hotel Imperial. The location is perfect if you want a snack after a concert at the Musikverein or the Konzerthaus, both just a couple of minutes away. Wall-to-wall mirrors reflect the elegant clientele perched on green leather seats. Open until midnight, this has a good choice of food and pastries, and even though the waiters can be a little condescending, the overall atmosphere is still nice enough to encourage longer stays. Piano music can be heard until late on Wednesday and Friday and from 5 until 7 PM on weekends. ⊠ *Kärntnerring 17, 1st District* ☎ *01/512–8998* Ⓤ *U2/Schottentor.*

¢–$ ✕ **Haas & Haas Colonial Teahouse.** Have you tired of coffeehouses? Are you longing for a decent cuppa? If this is the case, then head for the far end of the Ringstrassen-Galerien, where one the coziest tea parlors in town offers a selection of more than 200 teas and an afternoon tea to die for. Presented on the obligatory three-tier tea rack, traditional finger sandwiches come with all sorts of fillings accompanied by scones with strawberry jam and clotted cream and a selection of petits fours. Yummy! It's open Monday through Saturday, 9:30–7. ⊠ *Kärntnerring 9–13, Ringstrassen Galerien Top 65, 1st District* ☎ *01/512–6817* Ⓤ *U1, U2, or U4 Karlsplatz.*

WHERE TO STAY

If you're lucky enough to stay at one of Vienna's better hotels, chances are you'll be deposited at one of those grand Ringstrasse palaces that once housed assorted Imperial Highnesses. Their red velvet–gilt mirror–and–crystal chandelier opulence still stands supreme even in today's world of lavish hospitality, and these establishments pride themselves on staff that appear to anticipate, like fairy guardians, your every desire. Of course, for those with more modest requirements and purses, ample rooms are available in less costly but still alluring hotels. Our lower-price options offer the best in location, value, and, in many instances, a quaint echo of Alt Wien (Old Vienna) atmosphere.

When you have only a short time to spend in Vienna, you will probably choose to stay in the inner city (the 1st District, or 1010 postal code), to be within walking distance of the most important sights, restaurants, and shops. But outside of the 1st, there are any number of other delightful neighborhoods in which to rest your head. The "Biedermeier" quarter of Spittelberg, in the 7th District of Neubau, has cobblestone streets, lots of 19th-century houses, and a wonderful array of art galleries and restaurants and, increasingly, hotel options. Just to its east is the fabulous MuseumsQuartier, an area that has some nice hotel finds. Schwedenplatz is the area fronted by the Danube Canal—a neighborhood that is one of the most happening in the city, although just a stroll from the centuries-old lanes around Fleischmarkt. Other sweet hotel options are set in the 8th District of Josefstadt, an area noted for antiques shops, good local restaurants, bars, and theater.

Because of the famous Christmas markets, the weeks leading up to the holidays are a popular time to visit, as is the week around New Year's (*Silvester*), with all the orchestral concerts. Expect to pay accordingly, and, at the very top hotels, a lot (around €300–€550 a night). Surprisingly, summer months are not as busy, perhaps because the opera is not in season. You'll find good bargains at this time of year, especially in August. Air-conditioning is customary in the top categories only, but since Vienna has very few extremely hot days, with temperatures cooling off at night, it's usually not necessary.

If you need a room upon arrival and have not made previous reservations, go to **Information-Zimmernachweis** (☎ 01/892–3392 in Westbahnhof), operated by the Verkehrsbüro in the Westbahnhof. At the airport the information and room-reservation office in the arrivals hall is open daily 8:30 AM–8:30 PM. If you're driving into Vienna, get information or book rooms through the Vienna Tourist Board's hotel assistance **hotline** (☎ 01/24555 🖷 01/24–555–666 ⊕ www.info.wien.at). It's open daily from 9 to 7. Assume that all guest rooms have air-conditioning, room phones, and room TVs unless noted otherwise.

WHAT IT COSTS In euros					
	$$$$	$$$	$$	$	¢
FOR 2 PEOPLE	over €270	€170–€270	€120–€170	€80–€120	under €80

Prices are for two people in a standard double room. Assume that hotels operate on the European Plan (EP, with no meal provided) unless we note that they use the Breakfast Plan (BP).

$$$$ ▣ **Ambassador.** Franz Lehár, Marlene Dietrich, the Infanta Isabel of Spain, and Mick Jagger are just a few of the celebrities who have stayed at this old dowager (from 1866). The lobby is small but grand, and the high-ceiling guest rooms, differing only in size, are uniformly decorated with pale yellow–stripe wallpaper, deep blue carpets, and faux Empire furniture. Unless you want the excitement of a direct view onto the lively pedestrian Kärntnerstrasse, ask for one of the quieter rooms on the Neuer Markt side. The Ambassador also houses the top-flight restaurant Mörwald, which offers stunning views of the square. ⊠ *Kärntnerstrasse 22/ Neuer Markt 5, A-1010, 1st District* ☎ *01/961610* 🖷 *01/5132–999*

1

⊕ *www.ambassador.at* ⬤ *86 rooms* △ *Restaurant, minibars, bar, Internet* ⊟ *AE, DC, MC, V* ⦿ *EP.*

★ **$$$$**   ▦ **Bristol.** A Bösendorfer grand of a hotel, this venerable landmark dating from 1892 has one of the finest locations in the city, on the Ring next to the Opera. The accent here is on tradition—a note struck by the lobby, which is fairly and disappointingly standard-issue when it comes to luxe: the usual oval salons, domed ceilings, traditional overstuffed chairs, modern wood paneling, and potted palms. There are enough chandeliers, surely, but too bad there are so many ugly recessed ceiling lights. For real grandeur, you have to book one of the top penthouses and suites, gloriously furnished in Biedermeier style with decorative fireplaces, thick carpets, wing-back chairs, crystal chandeliers, and lace curtains. Penthouse rooms have terraces with staggering views of the Opera. Other rooms miss out on this Ringstrasse splendor but are most comfortable and stylish nevertheless. The Bristol also houses the acclaimed Korso restaurant and a music salon complete with a pianist playing tunes on a time-burnished—yes—Bösendorfer. ⊠ *Kärntner Ring 1, A-1010, 1st District* ☎ *01/515–16–0* 🖷 *01/515–16–550* ⊕ *www.westin.com/bristol* ⬤ *141 rooms* △ *2 restaurants, minibars, health club, bar, Internet, business services* ⊟ *AE, DC, MC, V* ⦿ *EP.*

$$$$ ▦ **Grand Hotel Wien.** One of the great locations on the magnificent
Fodor'sChoice   Ringstrasse, just across from the Musikverein and a minute on foot from
★   the Opera, the Grand Hotel Wien (the first luxury hotel in Vienna) was to rise in new splendor in the early 1990s. Built in 1870, it was re-erected almost from scratch. Rooms have elegant, dark-wood walls and pastel accents. Le Ciel, Unkai, the Japanese restaurant, and the Grand Café offer culinary delights for every palate. The interior really does appear palatial thanks to its exquisite fabrics and rare antiques. An additional boon here is the adjoining shopping mall: Ringstrassen-Galerien comprises two buildings connected by a glass bridge. ⊠ *Kärntnerring 9, A-1010, 1st District* ☎ *01/515–800* 🖷 *01/515–1310* ⊕ *www.grandhotelwien.com* ⬤ *205 rooms* △ *Restaurant, café, minibars, gym, bar, Internet, no-smoking rooms* ⊟ *AE, DC, MC, V.*

$$$$ ▦ **Imperial.** One of the great landmarks of the Ringstrasse, this hotel
Fodor'sChoice   has exemplified the grandeur of imperial Vienna ever since Emperor Franz
★   Josef formally opened its doors in 1873. Adjacent to the famed Musikverein concert hall and two blocks from the Staatsoper, the emphasis here is on Old Vienna elegance and privacy, which accounts for a guest book littered with names like Elizabeth Taylor, José Carreras, and Bruce Springsteen. Originally the home of Philipp Duke of Württemberg, this remains a symphony of potted-palm luxe. Don't overlook, as if you could, the grand marble staircase, a wonder in colored marbles modeled on the one in Munich's court library. The main lobby looks as opulent as a Hofburg ballroom. On the ground floor is the true showpiece: the Marmorsaal, or Marble Hall, where you can now dine amid Corinthian columns. Upstairs, the reception floor is filled with rooms done in whipped-cream neo-Rococo. As for the beautiful guest rooms, they are furnished with sparkling chandeliers, gorgeously swagged fabrics, and original 19th-century paintings. The larger suites are found on the lower floor; as you ascend, guest rooms get smaller, but those on

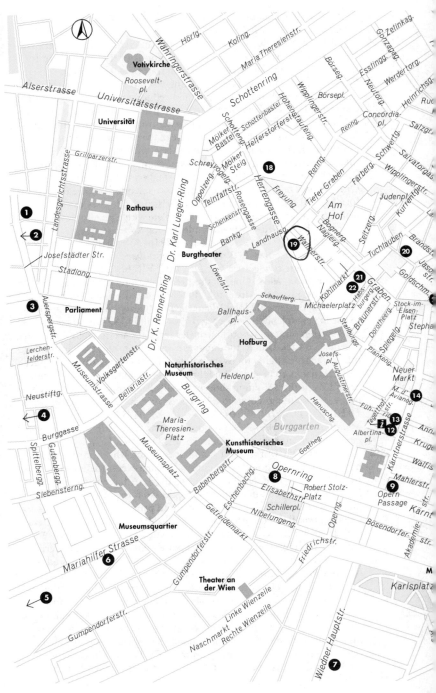

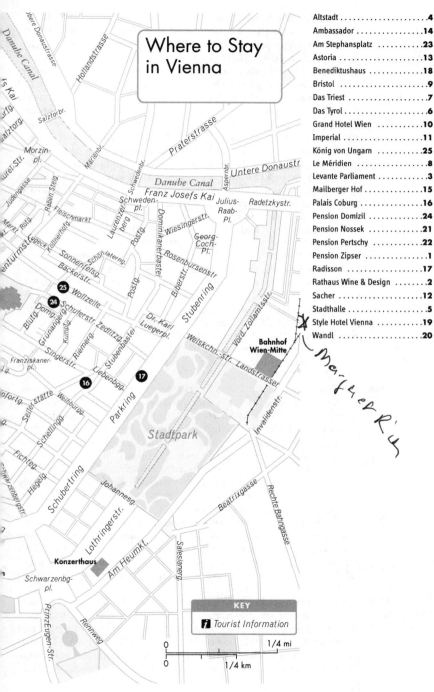

Where to Stay in Vienna

the top floor (the former attic) are done in an enchanting Biedermeier style, and several have small terraces offering amazing views of the city. Suites come with a personal butler. ⊠ *Kärntnerring 16, A-1010, 1st District* ☎ *01/501–10–0* ⊟ *01/501–10–410* ⊕ *www.luxurycollection.com/ imperial* ⇱ *138 rooms* ⚬ *Restaurant, café, minibars, gym, piano bar, Internet, no-smoking rooms* ⊟ *AE, DC, MC, V* ❖❖ *EP.*

★ **$$$$** ▦ **Le Méridien.** One of Le Méridien's super-cool "art and tech" ventures, their Vienna outpost occupies three former 19th-century Ringstrasse palaces, but you'd never know it after one step inside the front door. The lobby is minimalist, but adorned with Mies van der Rohe–style sofas and ottomans, acres of nouvelle fluorescent-light panels, and contemporary art renditions of Austrian actors Oskar Werner and Romy Schneider. Ideally located two minutes from the Staatsoper, the hotel is also home to Shambala, the luxe restaurant masterminded by Michel Rostang, the Parisian chef-guru, so you can enjoy the latest in Austrian/Asian fusion cuisine. Adjacent is a hip bar with a DJ. Guest rooms are white and strikingly decorated with glass headboards, contempo vases, and other cutting-edge items. Cloudlike mattresses, flat-screen plasma TVs, and roomy "tower of power" showers with three massaging jets pour on the luxe. Outside, visual excitements continue, as the tranquil, soundproofed rooms offer views of the Hofburg, Burggarten, and Ring. Add to this a complimentary minibar and Internet service, and you have the makings for a truly pampered stay, which you can enjoy from the get-go: the buffet breakfast is arguably the best in the country. ⊠ *Opernring 13, A-1010, 1st District* ☎ *01/588–900* ⊟ *01/588–9090–90* ⊕ *www.lemeridien.com/austria* ⇱ *294 rooms* ⚬ *Restaurant, café, minibars, indoor pool, gym, bar, Internet, no-smoking rooms* ⊟ *AE, DC, MC, V* ❖❖ *EP.*

$$$$ ▦ **Palais Coburg.** In this 19th-century regal residence, originally built for the princes of Saxe-Coburg-Kohary, Johann Strauss conducted his orchestra as dancers waltzed across the parquet of the opulent pink and yellow marble ballroom. The ballroom remains, but the lobby is all white stone and plate glass modernism. There are no double rooms, only deluxe modern or imperial-style suites, all named after Coburg titles. Many of them are spectacular two-story showpieces, the best done in a gilded-yellow Biedermeier or Empire style. All offer fresh flowers, fully equipped kitchenettes with a complimentary stock of champagne, wine, beer, and soft drinks, espresso makers, laptops with free Internet, and two bathrooms, some with gigantic whirlpool baths and saunas. Popular in its own right is the house restaurant, manned by one of the most famous chefs in the country, Christian Petz. ⊠ *Coburgbastei 4, A-1010, 1st District* ☎ *01/51818–0* ⊟ *01/51818–1* ⊕ *www.palaiscoburg.at* ⇱ *33 suites* ⚬ *Restaurant, minibars, indoor pool, gym, bar, Internet* ⊟ *AE, DC, MC, V* ❖❖ *EP.*

$$$$ ▦ **Sacher.** The legendary Sacher dates from 1876. Adding two extra floors
Fodor'sChoice and a spa on the fifth floor, the hotel has augmented its historic aura
★ with luxurious, modern-day comfort. It hardly comes as a surprise to learn that the spa's top billing is "Hot Chocolate Treatments." The corridors serve as a veritable art gallery, and guest rooms are exquisitely furnished with antiques, heavy fabrics, and original artwork. The loca-

tion directly behind the Opera House could hardly be more central, and the ratio of staff to guests is more than two to one. Meals in the Anna Sacher Room are first-rate and the Rote Bar restaurant has garnered culinary awards. The Café Sacher, of course, is legendary. Then there's the Sacher Eck, a new, elegant, and airy snack-bar where the ultrafashionable meet. ⊠ *Philharmonikerstrasse 4, A-1010, 1st District* ☎ *01/514–56–0* 🖷 *01/514–56–810* ⊕ *www.sacher.com* ↩ *152 rooms* ⚒ *2 restaurants, 2 cafés, minibars, bar, Internet, no-smoking rooms* ▤ *AE, DC, MC, V* |◎| *EP.*

\$\$\$–\$\$\$\$ 🏨 **Am Stephansplatz.** You can't get a better location than this, directly across from the magnificent front entrance of St. Stephen's Cathedral. And after a recent renovation, a sleek, peaceful and stunning hotel has emerged. What for the Viennese is a great loss is the hotel guest's great gain: the former delightful Dom Café on the first floor in now a showy, ultrachic breakfast lounge. Your breakfast chair is the best spot in Vienna from which to admire the "Giant's Gate" and the throngs of worshippers entering into the church. Parquet flooring, light oak furniture paired with dark brown leather, light-color walls and triple-glaze windows make this a fine hotel with flair. ⊠ *Stephansplatz 9, A-1010, 1st District* ☎ *01/53405–0* 🖷 *01/53405–710* ⊕ *www.hotelamstephansplatz. at* ↩ *56 rooms* ⚒ *Café, minibars, gym, bar, Internet* ▤ *AE, DC, MC, V* |◎| *BP.*

\$\$\$ 🏨 **Astoria.** Built in 1912 and still retaining the outward charm of that era, the Astoria is one of the grand old Viennese hotels and enjoys a superb location on the Kärntnerstrasse between the Opera and St. Stephen's. The wood-paneled lobby is an essay in Wiener Werkstätte style. All four floors have a soft contemporary style with pretty fabrics in beige tones, polished dark wood, and Oriental rugs. ⊠ *Kärntnerstrasse 32–34, A-1010, 1st District* ☎ *01/51577* 🖷 *01/515–7782* ⊕ *www.austria-trend. at/asw* ↩ *118 rooms* ⚒ *Minibars, bar, Internet; no a/c* ▤ *AE, DC, MC, V* |◎| *BP.*

\$\$\$ 🏨 **Das Triest.** An ultrasleek ocean-liner look is Sir Terrence Conran's nod
Fodor's Choice   to the past of this former postal coach station on the route between Vi-
★   enna and the port city of Trieste. The original cross vaulting remains in the lounges and some suites, but otherwise the interior and furnishings are Conran. In rooms, beige-on-beige fabrics are offset by glowing pine headboards the size of walls. Decor is delightful—linen-fresh, with accents of blue carpeting and honey-hue woods, and high-style as only a Conran hotel can be; even doorknobs feel nice to the touch. The hotel also allures with an excellent Austro-Italian restaurant, Collio. Das Triest may be a little off the beaten track, but is still within easy walking distance of the city center. ⊠ *Wiedner Hauptstrasse 12, A-1040, 4th District/Wieden* ☎ *01/589–180* 🖷 *01/589–1818* ⊕ *www.dastriest.at.* ↩ *72 rooms* ⚒ *Restaurant, café, minibars, health club, bar, Internet; no a/c in some rooms* ▤ *AE, DC, MC, V* |◎| *BP.*

\$\$\$ 🏨 **König von Ungarn.** In a dormered, 16th-century house in the shadow of St. Stephen's Cathedral, this hotel began catering to court nobility in 1815. Famously, the complex is joined to the Mozarthaus, where Mozart lived when he wrote *The Marriage of Figaro.* Wolfie would undoubtedly cotton to this hostelry, now outfitted with the glowing Mozartstuberl restaurant that is beautifully aglow in "Maria Theresa yellow"; a courtyard-atrium (so gigantic a tree sprouts in the middle of it); and guest rooms that radiate charm. Some rooms with Styrian wood-paneled walls are furnished with country antiques and have walk-in closets and double sinks in the sparkling bathrooms. The eight suites are two-storied, and two have balconies with rooftop views of Old Vienna. ⊠ *Schulerstrasse 10, A-1010, 1st District* ☎ *01/515–840* 🖷 *01/515–848* ⊕ *www. kvu.at* 🛏 *33 rooms* 🗘 *Restaurant, minibars, bar, Internet* ☰ *DC, MC, V* ⦿ *BP.*

$$$ ▦ **Levante Parliament.** This extravagant design hotel caters to seekers of luxury and high-tech. Arty indeed, since top photographer Curt Themessl exhibits his wonderful black-and-white ballet pics and Romanian glass artist Ioan Nemtoi decorates the hotel spaces with fantastic glass work. Breathing Bauhaus, the building from 1911 is as perfectly polished outside as it is within. Bright natural stone, glass, chrome, and dark wood harmonize well with the classical design of the house. The room furnishings emphasize rectangular formalism, but warm with splashes of orange and red. The huge courtyard garden acts as a oasis of peace. The Nemtoi Restaurant offers fabulous fusion cuisine, and the bar is an eyecatcher. You get five-star luxury here for the price of four. ⊠ *Auerspergstrasse 9, A-1080, 1st District* ☎ *01/228–280* 🖷 *01/228–2828* ⊕ *www.thelevante.com* 🛏 *74 rooms* 🗘 *Minibars, bar, gym, Internet* ☰ *AE, DC, MC, V* ⦿ *BP.*

$$$ ▦ **Mailberger Hof.** The Knights of Malta—the famous Hospitallers—knew something about hospitality, and their Baroque mansion, now familyrun, continues to offer travelers a comforting welcome mat. An atmospheric carriage entrance and a cobblestoned courtyard greet you in this wonderfully tranquil location just off Kärntnerstrasse, away from the crowded shopping streets. The traditional hotel offers attractive and airy rooms with golden and crimson bedspreads, reproduction furniture, and soft carpets. The rooms on the first floor are the most attractive; try to get one facing the pretty Baroque street. In summer the inner courtyard is set with tables for dining; at other times you'll dine on Vienna specialties and *Naturküche* under rather regal vaulted arches. ⊠ *Annagasse 7, A-1010, 1st District* ☎ *01/512–0641* 🖷 *01/512–0641–10* ⊕ *www. mailbergerhof.at* 🛏 *40 rooms, 5 apartments with kitchenettes (available by the month)* 🗘 *Restaurant, minibars, Internet; no a/c in some rooms* ☰ *AE, DC, MC, V* ⦿ *BP.*

$$$ ▦ **Radisson.** One of the handsomest of all Ringstrasse palace hotels combines the fin-de-siècle Palais Leitenberger and the Palais Henckel von Donnersmarck. The latter, built in 1872, was occupied by an exceedingly patrician family, and their taste shows in the superbly designed facade, articulated with window pediments and caryatids. Inside, a grand staircase leads up to a gallery of ancestral portraits, spotlighted in a sober marble hall. The location is also princely—directly across from the Stadtpark, Vienna's main city park. Inside, the rooms are done in an understated, traditional, and soigné manner. Quiet and comfortable, some have pretty floral drapes and matching bedspreads, others allure with a more masculine Biedermeier look. Le Siecle restaurant offers celebrated food as stylish as its decor. ⊠ *Parkring 16, A-1010, 1st District* ☎ *01/515170*

🕾 *01/512–2216* 🌐 *www.radissonsas.com* 🛏 *246 rooms* ♨ *2 restaurants, café, minibars, gym, bar, Internet, spa* ▭ *AE, DC, MC, V* � *EP.*

$$$ ✕ **Style Hotel Vienna.** Within the hotel's Art Nouveau shell London in-
Fodor'sChoice terior designer Maria Vafiadis has paid tribute to Viennese Art Deco.
★ Quite an eye-catcher is the tremendous glass-enclosed vault, smack
bang in the middle of the lobby. You would never have guessed the ed-
ifice was previously a bank and the big bucks were stashed right here.
Today this wonderful feature serves as a wine cellar. Have your favorite
vintage served up at the push of a button. Enjoy your glass of wine in
the elegant marble-and-wood wine bar, which has an enormous open
fire and the dreamiest of contemporary music playing. Rooms are full
of streamlined, sedate furnishings. Step out of the hotel and you're in
the venerable Café Central in a flash, and just down the cobbled street
is the Hofburg palace. ⊠ *Herrengasse 12, A-1010, 1st District* 🕾 *01/
22–780–0* 🖷 *01/22–780–77* 🌐 *www.stylehotel.at* 🛏 *78 rooms* ♨ *1
restaurant, minibars, health club, bar, Internet, business services* ▭ *AE,
DC, MC, V* 101 *BP.*

★ **$$–$$$** 🖭 **Das Tyrol.** On a busy Mariahilferstrasse corner, this small, luxurious
hotel is a good choice for those who want to be close to the Museums-
Quartier and some fun shopping, too. Rooms are exceptionally pleas-
ing, with fabrics and tony furniture from posh Viennese stores like
Backhausen, Thonet, and Wittmann. There are many nice touches,
from the exquisite bedcovers, stylish high-backed chairs and fashion-
able, elongated lamps, to the elegant, subtle drapes that dress the long
windows. It's in a neighborhood that has everything, including a host
of good restaurants. ⊠ *Mariahilferstrasse 15, A-1060* 🕾 *01/587–5415*
🖷 *01/587–5415–9* 🌐 *www.das-tyrol.at* 🛏 *30 rooms* ♨ *Minibars, bar,
Internet* ▭ *AE, DC, MC, V* 101 *BP.*

$$–$$$ 🖭 **Pension Domizil.** Around the corner from the house where Mozart wrote
The Marriage of Figaro, the Domizil offers quiet, well-equipped rooms
with rather bland contemporary furniture. Breakfast is a notch above
the average, with both hot and cold selections. Another nice thing about
staying here is free access to the Internet in the lobby. The staff is pleas-
ant, and you're right in the middle of a series of charming Old World
cobblestone streets near St. Stephen's. ⊠ *Schulerstrasse 14, A-1010, 1st
District* 🕾 *01/513–3199–0* 🖷 *01/512–3484* 🌐 *www.hoteldomizil.at*
🛏 *47 rooms* ♨ *Internet; no a/c* ▭ *AE, DC, MC, V* 101 *BP.*

★ **$–$$$** 🖭 **Wandl.** The restored facade identifies a 300-year-old house that has
been in family hands as a hotel since 1854. You couldn't find a better
location, tucked behind St. Peter's Church, just off the Graben. The hall-
ways are punctuated by cheerful, bright openings along the glassed-in
inner court. The rooms are modern, but some are a bit plain and charm-
less, despite parquet flooring and red accents. If you can, ask for one of
the rooms done in period furniture, with decorated ceilings and gilt mirrors; they're rather palatial, with plush Victorian chairs, carved-wood
trim, and velvet throws. ⊠ *Petersplatz 9, A-1010, 1st District* 🕾 *01/
534–55–0* 🖷 *01/534–55–77* 🌐 *www.hotel-wandl.com* 🛏 *138 rooms*
♨ *Bar, Internet; no a/c* ▭ *AE, DC, MC, V* 101 *BP.*

$$ 🖭 **Altstadt.** A cognoscenti favorite, this small hotel was once a patrician
home, and is in one of Vienna's most pampered neighborhoods—and

we mean neighborhood: a plus here is being able to really interact with real Viennese, their stores (hey, supermarkets!), and residential streets. In fact, you are lucky enough to be in the chic and quaint Spittelberg quarter. The Altstadt is blessed with a personable and helpful management. Palm trees, a Secession-style wrought-iron staircase, modernist fabrics, and halogen lighting make for a very design-y interior. Guest rooms are large with all the modern comforts, though they retain an antique feel. The English-style lounge has a fireplace and plump floral sofas. Upper rooms have lovely views out over the city roofline. Last but not least, you are one streetcar stop or a pleasant walk from the main museums. ✉ *Kirchengasse 41, 7th District/Neubau* ☎ *01/526–3399–0* 📠 *01/523–4901* 🌐 *www.altstadt.at* *25 rooms* *Minibars, bar; no a/c* 💳 *AE, DC, MC, V* 🍽 *BP.*

$$ **Pension Pertschy.** Housed in the former Palais Cavriani, just off the Graben, this pension is as central as you can get—just behind the Hofburg and down the street from the Spanish Riding School. One of those typical Viennese mansion-turned-apartment houses, the structure is still graced with a massive arched portal and yellow-stone courtyard, around which the 18th-century edifice was built. A few guest rooms contain lovely old ceramic stoves (just for show). Most rooms are spacious, and each one is comfortable. Some rooms are sweet, with bed canopies and chandeliers, although others are decorated with "repro"–antique furniture that verges on the kitsch. As for noise, the street outside gets a lot of horse-drawn fiaker carriages (and street sweepers at night), so opt for a courtyard room if you need complete peace and quiet. Use the elevator, but don't miss the palatial grand staircase. ✉ *Habsburgergasse 5, A-1010, 1st District* ☎ *01/534–49–0* 📠 *01/534–49–49* 🌐 *www.pertschy.com* *43 rooms* *Minibars; no a/c* 💳 *AE, DC, MC, V* 🍽 *BP.*

★ **$$** **Rathaus Wine & Design.** The friendliest staff and the most salutiferous breakfast buffet in town—see to it that your schedule allows you to savor the spread—make this abode a worthwhile choice. The brainchild of entrepreneurs Petra und Klaus Fleischhaker of Salzburg, this exclusive boutique hotel pays homage to the winemakers of Austria. The spacious, high-ceiling, ultramodern guest rooms have polished wooden floors and accent wood walls, with warm orange, yellow, ocher, and cream colors. On each door is the name of a different winemaker, with a bottle of the vintner's wine inside (sorry, it's not included in the room price), and some of the greatest Austrian winemakers are represented, such as Bründelmayer, Gesellmann, Sattlerhof, and Markowitsch. Guests can take a grape escape in the chic, minimalist lounge, where vintages and snacks are served. ✉ *Langegasse 13, A-1080* ☎ *01/400–1122* 📠 *01/400–1122–88* 🌐 *www.hotel-rathaus-wien.at* *33 rooms* *Minibars, wine bar, Internet* 💳 *AE, DC, MC, V* 🍽 *BP.*

$–$$ **Pension Nossek.** A family-run establishment on the upper floors of a 19th-century office and apartment building, the Nossek lies at the heart of the pedestrian and shopping area. The rooms have high ceilings and are eclectically but comfortably furnished; those on the front have a magnificent view of the Graben. Mozart worked on *The Abduction from the Seraglio* while he lived here in the early 1780s. Do as the many regular guests do: book early. ✉ *Graben 17, A-1010, 1st District* ☎ *01/*

533–7041–0 🖨 *01/535–3646* ⊕ *www.pension-nossek.at* ⊃ *32 rooms* ☖ *Internet; no a/c* ☰ *No credit cards* ⍥ *BP.*

★ **$** ⊞ **Stadthalle.** This budget hotel close to Vienna's main Westbahnhof railway station was awarded the Austrian environment-friendly label from the Ministry for Economic Affairs in 2005. Water is heated by solar cells, rainwater is recycled, and the flat roofs are used for gardening. Energized tap water gushes from the faucets, and in summer there's the lovely courtyard abounding with plants and flowers for that breakfast-in-the-garden feel. Breakfast is made up entirely of produce, which is pointedly free of any genetically modified products. The homey rooms are quiet and individually styled. Some of Austria's well-known artists have had a hand in embellishing the interiors. For that additional health kick, try out the biking path that runs straight by the front door into the center of town. ⊠ *Hackengasse 20, A-1150/Rudolfsheim–Fünfhaus* 🕿 *01/982–4272* 🖨 *01/98–7232–56* ⊕ *www.hotelstadthalle.at* ⊃ *46 rooms* ☖ *Internet; no a/c* ☰ *MC, V* ⍥ *BP.*

¢–**$** ⊞ **Benediktushaus.** You can stay in this guesthouse of a monastery without following the dictum *ora et labora* (pray and work). Stay in the Benedictene house and see how the monks live, pray, and work. It's guaranteed to be one of the most tranquil stays you've ever had. The rooms are simply furnished and without frills—no TV set either—so switch on to relax mode and go chant with the fratres in the Freyung. The picturesque square is but a minute from Café Central if you think you're missing out on some of the fun. ⊠ *Freyung 6a, A-1010, 1st District* 🕿 *01/534–98–900* 🖨 *01/534–98–905* ⊕ *www.schottenstift.at* ⊃ *21 rooms* ☖ *No a/c* ☰ *AE, DC, MC, V* ⍥ *BP.*

¢–**$** ⊞ **Pension Zipser.** With an ornate facade and gilt-trimmed coat of arms, this 1904 house is one of the city's better values. It's in the picturesque Josefstadt neighborhood of small cafés, shops, bars, and good restaurants, yet within steps of the J streetcar line to the city center. The rooms are in browns and beiges, with modern furniture and well-equipped baths. The balconies of some of the back rooms overlook tree-filled neighborhood courtyards. The accommodating staff will help get theater and concert tickets. ⊠ *Langegasse 49, A-1080, 8th District/Josefstadt* 🕿 *01/404–540* 🖨 *01/404–5413* ⊕ *www.zipser.at* ⊃ *47 rooms* ☖ *Bar, Internet; no a/c* ☰ *AE, DC, MC, V* ⍥ *BP.*

NIGHTLIFE & THE ARTS

Vienna's nightlife and arts scenes present you with myriad tantalizing choices, so only by combining Admiral Byrd-ish foresight with a movie editor's ruthless selectivity can you hope to ride herd on it all. Do you want to time-warp back to the 18th century at Mozart concerts featuring bewigged musicians in the opulent surroundings of the court theater at Schönbrunn Palace? Or at the tiny jewelbox Sala Terrena that shimmers with Venetian-style frescoes? Or cheer the divas at the grandest of grand opera at the Staatoper? Or dive into the Franz Josef splendor of an evening concert of Strauss waltzes? Or catch a recital of the greatest early-music ensemble, Nikolaus Harnoncourt's Concentus Musicus? Or enjoy a trombone troupe at a *Jazzkeller*? Or do you want to catch a Broadway-musical extravaganza devoted to the life of the tragic empress Elisabeth at the Raimund Theater? Or will it be a summer opera, dance, or concert performance at the Theater an der Wien (where Beethoven's *Fidelio* premiered in 1805)? Or take in an operetta at the beloved Volksoper? Or, or, or . . . ?

The Arts

Tickets

With a city as music mad and opera crazy as Vienna, it is not surprising to learn that the bulk of major performances are sold out in advance. But with thousands of seats to be filled every night, you may luck out with a bit of planning and the help of the State Theater Booking Office, or **Österreichischer Bundestheaterkassen** (✉ Theaterkassen, back of Opera, Hanuschgasse 3, in courtyard ☎ 01/513–1513 ⊕ www.bundestheater. at). They sell tickets for the Akademietheater, Schauspielhaus, Staatsoper, Volksoper, and Burgtheater. Call the (frequently busy) phone line weekdays 8–5. To purchase tickets at the box office, the above address also operates as a central clearing house, open weekdays 8–6, weekends from 9 AM to noon. Tickets for the Staatsoper and Volksoper go on sale one month before the date of performance; credit-card reservations are taken up to six days before the performance. You can also purchase tickets using the **Web site** (⊕ www.culturall.at). As for other ticket agencies, the most trusted is **Liener Brünn** (☎ 01/533–0961 ⊕ www.ims.at/lienerbruenn)—charging a minimum 22% markup and generally dealing in the more expensive seats. Tickets to musicals and some events including the Vienna Festival are available at the **"Salettl" gazebo** kiosk alongside the Opera House on Kärntnerstrasse, open daily 10 AM to 7 PM. Tickets to that night's musicals are reduced by half after 2 PM.

Dance

A small revolution has been brewing on the modern dance front, thanks to **Tanzquartier Wien** (✉ Museumsplatz 1, 7th District/Neubau ☎ 01/581-35-91 ⊕ www.tqw.at). DanceQuarter Vienna is now Austria's foremost center for contemporary dance performances. The Tanzquartier season lasts from October through April. In May and June it is followed by the so-called "Factory Season," when the center concentrates solely on the projects presented in its dance studios. The **ballet evenings** (☎ 01/514-44-0 ⊕ www.wiener-staatsoper.at) on the Staatsoper and Volksoper seasonal schedule feature mostly contemporary choreography. **dietheater Wien Künstlerhaus** (✉ Karlsplatz 5, 1st District ☎ 01/587–0504–0) is a popular venue for cutting-edge dance arts (don't confuse it with its sister venue, dietheater Wien Konzerthaus on Lothringer Strasse 20).

Film

The film schedules in the daily newspapers *Der Standard* and *Die Presse* list foreign-language films (*Fremdsprachige Filme*) separately. In film listings, *OmU* means original language with German subtitles. Vienna has a thriving film culture, with viewers seeking original rather than German-dubbed versions. There are several theaters offering English-language films.

Just around the corner from Tuchlauben street, the **Artis** (✉ Corner of Shultergasse/Jordangasse, 1st District ☎ 01/535–6570) has six screens altogether, showing the latest blockbusters three to four times a day. The **Burg Kino** (✉ Opernring 19, 1st District ☎ 01/587–8406) features Carol Reed's Vienna-based classic *The Third Man,* with Orson Welles and Joseph Cotton, Tuesday, Friday, and Sunday. Otherwise all new releases are usually shown in the original English version. The **Haydn** (✉ Mariahilferstrasse 57, 6th District/Mariahilf ☎ 01/587–2262) is a multiplex theater. Most English films are shown with German subtitles. Set in the famous Albertina museum, the **Filmmuseum** (✉ Augustinerstrasse 1, 1st District ☎ 01/533–7054 ⊕ www.filmmuseum.at) has one of the most ambitious and sophisticated schedules around, with original-version classics and a heavy focus on English-language films. The theater is closed July–September. The arty **Votiv-Kino** (✉ Währingerstrasse 12, 9th District/Alsergrund ☎ 01/317–3571) usually features less mainstream, more alternative fare, most films being shown in their original version with German subtitles. In winter the Votiv Kino offers a leisurely Sunday-brunch/feature-film package.

Galleries

With new and hip contemporary art museums springing up across Austria (notably the Kunsthaus in Graz and the Museum der Moderne Kunst in Salzburg), art in Vienna needs to remain cutting-edge, and it succeeds in doing so in notable galleries in two city quarters. The first is behind the MQ (MuseumsQuartier) complex, while the second is in the 4th District—the Freihaus-Quartier, where some of the most exciting contemporary galleries in town have set up shop, appropriately within range of the famed Secession Pavilion. Today Freihaus has become one of the hottest areas in Vienna for everything that's trendy, fashionable, and fun. The more traditional art galleries are still grouped around the now privatized Dorotheum auction house (⇨ Shopping) in the city center.

The leading address for contemporary galleries in the Freihaus-Quartier is Schleifmühlgasse. Here is where you'll find, in a former printing shop, **Gallery Georg Kargl** (✉ Schleifmühlgasse 5, 4th District/Wieden ☎ 01/585–4199), which shows art that sidesteps categorization and is a must for serious art collectors. Another of the Schleifmühlgasse galleries is **Gallery Christine Koenig** (✉ Schleifmülgasse 1a, 4th District/Wieden ☎ 01/585–7474). A presence at cutting-edge art fairs around the world, **Krinzinger Gallery** (✉ Schottenfeldgasse 45, 7th District ☎ 01/513–30 06) has been going strong since the 1970s, when it pushed Vienna Actionism. Its Krinzinger Projects are among the most important blips on the contemporary Austrian art radar screen, and it is close to the MQ (MuseumsQuartier). **Gallery Julius Hummel** (✉ Bäckerstrasse 14, 1st District ☎ 01/512–1296) concentrates mainly on themes concerning the human body in art. It is in an old Gothic building in one of the most charming spots in Vienna, nestled between such venerable institutions as Café Alt-Wien and Oswald & Kalb. Franz West is one of the artists shown here. While her father, Baron H. H. Thyssen-Bornemiesza, amassed one of the greatest collections of Old Master paintings, Francesca von Habsburg has chosen to spearhead Austria's avant-garde scene at her

TB A-21 (✉ Himmelpfortgasse 13, 1st District ☎ 01/513–9856). New media installations, puppet-rock operas, and exhibitions by hot new Turkish and Croatian artists keep people talking about Thyssen-Bornemieza Art Contemporary.

Music

Vienna is one of the main music centers of the world. Contemporary music gets its due, but it's the hometown standards—the works of Beethoven, Brahms, Haydn, Mozart, and Schubert—that draw the Viennese public and make tickets to the Wiener Philharmoniker the hottest of commodities. A monthly printed program, the *Wien-Programm,* put out by the city tourist board and available at any travel agency or hotel, gives a general overview of what's going on in the worlds of opera, concerts, jazz, theater, and galleries, and similar information is posted on billboards and fat advertising columns around the city. Vienna is home to four full symphony orchestras: the great Wiener Philharmoniker (Vienna Philharmonic), the outstanding Wiener Symphoniker (Vienna Symphony), the broadcasting service's ORF Symphony Orchestra, and the Niederösterreichische Tonkünstler. There are also hundreds of smaller groups, from world-renowned trios to chamber orchestras.

★ The most important concert halls are in the buildings of the Gesellschaft der Musikfreunde, called the **Musikverein** (✉ Dumbastrasse 3, ticket office at Karlsplatz 6 ☎ 01/505–8190 🖷 01/505–8190–94 ⊕ www. musikverein.at). There are actually six halls in this magnificent theater, but the one that everyone knows is the venue for the annually televised New Year's Day Concert—the Goldene Saal, the Gold Hall, officially called the Grosser Musikvereinssaal. Possibly the most beautiful in the world, this Parthenon of a music hall was designed by the Danish 19th-century architect Theophil Hansen, a passionate admirer of ancient Greece. For his 1869 design of the hall, he arrayed an army of gilded caryatids in the main concert hall, planted Ionic columns in the 660-seat Brahmssaal, and placed the figure of Orpheus in the building pediment. But the surprise is that his smaller Brahmssal is even more sumptuous—a veritable Greek temple with more caryatids and lots of gilding and green malachite. What Hansen would have made of the four newly constructed (2004) subsidiary halls, set below the main theater, must remain a mystery, but the avant-garde Glass, Metal, Wooden, and Stone Halls (Gläserne, Hölzerne, Metallene, Steinerne Säle) make fitting showcases for contemporary music concerts. The Musikverein, in addition to being the main venue for such troupes as the Wiener Philharmoniker and the Wiener Symphoniker, also hosts many of the world's finest orchestras. A three-minute walk from the Musikverein, crossing ★ Schwarzenbergplatz, is the **Konzerthaus** (✉ Lothringerstrasse 20, 1st District ☎ 01/242002 🖷 01/242–0011–0 ⊕ www.konzerthaus.at), home to the Grosser Konzerthaussaal, Mozartsaal, and Schubertsaal. The first is a room of magnificent size, with red-velvet and gold accents. The calendar of Grosser Konzerthaussaal is packed with goodies, including the fabulous early-music group Concentus Musicus Wien, headed by Nicolaus Harnoncourt, and concerts of the Wiener Philharmoniker and the Wiener Symphoniker.

CLOSE UP

The Sound—and Sights—of Music

1

WHAT CLOSER ASSOCIATION TO VIENNA is there than music? Saturated with musical history and boasting one of the world's greatest concert venues (the Musikverein), two of the world's greatest symphony orchestras (Vienna Philharmonic and Vienna Symphony), and one of the top opera houses (the Staatsoper), it's no wonder that music and the related politics are subjects of daily conversation.

Music lovers can tread in the footsteps of the mighty, seeing where masterpieces were committed to paper or standing where a long-loved work was either praised or damned at its first performance. Many former musicians' residences are open as museums. The most famous apartments are where Mozart wrote his last three symphonies (⇨ *see* Mozarthaus *in* From St. Stephen's to the Opera House) and Beethoven's Pasqualatihaus (⇨ *see* Baroque Gems & Cozy Cafés). Unlike most of Vienna's composers, Schubert was a native of Vienna and you can visit **Schubert's Birthplace** (✉ Nussdorferstrasse 54, 9th District ☎ 01/317-3601 Ⓤ U2/Schottenring; Streetcar 37 or 38 to Canisiusgasse) as well as where he

died at **Kettenbrückengasse 6** (✉ 4th District ☎ 01/581-6730 Ⓤ U4/Kettenbrückengasse). **Joseph Haydn's house** (✉ Haydngasse 19, 6th District ☎ 01/596-1307 Ⓤ U4/Pilgramgasse or U3/Zieglergasse) includes a Brahms memorial room and is open Wednesday and Thursday 10-1 and 2-6, Friday–Sunday 10-1. **Beethoven's Heiligenstadt residence** (✉ Probusgasse 6, 19th District ☎ 01/370-5408 Ⓤ U4/Heiligenstadt; Bus 38A to Wählamt) is where at age 32 he wrote the "Heiligenstadt Testament," an anguished cry of pain and protest against his ever-increasing deafness. All the above houses contain commemorative museums. Admission is €2. Most are open Tuesday–Sunday 10-1 and 2-6, but note there are exceptions. The home of the most popular composer of all, waltz king Johann Strauss the Younger, can be visited at **Praterstrasse 54** (✉ 2nd District ☎ 01/214-0121 Ⓤ U4/Nestroyplatz); he lived here when he composed "The Blue Danube Waltz" in 1867. Opening times here are Tuesday–Thursday 2-6, Friday–Sunday 10-1. On Sunday morning all houses but the Mozarthaus offer free admission.

If the whirling waltzes of Strauss are your thing, head to the Johann Strauss concerts at the **Wiener Kursalon** (✉ Johannesgasse 33, 1st District ☎ 01/513–2477 🖷 01/512–5791 ⊕ www.strauss-konzerte.at/), a majestic palacelike structure built in the Italian Renaissance Revival style in 1865 and set in Vienna's sylvan Stadtpark. Here, in gold-and-white salons, the Salonorchester Alt Wien performs concerts, accompanied at times by dancers, of the works of "Waltz King" Johann Strauss and his contemporaries, with waltzes, polkas, parade themes, operetta melodies, traditional *Schrammeln,* and *Salonmusik* at the fore. In addition, the Wiener Johann Strauss Capelle, dressed in period costume, also presents concerts of the Strauss era in Original Viennese Waltz Show evenings, replete with singers, dancers, and your very own glass of champagne (no dancing by the audience allowed).

Happily, there is a plethora of period-era, chocolate-box, jeweled concert salons in Vienna. Perhaps the most opulent is the **Schlosstheater Schönbrunn** (✉ Schönbrunner Schloss-Strasse, 13th District/Hietzing ☎ 01/71155–158 ⊕ www.mdw.ac.at), built for Empress Maria Theresa in the palace's Valerie Wing, with glittering chandeliers and a gigantic ceiling fresco. For a grand evening of Strauss and Mozart in imperial surroundings, head to the Wiener Hofburgorchester concerts given in the Hofburg palace's Redoutensaal and mammoth 19th-century **Festsaal** (✉ Heldenplatz, 1st District ☎ 01/587–2552 🖷 01/587–4397 ⊕ www.hofburgorchester.at/). The concerts are offered Tuesday, Thursday, and Saturday, May through October. The most enchanting place to hear Mozart in Vienna (or anywhere, for that matter?) is the exquisite 18th-century Sala Terrena of the **Deutschordenskloster** (✉ Singerstrasse 7, 1st District ⊕ www.mozarthaus.at). Here, in a tiny room—seating for no more than 50 people—a bewigged chamber group offers Mozart concerts in a jewel box overrun with Rococo frescoes in the Venetian style. The concerts are scheduled by the nearby Mozarthaus. Said to be the oldest concert "hall" in Vienna, the Sala Terrena is part of the German Monastery, where, in 1781, Mozart worked for his despised employer, Archbishop Colloredo of Salzburg.

Although the well-known mid-May to mid-June Vienna Festival, the **Wiener Festwochen** (☎ 01/589–22–11 ⊕ www.festwochen.at), wraps up the primary season, the rest of the summer musical scene, from mid-July to mid-August, nowadays brims with activities. One top event is the **Festival KlangBogen** (✉ Stadiongasse 9, 1st District ☎ 01/42717 ⊕ www.klangbogen.at), which features rare and contemporary operas starring some famous singers and performers.

The beloved Vienna Boys' Choir, the **Wiener Sängerknaben** (✉ Hofburg, Schweizer Hof, 1st District ☎ 01/533–9927 🖷 01/533–9927–75 ⊕ www.wsk.at) are far from just being living "dolls" out of a Walt Disney film (remember the 1962 movie *Almost Angels?*). Their pedigree is royal, and their professionalism such that they regularly appear with the best orchestras around the world. The troupe originated as a choir founded by Emperor Maximilian I in 1498, but with the demise of the Habsburg empire in 1918 they were on their own and became a private outfit, subsidizing themselves by giving public performances starting in the 1920s. When the troupe lost its imperial patronage, they traded in their court costume for these charming costumes, then the height of fashion (a look even sported by Donald Duck, who was also born in that era).

From mid-September to late June, the apple-cheeked lads sing mass at 9:15 AM Sunday in the **Hofburgkapelle** (✉ Verwaltung der Hofmusikkapelle, Hofburg, A-1010 Vienna). Written requests for seats should be made at least eight weeks in advance. You will be sent a reservation card, which you exchange at the box office (in the Hofburg courtyard) for your tickets. Tickets are also sold at ticket agencies and at the box office (open Friday 11–1 and 3–5; any remaining seats may be available Sunday morning, 8:15 to 8:45). General seating costs €5, prime seats in the front of the church nave €29. It's important to note that only the 10 side balcony seats allow a view of the actual choir; those who purchase floor seats, standing room, or center balcony will not have a view of the boys. On Sunday at 8:45 AM any unclaimed, preordered tickets are sold. You can also opt for standing room, which is free. If you miss hearing the choir at a Sunday mass, you may be able to catch them in a more popular program in the Musikverein or Konzerthaus or, in August, at Schönbrunn Palace.

Opera & Operetta

★ The **Staatsoper** (State Opera House; ✉ Opernring 2, 1st District ☎ 01/514–440 ⊕ www.wiener-staatsoper.at), one of the world's great opera houses, has been the scene of countless musical triumphs and a center of unending controversies over how it should be run and by whom. (When Lorin Maazel was unceremoniously dumped as head of the opera not many years ago, he pointed out that the house had done the same thing to Gustav Mahler almost a century earlier.) A performance takes place virtually every night September–June, drawing on the vast repertoire of the house, with emphasis on Mozart and Verdi works. Guided tours of the opera house are given year-round.

★ Opera and operetta are also performed at the **Volksoper** (✉ Währingerstrasse 78 ☎ 01/514–440 ⊕ www.volksoper.at), outside the city center at Währingerstrasse and Währinger Gürtel (third stop on Streetcars 41, 42, or 43, which run from "downstairs" at Schottentor, U2, on the Ring). Prices here are significantly lower than at the Staatsoper, and performances can be every bit as rewarding. This theater has a fully packed calendar, with offerings ranging from the grandest opera, such as Mozart's *Don Giovanni,* to an array of famous Viennese operettas, such as Johann Strauss's *Wiener Blut* and *Die Fledermaus,* to modern Broadway musicals (during 2004, Rodgers and Hammerstein's *Sound of Music* finally received its first Austrian staging here ever). Most operas are sung here in German.

You'll also find musicals and operetta at a couple of theaters. The **Raimundtheater** (✉ Wallgasse 18 ☎ 01/599–77–0 ⊕ www.musicalvienna.at) mostly offers musicals by local composers. For decades the **Theater an der Wien** (✉ Linke Wienzeile 6 ☎ 01/588—30–660 ⊕ www.theater-wien.at), an historic theater dating to 1801, was misused as a contemporary musical venue. Now this building closely linked to Beethoven—who lived here—and to Schikaneder, the librettist who wrote *The Magic Flute* for Mozart, has renewed its role as a opera house. It will be open year-round with a premiere every month. Each opera is to be performed by the same cast, to guarantee the highest standard possible. Also on the schedule will be concerts, dance performances, and the occasional operetta—such as Johann Strauss's *Die Fledermaus,* which premiered here. The Vienna Summer of Music is held here in July and August. Opera and operetta are performed on an irregular schedule at the **Kammeroper** (✉ Fleischmarkt 24 ☎ 01/512–01–000 ⊕ www.wienerkammeroper.at). In summer, light opera or operetta performances by the Kammeroper ensemble are given in the exquisite **Schlosstheater** at Schönbrunn. Send a fax to 01/51201–00–30 for details.

Theater

Vienna's **Burgtheater** (✉ Dr.-Karl-Lueger-Ring 2, 1st District, Vienna) is one of the leading German-language theaters of the world. The repertoire has recently begun mixing German classics with more modern and controversial pieces. The Burg's smaller house, the **Akademietheater** (✉ Lisztstrasse 1), draws on much the same group of actors for classical and modern plays. Both houses are closed during July and August. The **Kammerspiele** (✉ Rotenturmstrasse 20 ☏ 01/42700–304) does modern plays. The **Theater in der Josefstadt** (✉ Josefstädterstrasse 26, 8th District/Josefstadt ☏ 01/42700–306) stages classical and modern works year-round in the house once run by the great producer and teacher Max Reinhardt. The **Volkstheater** (✉ Neustiftgasse 1, 7th District/Neubau ☏ 01/523–3501–0) presents dramas, comedies, and folk plays.

For theater in English (mainly standard plays), head for **Vienna's English Theater** (✉ Josefsgasse 12, 8th District/Josefstadt ☏ 01/402–1260). Another option is the equally good **International Theater** (✉ Porzellangasse 8, 9th District/Alsergrund ☏ 01/319–6272).

Nightlife

Balls

The gala Vienna evening you've always dreamed about can become a reality: among the many **balls** given during the Carnival season, several welcome the public—at a wide range of prices, from about €65 to €350 and up per person. Dates change every year, but most balls are held in January and February. The dress code for all is "full dress," and they usually run between 8 or 9 PM and 3 or 4 AM. Food and drink is always available. Some of the more popular balls are the Blumen Ball (Florists' Ball), the Kaffeesieder Ball (Coffee Brewers' Ball), the Bonbon Ball (Confection Ball), and the most famous and expensive of them all, the Opernball (Opera Ball). You can book tickets through **hotel concierges** (☏ 01/211140 for more information 🖷 01/216–8492).

Bars, Lounges & Nightclubs

Where once night-owls had to head to Vienna's *Bermuda Dreieck* (Bermuda Triangle, around St. Ruprecht's church on the Ruprechtsplatz, two blocks south of the Danube Canal), today's nightclub scene has blossomed with a profusion of delightful and sophisticated bars, clubs, and lounges. Many of the trendoisie like to head to the clubs around the Naschmarkt area, then move on to nearby Mariahilferstrasse to shake their groove thing. The Freihaus Quarter sizzles with cafés and shops. For the run-down of options, log on to ⊕ www.freihausviertel.at.

A sort of spaceship has landed smack between the Hofburg palace and the Kunsthistorisches Museum—just look for the glowing orange kiosk at the intersection of the Ring and Mariahilferstrasse and head downstairs to find **Babenberger Passage** (✉ Ringstrasse at Babenbergerstrasse, 1st District ☏ 01/961–8800 ⊕ www.sunshine.at/ Ⓤ U2/MuseumsQuartier), one of the hippest places in Vienna these days. State-of-the-art lighting systems, futuristic decor, and adaptable design elements come together in a blush-hue bar and a sizzling-blue dance room. One

CLOSE UP

Stepping Out in Three-Quarter Time

1

EVER SINCE THE 19TH-CENTURY Congress of Vienna—when pundits laughed "*Elle danse, mais elle ne marche pas*" (the city "dances, but it never gets anything done")—Viennese extravagance and gaiety have been world-famous. Fasching, the season of Carnival, was given over to court balls, opera balls, masked balls, chambermaids' and bakers' balls, and a hundred other gatherings, many held within the glittering interiors of Baroque theaters and palaces. Presiding over the dazzling evening gowns and gilt-encrusted uniforms, towering headdresses, flirtatious fans, *chambres séparées*, "Wine, Women, and Song," *Die Fledermaus*, "Blue Danube," hand kissing, and gay abandon was the baton of the waltz emperor, Johann Strauss. White-gloved women and men in white tie would glide over marble floors to his heavenly melodies. They still do. Now, as in the days of Franz Josef, Vienna's old three-quarter-time rhythm strikes up anew each year during Carnival, from New Year's Eve until Mardi Gras.

During January and February as many as 40 balls may be held in a single evening. Many events are organized by a professional group, including the Kaffeesiederball (Coffee Brewers' Ball), the Zuckerbaeckerball

(Confectioners' Ball), or the Opernball (Opera Ball). The latter is the most famous—some say too famous. This event transforms the Vienna Opera House into the world's most beautiful ballroom (and transfixes all of Austria when shown live on national television). The invitation reads "*Frack mit Dekorationen*," which means that ball gowns and tails are usually required for most events (you can always get your tux from a rental agency) and women mustn't wear white (reserved for debutantes). But there's something for everyone these days, including the "Ball of Bad Taste" or "Wallflower Ball." Other noted venues are the imperial Hofburg palace and the famous Musikverein concert hall. Prices usually run from about €75 to €450 and up per person. For a calendar of the main balls, visit www.top.wien.at/ ballkalender, or ask your discerning hotel concierge for tips and pointers. If you go, remember that you must dance the *Linkswalzer*—the counterclockwise, left-turning waltz that is the only correct way to dance in Vienna. After your gala evening, finish off the morning with a *Kater Frühstuck*—hangover breakfast—of goulash soup.

---

of the most dazzling settings for a Viennese club is in one of the city's cavernous subway stations, and **Café Carina** (✉ Josefstädterstrasse 84/ Stadtbahnbogen, 8th District/Josefstadt ☎ 01/406–4322 Ⓤ U6/Josef-städterstrasse) has one of the best—an actual Otto Wagner original. Vienna's new subway-station clubs are proof positive that nightlife is no longer centered in and around the old city center. Carina is very off-beat, artistic, and action-packed—anything can happen here, from an airgui-tar competition to an evening with 1980s hits. Near the Naschmarkt, **Kaleidoskop** (✉ Schleifmühlgasse 13, 4th District/Wieden ☎ 01/920–3343 Ⓤ U4/Kettenbrückengasse) sits shoulder to shoulder with a number of top art galleries, so the hip and happening art crowd tends to come here. Chic, chic, and once again chic, the designer café-bar **Shultz** (✉ Siebensterngasse 31, 7th District/Neubau ☎ 01/522–9120 ⊕ www.schultz.at Ⓤ U4/Kettenbrückengasse) seduces fashionable folk with its long drinks, retro cocktails, and its Vienna Moderne setting. Back in 1870, Viennese used to come to the **Volksgarten** (✉ Burgring 2, 1st District ☎ 01/532–0907 ⊕ www.volksgarten.at Ⓤ U2/3 MuseumsQuartier) to waltz, share champagne, and enjoy the night in a candlelit garden. Today they come to the same site to *diskothek* the night away under pink strobes, enjoy some boogie-woogie or tango dancing in the Tanzcafe (Dance Café), and sip a beer against the greenery. A best bet when you don't know where else to head, this one-in-all club complex is set within a lush garden and has a pretty, vaguely Jugendstil dining salon with a vast curved wall of windows overlooking a terrace set with tables. Beyond lies the Pavilion, a 1950s jewel that looks airlifted from California, which serves brews and nibbles.

Dance Clubs

In the MuseumsQuartier, **Café Leopold** (✉ Museumsplatz 1, MuseumsQuartier, 1st District ☎ 01/523–6732 ⊕ www.cafe-leopold.at/ Ⓤ U2 or 3/MuseumsQuartier) is in the big modern white cube that is the Leopold Museum. After enough house and electro music, you can escape to a table outdoors in the plaza. "U" stands for underground and **Club U im Otto-Wagner-Café** (✉ Karlsplatz/Kuenstlerhauspassage, 4th District/Wieden ☎ 01/505–9904 ⊕ www.club-u.at Ⓤ U1, U2, or U4/Karlsplatz) is just underneath one of the two celebrated Jugendstil pavilions that Otto Wagner built on the Karlsplatz square when designing Vienna's subway. Which means this disco is easy to find. One of the best dance halls for alternative music, it is open on Sunday, has outdoor seating, live music, a great atmosphere, and excellent DJs who turn this place into a real Soul City most nights. In the middle of the Freihaus Quarter, **Club Schikaneder** (✉ Margaretenstrasse 22–24, 4th District/Wieden ☎ 01/585–2867 ⊕ www.schikaneder.at Ⓤ U1, U2, or U4/Karlsplatz) is a former movie theater that has become a multimedia art and dance center. It still screens three to five art films daily, has exhibitions, and first-class DJ line-ups. **Flex** (✉ Donaukanal/Augartenbrücke, 1st District ☎ 01/533–7525 ⊕ www.flex.at Ⓤ U1, U2, or U4/Karlsplatz) is an alternative rock venue set in a dark, dungeonlike cave—with a famous sound system. Practically an institution, the disco **Queen Anne** (✉ Johannesgasse 12, 1st District ☎ 01/512–0203 Ⓤ U4/Stadtpark) offers a retro trip, complete with a marble dance floor and a bar where the tunes date from the '50s.

Jazz Clubs

The jazz scene in Vienna is one of the hottest in Europe. The stage might be small at **Birdland** (✉ Am Stadtpark 3 [enter Landstrasser Hauptstrasse 2], 3rd District ☎ 01/2196–39315 ⊕ www.birdland.at), but the stars are major. The club under the Hilton Hotel Stadtpark hosts some of the best in the world of jazz. Jazz legend Joe Zawinul named it after one of his most renowned compositions and New York City's legendary temple of jazz. Set in a cellar under St. Ruprecht's church and the granddaddy of

Vienna's jazz clubs, **Jazzland** (✉ Franz-Josefs-Kai 29, 1st District ☎ 01/
533–2575 ⊕ www.jazzland.at) opened more than 30 years ago when there
was just a small local jazz scene. But thanks to the pioneering work of
the club's founder, Axel Melhardt, Austrian jazz musicians have vibed
with the best American stars. The club also serves excellent and authen-
★ tic Viennese cuisine. In the course of a few years, **Porgy & Bess** (✉ Riemer-
gasse 11, 1st District ☎ 01/512–8811 ⊕ www.porgy.at) has become a
fixed point in the native and international jazz scene.

SPORTS & THE OUTDOORS

Bicycling

Look for the special pathways either in red brick or marked with a stylized cyclist image in yellow. Note and observe the special traffic signals
at some intersections. You can take a bike on the subway (except during rush hours) for an additional half fare, but only in cars with a blue
shield on the door, and only on stairs or elevators with the "bike"
shield, not on escalators. The city tourist office has a brochure in German with useful cycling maps, plus a leaflet, "See Vienna by Bike," with
tips in English. At most bookstores you can purchase a cycling map of
Vienna put out by a local cycling organization known as ARGUS.

It's possible to rent a bike in the Prater. **Radverleih Hochschaubahn** (☎ 12/
729–5888) is open mid-March–October and is in the Prater amusement
park by the Hochschaubahn, slightly right after the Ferris wheel. **Radverleih Praterstern** is open April–October and can be found at street level
under the Praterstern North rail station.

Pedal Power (✉ Ausstellungsstrasse
3, 2nd District/Leopoldstadt ☎ 01/
729–7234 🖷 01/729–7235) offers
guided bike tours of Vienna and
the surrounding vicinity in English
from April to October, including
the main sights of the city, or tours
to the outlying vineyards for a glass
of wine. It's also possible to rent a
bike and do your own exploring.
Rentals cost €5 per hour; a three-
hour guided tour costs €23 (€19 for
students); a four-hour bike rental on
your own is €17; for a full day,
€27. Pedal Power will also deliver
a bike to your hotel for an additional fee.

The cheapest way to discover Vienna in a saddle is with one of the
handy **Citybikes,** available only with
a Citybike Tourist Card, which itself can be borrowed for €2 a day
plus deposit from your hotel, Pedal

BADESCHIFF

When the going gets hot and
you're desperate for a cool dip,
head to **Badeschiff** (bathing ship).
Anchored between Urania and
Schwedenplatz on the Donau
Canal, this converted cargo ship,
with its huge open-air pool and
sundeck, is quite the hip social
scene. 🖾 Pool €5 ☉ June-
Aug., daily 10–2 Ⓤ U1 or U4/
Schwedenplatz.

If pools cramp your style, try the
24 km- (15 mi-) long **Neue Donau,**
a channel of the larger Danube,
where you can swim for free (as
long as no red flag is posted). If
you forget your swim things, no wor-
ries, there's nude bathing there,
too. Food stalls dot its length.

Power, or **Royal Tours** (✉ Herrengasse 1–3, 1st District ☎ 01/710–4606), open daily 9–11:30, 1–6. Pick up the bike at one of the 50 Citybike stations all over the city. When you're finished, just deposit it at a vacant station anywhere you like. The first hour on your bike is free, the second costs €1, the 3rd €2, and the 4th to 120th hours are €4. Note that for each card borrowed only one bike can be hired.

Ice-Skating

The **Wiener Eislaufverein** (✉ Lothringerstrasse 22, behind InterContinental Hotel, 3rd District ☎ 01/713–6353–0) has outdoor skating with skate rentals October–mid-March. Weekends are crowded.

SHOPPING

Shopping Districts

The Kärntnerstrasse, Graben, and Kohlmarkt pedestrian areas in the 1st District, **Inner City,** claim to have the best shops in Vienna, and for some items, such as jewelry, some of the best anywhere, and prices are appropriately steep. The side streets within this area have developed their own character, with shops offering antiques, art, clocks, jewelry, and period furniture. **Ringstrasse Galerie,** the indoor shopping plaza at Kärntner Ring 5–7, brings a number of shops together in a modern complex, although many of these stores have other, larger outlets elsewhere in the city. Outside the center, concentrations of stores are on **Mariahilferstrasse,** straddling the 6th and 7th districts; **Landstrasser Hauptstrasse** in the 3rd District; and, still farther out, **Favoritenstrasse** in the 10th District.

A collection of attractive small boutiques can be found in the **Palais Ferstel** passage at Freyung 2 in the 1st District. A modest group of smaller shops has sprung up in the **Sonnhof** passage between Landstrasser Hauptstrasse 28 and Ungargasse 13 in the 3rd District. The **Spittelberg** market, on the Spittelberggasse between Burggasse and Siebensterngasse in the 7th District, has drawn small galleries and handicrafts shops and is particularly popular in the weeks before Christmas and Easter. Christmas is the time also for the tinselly **Christkindlmarkt** on Rathausplatz in front of City Hall; in protest over its commercialization, smaller markets specializing in handicrafts have sprung up on such traditional spots as Am Hof and the Freyung (1st District), also the venue for other seasonal markets.

Vienna's **Naschmarkt** (between Linke and Rechte Wienzeile, starting at Getreidemarkt) is one of Europe's great and most colorful food and produce markets. Stalls open at 5 or 6 AM, and the pace is lively until 5 or 6 PM. Saturday is the big day, when farmers come into the city to sell at the back end of the market, but shops close around 3 PM. Also Saturday there's a huge flea market at the Kettenbrückengasse end. It is closed Sunday.

Flea Markets

Every Saturday (except holidays), rain or shine, from about 7:30 AM to 4 or 5, the **Flohmarkt** in back of the Naschmarkt, stretching along the Linke Wienzeile from the Kettenbrückengasse U4 subway station, offers a stag-

gering collection of stuff ranging from serious antiques to plain junk.
■ TIP→ **Haggle over prices.** On Thursday and Friday from late spring to
mid-fall, an outdoor combination arts-and-crafts, collectibles, and flea
market takes place on **Am Hof.** On weekends in summer from about 10
to 6, an outdoor **art and antiques market** springs up along the Danube
Canal, stretching from the Schwedenbrücke to beyond the Salztorbrücke.
Lots of books are sold, some in English, plus generally better goods and
collectibles than at the Saturday flea market. Bargain over prices.

Department Stores

Steffl (⊠ Kärntnerstrasse 19, 1st District) is moderately upscale without being overly expensive. The larger department stores are concentrated in Mariahilferstrasse. By far the best is **Peek & Cloppenburg**
(⊠ Mariahilferstrasse 26–30, 6th District). Farther up the street you will
find slightly cheaper goods at **Gerngross** (⊠ Mariahilferstrasse and
Kirchengasse, 6th District).

Specialty Stores

ANTIQUES You will find the best antiques shops in the 1st District, many clustered
close to the Dorotheum auction house in the Dorotheergasse, Stallburggasse, Plankengasse, and Spiegelgasse. You'll also find interesting
shops in the Josefstadt (8th) District, where prices are considerably
lower than those in the center of town. Wander up Florianigasse and
back down Josefstädterstrasse, being sure not to overlook the narrow
side streets.

Just around the corner from the Opera House, **Gallery Dr. Sternat**
(⊠ Lobkowitzplatz 1 ☎ 01/512–2063) is one of the most traditional
art galleries, with a focus on fine Austrian paintings, Viennese bronzes,
Thonet furniture, and beautiful Biedermeier pieces. **Bel Etage** (⊠ Mahlerstrasse 15 ☎ 01/512–2379) has wonderful works by Josef Hoffmann,
Dagobert Peche, and other Wiener Werkstätte masters, all of which en-
tice onlookers to spend more than just time here. **D & S Antiquitäten**
(⊠ Dorotheergasse 13 ☎ 01/512–5885) has a striking entrance designed by Oskar Hoefinger; inside are rare Austrian clocks, 18th-cen-
tury paintings, and beautiful 19th-century furniture. Set in a beautiful
historic palais, the **Dorotheum** (⊠ Dorotheergasse 17 ☎ 01/515–60–0
⊕ www.dorotheum.at) is a state institution dating from 1707, when Emperor Josef I determined that he didn't want his people being exploited
by pawnbrokers. The place is intriguing, with goods ranging from furs
to antique jewelry to paintings and furniture auctioned almost daily. Information on how to bid is available in English. Some items are for immediate cash sale. Also check out **Palais Kinsky** (⊠ Freyung 4 ☎ 01/532–
42009) for paintings and antiques.

AUSTRIAN For military memorabilia, including uniforms, medals, and weapons from
CLOTHING & the Austrian monarchy through World War I, go to **Doppeladler** (⊠ Opern-
TRACHTEN ring 9 ☎ 01/581–6232). If you want to dress like Captain von Trapp
and Maria, perhaps the best place for that extra special piece of folklore wear is **Loden-Plankl** (⊠ Michaelerplatz 6 ☎ 01/533–8032), which
stocks hand-embroidered jackets and the *Lederhosen* for kids (famed
for being just about indestructible). The building, opposite the Hofburg,

A Glittering Trove

IF YOU ARE LOOKING FOR THAT SOMETHING truly special—an 18th-century oil portrait or a fake fur, a Rococo mirror or a fine silk fan, modern or retro jewelry, a china figurine or sterling-silver spoon, an old map of the Austrian Empire or even a stuffed parrot—the one place that may have the answer is the **Dorotheum** (✉ Dorotheergasse 17, 1st District ☎ 01/515-60-0 ⊕ www.dorotheum.at), Vienna's fabled auction house. Have you ever wanted to see how the Austrian aristocracy once lived, how their sumptuous homes were furnished? Well, don't bother with a museum—you can inspect their antique furnishings, displayed as if in use, for free, and without the eagle eyes of sales personnel following your every move, in peace and quiet in the gilded salons here. This was the first imperial auction house (*oops*, pawn-shop), established in 1707 by Emperor Joseph

I. Occupying the former site of the Dorothy Convent (hence the name), the Dorotheum has built up a grand reputation since it was privatized in the early 1990s. The neo-Baroque building was completed in 1901 and deserves a walk-through (you can enter from Spiegelgasse and exit on Dorotheergasse) just to have a look, even if it is only to admire the gorgeous stuccoed walls and palatial interiors, or to take a peek into the glass-roofed patio stocked with early-20th-century glass, furniture, and art. With more than 600 auctions a year, this has become one of the busiest auction houses in Europe. There are auctions held daily except Sunday. And if you don't fancy bidding for something, there are large cash-sale areas on the ground and second floors where loads of stuff (that didn't sell at auction) can simply be bought off the floor.

---

is a centuries-old treasure. Dirndls and *Trachten* (the typical Austrian costume with white blouse, print skirt, and apron) for toddlers to dames and cute hand-embroidered cardigans for the kids are all found at **Giesswein** (✉ Kärntnerstrasse 5–7 ☎ 01/512–4597), famed for some of the best traditional clothing in town. **Resi Hammerer** (✉ Kärntnerstrasse 29–31 ☎ 01/512–6952) offers folklore fashion with a touch of the trendy. The color and fabric mix has that certain casual, sportive touch but still is conservative enough to suit most any *Frau*. Fancy having your very own tailor-made Austrian dirndl dress? **Tostmann** (✉ Schottengasse 3a ☎ 01/533–5331) is the place to exquisitely fulfill your wishes.

★

BOOKS The biggest Harry Potter launch in Austria took place at the **British Bookshop** (✉ Weihburggasse 24 ☎ 01/512–1945 ⊕ www.britishbookshop. at), which is always well stocked with the latest editions and best-sellers. The staff encourages browsing. If you are planning a hiking holiday in Austria, stock up on the necessary maps at **Freytag & Berndt** (✉ Kohlmarkt 9 ☎ 01/533–8685 ⊕ www.freytagberndt.at), the best place for maps and travel books in Vienna. The biggest book store in Vienna, **Morawa** (✉ Wollzeile 11 ☎ 01/513–7513 ⊕ www.morawa.at), has titles on everything under the sun. Thankfully, help is always at hand if you can't find that one book. The magazine and newspaper section is vast, and don't pass over some of the cute printed gifts, such as a calendar made out of paper shopping bags (put the bags to good use when the year has passed.) If you're an art book lover, **Wolfrum** (✉ Augustinerstrasse 10 ☎ 01/512–5398) will be your home away from home. If you have money to burn, you can also spring for a Schiele print or special art edition to take home.

CERAMICS, GLASS & PORCELAIN The best porcelain in town can be found at **Augarten** (✉ Graben/Stockim-Eisen-Platz 3 ☎01/512–1494–0 ⊕ www.augarten.at). The Lipizzaner stallion balancing on two hind hoofs is an expensive piece but an eye-catcher. The manufactory in the 2nd District in Vienna offers tours of the palais Augarten is housed in, and you can study the steps involved in making these precious pieces. Is it a "Maria-Theresia," ornately cut diamanté chandelier with a 30%–34% lead content you're looking for? If it is, head and hunt here at **Lobmeyr** (✉ Kärntnerstrasse 26 ☎ 01/512–0508–0 ⊕ www. lobmeyr.at), one of the world's finest addresses for the best in glass and crystal. Even if you're not buying, go upstairs and have a look at the museum on the second floor. Pottery from **Berger** (✉ Weihburggasse 17 ☎ 01/512–1434) may be just the great gift you're looking for—how about a decorative wall plate blooming with a hand-painted flowering gentian? If you want to enter an old-fashioned interior that makes time stand still and is little changed from the time when Empress Elisabeth shopped here, **Albin Denk** (✉ Graben 13 ☎ 01/512–4439 ⊕ www.albindenk.at) is the place. The shop entrance itself is a vitrine, as it is lined with glass cases and filled with a wonderful if kitschy army of welcoming porcelain figurines. Gmunden ceramics have been the Hausfrau's favorite for centuries. The typical green-and-white design with the tiny painted buttercups or the irregular bands of color are found in nearly every Austrian country home. Stock up on these quaint rustic pieces at **Pawlata** (✉ Kärntnerstrasse 14 ☎ 01/512–1764). Ireland has its Waterford, France its Baccarat, and Austria has **Swarovski** (✉ Kärntnerstrasse 8 ☎ 01/5129032 ⊕ www. swarovski.com), purveyors of some of the finest cut crystal in the world and, thanks to the newer generation of Swarovskis, trinkets increasingly fashionable in style and outlook. There are your typical collector items and gifts here, but also high-style fashion accessories (Paris couturiers now festoon their gowns with Swarovski crystals the way they used to with ostrich feathers), crystal figurines, jewelry, and home accessories. This flagship store is a cave of coruscating crystals that gleam and glitter.

GIFTS THAT SAY "VIENNA" Are you looking for an old postcard, a hand-carved walking stick, an old record or ball gift, or even an old photograph of the Opera House from before the war? Head to **Alt-Österreich** (✉ Himmelpfortgasse 7 ☎ 01/5121296)—its name translates as "Old Austria," and this treasure trove has just about everything dealing with that time-burnished subject. Austria's one and only cooperative for art and crafts, **Österreichische Werkstätten** (✉ Kärntnerstrasse 6 ☎01/512–2418), stocks Austrian handicrafts of the finest quality. The range covers home accessories, from brass or pewter candlesticks to linen tablecloths, to quality souvenirs, ranging from enamel jewelry to embroidered brooches. For that Alt Wien flourish, choose a needlepoint handbag, pill box, or brooch from **Petit Point Kovalcec** (✉ Kärntnerstrasse 16 ☎ 01/512–4886). Fancy a composers' portrait–bust collection? Schubert, Mozart, Beethoven, Haydn, and the rest of the gang can be had at **Souvenir in der Hofburg** (✉ Hofburgpassage 1 and 7 ☎ 01/533–5053). While you're at it, you might want to go for a ceramic figure of a Lipizzaner stallion, too (it may not be an Augarten porcelain original, but it is certainly more affordable). Postcards, vintage booklets on Vienna, imperial memorabilia, small busts of former Habsburg rulers, and petite gifts for the folks back home will tempt one and all connoisseurs at **Stransky** (✉ Hofburgpassage 2 ☎ 01/533–6098).

CHRISTKINDL-MÄRKTE
Vienna keeps the Christmas flame burning perhaps more brightly than any other metropolis in the world. Here, during the holiday season, no fewer than five major *Christkindlmärkte* (Christmas Markets) proffer their wares, with stands selling enough wood-carved Austrian toys, crèche figures, and Tannenbaum ornaments to tickle anybody's mistletoes. Many of the markets offer food vendors selling *Glühwein* (mulled wine) and *Kartoffelpuffer* (potato patties). Here are the best of the markets. The **Altwiener Christkindlmarkt** (✉ The Freyung ☎ 01/5121296) is held on one of Vienna's biggest squares. **Karlsplatz** (✉ Karlsplatz) has some of the more refined stands in town. The biggest holiday market is the one on **Rathausplatz,** in front of the magnificently Gothic fantasy that is Vienna's city hall. All the glitter and gilt of the season frames the market held at the Habsburgs' splendid **Schönbrunn** (✉ Schönbrunn Palace). The cognoscenti love the arty market held in the enchanting Biedermeier quarter of **Spittelberg** (✉ Burggasse and Siebensterngasse).

JEWELRY
The finest selection of watches in Vienna can be found at **Haban** (✉ Kärntnerstrasse 2 ☎ 01/512–6730–0 ✉ Kärntnerstrasse 17 ☎ 01/512–6750), and the gold and diamond jewelry selection is top-notch, too. In the city of Freud, father of psychoanalysis, what else can you expect but the sort of jewelry at the **Golden Genius** (✉ Kohlmarkt 3 ☎ 01/470–94–82), where dream symbols are individually cast in different shades of gold as a surround for colorful precious stones. One of Vienna's fabled purveyors to the imperial court, **A. E. Köchert** (✉ Neuer Markt 15 ☎ 01/512–5828–0), has been Vienna's jeweler of choice for nearly two centuries. Almost 150 years ago Empress Elisabeth ordered some diamond-studded stars here to adorn her legendary auburn hair (so long she could sit on it). Guess what? Those diamonded stars are more fashionable than ever, since Köchert has started reissuing them. And if you're ever in need of a crown, Köchert will even craft your very own. Discover interesting pieces of Austrian jade at **Burgenland** (✉ Opernpassage ☎ 01/587–6266).

MEN'S CLOTHING
Grandits (✉ Rotenturmstrasse 10 ☎ 01/512 63 89) has a great selection from Armani, Boss, Joop, Ralph Lauren, Versace. and Zegna, all displayed in a stylish ambience. **Peek & Cloppenburg** (✉ Mariahilferstrasse 26–30 ☎ 01/525610 ⊕ www.peekundcloppenburg.at) is the right place for those who hate having to go to various shops to find what they're looking for. It's all here with brand names, designer labels, and excellent value for money. Austrians love their hats, and **Collins Hüte** (✉ Opernpassage ☎ 01/587–1305) is one of the best sources in town—not only for hats but also for accessories such as scarves, gloves, and the stray sombrero (for that glaring summer sun on the slopes at Lech). For that

high classic look, **Sir Anthony** (⊠ Kärntnerstrasse 21–23, 1st District ☎ 01/512–6835) is the place.

MUSIC You just might bump into Placido, Jose, or even Dame Joan Sutherland—and if you do, you know where to buy that picture postcard and then
★ run and have it autographed—at Vienna's noted **Arcardia** (⊠ Staatsoper Opera House, Opernring 2 ☎ 01/513–9568–0), which is stocked with not only a grand selection of latest CD releases from the operatic world but quite a few classic rarities, too. Helpful sales assistants are at the ready if you're looking for any special titles at **EMI** (⊠ Kärntnerstrasse 30 ☎ 01/512–3675)—one of the big mainstays for classical music (find it upstairs), plus the whole gamut from ethno to pop.

Toys

Emperor Franz Josef in his horse-drawn carriage, the infantry cheering him on, and the Prussian emperor to meet him at the battlefield—here at **Kober** (⊠ Graben 14–15 ☎ 01/533–6018) you can find all the historic tin soldiers you'll ever need to relive those eventful last years of the empire. If you prefer something a little less military, go for the full Johann Strauss Orchestra, it's a scream. Mozart, that "eternal child," would have loved **Spielzeugschachtel** (⊠ Rauensteingasse 5 ☎ 01/512–3994)—he lived just across the street.

WOMEN'S **Doris Ainedter** (⊠ Jasomirgottstrasse 5 ☎ 01/532 03 69). Business and
CLOTHING leisure fashion for the trend-conscious woman from the hand of one of Vienna's most successful designers. There's also help at hand for the matching accessories. **Wiener Blut** (⊠ Spiegelgasse 19 ☎ 01/5132015) has lots of temptations. Monika Bacher's zippy knitwear, striking pieces by Berlin designers, zany shoes from Canada, and the finest crafted handbags from Italy. Fashionistas make a bee line for the studio of Austrian designer **Schella Kann** (⊠ Singerstrasse 14/2 ☎ 01/513–2287)—extravagant and trendy, these are clothes you never want to take off. For conservative, high-quality clothing, go to the **Geiger Boutique** (⊠ Kärntnerstrasse 19 ☎ 01/513–1398) in the Steffl Department Store.

VIENNA ESSENTIALS

Transportation

BY AIR

Vienna's airport is at Schwechat, about 19 km (12 mi) southeast of the city. Austrian Airlines flies into Schwechat from North America.

🛈 **Schwechat Airport (VIE)** ☎ 01/7007–0 for flight information ⊕ www.viennaairport.com.

GROUND The fastest way into Vienna from Schwechat Airport is the sleek, dou-
TRANSPORTATION ble-decker **CAT, or City Airport Train.** The journey from the airport to Wien–Mitte (the center of the city) takes only 16 minutes, and trains operate daily every 30 minutes between 5:30 AM and midnight. The cost is €8 one-way and €15 round-trip.

The cheapest way to get to Vienna from the airport is the **S7 train,** called the *Schnellbahn,* which shuttles twice an hour between the station beneath the airport and the Landstrasse/Wien–Mitte (city center) and Wien–Nord (north Vienna) stations; the fare is €3, and it takes about 35 minutes (19 minutes longer than the CAT). Your ticket is also good for an immediate transfer to your destination within the city on streetcar, bus, or U-Bahn.

Another cheap option is the **bus,** which has two separate lines. One line goes to Schwedenplatz/Postgasse (1st District, city center) every 30 minutes between 5 AM and 12:30 AM; traveling time is 20 minutes. The second line goes to the South and West train stations (Südbahnhof and Westbahnhof) in 20 and 35 minutes, respectively. Departure times are every 30 minutes from 5:30 AM to 11:10 PM. Fare is €6 one-way, €11 for a round-trip.

🏳 Taxis **Airport Driver** ☎ 01/22822-0 🖷 01/22822-8 ⊕ www.airportdriver.at.

BY BOAT & FERRY

For information about Danube River cruises, *see* Danube River Cruises *in* Chapter 4, The Danube Valley. When you arrive in Vienna via the Danube, the Blue Danube Steamship Company/DDSG will leave you at Praterlände near Mexikoplatz. The Praterlände stop is a two-block taxi ride or walk from the Vorgartenstrasse U1/subway station, or you can take a taxi directly into town.

An effortless way to travel from Vienna to Bratislava, Slovakia, was inaugurated in the summer of 2006. The Twin City Liner (a comfortable 102-seat catamaran) departs from Schwedenplatz in the center of Vienna daily at 8:30, 12:30, and 4:30 from June 1 until late October. The round-trip costs €30, and a one-way journey costs between €15 and €23, depending on the day, direction (upstream or down), and departure time. Bring your passport; check-in is 30 minutes prior to departure. The one-way downriver trip takes 75 minutes, the trip back is a little longer. The fully air-conditioned catamaran has an onboard buffet and allows passengers to bring bikes.

🏳 Boat & Ferry Information **Blue Danube Schiffahrt (Steamship Company)/DDSG** ✉ Friedrichstrasse 7, A-1010 Vienna ☎ 01/588-80 🖷 01/588-8044-0 ⊕ www.ddsg-blue-danube.at. **Twin City Liner** ☎ 01/588-80 🖷 01/588-8044-0 ⊕ www.twincityliner.com.

BY BUS

International long-distance bus service (Bratislava, Brno) and most postal (local) and railroad buses arrive at the Wien-Mitte central bus station, across from the Hilton Hotel on the Stadtpark.

🏳 Bus Information **Wien-Mitte** ✉ Landstrasser Hauptstrasse 1b ☎ 01/711-01.

BY CAR

Vienna is 300 km (187 mi) east of Salzburg, 200 km (125 mi) north of Graz. Main routes leading into the city are the A1 Westautobahn from Germany, Salzburg, and Linz and the A2 Südautobahn from Graz and points south. Rental cars can be arranged at the airport or in town. Buchbinder is a local firm with particularly favorable rates and clean cars.

On highways from points south or west or from Vienna's airport, ZEN-TRUM signs clearly mark the route to the center of Vienna. From there, however, finding your way to your hotel is a challenge, for traffic planners have installed a devious scheme prohibiting through traffic in the city core (the 1st District). Traffic congestion within Vienna has gotten out of hand, and driving to in-town destinations generally takes longer than public transportation. In the city itself a car is a burden, though very useful for trips outside town.

📻 Local Contacts **Buchbinder** ✉ Schlachthausgasse 38 ☎ 01/71750-0.

PARKING The entire 1st through 9th districts and part of the 15th are limited-parking zones and require that a *Parkschein*, a paid-parking chit available at most newsstands and tobacconists, be filled in and displayed on the dash during the day. At this writing, Parkscheine cost €0.40 for 30 minutes, €0.80 for 1 hour, and €1.20 for 90 minutes. You can park 10 minutes free of charge, but you must get a violet "gratis" sticker (check for one at a newsstand, tobacconist, or bank) to put in your windshield. You can also park free in the 1st District on weekends, but not overnight. Overnight street parking in the 1st and 6th through 9th districts is restricted to residents with special permits; all other cars are subject to expensive ticketing or even towing, so in these districts be sure you have off-street, garage parking.

BY PUBLIC TRANSIT: BUS, TRAM & U-BAHN

When it comes to seeing the main historic sights, Vienna is a city to tackle on foot. With the exception of the Schönbrunn and Belvedere palaces and the Prater amusement park, most sights are concentrated in the center, the 1st District (A-1010), much of which is a pedestrian zone anyway. Happily, Vienna's subway system, called the U-Bahn, does service the core of the inner city. The main city center subway stops in the 1st District are Stephansplatz, Karlsplatz, Herrengasse, Schottenring, and Schwedenplatz. Stephansplatz is the very heart of the city, at St. Stephen's cathedral, with exits to the Graben and Kärntnerstrasse. You can reach the famous amusement park of the Prater from Stephansplatz by taking the U1 to Praterstern. Near the southern edge of the Ringstrasse, the major Karlsplatz stop is right next to the Staatsoper, the pedestrian Kärntnerstrasse, and the Ringstrasse, with an easy connection to Belvedere Palace via the D Tram. You can also take the U4 from Karlsplatz to Schönbrunn Palace (Schönbrunn stop). Herrengasse is also directly in the city center, close to the Hofburg and Graben. Schottenring is on the Ringstrasse, offering quick tram connections or a short walk on foot to the Graben. Schwedenplatz is ideally situated for a 10-minute walk to St. Stephen's through some of Vienna's oldest streets, or you can hop on a tram and be on the Ringstrasse in five minutes. You can also take the U1 from Schwedenplatz to the Prater, getting off at Praterstern. Karlsplatz is serviced by the train lines U4, U2, U1, while U3 goes to Herrengasse and U2 to Schottentor. In addition, there are also handy U-Bahn stops along the rim of the city core, such as MuseumsQuartier, Stadtpark, Volkstheater, and Rathaus. You can also hop around the 1st District by using bus lines 1A, 2A, and 3A, and there are useful crosstown buses if you don't want to walk 10 minutes from one U-Bahn stop to another.

Vienna's public transportation system is fast, clean, safe, and easy to use. Get public transport maps at a tourist office or at the transport-information offices (*Wiener Verkehrsbetriebe*), underground at Karlsplatz, Stephansplatz, and Praterstern. You can transfer on the same ticket between subway, streetcar, bus, and long stretches of the fast suburban railway, or *Schnellbahn* (*S-Bahn*).

Five subway (*U-Bahn*) lines, whose stations are prominently marked with blue U signs, crisscross the city. Karlsplatz and Stephansplatz are the main transfer points between lines. The last subway (U4) runs at about 12:30 AM. Track the main lines of the U-Bahn system by their color codes on subway maps: U1 is red; U2, purple; U3, orange; U4, green; and U6, brown. Note that you have to open the subway door when the train stops, either by pushing a lighted button or pulling the door handle aside.

The first streetcars (*Strassenbahnen*) run from about 5:15 AM. From then on service is regular and reliable (barring gridlock on the streets), and most lines operate until about midnight. The most famous tram lines are No. 1, which travels the great Ringstrasse avenue clockwise, and No. 2, which travels it counter-clockwise; each offers a cheap way to admire the glories of Vienna's 19th-century Ringstrasse monuments. Where streetcars don't run, buses—*Autobusse*—do; route maps and schedules are posted at each bus or subway stop.

Within the heart of the city, bus lines 1A, 2A, and 3A are useful crosstown routes. Should you miss the last streetcar or bus, special night buses with an N designation operate at half-hour intervals over several key routes; the starting (and transfer) points are the Opera House and Schwedenplatz. These night-owl buses now accept all normal tickets. There is no additional fare.

Tickets for public transportation are valid for all public transportation—buses, trams, and the subway. It's best to buy your ticket at a U-Bahn stop before boarding a bus or tram. Though there are ticket machines on trams, and bus drivers sell tickets, you'll pay €0.50 more. Passengers can enter and exit buses and trams through any door. You'll need to punch your ticket before entering the boarding area at U-Bahn stops, but for buses and trams you punch it on board. Though Vienna's public transportation operates on the honor system, if you're caught without a ticket you'll pay a hefty fine.

Buy single tickets for €2 from dispensers on the streetcar or from your bus driver; you'll need exact change for the former. Note that it's €0.50 cheaper to buy your ticket in advance from ticket machines at subway stations. The ticket machines (labeled *VOR-Fahrkarten* at subway stations give change and dispense 24-hour, 72-hour, and eight-day tickets, as well as single tickets separately and in blocks of two and five. Tickets are sold singly or as strip tickets, *Streifenkarten*. At Tabak-Trafik (cigarette shops/newsstands) or the underground Wiener Verkehrsbetriebe offices you can get a block of five tickets for €7.50, each ticket good for one uninterrupted trip in more or less the same general direction with unlimited transfers. Or you can get a three-day ticket for €12, good on all lines for 72 hours from the time you validate the ticket; there's also a 24-hour ticket for €5. If you're staying longer, get an eight-day ticket (€24), which can be used on eight separate days or by any number of persons (up to eight) at any one time. Prices, current at this writing, are subject to change. Children under six travel free on Vienna's public transport system; children under 15 travel free on Sunday, public holidays, and during Vienna school holidays. If you don't speak German, opt to purchase your transport tickets from a person at a Tabak or main U-Bahn station.

As with most transport systems in European cities, it is essential to "validate," or punch, your ticket when you start your trip. You'll find the validation machines on all buses, trams, and at the entrance of each U-Bahn station—look for the blue box and slide your ticket into the machine until you hear a "punch." Public transportation is on the honor system, but if you're caught without a punched ticket the fine is €62, payable within three days, or €127 afterward. Tabak-Trafik Almassy is open every day from 8 AM to 7 PM, and has tickets as well as film and other items.

🚹 **Tabak-Trafik Almassy** ⊠ Stephansplatz 4, to right behind cathedral ☎ 01/512–5909. **VOR, or Vorverkaufsstellen der Wiener Linien** ☎ 7909/105 ⊕ www.wienerlinien.at.

BY TAXI

Taxis in Vienna are relatively reasonable. The initial charge is €2.50 for as many as four people daytime, and about 5% more from 11 PM until 6 AM. Radio cabs ordered by phone have an initial charge of €6. They also may charge for each piece of luggage that must go into the trunk, and a charge is added for waiting beyond a reasonable limit. It's customary to round up the fare to cover the tip. You can't flag a cab down in the street in Vienna. Look for a taxi stand. Service is usually prompt, but when you hit rush hour, the weather is bad, or you need to keep to an exact schedule, call ahead and order a taxi for a specific time. If your destination is the airport, ask for a reduced-rate taxi. There are several companies that offer chauffeured limousines, which are listed below.

■ TIP➔ **Taxi drivers may need to know which of the 23 districts you seek, as well as the street address.** The district number is coded into the postal code with the second and third digits; thus A-1010 (the "01") is the 1st District, A-1030 is the 3rd, A-1110 is the 11th, and so on. Some sources and maps still give the district numbers, either in Roman or Arabic numerals, as Vienna X or Vienna 10.

🚹 Taxi Companies **Göth** ☎ 01/713-7196. **Mazur** ☎ 01/604-2530. **Peter Urban** ☎ 01/713-5255.

BY TRAIN

Trains from Germany, Switzerland, and western Austria arrive at the Westbahnhof (West Station), on Europaplatz, where Mariahilferstrasse crosses the Gürtel. If you're coming from Italy or Hungary, you'll generally arrive at the Südbahnhof (South Station). There are two current stations for trains to and from Prague and Warsaw: Wien Nord (North Station) and Franz-Josef Bahnhof. Central train information will have schedule information for train departures all over Austria. However, it's hard to find somebody who can speak English, so it's best to ask your hotel for help in calling.

🚩 Train Information **Central train information** ☎ 05/1717. **Westbahnhof** ✉ Westbahnhof, 15th District/Fünfhaus. **Franz-Josef Bahnhof** ✉ Julius-Tandler-Platz, 9th District/Alsergrund. **Südbahnhof** ✉ Wiedner Gürtel 1, 4th District/Wieden. **Wien Nord** ✉ Praterstern, 2nd District/Leopoldstadt.

Contacts & Resources

EMERGENCIES

If you need a doctor and speak no German, ask your hotel, or in an emergency, phone your consulate. In each area of the city one pharmacy stays open 24 hours; if a pharmacy is closed, a sign on the door will tell you the address of the nearest one that is open. Call the number listed below for names and addresses (in German) of the pharmacies open that night.

🚩 Emergency Services **Ambulance** ☎ 144. **Fire** ☎ 122. **Police** ☎ 133.
🚩 Late-night Pharmacies **Pharmacy information** ☎ 01/1550.

MAIL & SHIPPING

Post offices are scattered throughout every district in Vienna and are recognizable by a square yellow sign reading "Post." They are usually open weekdays 9–noon and 2–6, Saturday 8–10 AM. The main post office, near Schwedenplatz, is open 6 AM–10 PM daily, and the offices at the South and West railway stations are open until 10 PM weekdays, 8 PM weekends.

You can have mail held at any Austrian post office; letters should be marked *Poste Restante* or *Postlagernd*. You will be asked for identification when you collect mail. In Vienna, if not addressed to a specific district post office, this service is handled through the main post office.

🚩 **Main Post Office** ✉ Fleischmarkt 19, A-1010 Vienna.

MEDIA

BOOKS In Vienna and Salzburg it's fairly easy to find English-language bookstores. For a vast selection of American magazines, go to the bookstore Morawa.

🚩 Bookstores **British Bookstore** ✉ Weihburggasse 24–26, 1st District, Vienna ☎ 01/512-1945-0 ✉ Mariahilferstrasse 4, 7th District, Vienna ☎ 01/522-6730. *Morawa* ✉ Wollzeile 11, Vienna. **Shakespeare & Co.** ✉ Sterngasse 2, 1st District, Vienna ☎ 01/535-5053.

TOUR OPTIONS

BUS TOURS When you're pressed for time, a good way to see the highlights of Vienna is via a sightseeing bus tour, which gives you a once-over-lightly of the heart of the city and allows a closer look at Schönbrunn and Belvedere palaces. You can cover almost the same territory on your own by taking either Streetcar 1 or 2 around the Ring and then walking through the heart of the city. For tours, there are a couple of reputable firms: Vienna Sightseeing Tours and Cityrama Sightseeing. Both run daily "get acquainted" tours lasting about three hours (€34), including visits to the Schönbrunn and Belvedere palace grounds. The entrance fee and guided tour of Schönbrunn is included in the price, but not a guided tour of the Belvedere, just the grounds. Both firms offer a number of other tours as well (your hotel will have detailed programs) and provide hotel pickup for most tours. These tour operators also offer short trips outside the city. Check their offerings and compare packages and prices to be sure you get what you want. Your hotel will have brochures.

You can tour at your own pace with Vienna Sightseeing's Hop On, Hop Off bus tour. There are 13 stops, and a day ticket purchased after 3 PM is valid for the whole next day, too. A running commentary describes the sights as you go along, and you can leave the tour at any of the stops and join again when you please. The short city tour costs €13 and does a run around the major sites in about an hour. There is a two-hour tour for €16, but the day ticket for €20 allows far more freedom. All tickets can be purchased at hotels, directly at the stops, and on the bus. The first bus leaves the Opera stop at 10 AM and leaves every hour after that until 6 PM (Friday through Sunday on the half-hour).
🖪 Fees & Schedules **Cityrama Sightseeing** ✉ Börsegasse 1 ☎ 01/534–130 🖷 01/534–13–28 ⊕ www.cityrama.at. **Vienna Sightseeing Tours** ✉ Graf Starhemberggasse 25 ☎ 01/712–4683–0 🖷 01/714–1141 ⊕ www.viennasightseeingtours.com.

FIAKER/HORSE CARRIAGE TOURS A *Fiaker,* or horse carriage, will trot you around to whatever destination you specify, but this is an expensive way to see the city. A short tour of the inner city takes about 20 minutes and costs €40; a longer one including the inner city and part of the Ringstrasse lasts about 40 minutes and costs €65, and an hour-long tour of the inner city and the whole Ringstrasse costs €95. The carriages accommodate four (five if someone sits next to the coachman). Starting points are Heldenplatz in front of the Hofburg, Stephansplatz beside the cathedral, and across from the Albertina, all in the 1st District. For longer trips, or any variation of the regular route, agree on the price first.

STREETCAR TOURS From early May to early October, a 1929 vintage streetcar leaves Saturdays at 11:30 AM and 1:30 PM and Sunday and holidays at 9:30, 11:30 AM, and 1:30 PM from the Otto Wagner Pavilion at Karlsplatz for a guided tour. For €15 (€13.50 if you have the Vienna-Card), you'll go around the Ring, out past the big Ferris wheel in the Prater, and past Schönbrunn and Belvedere palaces in the course of the two-hour trip. The old-timer trips are popular, so make your reservation at the transport-information office underground at Karlsplatz, weekdays 7 AM–6 PM, weekends and holidays 8:30–4. You must buy your ticket on the streetcar.
🖪 Fees & Schedules **Transport-information office** ☎ 01/7909–43426.

WALKING TOURS Guided walking tours (in English) are a great way to see the city highlights. The city tourist office offers around 40 tour topics, ranging from "Unknown Underground Vienna" to "Hollywood in Vienna," "For Lovers of Music and Opera," "Old World Vienna–Off the Beaten Track," "Jewish Families and Their Past in Vienna," and many more. Vienna Walks and Talks offers informative walks through the old Jewish Quarter and a *Third Man* tour from the classic film starring Orson Welles, among other subjects. Tours take about 1½ hours, are held in any weather provided at least three people turn up, and cost €11, plus any entry fees. No reservations are needed for the city-sponsored tours.

Get a full list of the guided-tour possibilities at the city information office. Ask for the monthly brochure "Walks in Vienna," which details the tours, days, times, and starting points. You can also arrange to have your own privately guided tour for €120 for a half day.

If you can, try to get a copy of Henriette Mandl's "Vienna Downtown Walking Tours" from a bookshop. The six tours take you through the highlights of central Vienna, with excellent commentary and some entertaining anecdotes that most of your Viennese acquaintances won't know. The booklet "Vienna from A–Z" (in English, €3.60; available at bookshops and city information offices) explains the numbered plaques attached to all major buildings.

🖪 **City information office** ⊠ Am Albertinaplatz 1. **Vienna Guide Service** ⊠ Werdertorgasse 9/2 ☎ 01/774-8901 ⊕ www.wienguide.at. **Vienna Walks and Talks** ⊠ Werdertorgasse 9/2, 1st District ☎ 01/774-8901 🖨 01/774-8933 ⊕ www.viennawalks.tix.at.

TRAVEL AGENCIES
American Express and the Österreichisches Verkehrsbüro serve as general travel agencies. American Express and Vienna Ticket Service/Cityrama are agencies that offer tickets to various sights and events in Vienna.

🖪 Local Agent Referrals **American Express** ⊠ Kärntnerstrasse 21-23, 1st District ☎ 01/515-40-0 🖨 01/515-40-777. **Österreichisches Verkehrsbüro** ⊠ Friedrichstrasse 7, 4th District, opposite Secession Bldg. ☎ 01/588-00-0 🖨 01/588-000-280. **Vienna Ticket Service/Cityrama** ⊠ Börsegasse 1, 1st District ☎ 01/534130 🖨 01/534-1328.

VISITOR INFORMATION
The main center for information (walk-ins only) is the Vienna City Tourist Office, open daily 9–7 and centrally located between the Hofburg and Kärntnerstrasse.

Ask at tourist offices or your hotel about a Vienna-Card; costing €18.50, the card combines 72 hours' use of public transportation and more than 200 discounts listed in the 104-page Vienna-Card Coupon Book, which every Vienna-Card purchaser receives free of charge. The Vienna-Card is also available at all sales offices or information booths of the Vienna Transportation System (for example, Stephansplatz, Karlsplatz, Westbahnhof, Landstrasse/Wien-Mitte) or from outside Austria with credit card, call (0043–1–798–44–00–148).

If you've lost something valuable, check with the municipal Zentrales Fundservice. If your loss occurred on a train in Austria, call the central number and ask for *Reisegepäck*. Losses on the subway system or streetcars can be checked by calling the Fundstelle U-Bahn.

🖪 Lost & Found **Fundstelle U-Bahn** ☎ 01/7909-43500. **Reisegepäck (Central Train Information)** ☎ 05/1717. **Zentrales Fundservice** ⊠ Bastiengasse 36-38 18th District/ Währing ☎ 01/4000-8091, 0900-600-200 from elsewhere in Austria ⊙ Mon.-Wed., Fri. 8-3:30, Thurs. 8-5:30.

🖪 Tourist Information **Vienna City Tourist Office** ⊠ Am Albertinaplatz 1, 1st District ☎ 01/24-555 🖨 01/216-84-92 or 01/24555-666.

The Danube Valley to the Salzkammergut

WORD OF MOUTH

"Hop a boat to Dürnstein, trek up to a ruined castle where Richard the Lion-Hearted was once jailed on his way back from a Crusade after being waylaid and held for ransom. Dürnstein is a cute wine town around which swirls a carpet of vineyards in the heart of the Wachau Valley."

—PalQ

"From St. Wolfgang a famous steam train climbs a mountain for a stupendous view of the lake-full Alpine wonderland. St. Wolfgang is a lovely chalet- and flowerbox-studded town."

—PalQ

Diane Naar-
Elphee &
Horst Earns
Reischenböck

IF AUSTRIA WERE RATED ON A BEAUTY-MEASURING GAUGE, the needle
would fly off the scale in the regions that stretch east-to-west and lie directly between Vienna and Salzburg. Here, conveniently linking these
two great Austrian metropolises, are two areas that have been extraor-
dinarily blessed by nature. Ready your camera, dust off your supply of
wunderschöns, and prepare for enchantment just 8 km (5 mi) northwest of Vienna's city borders, where the Danube Valley starts to unfold
like a picture book. Roman ruins (some dating to Emperor Claudius),
medieval castles-in-air, and Baroque monasteries with "candle-snuffer"
cupolas perching precariously above the river stimulate the imagination
with their historic legends and myths. This is where Isa—cousin of the
Lorelei—lured sailors onto the shoals; where Richard the Lion-Hearted
was locked in a dungeon for a spell; and where the Nibelungs—later
immortalized by Wagner—caroused operatically in battlemented forts.
Here is where Roman sailors threw coins into the perilous whirlpools
near Grein, in hopes of placating Danubius, the river's tutelary god. The
route that brought the ancient Romans to the area and contributed to
its development remains one of Europe's most important waterways.
As the saying went, "Whoever controls the Danube controls all Europe."

From the greatest sight of the Danube Valley, Melk Abbey, we head south-
ward down to the Salzkammergut (literally, "salt estates"), which presents the traveler with soaring mountains and needlelike peaks, forested
valleys that are populated with the *Rehe* (roe deer) immortalized by Felix
Salten in *Bambi,* and a glittering necklace of turquoise lakes. The Wolfgangsee, the Mondsee, and the Attersee (*See* is German for "lake") are
the best known of the region's 76 lakes. The entire region remains idyllic and largely unspoiled because of its salt mines, which date back to
the Celtic era; with salt so common and cheap nowadays, many forget
it was once a luxury item mined under strict government monopoly. The
Salzkammergut was closed to the casually curious for centuries, opening up only after Emperor Franz Josef I made it his official summer residence in 1854 and turned it into the "drawing room" of the Lake District.
Today, thanks to those famous scenes in *The Sound of Music,* the
Salzkammergut's castles fronting on water, mountains hidden by whipped-
cream clouds, and flower-strewn valleys crisped with cool blue lakes represent Austria in all its Hollywoodian splendor.

Exploring the Danube Valley & the Salzkammergut

Although much of the river is tightly wedged between steep hills rising
from a narrow valley, the north and south banks of the Danube present differing vistas. The hills to the north are terraced to allow its famous vineyards to catch the full sun; to the south, the orchards, occasional
meadows, and shaded hills have just as much visual appeal, if a less dramatic sight. Upstream from the Wachau region the valley broadens, giving way to farmlands and, straddling the river, the bustling city of Linz,
which we pass, eyes averted (there are more than enough cosmopolitan
pleasures to enjoy in Vienna and Salzburg). As for the Salzkammergut,
our journey passes through the land of operetta: the 19th-century resort towns of Bad Ischl and St. Wolfgang, before heading westward to

GREAT ITINERARIES

2

IF YOU HAVE 3 DAYS

Start out early from Vienna, planning for a stop to explore the medieval center of **Krems** ❷. The Weinstadt Museum Krems will give you a good idea of the region's best wines. Along the northern, Krems side of the Danube, you can opt to spend a night in a former cloister, now an elegant hotel, in ▦ **Dürnstein** ❸, probably the most famous town of the Danube Valley. Here you'll find the ruined castle where Richard the Lion-Hearted was imprisoned—an early-morning climb up to the ruin will reward you with great views. Take time to explore enchanting Dürnstein before heading west along the Danube crossing over to ▦ **Melk** ❹, rated one of the greatest abbeys in Europe. This is high Baroque at its most glorious. Then for your third day, head to regal ▦ **Bad Ischl** ❾, a town proud of its links with Emperor Franz Josef and filled with villas that seem right out of an operetta set (not surprisingly, the composer Lehár often vacationed here).

IF YOU HAVE 8 DAYS

A more leisurely schedule would follow the same basic route but permit some magical detours, including a stop at the fairy-tale castle of Burg Kreuzenstein, near

Korneuburg ❶, before continuing on to attractive **Krems** ❷ to tour its wine museum, the Weinstadt Museum Krems. Overnight in gorgeous ▦ **Dürnstein** ❸. Spend the morning exploring Dürnstein, including the colorfully restored Baroque Stiftskirche. On Day 3, take in the grandest abbey of all, ▦ **Melk** ❹. On Day 4, continue east to another magnificent abbey, **St. Florian** ❺, then head south to the enchanting medieval town of ▦ **Steyr** ❻. On Day 5, head southeast to the Salzkammergut, with a stopover at the abbey in **Kremsmünster** ❼, before enjoying an idyllic overnight in the gateway town to the Lake District, ▦ **Gmunden** ❽, beloved of Brahms. On Day 6, make a beeline for the heart of the region, the elegant 19th-century spa town of ▦ **Bad Ischl** ❾, Emperor Franz Josef's old stomping ground. On Day 7, head for ▦ **St. Wolfgang** ❿. The inn near the dock—now Hotel Weisses Rössl (White Horse)—spread the little Alpine town's fame (and made its fortune): It became the subject of a very popular operetta, *Im Weissen Rössl*. On Day 8, head north to **St. Gilgen** ⓫. The town gets very crowded in summer, especially along the shore, which is lined with ice-cream parlors and souvenir shops.

St. Gilgen, birthplace of Mozart's mother, and Fuschl, on the very doorstep of Salzburg itself.

About the Restaurants & Hotels

Wherever possible, restaurants along the Danube Valley make the most of the river view, and alfresco dining overlooking the Danube is one of the region's unsurpassed delights. Simple *Gasthäuser* are everywhere, but better dining is more often found in country inns. The cuisine usually runs along traditional lines, but the desserts are often brilliant inventions, including the celebrated Linzertorte and Linzer Augen, jam-filled cookies with three "eyes" planted in the top layer. Wine is very much the thing on the north bank of the Danube in the Wachau region. Here you'll find many of Austria's best white wines, slightly dry with a hint of fruitiness. In some of the smaller villages, you can sample the vintner's successes right on the spot in his cellars. Restaurants, whether sophisticated and stylish or plain and homey, are often rated by their wine offerings as much as by their chef's creations.

In the Salzkammergut, fresh, local lake fish is on nearly every menu in the area, so take advantage of the bounty. The lakes and streams are home to several types of fish, notably trout, carp, and perch. They are prepared in numerous ways, from plain breaded (*gebacken*), to smoked and served with *Kren* (horseradish), to fried in butter (*gebraten*). Look for *Reinanke,* a mild whitefish straight from the Hallstättersee. Sometimes at country fairs you will find someone charcoaling fresh trout wrapped in aluminum foil with herbs and butter: it's worth every euro. *Knödel*—bread or potato dumplings usually filled with either meat or jam—are a tasty specialty. Desserts are doughy as well, though *Salzburger Nockerl* consist mainly of air, sugar, and beaten egg whites. And finally, keep an eye out for seasonal specialties: in summer, restaurants often serve chanterelle mushrooms (*Eierschwammerl*) with pasta, and in October it's time for delicious venison and game during the *Wildwochen* (game weeks).

As for accommodations, your choices range from castle-hotels, where you'll be treated like royalty, to the often family-managed, quiet and elegant country inn. There are also luxurious lakeside resorts, small country river-town inns, even guesthouses without private baths; in some places, the *Herr Wirt,* his smiling wife, and his grown-up children will do everything to make you feel comfortable. Some hotels offer half-board, with dinner included in addition to buffet breakfast (although most $$$$ hotels charge extra for breakfast). The half-board room rate is usually an extra €15–€30 per person. Occasionally, quoted room rates for hotels already include half-board, though a "discounted" rate may be available if you prefer not to take the evening meal. Inquire about any pension food plans when booking. Assume all rooms have TV, telephones, and private bath, unless otherwise noted; air-conditioning, in rare instances, is noted. Happily, these hotels do not put their breathtakingly beautiful natural surroundings on the bill.

WHAT IT COSTS In euros				
$$$$	**$$$**	**$$**	**$**	**¢**
RESTAURANTS over €22	€18–€22	€13–€17	€7–€12	under €7
HOTELS over €175	€135–€175	€100–€135	€70–€100	under €70

Restaurant prices are per person for a main course at dinner. Hotel prices are for a standard double room in high season, including taxes and service. Assume that hotels operate on the European Plan (EP, with no meal provided) unless we note that they use the Breakfast Plan (BP), Modified American Plan (MAP, with breakfast and dinner daily, known as "halb pension"), or Full American Plan (FAP, or "voll pension," with three meals a day). Higher prices (inquire when booking) prevail for any meal plans.

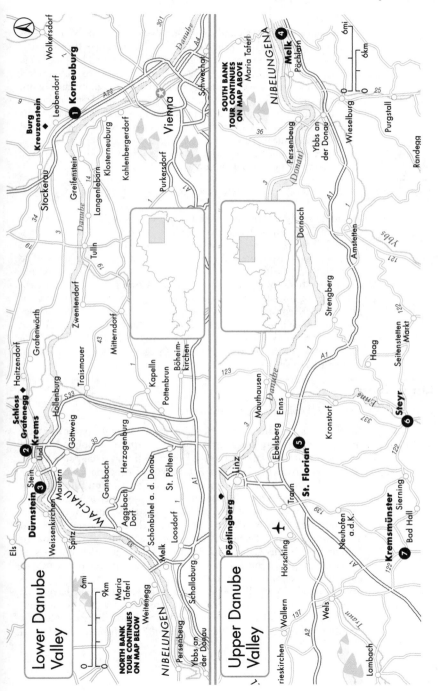

Lower Danube Valley

NORTH BANK TOUR CONTINUES ON MAP BELOW

Upper Danube Valley

SOUTH BANK TOUR CONTINUES ON MAP ABOVE

Timing

The Wachau—both north and south Danube banks—is packed wall-to-wall with crowds in late April to early May, but of course there's a reason: apricot and apple trees are in glorious blossom, and bright orange poppies blanket the fields. Others prefer the chilly early- to mid-autumn days, when a blue haze curtains the vineyards. Throughout the region, winter is drab. Year-round, vacationers flock to the Salzkammergut Lake District; however, late fall is the worst time to visit the region, for it is rainy and cold, and many sights are closed or operate on a restricted schedule. By far the best months are July and September. August, of course, sees the countryside overrun with families on school holidays and music lovers from the nearby Salzburg Music Festival.

THE WACHAU: JEWEL OF THE DANUBE VALLEY

Unquestionably the loveliest stretches of the Danube's Austrian course run from the outskirts of Vienna, through the narrow defiles of the Wachau to the Nibelungengau—the region where the mystical race of dwarfs, the Nibelungs, are supposed to have settled, at least for a while. The Danube River itself is a marvel—on a summer day it can take on the authentic shade of Johann Strauss blue. Continuing south toward Salzburg, explore the Gothic and Baroque sights found in the towns of St. Florian, Kremsmünster, and Steyr, the latter a gorgeously Gothic-flavor town once home to the great composer Anton Bruckner that certainly merits an overnight stay. Along the way you'll be dazzled by two masterworks of the Austrian Baroque, the great abbeys of St. Florian and Stift Kremsmünster.

Korneuburg

❶ *18 km (11¼ mi) northwest of Vienna.*

Castle lovers, prepare yourself. Seemingly lifted from the pages of a Germanic fairy tale, **Burg Kreuzenstein,** bristling with storybook turrets and towers, might have made Albrecht Dürer drop his sketch pad in a second. Sitting atop a hillside 3 km (2 mi) beyond Korneuburg along Route 3, "Castle Cross-stone," in fact, is a 19th-century architectural fantasy built to conjure up "the last of the knights"—Emperor Maximilian I himself. Occupying the site of a previously destroyed fort, the enormous structure was built by Count Nepomuk Wilczek between 1879 and 1908 to house his collection of Late Gothic art objects and armor, including the "Brixner Cabinet" dating from 15th-century Salzburg. Using old elements and Gothic and Romanesque bits and pieces, the castle was carefully laid out according to the rules of yore, complete with a towering Burgtor, "kennel" corridor (where attackers would have been cornered), Gothic arcades, and tracery parapet walls. The Burghof courtyard, with its half-timbered facade and Baltic loggia, could be a stand-in for a stage set for Wagner's *Tannhäuser*. Inside, the medieval

FodorsChoice
★

thrills continue with rooms full of armaments, a festival and banquet hall, a library, a stained-glass chapel (available for weddings), vassal kitchens, and the Narwalzahn, a room devoted to hunting trophies (if you've ever wanted to see a "unicorn horn," here's your chance).

A group of falconers keeps peregrine falcons and other birds of prey near the castle grounds. ■ TIP→ **Eagles and falcons take flight, hunt, and return to their trainer's arm with the catch at least twice a day, taking part in a sport that goes back nearly 4,000 years.** Shows, which run from April through October, are scheduled Tuesday through Saturday at 11 AM and 3 PM and Sunday at 11 AM and 2 and 4 PM. Tickets cost €7 each.

It is possible to reach Kreuzenstein from Vienna via the suburban train (S-Bahn) to Leobendorf, followed by a ¾-hour hike up to the castle. Until recently, the town of Korneuburg was the center of Austrian shipbuilding, where river passenger ships, barges, and transfer cranes were built to order for Russia, among other customers. Stop for a look at the imposing neo-Gothic city hall (1864), which dominates the central square and towers over the town. ☒ *Leobendorf bei Korneuburg* ☎ *0664–422–53–63, 01/283–0308 falconers phone* ⊕ *www.kreuzenstein. com* ☒ *€8* ☉ *Apr.–Oct. daily 10–4; guided tour on the hr.*

Krems

❷ *63 km (39 mi) west of Korneuburg, 80 km (50 mi) northwest of Vienna.*

Krems marks the beginning (when traveling upstream) of the Wachau section of the Danube. The town is closely tied to Austrian history; here the ruling Babenbergs set up a dukedom in 1120, and the earliest Austrian coin was struck here in 1130. In the Middle Ages Krems looked after the iron trade, while neighboring Stein traded in salt and wine, and over the years Krems became a center of culture and art. Today the area is the heart of a thriving wine production, and Krems is most famed for the cobbled streets of its Altstadt (Old Town), which is virtually unchanged since the 18th century. The lower Old Town is an attractive pedestrian zone, while up a steep hill (a car can be handy) you'll find the upper Old Town, with its Renaissance Rathaus and a parish church that is one of the oldest in Lower Austria.

The **Karikaturmuseum** (Caricature Museum) houses more than 250 works of cartoon art from the 20th century to the present, including a large collection of English-language political satire and caricature. ☒ *Steiner Landstrasse 3a* ☎ *02732/908020* ⊕ *www.karikaturmuseum.at* ☒ *€8* ☉ *Daily 10–6.*

A 14th-century former Dominican cloister now serves as the **Weinstadt Museum Krems,** a wine museum that holds occasional tastings. ☒ *Körnermarkt 14* ☎ *02732/801–567* ⊕ *www.weinstadtmuseum.at* ☒ *€4* ☉ *Mar.–Nov., Tues.–Sun. 10–6.*

Where to Stay & Eat

$$–$$$$ ✕ **Zum Kaiser von Österreich.** At this landmark in Krems's Altstadt (Old Town) district, you'll find excellent regional cuisine along with an outstanding wine selection (some of these vintages come from the backyard). The inside rooms are bright and pleasant, and the outside tables in summer are even more inviting. Owner-chef Haidinger learned his skills at Bacher, across the Danube in Mautern, so look for fish dishes along with specialties such as potato soup and roast shoulder of lamb with scalloped potatoes. ⊠ *Körnermarkt 9* 🕾 *02732/86001* 🖷 *02732/86001–4* ⚑ *Reservations essential* 🗁 *AE, DC, V* ☉ *Closed Sun., Mon., last 2 wks in July, and 1st wk in Aug.*

$–$$$ ✕ **Jell.** Located in the heart of Krems's medieval Altstadt (Old Town), this storybook stone cottage run by Ulli Amon-Jell (pronounced "Yell") is a cluster of cozy rooms with lace curtains, dark-wood banquettes, candlelight, and Biedermeier knickknacks on the walls, making it seem like you've stepped into an early-20th-century grandmother's house. Your meal begins with tantalizing breads and dips, fine starters like cream of asparagus soup, then proceeds to delicious main courses like the pheasant breast wrapped in the restaurant's own home-cured bacon. For vegetarians there's a superb dish of peppers stuffed with smoked tofu in a sweet, organic tomato sauce. And for that warm glow at the end of your repast, have a glass of homemade apricot schnapps. In summer, book ahead for a table under the grape arbor in the small, secluded outdoor dining area. ⊠ *Hoher Markt 8–9* 🕾 *02732/82345* 🖷 *02732/ 82345–4* ⚑ *Reservations essential* 🗁 *AE, DC, MC, V* ☉ *Closed Mon. No dinner weekends.*

★ $–$$$ ✕ **M. Kunst. Genuss.** Another popular, hip restaurant belonging to entrepreneur Toni Mörwald (who owns a string of hot dining spots), this strikingly minimalistic, cathedral-roofed, glass-sided structure is situated at the Karikaturmuseum and has a name that signifies "Mörwald, Art, and Pleasure." Look for the big salad of field greens topped with a generous skirt steak, or the perfectly cooked wild salmon fillet with basmati rice and a profusion of colorful grilled vegetables. Service is without fault. ■ TIP➔ **This is one of the few restaurants in the area open for lunch all day.** ⊠ *Franz-Zeller-Platz 3* 🕾 *02732/908–0102–1* 🖷 *02732/908011* 🗁 *AE, DC, MC, V.*

★ $$–$$$ ✕🖭 **Am Förthof.** An inn has stood on the riverside site of this small, multi-windowed hotel for hundreds of years. Comfortably set back from the busy main road, it gives a sense of seclusion because of the large front garden shaded by 200-year-old chestnut trees and a multitude of flowers. The charming rooms are done in pale yellow, blue, or pink, and have antique pieces and soft carpets. Those in front have views of the Danube and Göttweig Abbey across the river, whereas the back rooms overlook a swimming pool. Rooms on the second floor have more sweeping views of the river but are a bit smaller. At dinnertime there's no need to leave the premises, as the kitchen is nearly more touted than the hotel. Breakfast is a sumptuous feast of organic products and fresh-baked *Wachauer Semmeln,* as well as silver tureens of sweet strawberries, red currants, and apricots picked from the *Marillen* trees of the neighboring medieval village of Stein. ⊠ *Förthofer Donaulände 8, A-3500* 🕾 *02732/83345* 🖷 *02732/83345–40* ➴ *20 rooms* ⚐ *Restaurant, mini-*

bars, pool, sauna, Internet, free parking, some no-smoking rooms; no a/c ☐ *AE, DC, MC, V* ⊗ *Closed. Jan. and Feb.* ⦿ *BP.*

★ $ ✕⊡ **Alte Post.** The oldest inn in Krems, for centuries the mail-route post house for the region, this hostelry is centered around an adorable Renaissance-style courtyard, which is topped with a flower-bedecked arcaded balcony and storybook mansard roof. If you're a guest here, you'll be able to drive into the pedestrian zone of the Altstadt (Old Town) and pull up next to the Steinener Tor (Stone Gate) to find this inn. The rooms are in comfortable yet elegant country style (full baths are scarce), but the real draw here is dining on regional specialties or sipping a glass of the local wine in the courtyard. The staff is friendly (though English is a struggle), and cyclists are welcome. ☒ *Obere Landstrasse 32, A-3500 Krems* ☎ *02732/82276–0* 🖷 *02732/84396* ⊕ *www.altepost-krems.at* ↪ *23 rooms, 4 with bath* ⚹ *Restaurant; no a/c* ☐ *No credit cards* ⊗ *Closed Dec.–Mar.* ⦿ *BP.*

Dürnstein

★ ❸ *8 km (5 mi) west of Krems, 90 km (56 mi) northwest of Vienna.*

If a beauty contest were held among the towns along the Wachau Danube, chances are Dürnstein would be the winner hands down—as you'll see when you arrive along with droves of tourists. The town is small; leave the car at one end and walk the narrow streets. The main street, Hauptstrasse, is lined with picturesque 16th-century residences. ▪ TIP➡ **The trick is to overnight here—when the day-trippers depart, the storybook spell of the town returns.** The top night to be here is the summer solstice, when hundreds of boats bearing torches and candles sail down the river at twilight to honor the longest day of the year—a breathtaking sight best enjoyed from the town and hotel terraces over the Danube. In October or November the grapes from the surrounding hills are harvested by volunteers from villages throughout the valley—locals garnish their front doors with straw wreaths if they offer tastes of the new wine, as members of the local wine cooperative, the Winzergenossenschaft Wachau.

Set among terraced vineyards, the town is landmarked by its gloriously Baroque **Stiftskirche,** dating from the early 1700s, which sits on a cliff overlooking the river—this cloister church's combination of luminous blue facade and stylish Baroque tower is considered the most beautiful of its kind in Austria. After taking in the Stiftskirche, head up the hill, climbing 500 feet above the town, to the famous **Richard the Lion-Hearted Castle** where Leopold V held Richard the Lion-Hearted of England, captured on his way back home from the Crusades. Leopold had been insulted, so the story goes, by Richard while they were in the Holy Land and when the English nobleman was shipwrecked and had to head back home through Austria, word got out—even though Richard was disguised as a peasant—and Leopold pounced. In the tower of this castle, the Lion-Hearted was imprisoned (1192–93) until he was located by Blondel, the faithful minnesinger. It's said that Blondel was able to locate his imprisoned king when he heard his master's voice completing the verse of a song Blondel was singing aloud—a bit famously re-

DANUBE RIVER CRUISES

A cruise up the Danube to the Wachau Valley is a tonic in any season. A parade of storybook-worthy sights—fairy-tale castles-in-air, medieval villages, and Baroque abbeys crowned with "candle-snuffer" cupolas—unfolds before your eyes. Remember that it takes longer to travel north: the trip upstream to Krems, Dürnstein, and Melk will be longer than the return back to Vienna, which is why many travelers opt to return to the city by train, not boat. Keep your fingers crossed: rumor has it that on the proper summer day the river takes on an authentic shade of Johann Strauss blue.

Blue Danube Schifffahrt/DDSG. The main company offering these sightseeing cruises is based in Vienna. Their boats leave from the company's piers at Handelskai 265 every Sunday between May 11 and September 28 at 8:45 AM. Departing from the Reichsbrücke (Vienna piers) on the city's Danube Canal, they arrive in Krems at 1:55 PM, Dürnstein at 2:30 PM, returning from Dürnstein at 4:30 PM, Krems at 4:50 PM, and get back to Vienna by 8:45 PM. One-way is €19.50—the ticket office is at the Vienna piers (take the U-Bahn line U1 to Vorgartenstrasse). ⊠ *Friedrichstrasse 7, A-1043 Vienna* ☎ *01/588-800* 🖷 *01/58880-440* ⊕ *www.ddsg-blue-danube.at.*

Brandner Schifffahrt. Another way to cruise the Danube is to leapfrog ahead by train from Vienna to Krems, where a short walk will lead you to the Schiffstation Krems piers, where river cruises run by Brandner Schifffahrt depart (10:15 AM, 1 PM, and 3:45 PM) for a ride to glorious Melk Abbey and Dürnstein. One-way tickets are €16.50, but their Web site offers an enticing array of extra goodies—"ump-pah" band concerts, wine cruises, and the like—for extra prices. ⊠ *Ufer 50, A-3313 Wallsee* ☎ *07433/2590-21* ⊕ *www.brandner.at.*

cycled in Sir Walter Scott's *Ivanhoe* (and the Robert Taylor MGM film). Leopold turned his prisoner over to the emperor, Henry VI, who held him for months longer until ransom was paid by Richard's mother, Eleanor of Aquitaine. ■ TIP➔ **The rather steep 30-minute climb to the ruins will earn you a breathtaking view up and down the Danube Valley and over the hills to the south.**

Where to Stay & Eat

★ $$$-$$$$ ✕ **Loibnerhof.** It's hard to imagine a more idyllic frame for a memorable meal, especially if the weather is fine and tables are set out in the invitingly fragrant apple orchard. The kitchen offers inventive variations on regional themes: Wachau fish soup, crispy roast duck, and various grilled fish or lamb specialties. The house is famous for its *Butterschnitzel,* an exquisite variation on the theme of ground meat (this one is panfried veal with a touch of pork). To reach Loibnerhof, look for the Unterloiben exit a mile east of Dürnstein. ⊠ *Unterloiben 7* ☎ *02732/82890-0* 🖷 *02732/82890-3* ⚹ *Reservations essential* ▤ *MC, V* ☺ *Closed Mon., Tues., and early Jan.–mid-Feb.*

★ **$$$$**   ✕🏨 **Schloss Dürnstein.** Once the preserve of the princes of Starhemberg, this 17th-century Early Baroque castle on a rocky terrace with exquisite views over the Danube is one of the most famous hotels in Austria. Its classic elegance and comfort have been enjoyed by King Juan Carlos of Spain, Prince Hirohito of Japan, Rudolf Nureyev, and a bevy of other celebs. The best guest rooms look onto the river, but all are elegantly decorated, some in grand Baroque or French Empire style. Biedermeier armoires, ceramic stoves, and country antiques grace public rooms. The restaurant is cozily nestled under coved ceilings—half-board is standard and a good value, but not required. The kitchen matches the quality of the excellent wines from the area, and the tables set outside on the large stone balcony overlooking the river make dining here a memorable experience, with pike perch from the Danube, Waldviertel beef, or roast pheasant stuffed with apricots among the menu's delights. Even if you don't stay at the hotel, it's worth a stop for lunch or a leisurely afternoon Wachauer Torte and coffee. ✉ *A-3601* ☎ *02711/ 212* 🖷 *02711/212–30* ⊕ *www.schloss.at* ⟿ *47 rooms* ⚴ *Restaurant, minibars, 2 indoor-outdoor pools, gym, sauna, bar, Internet; no a/c* ▤ *AE, DC, MC, V* ⊙ *Closed Nov.–Mar.* �۝ *BP.*

$$$–$$$$ ✕🏨 **Richard Löwenherz.** Built up around the former church of a vast 700-year-old convent, this noted inn occupies a fine point overlooking the Danube. If you can tear yourself away from its bowered terrace and balcony walkways, you'll enter the hotel and discover impressive, vaulted reception rooms beautifully furnished with antiques, reflecting the personal warmth and care of the family management. The inviting open fire, stone floors, grandfather clock, and bowls of fresh roses make this one of the most romantic of the Romantik Hotels group. Though all rooms are spacious and comfortable, the balconied guest rooms in the newer part of the house have more modern furnishings. Wander through the grounds among the roses, oleanders, and fig trees, all set against the dramatic backdrop of 600-year-old stone walls. The outstanding restaurant—with an impressively Danubian decor—is known for its local wines and regional specialties, such as crispy duck with dumplings and red cabbage. In summer, dine on that enchanting terrace under maple and chestnut trees, and admire the lushly wooded hills and languid Danube. ✉ *A-3601* ☎ *02711/222* 🖷 *02711/ 222–18* ⊕ *www.richardloewenherz.at* ⟿ *37 rooms* ⚴ *Restaurant, minibars, pool, bar; no a/c* ▤ *AE, DC, MC, V* ⊙ *Closed Nov.–Easter or mid–Apr.* �۝ *BP.*

FodorśChoice
★

$–$$ 🏨 **Sänger Blondel.** Nearly under the shadow of the exquisitely Baroque spire of Dürnstein's parish church, this *Gasthof-Pension* welcomes you with a lovely, sunny-yellow, flower-bedecked facade. Owned by the same family since 1729, the inn—named after the minstrel famous for tracking Richard the Lion-Hearted—has a large garden, quite the treat to enjoy in the heart of town. The simply furnished, country-style rooms are of medium size and have attractive paneling and antique decorations. The staff is particularly helpful and can suggest excursions in the area. The hotel's restaurant serves hearty Austrian food, and offers zither music on Thursday evenings. In summer, meals are served in the pretty courtyard under a huge chestnut tree. ✉ *No. 64, A-3601* ☎ *02711/253–0*

☎ 02711/253–7 ⊕ www.saengerblondel.at ⏎ 16 rooms ⚄ Restaurant; no a/c ⊟ V ⊗ Closed mid-Nov.–mid-Mar. ⛄ BP.

Melk

❹ *33 km (20¾ mi) southwest of Krems, 88 km (55 mi) west of Vienna.*

Unquestionably one of the most impressive sights in all Austria, the abbey of Melk is best approached in mid- to late afternoon, when the setting sun ignites the abbey's ornate Baroque yellow facade. As one heads eastward paralleling the Danube, the abbey, shining on its promontory above the river, comes into view. It easily overshadows the town—located along Route 1—but remember that the riverside village of Melk itself is worth exploring. A self-guided tour (in English, from the tourist office) will head you toward the highlights and the best spots from which to photograph the abbey.

Fodor'sChoice By any standard, **Stift Melk** (Melk Abbey) is a Baroque-era masterpiece.
★ Part palace, part monastery, part opera set, Melk is a magnificent vision thanks greatly to the upward-reaching twin towers capped with Baroque helmets and cradling a 208-foot-high dome, and a roof bristling with Baroque statuary. Symmetry here beyond the towers and dome would be misplaced, and much of the abbey's charm is due to the way the early architects were forced to fit the building to the rocky outcrop that forms its base. Erected on the site of an ancient Roman fort, used by Napoléon as his Upper Austrian redoubt, exploited as the setting for part of Umberto Eco's *Name of the Rose,* and still a working monastery, the Benedictine abbey has a history that extends back to the 11th century, as it was established in 1089. The glorious building you see today is architect Jakob Prandtauer's reconstruction, completed in 1736, in which some earlier elements are incorporated; two years later a great fire nearly totally destroyed the abbey and it had to be rebuilt. A tour of the building includes the main public rooms: a magnificent library, with more than 90,000 books, nearly 2,000 manuscripts, and a superb ceiling fresco by the master Paul Troger; the **Marmorsaal,** whose windows on three sides enhance the ceiling frescoes; the glorious spiral staircase; and the **Stiftskirche** (abbey church) of Saints Peter and Paul, an exquisite example of the Baroque style. Call to find out if tours in English will be offered on a specific day. The **Stiftsrestaurant** (closed November–April) offers standard fare, but the abbey's excellent wines elevate a simple meal to a lofty experience—particularly on a sunny day on the terrace. ⊠ *Abt Berthold Dietmayr-Strasse 1* ☎ *02752/555–232* ☎ *02752/555–249* ⊕ *www.stiftmelk.at* ☞ *€7, with tour €8.60* ⊗ *End of Mar.–Apr. and Oct., daily 9–5 (ticket office closes at 4); May–Sept., daily 9–6 (ticket office closes at 5).*

Where to Stay & Eat

★ **$$–$$$$** ✕ **Tom's.** The Wallner family has given son Tom full creative control of the kitchen in this Melk landmark, and to show their approval they even changed the name from Stadt Melk to Tom's. Nestled below the golden abbey in the center of the village square, the elegant outpost (whose guest roster includes the Duke and Duchess of Windsor) maintains its high standards, and the decidedly Biedermeier atmosphere remains unchanged. The seasonal menu may include zucchini Parmesan lasagna with truffles or fresh grilled crayfish dribbled with butter and lemon. The fried chicken is excellent. Desserts are irresistible, such as chocolate pudding with a Grand Marnier parfait or cheese curd soufflé with homemade pistachio ice cream. Upstairs there are (rather plain) bedrooms in the $ category, a good bet if you wish to overnight in magical Melk. ⊠ *Haupt-platz 1, A-3390* ☎ *02752/52475* 🖷 *02752/52475–19* ◔ *16 rooms* 🖃 *AE, DC, MC, V* ⊘ *Closed variable wks in winter.*

$–$$ 🏨 **Hotel zur Post.** Here in the center of town you're in a typical village hotel with the traditional friendliness of family management. The rooms are nothing fancy, though comfortable, and the restaurant offers solid, standard fare. ⊠ *Linzer Strasse 1, A-3390* ☎ *02752/52345* 🖷 *02752/52345–50* ◔ *27 rooms* ⚐ *Restaurant; no a/c* 🖃 *DC, MC, V* ⊘ *Closed Jan. and Feb.* ⦿ *BP.*

St. Florian

⑤ *81 km (50 mi) west of Melk.*

St. Florian is best known for the great Augustinian abbey, considered among the finest Baroque buildings in Austria. Composer Anton Bruckner (1824–96) was organist here for 10 years and is buried in the abbey. Built to honor the spot on the river Enns where St. Florian was drowned by pagans in 304 (he is still considered the protector against fire and flood by many Austrians), the **Stift St. Florian** (St. Florian Abbey) over the centuries came to comprise one of the most spectacular Baroque showpieces in Austria, landmarked by three gigantic "candle-snuffer" cupolas. In 1686 the Augustinian abbey was built by the Italian architect Carolo Carlone, then finished by Jakob Prandtauer. More of a palace than anything else, it is centered around a mammoth **Marmorsaal** (Marble Hall)—covered with frescoes honoring Prince Eugene of Savoy's defeat of the Turks—and a sumptuous library filled with 140,000 volumes. In this setting of gilt and marble, topped with ceiling frescoes by Bartolomeo Altomonte, an entire school of Austrian historiographers was born in the 19th century. Guided tours of the abbey begin with the magnificent figural gateway, which rises up three stories and is covered with symbolic statues. The Stiegenhaus, or Grand Staircase, leads to the upper floors, which include the **Kaiserzimmer,** a suite of 13 opulent salons (where you can see the "terrifying bed" of Prince Eugene, fantastically adorned with wood-carved figures of captives). The tour includes one of the great masterworks of the Austrian Baroque, Jakob Prandtauer's **Eagle Fountain Courtyard,** with its richly sculpted figures. In the over-the-top **abbey church,** where the ornate surroundings are somewhat in contrast to Bruckner's music, the Krismann organ (1770–74) is one of the largest and best of its period, and Bruckner used it to become a master organist and composer. Another highlight is the **Altdorfer Gallery,** which contains several masterworks by Albrecht Altdorfer, the leading master of the 16th-century Danube School and ranked with Dürer and Grunewald as one of the greatest northern painters. ⊠ *Stiftstrasse 1* ☎ *07224/8902-0* 🖷 *07224/8902-31* ⊕ *www.stift-st-florian.at* 🖃 *€6* ⊘ *70-min tour Easter–Oct., daily at 10, 11, 2, 3, and 4.*

Fodor's Choice ★

Nightlife & the Arts

Summer concerts are held weekends in June and July at St. Florian Abbey; for tickets, contact **Oberösterreichische Stiftskonzerte** (✉ Domgasse 12 ☎ 0732/776127 ⊕ www.stiftskonzerte.at). A series of **concerts** (☎ 0732/ 221022 🖷 0732/727–7701 ⊕ www.florianer.at ⊙ May–Sept., weekdays at 2:30 📧 €3) on the Bruckner organ are given in the church of St. Florian during the summer months. Also look for the annual Christmas concert by the St. Florian choirboys (*Sängerknaben*).

Steyr

★ ⑥   *18 km (11 mi) southeast of St. Florian.*

Steyr is one of Austria's best-kept secrets, a stunning Gothic market town that watches over the confluence of the Steyr and Enns rivers. Today the main square is lined with Baroque facades, many with Rococo trim, all complemented by the castle that sits above. The Bummerlhaus at No. 32, in its present form dating from 1497, has a Late Gothic look. On the Enns side, steps and narrow passageways lead down to the river. Across the River Steyr, St. Michael's Church, with its Bohemian cupolas and gable fresco, presides over the postcard-perfect scene. In the center of town is the Stadtplatz, lined with arcaded houses, along with a Rococo-era town hall and a Late Gothic burgher's house. Elsewhere in town are a bevy of lovely Gothic, Baroque, and Rococo churches.

In Steyr you are close to the heart of Bruckner country. He composed his Sixth Symphony in the parish house here, and there is a Bruckner room in the Meserhaus, where he composed his "sonorous music to confound celestial spheres." Schubert also lived here for a time. So many of the houses are worthy of attention that you will need to take your time and explore. Excitement is guaranteed if you accompany the night watchman on his tour of the historic center (for info, contact the tourist board). Given the quaintness of the town center, you'd hardly guess that in 1894 Steyr had Europe's first electric street lighting.

The **Steyrertalbahn** (☎ 0664–3812298), a narrow-gauge vintage railroad, wanders 17 km (10½ mi) from Steyr through the countryside from late May to late September. It also runs in December on weekends, on the 6th (as the St. Nikolaus train), and on the 31st.

In a Gothic building on Michaelerplatz, the **Austrian Christmas Museum** houses the world's largest private collection of antique Christmas-tree decorations. There are more than 10,000 ornaments created out of glass, porcelain, metal, and many other materials. In addition, there are more than 200 parlor dolls, dollhouses, and doll tea cozies from Biedermeier time to post World War II. A thoroughly eccentric Viennese lady named Elfriede Kreuzberger collected this treasure and decided that Steyr was the right place to deposit her hoard. There's also a cute, tiny, single-seater train that takes you up two floors, past Nativity scenes, to the attic with its angel workshop. ✉ *Michaelerplatz 2* ☎ *07252/80659, 07252/53229 tourist board* 📧 *€3, combination of train and museum €7* ⊙ *Late Nov.–early Jan. For visits outside these dates call the tourist board.*

BIKING ALONG THE RIVERBANK

You don't have to be Lance Armstrong to bike the Danube River trail. The stretch of relatively even terrain from Upper Austria to Vienna is an "almost" effortless pleasure, even for the inexperienced cyclist. From mid-April until the end of October, from the budding apricot orchards in spring to the copper-red leaves in the vineyards in fall, the natural beauty of this river landscape, not to mention its historic sites and towns, makes this route the most popular Austrian cycle track.

From Passau, Germany, or Schärding, Austria (a pretty place with a beautiful Baroque city center roughly 17 km [10½ mi] south of Passau), the circa 330-km (205-mi) trip can take up to one week, depending on your sightseeing urges, stamina, and curiosity. For much of the way (the exception being the Korneuburg–Krems stretch) you can bike along either side of the river.

The best Web site for planning a trip is ⊕ www.upperaustria.at. It's the official site for the tourist office of Upper Austria, and it has comprehensive advice in English on cycling tours in Austria in general and on the Danube route in particular. The Tourist Office of Lower Austria also has a Web site, ⊕ www.niederoesterreich.at, which offers a brochure in English, the "Danube Cycle Track." The brochure "Radfahren" is in German, but lists contact numbers for cycle rentals throughout Austria. Another site, ⊕ www.donauradweg.com, covers the whole of Upper Austria and offers lots of information about bike rental agencies and hotels.

The Upper Austria Web site does offer tailor-made packages and deals for cycle adventures in Austria, but, if you are adventurous enough, it is not difficult to tackle the bike routes alone. Paths are well signposted, and there are outfitters and repair stations along most tracks. Many hotels and bed-and-breakfasts will even arrange to pick up you and your bike from the cycle path and/or from the train station. Since cycling has become so popular bikes for hire can be found in most towns.

If you decide to return to your starting point by train or to take a short cut on the rails, it is best to check in advance whether or not there is room for bikes, as space can be limited. Call the Austrian Rail enquiries in advance. The ÖBB call center, 0043/05–1717, will help with reservations if necessary.

BIKE RENTALS & TOURS

Donau Touristik. This operator offers easygoing seven-day Danube trips from Passau to Vienna, including B&Bs, bike hire, baggage transfer, and more at reasonable prices. Depending on the season, costs per person for double room occupancy run €422–€503. ⊠ *Lederergasse 4–12, A-4020 Linz* ☎ *0732/20800* 🖶 *0732/20808* ⊕ *www.donautouristik.com.*

Pedal Power. Based in Vienna, this venerable outfitter has a very good reputation and a great guidebook in English, *The Danube Bike Trail*, for €13 (€21 if mailed to the United States). They have bikes for hire and guided bike tours of Vienna. ⊠ *Ausstellungsstrasse 3, A-1020 Vienna* ☎ *01/729-7234* 🖶 *01/729-7235* ⊕ *www.pedalpower.at.*

2

The **Museum Industrielle Arbeitswelt** (Industrial Museum), set in former riverside factories, is a reminder of the era when Steyr was a major center of iron making and armaments production; hunting arms are still produced here, but the major output is powerful motors for BMW cars, including some assembled in the United States. Interactive installations and exhibitions make for a worthwhile visit. ☒ *Wehrgrabengasse 7* ☏ *07252/77351* ⊕ *www.museum-steyr.at* ☒ *€5* ☽ *Tues.–Sun. 9–5.*

Where to Stay & Eat

★ $$–$$$$ ✕ **Rahofer.** You'll have to search for this popular restaurant, which is hidden away at the end of one of the passageways off the main square. Inside it's warm and cozy, with dark-wood accents and candlelight. The focus here is Italian, from the Tuscan bread and olives brought to your table on your arrival to the selection of fresh pastas and lightly prepared meat and fish dishes. Individual pizzas are baked to perfection with a thin, crispy crust and toppings ranging from arugula and shaved Parmesan to tuna and capers. ☒ *Stadtplatz 9* ☏ *07252/54606* ▭ *MC, V* ☽ *Closed Sun. and Mon.*

$$–$$$ ✕▦ **Minichmayr.** From this traditional hotel the view alone—out over the confluence of the Enns and Steyr rivers, up and across to the Schloss Lamberg and the Baroque cupolas of St. Michael's Church—will make your stay memorable. And what could be more wonderful than falling asleep while listening to the river outside your window? Some rooms have modern-style Biedermeier furnishings, complementing the old-world charm of the building's exterior and public rooms; others have traditional cherrywood furniture. Try to get a room on the river side—the front of the hotel overlooks a busy street. The restaurant, with a secession-style bar, offers classic Austrian cuisine, specializing in fresh fish. ☒ *Haratzmüllerstrasse 1–3, A-4400* ☏ *07252/53410–0* ☐ *07252/48202* ⊕ *www.hotel-minichmayr.at* ☜ *47 rooms* ఓ *Restaurant, bar, Internet; no a/c* ▭ *AE, DC, MC, V* ▢◎▢ *BP.*

$$ ✕▦ **Mader/Zu den Drei Rosen.** In this very old family-run hotel with small but pleasant modern rooms you're right on the attractive town square. The restaurant offers solid local and traditional fare, with outdoor dining in a delightful garden area within the ancient courtyard. ☒ *Stadtplatz 36, A-4400* ☏ *07252/53358–0* ☐ *07252/53358–6* ⊕ *www.mader.at* ☜ *62 rooms* ఓ *Restaurant, some minibars; no a/c* ▭ *AE, DC, MC, V* ▢◎▢ *BP.*

OFF THE BEATEN PATH

WAIDHOFEN AN DER YBBS – Well worth a slight detour from the more traveled routes, this picturesque river town (30 km [18 mi] east of Steyr) developed early as an industrial center, turning Styrian iron ore into swords, knives, sickles, and scythes. These weapons proved successful in the defense against the invading Turks in 1532; marking the decisive moment of victory, the hands on the north side of the town tower clock remain at 12:45. In 1871 Baron Rothschild bought the collapsing castle and assigned Friedrich Schmidt, architect of Vienna's City Hall, to rebuild it in neo-Gothic style. Stroll around the two squares in the Altstadt (Old Town) to see the Gothic and Baroque houses and to the Graben on the edge of the Old Town for the delightful Biedermeier houses and churches and chapels.

Kremsmünster

❼ *32 km (20 mi) west of Steyr.*

★ The vast Benedictine **Stift Kremsmünster** was established in 777 and remains one of the most important abbeys in Austria. Inside the church is the Gothic memorial tomb of Gunther, killed by a wild boar, whose father, Tassilo, duke of Bavaria (and nemesis of Charlemagne), vowed to build the abbey on the site. Centuries later, the initial structures were replaced in the grand Baroque manner, including the extraordinary tower. Magnificent rooms include the Kaisersaal and the frescoed library with more than 100,000 volumes, many of them manuscripts. On one side of the Prälatenhof courtyard are Jakob Prandtauer's elegant fish basins, complete with sculpted saints holding squirming denizens of the deep, and opposite is the Abteitrakt, whose art collection includes the Tassilo Chalice, from about 765. The seven-story observatory (*Sternwarte*) houses an early museum of science, which includes (among lots of other treasures) the sextant used by Johannes Kepler. Most travelers arrive here by taking Route 139 (or the train) heading southwest from Linz. ☎ *07583/5275–151* ⊕ *www.kremsmuenster.at* ✉ *Rooms and art gallery €5, observatory and tour €6.50* ⊗ *Rooms and art gallery tour (minimum 5 people) Easter–Oct., daily at 10, 11, 2, 3, and 4; Nov.–Easter, Tues.–Sun. at 11 and 2. Observatory tour (minimum 5 people) May–Oct., daily at 10 and 2.*

Schloss Kremsegg has a collection of rare musical instruments, including Friedrich Gulda's personal collection. A number of rooms are dedicated to Franz Schubert, with personal letters and an audio room for listening to his works. ✉ *Kremseggerstrasse 59* ☎ *07583/52470* 🖷 *07583/6830* ✉ *€5* ⊗ *Apr.–Oct., Wed.–Mon. 10–5. Open in winter by arrangement.*

Where to Eat

★ **$$–$$$** ✕ **Gasthof Moser.** North of Kremsmünster on Highway 139 in the village of Neuhofen, the Moser is known throughout the countryside for its good cooking. Built in 1640, it retains a time-stained ambience with its vaulted ceilings, curving, thick white walls, and dark wood. The menu ranges from old standards like turkey cordon bleu to the innovative cannelloni stuffed with *Zanderfilet* (pike perch) on a bed of roasted zucchini and tomatoes. ✉ *Marktplatz 9, A-4501 Neuhofen an der Krems* ☎ *07227/4229* 🖷 *07227/42294* ⚠ *Reservations essential* ▤ *DC, V* ⊗ *Closed Mon. No lunch Tues.* ❧ *BP.*

SALZKAMMERGUT: THE LAKE DISTRICT

Remember the exquisite opening scenes of *The Sound of Music*? Castles reflected in water, mountains veiled by a scattering of downy clouds, flower-strewn valleys dotted with cool blue lakes: a view of Austria as dreamed up by a team of Hollywood's special-effects geniuses—so we thought. But, no, those scenes were filmed right here, not far from where the Trapp children "Do-Re-Mi"-ed. Here, we feature just a few

jewels from this scenic treasure box, including the delightfully picturesque towns of Gmunden, St. Wolfgang, St. Gilgen, and Bad Ischl,
which seems to be on sabbatical from an operetta set.

Gmunden

❽ *35 km (22 mi) southwest of Kremsmünster.*

Gmunden, at the top of the Traunsee, is an attractive town for strolling.
The tree-lined promenade along the lake is reminiscent of past days of
the idle aristocracy and artistic greats—the composers Franz Schubert,
Johannes Brahms, Béla Bartók, Arnold Schoenberg, and Erich Wolfgang
Korngold and the Duke of Württemberg were just some who strolled
under the chestnut trees. The gloriously ornate, arcaded yellow-and-white
town hall, its corner towers topped by onion domes, can't be overlooked; it houses a famous carillon, with bells fashioned not from the
local clay but from fabled Meissen porcelain (which gives a better
sound) decorated in the Gmunden style. Head to the upper town and
take in the parish church on Pfarrhofgasse. It has a beautiful high altar
dedicated to the Three Kings. You can easily walk to the **Strandbad,** the
swimming area, from the center of town. The beaches are good, and
you can sail, water-ski, or windsurf.

Be sure to head out to the town's historic castles: the "lake" castle, **Schloss
Orth,** on a peninsula known as Toskana, was originally built in the 15th
century. It was once owned by Archduke Johann, who gave up his title
after marrying an actress and thereafter called himself Orth. He disappeared with the casket supposedly holding the secret to the mysterious
deaths in 1889 of Crown Prince Rudolf, Emperor Franz Josef's only son,
and his mistress at Mayerling. The **Landschloss** on the shore is a simple
17th-century affair now operating as a government school of forestry;
you can visit the courtyard, with its coats of arms and Rococo fountain, daily 8 AM–dusk.

Music lovers will enjoy the Brahms memorial collection—the world's
largest—on display in the **Stadtmuseum** (City Museum) at the town
Kammerhof. Other exhibitions are devoted to the town's history and
the region's salt and mineral resources. ⊠ *Kammerhofgasse 8* 🏬 *07612/
794420* 🎫 *€4.20* ⊗ *May–Oct., Dec., and Jan., Mon.–Sat. 10–noon and
2–5, Sun. 10–noon.*

★ From Gmunden, take a lake trip on the *Gisela,* built in 1872, the oldest coal-fired steam side-wheeler running anywhere. It carried Emperor
Franz Josef and is now restored. For departure times, check with **Traun-
seeschiffahrt Eder** (🕾 *07612/66700* ⊕ www.traunseeschiffahrt.at). The
boat route crisscrosses the whole 12-km (7-mi) length of the lake.

From beyond the railroad station, a 12-minute cable-car ride brings you
to the top of the **Grünberg.** From here you will have a superb view over
the Traunsee, with the Dachstein glacier forming the backdrop in the
south. In winter there are good ski runs here. ⊠ *Freygasse 4* 🕾 *07612/
64977–0* 🎫 *Round-trip €11.20, one-way €7.80* ⊗ *Apr.–June and
Sept., daily 9–5; July and Aug., daily 9–6; Oct., daily 9–4:30.*

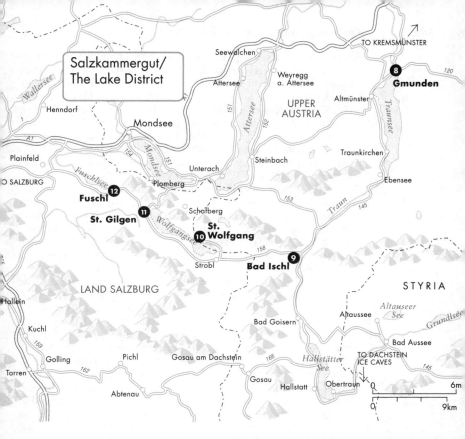

To get to Bad Ischl from Gmunden, take Route 145 along the western shore of the Traunsee—note the Traunstein, Hochkogel, and Erlakogel peaks on the eastern side, the latter nicknamed "Die schlafende Griechen" ("The Slumbering Greek Girl")—and then along the Traun River. At **Ebensee** is the chance to enjoy the overwhelming karst scenery of the limestone Alps from above by using the **cable car** (⌗ Rudolf-Ipplisch-Platz 4 ☎ 06133/5219 ☑ €16 ⊘ May 15–Oct. 10, daily) up the Feuerkogel mountain. You can also take a train to Gmunden via Attnang-Puchheim from Salzburg, or from the main station in Linz.

OFF THE BEATEN PATH
TRAUNKIRCHEN – About 4½ km (3 mi) north of Ebensee on Route 145 you'll come to Traunkirchen, a little village where Arnold Schoenberg invented his 12-tone method of composition; stop for a look at the famous "fishermen's pulpit" in the parish church next to a convent founded by the nuns from Nonnberg in Salzburg. This 17th-century Baroque marvel, carved from wood and burnished with silver and gold, portrays the astonished fishermen of the Sea of Galilee pulling in their suddenly full nets at Jesus's direction.

Where to Stay & Eat

$$ ✕⊡ **Hois'n Wirt.** This large, modern-chalet complex enjoys a swooningly idyllic Traunsee setting. Now run by the fourth generation of the

Schallmeiner family, it is geared to please. The restaurant has a glittering glass window wall overlooking the lakeside view, and the kitchen uses the lake as its larder, cooking up some of the best trout and Reinanke around. Guest rooms are pretty, light-filled, and casual-modern, with balconies overlooking the lakeside beach. Many guests check in and then immediately dive in. In a house not far away from the hotel, Arnold Schoenberg composed his first official string quartet and started painting. ⊠ *Traunsteinstrasse 277, A-4810* ☎ *07612/77333* ⊟ *07612/773–3395* ⊕ *www.hoisnwirt.at/hoisnwirt* ↩ *16 rooms* ♨ *Restaurant, beach; no a/c* ⊟ *AE, DC, MC, V* ⦿ *FAP, MAP.*

$$$ ▥ **Schloss Freisitz Hotel Roith.** Crowning the eastern shores of the Traunsee, this landmark Schloss draws all eyes, thanks to its flapping flag atop its white turret, its *Mitteleuropisch* Baroque pediments, and expansive "hunting lodge" facade. Gracing a castle site from 1550, it was renovated in 1887 by Gustav Faber. In 1964 the mansion became a hotel, and now anyone can experience the 19th-century luxe that Faber, the famous German pencil maker, once enjoyed—Oriental carpets, Art Nouveau furniture, and those breathtaking vistas down to the lake. The breakfast buffet is almost as beautiful. ⊠ *Traunsteinstrasse 87, A-4810* ☎ *07612/64905* ⊟ *07612/649–0517* ⊕ *www.schlosshotel.at* ↩ *14 rooms* ♨ *Restaurant, gym, sauna, steam room* ⊟ *AE, DC, MC, V.*

$$ ▥ **Grünberg am See.** This sprawling, multilevel chalet hotel makes a pretty picture along the lakeshore opposite Gmunden's city center. Rooms are spacious with contemporary blond-wood furniture, and many have balconies with stunning views. The popular restaurant serves good local cuisine, emphasizing fish fresh from the lake. The hotel offers superb sports opportunities, from hiking to cycling to swimming. Half-pension plans are offered for a stay of three days or more. ⊠ *Traunsteinstrasse 109, A-4810* ☎ *07612/777–00* ⊟ *07612/77700–33* ⊕ *www.gruenberg. at* ↩ *30 rooms* ♨ *Restaurant, beach, bicycles, hiking, bar; no a/c* ⊟ *AE, DC, MC, V* ⊘ *Closed 2 wks. in Feb.* ⦿ *MAP.*

$$ ▥ **Seehotel Schwan.** On the edge of the lake in the center of town, this grand old hotel is part of the Best Western chain. Rooms are standard, but the views make up for what they might be lacking in character. The restaurant, with huge windows overlooking the lake, has a creative menu with lots of fresh fish offerings. ⊠ *Rathausplatz 8, A-4810* ☎ *07612/63391-0* ⊟ *07612/63391-8* ↩ *30 rooms* ♨ *Restaurant, bar; no a/c* ⊟ *AE, DC, MC, V* ⦿ *FAP, MAP.*

Bad Ischl

❾ *35 km (22 mi) southwest of Gmunden, 56 km (35 mi) east of Salzburg.*

Many travelers used to think of Bad Ischl primarily as the town where Zauner's pastry shop is located, to which connoisseurs drove miles for the sake of a cup of coffee and a slice of *Guglhupf*, a lemon sponge cake studded with raisins and nuts. Pastry continues to be the best-known drawing card of a community that symbolizes, more than any other place except Vienna itself, the Old Austria of resplendent uniforms and balls and waltzes and operettas. Although the center is built up, the town is charmingly laid out on a peninsula between the Rivers Traun and Ischl, whose amazing waters still run crystal clear. Bad Ischl was the place where Emperor Franz Josef chose to establish his summer court: when he died in 1916 at an age of 85 he had spent 82 summers in Ischl (the story goes that his mother, Sophie, had stayed at the spa in 1829 at the time of his conception, thereby earning the ruler his nickname, the "Salt Prince"). And it was also here that Franz Josef met and fell in love with his future empress, the troubled Sisi, though his mother had intended him for Sisi's elder sister. Today you can enjoy the same sort of pastries *mit Schlag* (with whipped cream) that the emperor loved. Afterward, you can hasten off to the

> ### GMUNDEN CRAFTS
>
> Among the many souvenirs and handicrafts you'll find in Salzkammergut shops, the most famous are the handcrafted ceramics of Gmunden. The green-trimmed, white country ceramics are decorated with blue, yellow, green, and white patterns, including the celebrated 16th-century *Grüngeflammte* design, solid horizontal green stripes on a white background. You'll find them at **Gmundner Keramik** (✉ Keramikstrasse 24 ☎ 07612/786-0).

town's modern spa, one of the best known in Austria. The town initially grew up around the curative mineral salt springs. One of the town's main landmarks is the classic 19th-century *Kurhaus* (spa building), which is now a theater for operetta festivals (note the monuments to Lehár and Kálmán in the adjoining park), and is home to the town's Kurorchestra (spa orchestra), which can also be found at various venues around town, including the Esplanade. Nearby are buildings from the 1860s that still offer spa treatments.

You'll want to stroll along the shaded **Esplanade,** where the pampered and privileged of the 19th century loved to take their constitutionals, usually after a quick stop at the **Trinkhalle,** a spa pavilion in high 19th-century Austrian style, still in the middle of town on Ferdinand-Auböck-Platz.

★ In Bad Ischl the quickest way to travel back in time to the gilded 1880s is to head for the mammoth **Kaiservilla,** the imperial-yellow (signifying wealth and power) residence, which looks rather like a miniature Schönbrunn: its ground plan forms an "E" to honor the empress Elisabeth. Archduke Markus Salvator von Habsburg-Lothringen, great-grandson of Franz Josef I, still lives here, but you can tour parts of the building to see the ornate reception rooms and the surprisingly modest residential quarters (through which sometimes even the archduke guides guests with what can only be described as a very courtly kind of humor). It was at this villa that the emperor signed the declaration of war against Serbia, which officially marked the start of World War I. The villa is filled with Habsburg and family mementos, none more moving than the cushion on which the head of Empress Elisabeth rested after she was stabbed by an Italian assassin in 1898, which is on view in the villa's chapel. ✉ *Kaiserpark* ☎ *06132/23241* ⊕ *www.kaiservilla.at* ☎ *Grounds €3.50; combined ticket, including tour of villa, €9.50* ☉ *Easter, Apr. weekends, and May–mid-Oct., daily 9:30–4:45.*

Don't overlook the small but elegant "marble palace" built near the Kaiservilla for Empress Elisabeth, who used it as a teahouse; this now houses a **photography museum.** The marriage between Franz Josef and Elisabeth was not an especially happy one; a number of houses bearing women's names in Bad Ischl are said to have been quietly given by the emperor to his various lady friends (most prominently, Villa Schratt—*see* Where to Stay & Eat, *below*—given to Katharina Schratt, the emperor's nearly official mistress). You'll first need to purchase a ticket to the museum to enter the park grounds. ⊠ *Kaiserpark* ☎ *06132/24422* 🎟 *€1.50* ☉ *Apr.–Oct., daily 9:30–5.*

Fascinating is the only word to describe the **Museum der Stadt Ischl,** which occupies the circa 1880 Hotel Austria—the favored summer address for archduke Franz Karl and his wife Sophie (from 1834 on). More momentously, the young Franz Josef got engaged to his beloved Elisabeth here in 1853. After taking in the gardens (with their Brahms monument), explore the various exhibits, which deal with the region's salt, royal, and folk histories. Note the display of national folk costumes, which the emperor made presentable even for his court aristos by wearing them while hunting. From December until the beginning of February, the museum shows off its famous *Kalss Krippe,* an enormous mechanical Christmas crèche. Dating from 1838, it has about 300 figures. The townsfolk of Ischl, in fact, are famous for their Christmas "cribs," and you can see many of them in tours of private houses opened for visits after Christmas until January 6. ⊠ *Esplanade 10* ☎ *06132/30114* ⊕ *www.stadtmuseum.at* 🎟 *€4.50* ☉ *Jan.–Mar., Fri.–Sun. noon–5; Apr.–Oct. and Dec., Sun.–Tues. and Thurs.–Sat. 10–5, Wed. 2–7.*

In the center of town, **St. Nikolaus** parish church graces Ferdinand-Auböck-Platz. It dates back to the Middle Ages, but was enlarged to its present size during Maria Theresa's time in the 1750s. The decoration inside is in the typically gloomy style of Franz Josef's days (note the emperor's family portrayed to the left above the high altar). Anton Bruckner used to play on the old church organ.

A steady stream of composers followed the aristocracy and the court to Bad Ischl. Anton Bruckner, Johannes Brahms (who composed his famous *Lullaby* here as well as many of his late works), Johann Strauss the Younger, Carl Michael Ziehrer, Oscar Straus, and Anton Webern all spent summers here, but it was the Hungarian-born Franz Lehár, composer of *The Merry Widow,* who left the most lasting musical impression—today, Bad Ischl's summer operetta festival (⇨ Nightlife & the Arts, *below*) always includes one Lehár work. With the royalties he received from his operettas, he was able to afford his own vacation villa from 1912 on. Previously, he rented the Rosenvilla, set between the trees to the left of the Kongresshaus (a house in which Giacomo Meyerbeer composed parts of his opera *Le Prophete*). He finally settled into the sumptuous **Villa Lehár,** in which he lived from 1912 to his death in 1948. Now a museum, it contains a number of the composer's fin de siècle period salons, which can be viewed on guided tours. ⊠ *Lehárkai 8* ☎ *06132/ 26992* 🎟 *€4.80* ☉ *May–Sept., daily 9–noon and 2–5.*

2

Bad Ischl is accessed easily via various routes. From St. Wolfgang, backtrack south to Strobl and head eastward on Route 158. To get to the town directly from Salzburg, take the A1 to Mondsee, then Routes 151 and 158 along the Wolfgangsee and the Mondsee. There are many buses that depart hourly from Salzburg's main railway station; you can also travel by train via the junction of Attnang-Puchheim or Stainach-Irdning (several transfers are required)—a longer journey than the bus ride, which is usually 90 minutes. There are also many regular bus and train connections between Gmunden and Bad Ischl.

Where to Stay & Eat

$$–$$$$ ✕ **Villa Schratt.** About a mile outside Bad Ischl on the road to Salzburg
Fodor's Choice is this enchanting, secluded villa, fabled retreat of the actress Katharina
★ Schratt. "Kati"—star of Vienna's Hofburgtheater (Imperial and Royal Court Theater)—was Emperor Franz Josef's mistress in his later years, and almost every summer morning the emperor would stroll over here for his breakfast. Over the course of their time together, most of Europe's royalty dropped in for a visit. Nowadays the Villa Schratt is one of the best places to dine in the area. Choose between two dining rooms—one with a Jugendstil slant, the other country style with chintz curtains, a ceramic stove, and a hutch displaying homemade jams. Try the *Zanderfilet* (pike perch) on a bed of delicate beets soaked in port wine, or beef tenderloin strips with oyster mushrooms in a cream sauce. For dessert, order the traditional Guglhupf, Franz Josef's favorite—it even comes warm out of the oven. Upstairs are four lovely, antiques-filled bedrooms ($–$$) for overnighters. ✉ *Steinbruch 43, A-4820* ☎ *06132/27647 restaurant, 06132/23535 rooms* 🖷 *06132/27647–4* ⊕ *www.oberoesterreich.at/villa.schratt* ⚓ *Reservations essential* 🖃 *AE, MC* ⊘ *Closed Tues., Wed., early–mid-Nov., and varying wks in spring.*

$–$$ ✕ **Rettenbachmühle.** A shady walk of about 20 minutes east from Bad Ischl's town center follows a brook and deposits you at this former farmhouse, once thought to be the supplier of eggs and milk for the imperial breakfast table (a nice story, though probably not true). The Vierthaler family, the present owners, swear, however, that this was the very locale where the *Kaiserschmarrn* was born. The name literally translates to "emperor's nonsense," but many consider it to be the most delicious dessert in Austria—a raisin-studded pancake covered with powdered sugar. It makes for a lovely time to stop here to enjoy this treat along with an afternoon coffee. ✉ *Hinterstein 6* ☎ *06132/23586* ⊘ *Closed Mon. and Tues.*

★ **$–$$** ✕ **Weinhaus Attwenger.** Once the summer residence of composer Anton Bruckner (who journeyed here to be the emperor's organist in the town parish church), this turn-of-the-19th-century gingerbread villa is set in a shady garden overlooking a river, with the Villa Lehár perched just next door. The tranquil garden is ideal for summer dining, and inside the house the cozy, wood-paneled rooms are decorated with antique country knickknacks. Order the crispy duck in a honey-ginger sauce or the basket of country-fried chicken, or ask for seasonal recommendations; the fish and game dishes are particularly good. ✉ *Lehárkai 12* ☎🖷 *06132/ 23327* 🖃 *No credit cards* ⊘ *Closed Wed., Thurs., and 2 wks in Mar.*

★ ¢–$ ✕ **Café Zauner.** If you haven't been to Zauner, you've missed a true high-light of Bad Ischl. There are two locations, one on the Esplanade over-looking the River Traun (open only in summer) and the other a few blocks away on Pfarrgasse. ■ TIP→ **The desserts—particularly the house creation, Zaunerstollen, a chocolate-covered confection of sugar, hazelnuts, and nougat—have made this one of Austria's best-known pastry shops.** Emperor Franz Josef used to visit every day for a Guglhupf, a lemon sponge cake. ⊠ *Pfarrgasse 7* ☎ *06132/23522* ⊕ *www.zauner.at* ▭ *MC* ☾ *Closed Tues.*

$–$$ ▥ **Goldener Ochs.** The "Golden Ox" is in a superb location in the town center, with the sparkling River Traun just a few steps away. Rooms are modern with blond-wood furniture; some have balconies, and there are a few large rooms designed for families. The kitchen prides itself on its health-oriented cooking. ⊠ *Grazerstrasse 4, A-4820* ☎ *06132/235290* 🖷 *06132/235293* ⊕ *www.tiscover.com/goldener-ochs* ⇄ *48 rooms* ⌂ *Restaurant, gym, sauna, Internet; no a/c* ▭ *AE, DC, MC, V* ⦿ *FAP, MAP.*

Nightlife & the Arts

The main musical events of the year in the Salzkammergut are the July and August operetta festivals held in Bad Ischl. In addition, performances of at least two operettas (*The Merry Widow* is a favorite standard) take place every season in the **Kongress- und Theaterhaus** (☎ 06132/23420), where tickets are sold. For early booking, contact the **Operrettengemeinde** (⊠ Kurhausstrasse 8, A-4820 Bad Ischl ☎ 06132/23839 🖷 06132/23839–39).

St. Wolfgang

★ ⑩   *21 km (13 mi) northwest of Bad Ischl, 50 km (31 mi) east of Salzburg.*

A delightful way to enter the picture-book town of St. Wolfgang is to leave your car at Strobl, at the southern end of the Wolfgangsee, and take one of the steamers that ply the waters of the lake. Strobl itself is a delightful village but not as fashionable as St. Wolfgang; if you prefer a quiet vacation base, this may be its attraction for you. Between St. Wolfgang and Strobl the Wolfgangsee still retains its old name of "Abersee." One of the earliest paddleboats on the lake is still in service, a genuine 1873 steamer called the *Kaiser Franz Josef.* Service is regular from May to mid-October. The view of the town against the dramatic mountain backdrop is one you'll see again and again on posters and postcards. If you decide to drive all the way to town, be prepared for a crowd. Unless your hotel offers parking, you'll have to park on the fringes of town and walk a short distance, as the center is a pedestrian-only zone.

The town has everything: swimming and hiking in summer, cross-country skiing in winter, and natural feasts for the eye at every turn. Here you will find yourself in the Austria of operetta. Indeed, St. Wolfgang became known around the world thanks to the inn called the **Weisses Rössl,** which was built right next to the landing stage in 1878. It featured prominently in a late-19th-century play that achieved fame as an operetta by Ralph Benatzky in 1930. Ironically, the two original playwrights, Gustav Kadelburg and Oskar Blumenthal, had another, now destroyed, Weisses Rössl (along the road from Bad Ischl to Hallstatt) in mind. In the years following World War II the composers Samuel Barber and Gian Carlo Menotti spent summer vacations here, too.

You shouldn't miss seeing Michael Pacher's great altarpiece in the 15th-century **Wallfahrtskirche** (pilgrimage church), one of the finest examples of Late Gothic wood carving to be found anywhere. This 36-foot masterpiece took 10 years (1471–81) to complete. As a winged altar, its paintings and carvings were used as an *Armenbibel* (a Bible for the poor)—illustrations for those who couldn't read or write. The coronation of the Virgin is depicted in detail so exact that you can see the stitches in her garments. Gesturing, she invites the onlooker to pray and is surrounded by various saints, including the local patron, bishop St. Wolfgang from Regensburg in Bavaria. Since the 15th century his namesake town has been a place of pilgrimage. Pacher set his painted scenes in landscapes inspired by his homeland, South Tirol (now Italy). You're in luck if you're at the church on a sunny day, when sunlight off the nearby lake dances on the ceiling in brilliant reflections through the stained-glass windows. ⊙ *May–Sept., daily 9–5; Oct.–Apr., daily 10–4; altar closed to view during Lent.*

OFF THE BEATEN PATH

SCHAFBERG – The rack railway trip from St. Wolfgang to the 5,800-foot peak of the Schafberg offers a great chance to survey the surrounding countryside from what is acclaimed as the "belvedere of the Salzkammergut lakes." On a clear day you can almost see forever—at least as far as the Lattengebirge mountain range west of Salzburg. Figure on crowds, so reserve in advance or start out early. The **train** (☎ 06138/2232-0 📠 06138/2232–12) itself is a curiosity dating from 1893, and does not run in bad weather. It departs daily from May to October every hour from 8:25 AM to 7:55 PM. Allow at least a good half day for the outing, which costs €24.

Where to Stay & Eat

★ **$-$$$** ✕ **Hupfmühle.** A hot tip for any fish lovers: This romantic old mill is simply a must for either fresh trout or Reinanke, the mild, local fish, right out of the Hutterer family's own pond nearby. And the warm *Apfel-* or *Topfenstrudel* is the ideal dessert afterwards. Hupfmühle is a short distance along the rather steep road parallel to the Schafbergbahn. Then take a few steps down to the restaurant, by the murmuring water of the Dittelbach. It's well worth the walk. ✉ *Au 1, A-5360* ☎ *06138/2579* 📠 *06138/2500* ⚑ *Reservations essential* 🚫 *No credit cards* ⊙ *Closed Tues. except July and Aug.*

$$$$ ✕🏨 **Landhaus zu Appesbach.** Very secluded and quiet and offering excellent service, this old ivy-covered manor hotel is set away from the hubbub of the village. Public salons are charmingly furnished with Biedermeier pieces, while guest rooms are a mixture of country antiques and modern pieces, with grand overtones. Some have large balconies overlooking the lake. Both the Duke of Windsor and writer Thomas Mann once enjoyed respites here. The hotel has its own restaurant, for guests only, though it isn't at all stuffy. The menu is seasonal, but a staple is the fantastic antipasti buffet. Half-pension is included in the room price, or you can opt for a reduction without meals. ⊠ *A-5360, St. Wolfgang am See* ☎ *06138/2209* 🖷 *06138/2209–14* ⊕ *www.appesbach.com* 🛏 *26 rooms* 🍴 *Restaurant, minibars, tennis court, sauna, steam room, beach, dock; no a/c* ⊟ *AE, DC, MC, V* ☉ *Closed varying wks in Nov. and last 3 wks of Jan.* ¶⊙¶ *MAP.*

★ **$$$–$$$$** ⨉▥ **Weisses Rössl.** The "White Horse" has been featured in films and theater over the years, thanks to the famous operetta set here. Part of the Romantik Hotel group, it has been family-owned since the 1800s. Guest rooms are full of country charm, with pretty chintz fabrics and quaint furniture, and many have a balcony with a lake view. Baths are luxurious, complete with controls to set the exact water temperature you desire. The buffet breakfast is outstanding. An added attraction is the outdoor pool, situated directly on the lake and heated to a constant 86°F (30°C) year-round. The dining terraces, built to float over the water, are enchanting, where you can enjoy the noted leek cream soup with scampi, *Forelle Müllerin* (trout "miller's daughter," simply fried in butter), or corn-fed chicken in a rosemary gravy. The hotel is world famous, so book well in advance, especially in summer. ⊠ *Markt 74, A-5360* ☎ *06138/2306–0* 🖷 *06138/2306–41* ⊕ *www.weissesroessl.at* 🛏 *72 rooms* 🍴 *2 restaurants, minibars, tennis court, 2 pools (1 indoor), lake, sauna, windsurfing, boating, bar, Internet; no a/c* ⊟ *AE, DC, MC, V* ☉ *Closed Nov.–mid-Dec.* ¶⊙¶ *MAP.*

★ **$$–$$$** ▥ **Cortisen am See.** A large chalet-style structure with a glowing yellow facade, "At the Court" has become one of St. Wolfgang's most stylish and comfortable hotels. It has a lakeside perch, of course, with its own beach, rowboats, terrace dining, and plenty of mountain bikes. Inside, all is Gemütlichkeit nouvelle—chintz fabrics, tin lanterns, Swedish woods, and sash windows. The restaurant sparkles with a mix of 19th-century fabrics and gleaming white trim. The menu is mighty spiffy, and owner Roland Ballner is proud to offer not only the largest wine selection in the area but also its most exotic cigar collection. ⊠ *Markt 15, A-5360* ☎ *06138/2376–0* 🖷 *06138/236744* ⊕ *www.cortisen.at* 🛏 *36 rooms* 🍴 *Restaurant, gym, sauna, steam room, bar; no a/c* ⊟ *AE, DC, MC, V* ¶⊙¶ *MAP.*

$ ▥ **Gasthof Zimmerbräu.** This pretty, pleasant budget Gasthof is four centuries old and was once a brewery, though for the last hundred years it has been an inn run by the Scharf family. Centrally located, the Zimmerbräu is not near the lake but does maintain its own bathing cabana by the water. The decor is appealingly rustic in some rooms, contemporary in others, but all rooms have balconies, and there is a lovely sitting room with Biedermeier furnishings on the first floor. Half-pension is offered in the summer season only. ⊠ *Im Stöck 85, A-5360* ☎ *06138/2204* 🖷 *06138/2204–45* ⊕ *www.zimmerbraeu.com* 🛏 *25 rooms* 🍴 *Restaurant, bar; no a/c* ⊟ *MC, V* ☉ *Closed Nov.–Dec. 26* ¶⊙¶ *MAP.*

St. Gilgen

★ **⓫** *15 km (9 mi) northwest of St. Wolfgang, 34 km (21 mi) east of Salzburg.*

Though its modest charms tend to be overshadowed by neighboring St. Wolfgang, St. Gilgen has a pretty main square and a nice beach (the northernmost strand on the Wolfgangsee). ■ TIP→ A combination ticket sold in the village pairs a boat ride with a trip up the cable car for fantastic views. You can see just about every lake in the entire region as well as the pilgrimage church below.

A fountain of Mozart in the town square commemorates the fact that his mother, Anna Pertl, was born here on December 25, 1720. Later his sister Nannerl resided in the same house when she married a town magistrate, Baron Baptist von Berchtold zu Sonnenberg. Their house, the **Mozart-Gedenkstätte St. Gilgen,** stands near the dock and is devoted to the town's Mozart legacy. After exploring the small town—more than Mozart himself ever did, since he never came here—you can see its small Baroque parish church (where Mozart's grandparents and sister married and his mother was baptized), then take the Zwölferhornbahn cable car (next to the bus station) up to the summit of the majestic Zwölferhorn peak. ⊠ *Mozarthaus: Ischler Strasse 15* ☎ *06227/2642* ⊠ *€3.50* ☉ *June–Sept., Tues.–Sun. 10–noon and 2–6.*

Where to Stay & Eat

★ **$$$–$$$$** ✕ **Timbale.** Cozy (with only five tables) and cheerful, Timbale is one of the premier restaurants in the Salzkammergut, known far and wide for regional specialties done just so. The taste treats start with the corn, whole-wheat, and French breads baked on the premises, and dazzle on to the *Stubenküken* (chicken breast) stuffed with a cheese soufflé and wild mush-rooms, or the *Kalbsrücken* (veal) with risotto and grilled shallots. Your eyes, as well as your stomach, will be happy—the crocheted red flower petals on periwinkle-blue tablecloths make everyone smile. ⊠ *Salzburgerstrasse 2, A-5340* ☎☎ *06227/7587* ☓ *Reservations essential* ☐ *No credit cards* ☉ *Closed Thurs. No lunch Fri. except in Aug.*

$–$$ ✕▣ **Hotel Gasthof zur Post.** An inn since 1415, the family-owned Post is one of the most attractive houses in town, a former domicile of Mozart's grandfather. A beautiful old spruce-wood staircase leads to spacious rooms with contemporary furniture and stunning views of the village and the Wolfgangsee (most rooms have balconies). Owner Norbert Leitner is also a top chef—his seasonal menus might include a salad of wild greens with duck breast, spinach-and-garlic soup with slivers of smoked freshwater salmon, and *Tafelspitz* (boiled beef). On Friday evenings from September to mid-November the restaurant offers live folk music. Be sure to have a glass of wine in the Vinothek, with its original 12th-century entrance. And get to know the secret behind the old hunting-scene fresco in the main parlor (with hidden motifs symbolizing "hunted" Lutherans). ⊠*Mozartplatz 8, A-5340* ☎*06227/2157* ☐*06227/2157–600* ⊕ *www.gasthofzurpost.at* ☞*18 rooms* ⌂ *Restaurant, sauna; no a/c* ☐ *AE, DC, MC, V* ☉ *Closed 1 month (variable) in winter. Restaurant closed Wed. and Thurs., Nov.–Apr.* ☉ *MAP.*

$$$–$$$$ ▣ **Parkhotel Billroth.** Theodor Billroth was a member of the famous Viennese medical school, a surgeon who specialized in stomach ailments. He was musically talented, playing violin and viola and becoming president of Vienna's famous Gesellschaft der Musikfreunde (Society of Friends of Music) in Vienna: its chorus master Johannes Brahms often came to see his friend at this summer residence. After Billroth's death his house was replaced by this elegant villa, decorated in 19th-century style, set in a huge park 10 minutes from the town center but close to the lake. The house is pleasantly worn at the edges yet spaciously arranged and luxuriously appointed, with a fine dining room. Sun terraces are particularly inviting. ⊠ *Billrothstrasse 2, A-5340* ☎ *06227/2217* 🖷 *06227/2218–25* ⤧ *44 rooms* ⚏ *Restaurant, tennis court, massage, sauna, beach, boating, bar; no a/c* ⊟ *MC, V* ☉ *Closed mid-Dec.–mid-Jan.* ⊗ *MAP.*

★ **$–$$$** ▦ **Fürberg.** If you drive down from Winkl to the northeastern corner of the Wolfgangsee (not far from a famous pilgrimage route used to get to St. Wolfgang), you'll leave the crowds of St. Wolfgang far behind and immerse yourself in the peace and scenic splendors of the mountains. To savor it all, this old inn in the typical Salzkammergut style offers a perfect perch. Flower-decorated balconies and bathing jetties, comfortable guest rooms in elegant dark-brown woods, an excellent breakfast buffet, and the elegant Stüberl restaurant (with a finely carved wooded ceiling) are some of the allures here. Fishing is possible, the use of rowboats free, and the kitchen may even do the honors in cooking up your afternoon haul. ■ **TIP→** For beautiful views of the lakeshore, take a 30-minute walk along the old pilgrim's route. ⊠ *A-5340* ☎ *06227/2385–0* 🖷 *06227/238535* ⊕ *www.fuerberg.at* ⤧ *25 rooms* ⚏ *Restaurant, fishing, bicycles; no a/c, no smoking* ⊟ *AE, DC, MC, V* ⊗ *FAP, MAP.*

Sports & Outdoor Activities

SKIING **Zwölferhorn** (⊠ *A-5340 St. Gilgen* ☎ *06227/2348* 🖷 *06227/72679* 🚡 Cable car round-trip €17, one-way €12 ☉ Daily 9–5 [9–6 July and Aug.]), reached via cable car, has two runs totaling 10 km (6 mi) for ski experts, and offers a ski school.

Fuschl

⑫ *8 km (5 mi) northwest of St. Gilgen, 30½ km (19 mi) east of Salzburg.*

Fuschl is so close to Salzburg that many attendees of the Salzburger Festspiele choose to stay in a hotel here, enjoying urban comforts while getting to savor rural pleasures at the same time. Located on Route 158, the town is on the Fuschlsee—a gem of a very clear, small (only 3-km-long [2-mi-long]), deep lake whose bluish-green water is ideal for swimming and windsurfing—surrounded by a nature preserve that was once the hunting domain of Emperor Franz Josef himself. There's not much to do in Fuschl, the beaches being very limited in number, though those willing to hike can reach an extremely narrow strip on the northern shore that is especially popular with nudists. The town is noted for its many good places to eat and spend the night, including Schloss Fuschl, one of the finest establishments in the Salzkammergut.

Where to Stay & Eat

$$–$$$$ ✕ **Brunnwirt.** You'll have to knock to be admitted, but once inside you'll find elegantly set tables in this atmospheric 15th-century house. Frau Brandstätter presides over a kitchen that turns out good-size portions of excellent Austrian and regional dishes. You might be offered game (in season) or roast lamb, always prepared with a light touch. Fish fresh from the lake is a regular specialty. ⊠ *Brunn 8* ☎ *06226/8236* 🖷 *06226/8236* ⚑ *Reservations essential* ☰ *AE, DC, MC, V* ⊘ *Closed Mon. No lunch except Sun. and during Salzburg Festival wks.*

\$\$\$\$
Fodor's Choice
★

✕▦ **Schloss Fuschl.** Once one of the most legendary hotels in Europe—guests with names like Roosevelt and Nehru were common—this dramatic 15th-century towerlike castle enjoys a spectacular, mountain-ringed perch atop a promontory over the Fuschlsee. Sixteen kilometers (10 mi) from Salzburg, this former hunting lodge for the Salzburg prince-archbishops is a top address for posh festivalgoers. The main structure remains imposingly fortresslike, but warmed up with quaint red-and-white shutters. Inside, finely frescoed ceilings, intriguing passageways lined with antique furniture, and a sumptuously outfitted restaurant make a haute Alpine splash. Guest rooms vary in size from the baronial to the surprisingly small. The suites and superior rooms are regally splendid, and though the standard rooms are more modern, most have spectacular views of the lake. In fine weather dining is outdoors on the magically beautiful stone terrace—whether a guest or not, be sure to splurge on a meal here. Opt for the trout caught in the lake (which is unpolluted by motorboats) and then delicately smoked in the smokehouse on the premises. The hotel presides over an 85-acre estate, replete with 9-hole golf course, sailing, and a gorgeous private beach and pier. ⊠ *A-5322 Hof bei Salzburg* ☎ *06229/2253–0* 🖷 *06229/2253–531* ⊕ *www. starwoodhotels.com/schlossfuschl* ⇗ *84 rooms* ⚐ *Restaurant, minibars, pool, Internet; no a/c* ☰ *AE, DC, MC, V* ¶◯¶ *MAP.*

DANUBE VALLEY/SALZKAMMERGUT ESSENTIALS

Transportation

BY AIR

The air hub of the Danube Valley is Linz, served by Austrian Airlines, Lufthansa, Swissair, and Tyrolean. Regular flights connect with Vienna, Amsterdam, Berlin, Düsseldorf, Frankfurt, Paris, Stuttgart, and Zürich. The Linz airport is in Hörsching, about 12 km (7½ mi) southwest of the city. Buses run between the airport and the main train station according to flight schedules.

The Salzkammergut is closer to Salzburg than to Linz, but ground transportation is such that there is little preference for one departure point over the other. The Salzburg airport is about 53 km (33 mi) from Bad Ischl, heart of the Salzkammergut; the Linz airport (Hörsching) is about 75 km (47 mi).

🛈 **Linz airport** ☎ 07221/600–0.

BY BOAT & FERRY

You can take a day trip from Vienna or Krems and explore one of the stops, such as Dürnstein or Melk. Boats run from May to late September. There are two boat companies that ply the Danube. For full information on cruises offered by the Blue Danube Schifffahrt/DDSG (Vienna to Dürnstein) and Brandner Schifffahrt (Krems to Melk), *see* Danube River Cruises *earlier in this chapter.*

Bridges across the river are few along this stretch, so boats provide essential transportation. There are a number of independent tow ferries that are attached to cables which stretch across the river. Service across the river for people, cars, and bikes is available for a small fee.

BY BUS

If you link them together, bus routes will get you to the main points in the Danube Valley and even to the hilltop castles and monasteries, assuming you have the time. If you coordinate your schedule to arrive at a point by train or boat, you can usually make reasonable bus connections to outlying destinations. The main bus route links Krems and Melk. You can book bus tours in Vienna or Linz by calling central bus information, listed below.

The main bus routes through the Salzkammergut are: Bad Aussee to Gründlsee; Bad Ischl to Gosau, Hallstatt, Salzburg, and St. Wolfgang; Mondsee to St. Gilgen and Salzburg; St. Gilgen to Mondsee; Salzburg to Bad Ischl, Mondsee, St. Gilgen, and Strobl.

🚌 Bus Information **Central bus information** ☎ 01/71101.

BY CAR

A car is certainly the most comfortable way to see this region, as it conveniently enables you to pursue the byways. The main route along the north bank of the Danube is Route 3; along the south bank, there's a choice between the autobahn Route A1 and a collection of lesser but good roads. Roads are good and well marked, and you can switch over to the A1 autobahn, which parallels the general east–west course of the Danube Valley route.

Driving is also by far the easiest and most convenient way to reach the Lake District; traffic is excessive only on weekends (although it can be slow on some narrow lakeside stretches). From Salzburg you can take Route 158 east to Fuschl, St. Gilgen, and Bad Ischl. Coming from Vienna or Linz, the A1 passes through the northern part of the Salzkammergut; get off at the Steyermühl exit or the Regau exit and head south on Route 144/145 to Gmunden and Bad Ischl. Remember: gasoline is expensive in Austria.

BY TRAIN

Rail lines parallel the north and south banks of the Danube. Fast services from Vienna run as far as Stockerau; beyond that, service is less frequent. The main east–west line from Vienna to Linz closely follows the south bank for much of its route. Fast trains connect German cities via Passau with Linz.

All the larger towns and cities in the region can be reached by train, but the train misses the Wachau Valley along the Danube's south bank. The rail line on the north side of the river clings to the bank in places; service is infrequent. You can combine rail and boat transportation along this route, taking the train upstream and crisscrossing your way back on the river.

The geography of the Salzkammergut means that rail lines run mainly north–south. Trains run from Vöcklabruck to Seewalchen at the top end of the Attersee and from Attnang-Puchheim to Gmunden, Bad Ischl, Hallstatt, Bad Aussee, and beyond. Both starting points are on the main east–west line between Salzburg and Linz.

🚩 Train Information **ÖBB–Österreichisches Bundesbahn** ☎ 05/1717 ⊕ www.oebb. at.

Contacts & Resources

EMERGENCIES

If you need a doctor and speak no German, ask your hotel how best to obtain assistance.

🚩 Emergency Services **Ambulance** ☎ 144. **Fire** ☎ 122. **Police** ☎ 133.

GUIDED TOURS

Tours out of Vienna take you to Melk and back by bus and boat. These tours usually run about eight hours, with a stop at Dürnstein. Bus tours operate year-round except as noted, but the boat runs only April–October.

Daylong tours of the Salzkammergut, offered by Dr. Richard/Albus/ Salzburg Sightseeing Tours and Salzburg Panorama Tours, whisk you all too quickly from Salzburg to St. Gilgen, St. Wolfgang, and Mondsee.

🚩 Fees & Schedules **Dr. Richard/Albus/Salzburg Sightseeing Tours** ⊠ Mirabellplatz 2, A-5020 Salzburg ☎ 0662/881616 🖷 0662/878776. **Salzburg Panorama Tours** ⊠ Schrannengasse 2/2, A-5020 Salzburg ☎ 0662/883211 🖷 0662/871628.

VISITOR INFORMATION

Most towns in these areas have their own *Fremdenverkehrsamt* (tourist office), which are listed below by town name.

🚩 Tourist Information **Bad Ischl** ⊠ Bahnhofstrasse 6, A-4820 ☎ 06132/277570 🖷 06132/27757-77 ⊕ www.badischl.at. **Dürnstein** ⊠ Rathaus, A-3601 ☎ 02711/200. **Gmunden** ⊠ Am Graben 2, A-4810 ☎ 07612/64305 🖷 07612/71410 ⊕ www. oberoesterreich.at/gmunden. **Klosterneuburg** ⊠ Rathausplatz 1, A-3400 ☎ 02243/34396 ⊕ www.klosterneuburg.net/tourismus. **Krems/Stein** ⊠ Undstrasse 6, A-3500 ☎ 02732/ 82676 🖷 02732/70011 ⊕ www.krems.at. **Melk** ⊠ Babenbergerstrasse 1, A-3390 ☎ 02752/ 52307-410 🖷 02752/52307-490. **St. Gilgen** ⊠ Mozartplatz 1, A-5340 ☎ 06227/2348 🖷 06227/7267-9 ⊕ www.wolfgangsee.at. **St. Wolfgang** ⊠ Au 140, A-5360 ☎ 06138/ 8003 🖷 06138/8003-81 ⊕ www.wolfgangsee.at. **Salzkammergut/Salzburger Land** ⊠ Wirerstrasse 10, A-4820 Bad Ischl ☎ 06132/26909-0 🖷 06132/26909-14 ⊕ www. salzkammergut.at. **Steyr** ⊠ Stadtplatz 27, A-4400 ☎ 07252/53229-0 🖷 07252/53229-15. **Wachau** ⊠ Schlossgasse 3, A-3620 Spitz an der Donau ☎ 02713/300-6015 🖷 02713/ 300-6030 ⊕ www.wachau.at.

Salzburg

WORD OF MOUTH

"And be SURE to have the peach soufflé at the Stiftskeller St. Peter (next to St. Peter's Church). It is the oldest restaurant in Austria (it dates to before AD 803)."   —cheribob

"Last time we were in Salzburg we took the cheesy but fun 'Sound of Music Tour.' We really enjoyed the day since they showed us places where they had filmed scenes around Salzburg, then took us out into the countryside to small towns that had different things to do with the movie."

—tomc

Updated by
Horst Erwin
Reischenböck

"ALL SALZBURG IS A STAGE," Count Ferdinand Czernin once wrote. "Its beauty, its tradition, its history enshrined in the grey stone of which its buildings are made, its round of music, its crowd of fancy-dressed people, all combine to lift you out of everyday life, to make you forget that somewhere far off, life hides another, drearier, harder, and more unpleasant reality." Shortly after the count's book, *This Salzburg,* was published in 1937, the unpleasant reality arrived; but having survived the Nazis, Salzburg once again became one of Austria's top drawing cards. Art lovers call it the Golden City of High Baroque; historians refer to it as the Florence of the North or the German Rome; and, of course, music lovers know it as the birthplace of one of the world's most beloved composers, Wolfgang Amadeus Mozart (1756–91). If the young Mozart was the boy wonder of 18th-century Europe and Salzburg did him no particular honor in his lifetime, it is making up for it now. Since 1920 the world-famous Salzburger Festspiele (Salzburg Festival), the third-oldest on the continent, have honored "Wolferl" with performances of his works by the world's greatest musicians. To see and hear them, celeb-heavy crowds pack the city from the last week in July until the end of August. Whether performed in the festival halls—the Grosses Festspielhaus, the "House for Mozart," and the Felsenreitschule, to name the big three—or outdoors with opulent Baroque volutes and pilasters of Salzburg's architecture as background, Mozart's music serves as the heartbeat of the city.

Ironically, many who come to this golden city of High Baroque may first hear the instantly recognizable strains of music from the film that made Salzburg a household name: from the Mönchsberg to Nonnberg Convent, it's hard to go exploring without hearing someone humming "How Do You Solve a Problem Like Maria?" A popular tourist exercise is to make the town's acquaintance by visiting all the sights featured in that beloved Hollywood extravaganza *The Sound of Music,* filmed here in 1964. Julie Andrews may wish it wasn't so, but one can hardly imagine taking in the Mirabell Gardens, the Pferdeschwemme fountain, Nonnberg Convent, the Residenzplatz, and all the other filmed locations without imagining Maria and the von Trapp children trilling their hearts out. Oddly enough, just like Mozart, the Trapp family—who escaped the Third Reich by fleeing their beloved country—were little appreciated at home; Austria was the only place on the planet where the film failed, closing after a single week's showing in Vienna and Salzburg. It is said that the Austrian populace at large didn't cotton to a prominent family up and running in the face of the Nazis, and even now, locals are amazed by *The Sound of Music*'s popularity around the world. Austrians are slowly warming up to the film; in 2005 Vienna's Volksoper premiered the first Austrian stage production of the Broadway musical. It may just be a matter of time before the Panorama and Salzburg Sightseeing bus tours of Salzburg's *SoM* sites are crammed with as many Austrians as Americans.

But whether it is the arias of Mozart or the ditties of Rodgers and Hammerstein, no one can deny music is the element that shapes the life of the city. It is heard everywhere: in churches, castles, palaces, town house courtyards, and, of course, concert halls. During the five weeks of the Salzburger Festspiele there are as many as 10 concerts a day (most sold out months in advance). If the Salzburger Festspiele remain one of the world's most stirring musical events, this is also due to their perfect setting. Salzburg lies on both banks of the Salzach River, at the point where it is pinched between two mountains, the Kapuzinerberg on one side, the Mönchsberg on the other. In broader view are many beautiful Alpine peaks. Added to these many gifts of Mother Nature, man's contribution is a trove of buildings worthy of such surroundings. Salzburg's rulers pursued construction on a grand scale ever since Wolf-Dietrich von Raitenau—the "Medici prince-archbishop who preached in stone"—began his regime in the latter part of the 16th century. At the age of only 28, Wolf-Dietrich envisioned "his" Salzburg to be the Rome of the Alps, with a town cathedral grander than St. Peter's, a Residenz as splendid as a Roman palace, and his private Mirabell Gardens flaunting the most fashionable styles of Italianate horticulture. He employed only Italian architects to realize his dreams. After he was deposed by the rulers of Bavaria—he was imprisoned (very elegantly, thank you) in the Hohensalzburg fortress—other cultured prince-archbishops took over. Johann Ernst von Thun and Franz Anton von Harrach dismissed the Italian artists and commanded the masters of Viennese Baroque, Fischer von Erlach and Lukas von Hildebrandt, to complete Wolf-Dietrich's vision. The result is that Salzburg's many fine buildings blend into a harmonious whole. Perhaps nowhere else in the world is there so cohesive a flowering of Baroque architecture.

But times change and the Salzburgians with them. Museums of contemporary art are springing up as fast as edelweiss across Austria, so it is not surprising to learn that Salzburg is now home to one of the most striking: the Museum der Moderne. The avant-garde showcase stands on the very spot where Julie Andrews "do-re-mi"-d with the von Trapp brood; where once the fusty Café Winkler stood atop the Mönchsberg mount, a modern, cubical museum of cutting-edge art now commands one of the grandest views of the city.

EXPLORING SALZBURG

Making the acquaintance of Salzburg is not too difficult, for most of its sights are within a comparatively small area. The Altstadt (Old City) is a compact area between the jutting outcrop of the Mönchsberg and the Salzach River. The cathedral and interconnecting squares surrounding it form what used to be the religious center, around which the major churches and the old archbishops' residence are arranged (note that entrance into all Salzburg churches is free). The rest of the Old City belonged to the wealthy burghers: the Getreidegasse, the Alter Markt (old market), the town hall, and the tall, plain burghers' houses (like Mozart's Birthplace). The Mönchsberg cliffs emerge unexpectedly behind the Old City, crowned to the east by the Hohensalzburg Fortress. Across the river, in the small area between the cliffs of the Kapuzinerberg and the riverbank, is Steingasse, a narrow medieval street where working people lived. Northwest of the Kapuzinerberg lie Mirabell Palace and

GREAT ITINERARIES

Numbers in the text correspond to numbers in the margin and on the Exploring Salzburg map.

IF YOU HAVE 1 DAY

Start at the **Mozartplatz** ❶, not just to make a pit stop at the tourist information office, but to sweeten your tour with a few Mozartkugeln from the nearby chocolate manufacturers Fürst. Flower-bedecked cafés beckon, as does the palatial **Residenz** ❹, home to the great prince-archbishops and the center of Baroque Salzburg. Nearby is the **Dom** ❺, Salzburg's grand 17th-century cathedral. Across the Domplatz is the Francescan church, the **Franziskanerkirche** ❽. A bit to the south is the Romanesque-turned-Rococo **Stiftkirche St. Peter** ❼, where, under the cliffs, you'll find the famous **Petersfriedhof** ❻—St. Peter's Cemetery, whose wrought-iron grills and Baroque vaults shelter the final resting place of Mozart's sister and much of Old Salzburg. Take the Festungsbahn cable car (it's just behind the cathedral) up to the **Fortress Hohensalzburg** ❿—the majestic castle atop the Mönchsberg peak that overlooks the city. Enjoy a rest at the Stadt Alm restaurant or picnic in a quiet corner. Descend back to the city via the Mönchsberg express elevators. Head over to the **Pferdeschwemme** ⑬—the Baroque horse trough that is a somewhat bewildering tribute to the equine race—then over to the **Getreidegasse**. In this venerable merchant's quarter, posh shops set in pastel-covered town houses announce their wares through the overhanging wrought-iron scroll signs, and some of the houses have hidden courtyards set with timber-lined balconies. Next up is the most famous address in town: No. 9 Getreidegasse–**Mozarts Geburtshaus** ⑰, the birthplace of Mozart. After paying your respects, head over to the **Alter Markt** ⑱ to welcome twilight with a *Kaffee mit Schlag* (coffee with whipped cream) at Café Tomaselli.

IF YOU HAVE 3 DAYS

With three days, you can explore the **Altstadt**—the Old City—and the **New Town** as described in the two walking tours below. Try to catch an evening concert—perhaps of Mozart's music. For your third day, try one of four options: book a *Sound of Music* **tour**, then, in the afternoon, take a ride up the **Untersberg**; or opt for a boat trip along the Salzach river south to the 17th-century Hellbrunn Palace with its mischievous water fountains; or take an excursion to the the picture-book towns of the **Salzkammergut** (*see* Chapter 6). A fourth idea is to walk for about two hours over the Mönchsberg, starting in the south at the **Nonnberg Convent** ⑳ and continuing on to the **Richterhöhe** to enjoy the southwestern area of the city. Above the Siegmundstor, the tunnel through the mountain, there is a nice belvedere to take in a city view. But the most fascinating view is from the terrace in front of the new **Museum der Moderne** ⑯, which you reach after passing the old fortifications from the 15th century. Continue on to the Augustinerbrä, the large beer cellar at the northern end of the hill for some of the best brews and conviviality in town.

its gardens, now an integral part of the city but formerly a country estate on the outskirts of Salzburg.

It's best to begin by exploring the architectural and cultural riches of the Old City, then go on to the fortress and after that cross the river to inspect the other bank. Ideally, you need two days to do it all. An alternative, if you enjoy exploring churches and castles, is to stop after visiting the Rupertinum and go directly up to the fortress, either on foot or by returning through the cemetery to the funicular railway.

■ TIP→ **If you are doing this spectacular city in just one day, there is a flip-book approach to Salzburg 101: take a walking tour run by city guides every day at 12:15 PM, setting out from the tourist information office, Information Mozart-platz, at Mozart Square (closed on some Sundays during off-season).** There are also escorted bus tours through the city. However, as much of Salzburg's historic city center is for pedestrians only, the bus doesn't get you close to some of the best sights.

The Altstadt: In Mozart's Footsteps

Intent on becoming a patron of the arts, the prince-archbishop Wolf-Dietrich lavished much of his wealth on rebuilding Salzburg into a beautiful and Baroque city in the late 16th and early 17th centuries. In turn, his grand townscape came to inspire the young Joannes Chrysostomus Wolfgangus Amadeus (Theophilus) Mozart. It is no surprise that there is no better setting for his music than the town in which he was born. For, in point of fact, growing up in the center of the city and composing minuets already at five years of age, Mozart set lovely Salzburg itself to music. He was perhaps the most purely Austrian of all composers, a singer of the smiling Salzburgian countryside, of the city's gay Baroque and Rococo architecture. So even if you are not lucky enough to snag a ticket to a performance of *The Marriage of Figaro* or *Don Giovanni* in the Grosses Festspielhaus, you can still enjoy his melodies just by strolling through his streets and, as critic Erich Kästner once put it, "seeing a symphony."

Ever since the 1984 Best Film Oscar-winner *Amadeus* (remember Tom Hulse as "Wolfie"?), the composer has been the 18th-century equivalent of a rock star. Born in Salzburg on January 27, 1756, he crammed a prodigious number of compositions into the 35 short years of his life, many of which he spent in Salzburg (he moved to Vienna in 1781). Indeed, the Altstadt (or Old Town) revels in a bevy of important sights, ranging from his birthplace on the Getreidegasse to the abbey of St. Peter's, where the composer's "Great Mass in C Minor" was first performed. Beyond the Altstadt—the heart of the Baroque Salzburg familiar to the young prodigy—other Mozart-related sights are included in our second Salzburg tour. As you tour the composer's former haunts, why not listen to Papageno woo Papagena on your iPod?

A GOOD WALK

For this city there is no more appropriate center-of-it-all than **Mozart-platz** ❶ ▶, the square named to honor Salzburg's native genius. Get in the mood by noticing, near the statue of Mozart, the strolling street violinists, who usually play a Mozart sonata or two. Walk into the next

TOP REASONS TO GO

The view from Fortress Hohensalzburg: Go up to the fortress on the peak and realize, what the already romantic visitors in the 19th century enjoyed so much—the soul-stirring combination of gorgeous architecture in a stunning natural location.

A pilgrimage to the Rome of the North: See the magnificent Baroque churches built not only to honor God but also to document of the importance of the ruling prince-archbishops during the 17th century.

Concerts, operas, and more: Feel the spirit of 1,300 years of musical history as you listen to the music of Wolfgang Amadeus Mozart, the greatest composer who ever lived, in the Marble Hall of Mirabell

Palace. Or perhaps you would prefer an opera performed by marionettes or a mass sung in the cathedral. You will run out of time, not options, in Salzburg.

Medieval city: After exploring the Altstadt's grand churches and squares, cross the river Salzach to take in the completely different atmosphere of the narrow, 16th-century Steingasse, where working people once lived and shops, galleries, and clubs now beckon.

Rulers' delights: Drive, bike, walk, or take the boat out to Schloss Hellbrunn, a Renaissance-inspired pleasure palace with trick fountains and the gazebo that witnessed so much wooing in *The Sound of Music.*

square, the Residenzplatz, centered by the 40-foot-high Court Fountain, which is often illuminated at night. Take in the famous **Glockenspiel** ❷ (chances are the tunes it plays will be by you-know-who), set atop the Neubau Palace, now the city's **Salzburg Museum** ❸—at this writing, the doors are scheduled to open officially in June 2007. Then cross the plaza to enter the **Residenz** ❹, the opulent Baroque palace of Salzburg's prince-archbishops and Mozart's patrons. From the Residenzplatz, walk through the arches into Domplatz, the city's majestic Cathedral Square—in August, set out with seats for the annual presentation of Hofmannsthal's play *Jedermann.* The **Dom** ❺ (Salzburg Cathedral) is among the finest Italian-style Baroque structures in Austria. Walk into the Kapitelplatz through the arches across the square and go through two wrought-iron gateways into **St. Peter's Cemetery** ❻—one of the most historic and beautiful places in Salzburg. Enter the church of **Stiftkirche St. Peter** ❼. Above the main entrance the Latin inscription reads: "I am the door—by me if any man enters here, he shall be saved." If it's nearing lunchtime, be sure to stop at the Stiftskeller St. Peter—so legendary a restaurant that the story has it Mephistopheles met Faust here.

As you leave St. Peter's, look up to the right to see the thin Gothic spire of the **Franziskanerkirche** ❽. Leave the courtyard in this direction, cross the road, and enter around the corner by the main entrance (the side one is closed). It will bring you into the Gothic apse crowned by the or-

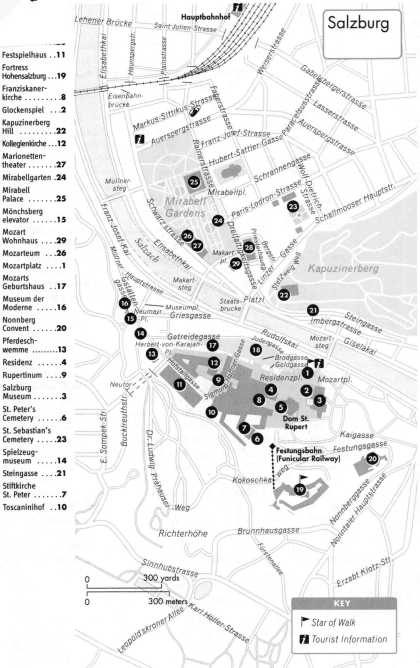

Salzburg

KEY

► *Star of Walk*

ℹ *Tourist Information*

nate red-marble altar designed by Fischer von Erlach. Return back up the Romanesque aisle and exit on Sigmund-Haffner-Gasse. Opposite is the rear entrance to one of Salzburg's galleries of contemporary art, the **Rupertinum** ⑨. Turn left around the corner into **Toscaninihof** ⑩, the square cut into the dramatic Mönchsberg cliff. The wall bearing the harp-shape organ pipes is part of the Haus für Mozart, one of three theaters that constitute the **Festspielhaus** ⑪. The carved steps going up the Mönchsberg are named for Clemens Holzmeister, architect of the new festival hall. If you climb them, you get an intimate view of the Salzburg churches at the level of their spires, and if you climb a little farther to the right, you can look down into the open-air festival hall, the Felsen-reitschule, cut into the cliffs. From Hofstallgasse—the main promenade (sometimes floodlighted and adorned with flags during the festival) connecting the main festival theaters—you can either walk directly up to Herbert-von-Karajan-Platz or, preferably, walk around by Universität-splatz to take a look at one of Johann Bernhard Fischer von Erlach's Baroque masterpieces, the **Kollegienkirche** ⑫, or Collegiate Church. In Herbert-von-Karajan-Platz is another point at which building and cliff meet: the **Pferdeschwemme** ⑬, a horse trough decorated with splendid Baroque-era paintings. To the left is the Siegmundstor, the impressive road tunnel blasted through the Mönchsberg in 1764. The arcaded Renaissance court on your left houses the **Spielzeugmuseum** ⑭ (Toy Museum), and a fine collection of ancient music instruments.

Pass by the tiny church of St. Blasius, built in 1350, and follow the road on through the Gstättentor to the **Mönchsberg elevator** ⑮ for a trip up the hill to Salzburg's most famous outlook, now the site of a large "white marble brick" (as critics carp), the **Museum der Moderne** ⑯, or Museum of Modern Art. After descending from the heights, turn left into the short street leading to Museumsplatz, where you could explore the Haus der Natur, one of the Europe's finest museums of natural history. Walk back toward the Blasius church, which stands at the beginning of the Old City's major shopping street, **Getreidegasse,** hung with numerous signs depicting little wrought-iron cobblers and bakers (few people could actually read centuries ago). Amid the boutiques and Salzburg's own McDonald's (featuring its own elegant sign) is **Mozarts Geburtshaus** ⑰, the celebrated composer's birthplace. Continue down the street past the Rathaus (Town Hall), and enter the **Alter Markt** ⑱, the old marketplace, adorned with historic buildings, including the Café Tomaselli (1703) and the Baroque Hofapotheke (prince-archbishop's court apothecary, 1591), still kept as it was back then. Finish up with some "I Was Here" photographs at the marble St. Florian's Fountain, then enjoy a finale back on Mozartplatz.

TIMING The Old City—the left bank of the Salzach River—contains many of the city's top attractions. Other than exploring by horse-drawn cabs (*Fi-akers*), available for rental at Residenzplatz, most of your exploring will be done on foot, since this historic section of town bans cars. The center city is compact and cozy, so you can easily cover it in one day. Note that many churches close at 6 PM, so unless you're catching a concert at one of them, be sure to visit them during the daylight hours.

Main Attractions

Alter Markt (Old Market). Right in the heart of the Old City is the Alter Markt, the old marketplace and center of secular life in past centuries. The square is lined with 17th-century middle-class houses, colorfully hued in shades of pink, pale blue, and yellow ocher. Look in at the old royal pharmacy, the **Hofapotheke,** whose incredibly ornate black-and-gold Rococo interior was built in 1760. Inside, you'll sense a curious apothecarial smell, traced to the shelves lined with old pots and jars (labeled in Latin). These are not just for show: this pharmacy is still operating today. You can even have your blood pressure taken—but preferably not after drinking a *Doppelter Einspänner* (black coffee with whipped cream, served in a glass) in the famous Café Tomaselli just opposite. In warm weather the café's terrace provides a wonderful spot for watching the world go by as you sip a *Mélange* (another coffee specialty, served with frothy milk), or, during the summer months, rest your feet under the shade of the chestnut trees in the Tomaselli garden at the top end of the square. Next to the coffeehouse you'll find the **smallest house in Salzburg,** now a crystal shop; note the slanting roof decorated with a dragon gargoyle. In the center of the square, surrounded by flower stalls, is the marble **St. Florian's Fountain,** dedicated in 1734 to the patron saint of firefighters.

★ ❺ **Dom** (Cathedral). When you walk through the arches leading from Residenzplatz into **Domplatz,** it is easy to see why Max Reinhardt chose it in August of 1920 as the setting for what has become the annual summer production of Hugo von Hofmannsthal's *Jedermann* (*Everyman*). The plaza is a complete, aesthetic concept and one of Salzburg's most beautiful urban set pieces. In the center rises the Virgin's Column, and at one side is the cathedral, considered to be the first early Italian Baroque building north of the Alps, and one of the finest. Its facade is of marble, its towers reach 250 feet into the air, and it holds 10,000 people (standing . . .). There has been a cathedral on this spot since the 8th century, but the present structure dates from the 17th century. The cathedral honors the patron saint of Salzburg, St. Rupert, who founded Nonnberg Abbey around 700, and also the Irish St. Virgil, the founder of the first cathedral consecrated in 774, whose relics lie buried beneath the altar. Archbishop Wolf-Dietrich took advantage of the old Romanesque-Gothic cathedral's destruction by fire in 1598 to demolish the remains and make plans for a huge new structure facing onto the Residenzplatz to reaffirm Salzburg's commitment to the Catholic cause. His successor, Markus Sittikus, and the new court architect, Santino Solari, started the present cathedral in 1614; it was consecrated with great ceremony in 1628 during the Thirty Years' War. The church's simple sepia-and-white interior, a peaceful counterpoint to the usual Baroque splendor, dates from a later renovation. To see remains of the old cathedral, go down the steps from the left-side aisle into the crypt where the archbishops from 1600 on are buried. Mozart's parents, Leopold and Anna-Maria, were married in this cathedral on November 21, 1747. Mozart was christened, the day after he was born, at the 14th-century font here, and he later served as organist from 1779 to 1781. Some of his compositions, such as the *Coronation Mass,* were written for the cathedral.

■ TIP→ **On Sunday and all catholic holidays, mass is sung at 10 AM—the most glorious time to experience the cathedral's full splendor.** This is the only house of worship in the world with no fewer than five independent fixed organs, which are sometimes played together during special church-music concerts. Many of the church's treasures are in a special museum on the premises. ⊠ *Domplatz* ☎ *0662/844189* 🖨 *0662/840442* ⊕ *www.kirchen.net/dommuseum* 💬 *Museum: €4.50* ◷ *Early May–late Oct., Mon.–Sat. 10–5, Sun. and holidays 1–6.*

★ **Getreidegasse.** As for centuries, this today is the main shopping street in the Old City center. According to historians, the name means "trade street"—not "grain street," as many people believe. Today it is the address of elegant fashion houses, international shoe chains, and a McDonald's (note its wrought-iron sign—one of many on the street—with classy bronze lettering: like all the other shops, it has conformed with Salzburg's strict Old City conservation laws). Other than coming to shop, crowds flock to this street because at No. 9 they'll find Mozart's birthplace, the **Mozarts Geburtshaus.** Needless to say, in summer the street is as densely packed with people as a corncob with kernels. You can always escape for a while through one of the many arcades—mostly flower-bedecked and opening into delightful little courtyards—that link the Getreidegasse to the river and the Universitätsplatz. At No. 37 you'll find one of the most glamorous hotels in the world, the Goldener Hirsch—just look for its filigree-iron sign showing a leaping stag with gilded antlers. ■ TIP→ **The Goldener Hirsch's interiors are marvels of Salzburgian gemütlichkeit so, if appropriately attired, you may wish to view the lobby and enjoy an aperitif in its gorgeous bar,** *the* **watering hole of chic Salzburg.** The southern end of Getreidegasse becomes Judengasse, part of the former Jewish ghetto area, which is also festooned with more of Salzburg's famous wrought-iron signs.

❷ **Glockenspiel** (Carillon). The famous carillon tower is perched on top of the **Neue Residenz** (New Residence), Prince-Archbishop Wolf-Dietrich's government palace. The carillon is a later addition, brought from today's Belgium in 1695 and finally put in working order in 1704. The 35 bells play classical tunes (usually by Mozart or Michael Haydn) at 7 AM, 11 AM, and 6 PM—with charm and ingenuity often making up for the occasional musical inaccuracy. From Easter to October, the bells are immediately followed by a resounding retort from perhaps the oldest mechanical musical instrument in the world, the 200-pipe "Bull" organ housed in the Hohensalzburg Fortress across town. Details about the music selections are listed on a notice board across the square on the corner of the Residenz building. ⊠ *Mozartplatz 1.*

⓯ **Mönchsberg Elevator.** Just around the corner from the Pferdeschwemme horse-fountain, at Neumayr Platz, you'll find the Mönchsberg elevator, which carries you up through solid rock not only to the new **Museum der Moderne** but also to wooded paths that are great for walking and gasping—there are spectacular vistas of Salzburg. In summer this can be a marvelous—and quick way—to escape the tiny crowded streets of the Old City. ⊠ *Gstättengasse 13* 💬 *Round-trip €2.90, one-way €1.80* ◷ *Open Oct.–May, daily 9–9; June–Sept., daily 9 AM–11 PM.*

⑯ Museum der Moderne. Enjoying one of Salzburg's most famous scenic spots, the dramatic museum of modern and contemporary art reposes atop the sheer cliff face of the Mönchsberg. The setting was immortalized in *The Sound of Music*—this is where Julie and the kids start warbling "Doe, a deer, a female deer . . ." Clad in minimalist white marble, the museum (2004) was designed by Friedrich Hoff Zwink of Munich. It has three exhibition levels, which bracket a restaurant with a large terrace—now, as always, the place to enjoy the most spectacular view over the city while sipping a coffee. ▓ TIP➔ **Visit in the evening to see the city illuminated.** The museum has an impressive calendar of temporary exhibitions of cutting-edge contemporary art. ⊠ *Mönchsberg 32* ☎ *0662/842220* ⊕ *www. museumdermoderne.at* ⊠ *€8* ☉ *Tues.–Sun. 10–6, Wed. 10–9.*

★ ④ Residenz. At the very heart of Baroque Salzburg, the Residenz overlooks the spacious Residenzplatz and its famous fountain. The palace in its present condition was built between 1600 and 1619 as the home of Wolf-Dietrich, the most powerful of Salzburg's prince-archbishops. The Kaisersaal (Imperial Hall) and the Rittersaal (Knight's Hall), one of the city's most regal concert halls, can be seen along with the rest of the magnificent **State Rooms** on a self-guided tour with headphones. Of particular note are the frescos by Johann Michael Rottmayr and Martino Altomonte depicting the history of Alexander the Great. Upstairs on the third floor is the **Residenzgalerie,** a princely art collection specializing in 17th-century Dutch and Flemish art and 19th-century paintings of Salzburg. On the state room floor, Mozart's opera *La Finta Semplice* was premiered in 1769 in the Guard Room. Mozart often did duty here, as, at age 14, he became the first violinist of the court orchestra (in those days, the leader, as there was no conductor). Today the reception rooms of the Residenz are often used for official functions, banquets, and concerts, and therefore might not always be open for visitors. The palace courtyard has been the lovely setting for Salzburg Festival opera productions since 1956—mostly the lesser-known treasures of Mozart. ⊠ *Residenzplatz 1* ☎ *0662/8042–2690, 0662/840451 art collection* ⊕ *www.residenzgalerie.at/* ⊠ *€7.30 for both museums; art collection only: €5* ☉ *Daily 10–5, closed 2 wks before Easter. Tours by arrangement. Art collection: daily 10–5, closed early Feb.–mid-Mar. and Wed., Oct.–Mar.*

③ Salzburg Museum (Neugebäude). The biggest "gift" to Mozart was the opening one day shy of his 250th birthday, when, on January 26, 2006, Salzburg's mammoth 17th-century **Neue Residenz** (New Residence) welcomed visitors after a year-long renovation to an exhibition entitled "Viva! Mozart." The setting is splendid, as this building was Prince-Archbishop Wolf-Dietrich's "overflow" palace (he couldn't fit his entire archiepiscopal court into the main Residenz across the plaza). As such, it features 10 state reception rooms that were among the first attempts at a *stil Renaissance* in the North. At this writing, the other wings of the building are closed but scheduled to reopen in June 2007, and to display the collections of the former Carolino-Augusteum Museum. These include Hallstatt Age relics, remains of the town's ancient Roman ruins, and the famous Celtic bronze flagon found earlier this century

Fodor'sChoice
★

on the Dürrnberg near Hallein (15 km [10 mi] south of Salzburg). The collection of Old Master paintings ranges from Gothic altarpieces to wonderful "view" paintings of 18th- and 19th-century Salzburg. Pride of place is given to the spectacular **Sattler Panorama,** one of the few remaining 360-degree paintings in the world, which shows the city of Salzburg in the early 19th century. Also here is the original composition of "Silent Night," composed by Franz Gruber and Josef Mohr in nearby Oberndorf in 1818. ⊠ *Mozartplatz 1* ☎ *0662/620808–200* 🖷 *0662/620808–220* ⊕ *www.smca.at* 🖼 *€8* ☉ *Mon.–Wed. and Fri.–Sun. 9–5, Thurs. 9–8.*

★ ❼ **Stiftkirche St. Peter** (Collegiate Church of St. Peter). The most sumptuous church in Salzburg, St. Peter's is where Mozart's famed *Great Mass in C Minor* premiered in 1783, with his wife, Constanze, singing the lead soprano role. Wolfgang often directed the orchestra and choir here, and also played its organ. During every season of the city's summer music festival in August, the *Great Mass in C Minor* is performed here during a special church music concert. The front portal of what was originally a Romanesque basilica dates from 1245. Inside, the low-ceiling aisles are charmingly painted in Rococo candy-box style. The porch has beautiful Romanesque vaulted arches from the original structure built in the 12th century; the interior was decorated in the characteristically voluptuous late-Baroque style when additions were made in the 1770s. Note the side chapel by the entrance, with the unusual crèche portraying the Flight into Egypt and the Massacre of the Innocents. Behind the Rupert Altar is the "Felsengrab," a rockface tomb where—according to a legend—St. Rupert himself was originally buried. To go from the sacred to the profane, head for the abbey's legendary Weinkeller restaurant, adjacent to the church. ⊠ *St. Peter Bezirk* ☎ *0662/844578–0* 🖼 *Free* ☉ *Apr.–Sept., daily 6:30 AM–7 PM; Oct.–Mar., daily 6:30 AM–6 PM.*

Also Worth Seeing

⓫ **Festspielhaus** (Festival Hall Complex). With the world-famous Salzburg Festival as their objective, music lovers head for the Hofstallgasse, the street where the three main festival theaters are located. Arrow-straight and framing a grand view of the Fortress Hohensalzburg, the street takes its name from the court stables once located here. Now, in place of the prancing horses, festival goers promenade along Hofstallgasse during the intervals of summer performances, showing off their suntans and elegant attire. ■ TIP→ **If you want to see the inside of the halls, it's best to go to a performance, but guided tours are given and group tours can be booked on request.** The festival complex consists of three theaters. The first is the new **Haus für Mozart** (House for Mozart). This was the former Kleines Festspielhaus, or Small Festival Hall. It now seats about 1,600 and is specially used for productions of Mozart's operas. The center ring is occupied by the famous **Grosses Festspielhaus** (Great Festival Hall, 1956–60), leaning against the solid rock of the Mönchsberg and opened in 1960, with a maximum stage width of 104 feet and a seating capacity of more than 2,150. In recent times the Grosses Festspielhaus, nicknamed the Wagner Stage because of its width (not to mention its headline-making productions of the *Ring of the Nibelungs*), has been the venue for spectacular productions of Modest Mussorgsky's *Boris Godunov* and Richard Strauss's *Der Rosenkavalier,* along with concerts by the world's most famous symphony orchestras. Stage directors are faced with the greatest challenge in the third theater, the **Felsenreitschule** (the Rocky Riding School), the former Summer Riding School, which—hewn out of the rock of the Mönchsberg during the 17th century by architect Fischer von Erlach—offers a setting that is itself more dramatic than anything presented on stage. Max Reinhardt made the first attempt at using the Summer Riding School for Salzburg Festival performances in 1926. With its retractable roof it gives the impression of an open-air theater; the three tiers of arcades cut into the rock of the Mönchsberg linger in the mind of fans of *The Sound of Music* film, for the von Trapps were portrayed as singing "Edelweiss" here in their last Austrian concert (according to Hollywood—in fact, this 1950 Festival farewell by the Trapp Family Singers, conducted by Franz Wasner, was given in the Mozarteum and at the cathedral square). The theaters are linked by tunnels (partially in marble and with carpeted floors) to a spacious underground garage in the Mönchsberg. ✉ *Hofstallgasse 1* ☎ *0662/849097* 🖨 *0662/847835* ⊕ *www.salzburgfestival.at* 🎫 *Guided tours: €5* ☉ *Group tour Jan.–May and Oct.–Dec. 20, daily at 2; June and Sept., daily at 2 and 3:30; July and Aug., daily at 9.30, 2, and 3:30.*

❽ Franziskanerkirche (Franciscan Church). The graceful, tall spire of the Franciscan Church stands out from all other towers in Salzburg; the church itself encompasses the greatest diversity of architectural styles. There was a church on this spot as early as the 8th century, but it was destroyed by fire. The Romanesque nave of its replacement is still visible, as are other Romanesque features, such as a stone lion set into the steps leading to the pulpit. In the 15th century the choir was rebuilt in Gothic style, then crowned in the 18th century by an ornate red-marble and gilt altar designed by Austria's most famous Baroque architect, Johann Bernhard Fischer von Erlach. Mass—frequently featuring one of Mozart's compositions—is celebrated here on Sunday at 9 AM. ✉ *Franziskanergasse 5* ☎ *0662/843629-0* 🎫 *Free* ☉ *Daily 6:30 AM–7 PM.*

⓬ Kollegienkirche (Kollegienkirche, or Collegiate Church). Completed by Fischer von Erlach in 1707, this church, sometimes called the Universitätskirche, is one of the purest examples of Baroque architecture in Austria. Unencumbered by Rococo decorations, the modified Greek cross plan has a majestic dignity worthy of Palladio. At this writing, the church was undergoing renovations. ✉ *Universitätsplatz* ☎ *0662/841–327–72* ☉ *Mon.–Sat. 9–7, Sun. 10–7 (winter closing hrs approximately 3 hrs earlier).*

❶ Mozartplatz (Mozart Square). In the center of the square stands the statue of Wolfgang Amadeus Mozart, a work by sculptor Ludwig Schwanthaler unveiled in 1842 in the presence of the composer's two surviving sons. It was the first sign of public recognition the great composer had received from his hometown since his death in Vienna in 1791. The statue, the first for a non-noble person in old Austria, shows a 19th-century stylized view of Mozart, draped in a mantle, holding a page of

Mozart: Marvel & Mystery

"MOZART IS SUNSHINE." So proclaimed Antonin Dvorak—and how better to sum up the prodigious genius of Wolfgang Amadeus Mozart (January 27, 1756–December 5, 1791)? Listening to his Rococo orchestrations, his rose-strewn melodies, and his insouciant harmonies, many listeners seem to experience the same giddiness as happiness. Scientists have found Mozart's music can cause the heart to pound, bring color to the cheeks, and provide the expansive feeling of being thrillingly alive. Yet, Mozart must have sensed how hard it is to recognize happiness, which is often something vaguely desired and not detected until gone. It is this melancholy undertow that makes Mozart modern. So modern that he is now the most popular classical composer, having banished Beethoven to second place. Shortly after *Amadeus* won the 1984 Oscar for Best Film—with its portrayal of Mozart as a giggling, foul-mouthed genius— *Don Giovanni* began to rack up more performances than *La Boheme*. The bewigged face graces countless "Mozartkugeln" chocolates, and Mostly Mozart festivals pay him homage. But a look behind the glare of the spotlights reveals that this blonde, slightly built tuning-fork of a fellow was a quicksilver enigma.

Already a skilled pianist at age three, the musical prodigy was dragged across Europe by his father Leopold to perform for empresses and kings. In a life that lasted a mere 35 years, he spent 10 on the road—a burden that contributed to making him the first truly *European* composer. Growing up in Salzburg, the *Wunderkind* became less of a *Wunder* as time went by. Prince-Archbishop Hieronymus von Colloredo enjoyed dissing his resident composer by commanding him to produce "table music" with the same, disdainful tone he commanded his chef's dinner orders. Being literally forced to sit with those cooks, Mozart finally rebelled. In March 1781 he married Constanze Weber and set out to conquer Vienna.

Hated by Mozart's father, Constanze is adored today, since we now know she was Mozart's greatest ally. Highly repressed by stuffy Salzburg, Mozart came to like his humor glandular (he titled one cantata "Kiss My XXX") and his women globular, a bill Constanze adequately filled. She no doubt heartily enjoyed the fruits of his first operatic triumph, the naughty *Abduction from the Seraglio* (1782). His next opera, *The Marriage of Figaro* (1786), to no one's surprise, bombed. Always eager to thumb his nose at authority, Mozart had adapted a Beaumarchais play so inflammatory in its depiction of aristos as pawns of their own servants, it soon helped ignite the French Revolution. In revenge, wealthy Viennese gave a cold shoulder to his magisterial *Don Giovanni* (1787). Mozart was relegated to composing, for a lowly vaudeville house, the now immortal *Magic Flute* (1790), and to ghosting a *Requiem* for a wealthy count. Sadly, his star only began to soar after a tragic, early death. But in company with fellow starblazers Vincent van Gogh and Marilyn Monroe, we assume he must be enjoying the last laugh.

–Robert I. C. Fisher

music and a copybook. A more appropriate bust of the composer, modeled by Viennese sculptor Edmund Heller, is found on the Kapuzinerberg. It contains the inscription *Jung gross, spät erkannt, nie erreicht*—"Great in youth, belatedly appreciated, never equaled."

⑰ Mozarts Geburtshaus (Mozart's Birthplace). As an adult, the great composer preferred Vienna to Salzburg, complaining that audiences in his native city were no more responsive than tables and chairs. Still, home is home, and this was Mozart's—when not on one of his frequent trips abroad—until the age of 17. Mozart was born on the third (in American parlance, the fourth) floor of this tall house, then owned by a family friend, one Johann Lorenz Hagenauer, on January 27, 1756, and the family lived on this floor, when they were not on tour, from 1747 to 1773. Like performing monkeys, the five- to seven-year-old Mozart and his slightly older sister were trotted around by their father to entertain the crowned heads of Europe for months at a stretch. Returning from the gilded splendor of royal palaces—not to say the archbishop's residence just across town—to this very modest domicile must have only whetted the young Mozart's taste for grandeur and fine living, which he managed to indulge to the utmost whenever he could afford to do so (not very often—he was a spendthrift).

As the child prodigy composed many of his first compositions in these rooms, it is fitting and touching to find Mozart's tiny first violin, his viola, and his clavicord on display. The second floor displays focus on the day-to-day living and traveling circumstances of his day, while the third floor has an exhibition called "Mozart on Stage." For the Mozart Year 2006, the American artist Robert Wilson redesigned the whole fourth floor. His sometimes surprising installation uses architecture, light, sound, and design objects with the intention of transforming the museum-like character of the apartment. Most of the rooms here are fitted out with modern museum vitrines and there is nothing extant from Mozart's time other than a cupboard on the landing of the fourth floor. ✉ *Getreidegasse 9* ☎ *0662/844313* ⊕ *www.mozarteum.at* ▧ *€6; combined ticket for Mozart residence and birthplace €9.50* ☉ *Sept.–June, daily 9–5:30; July and Aug., daily 9–6:30.*

⑬ Pferdeschwemme (Horse Pond). If Rome had fountains, so, too, would Wolf-Dietrich's Salzburg. The city is studded with them, and none is so odd as this monument to the equine race. You'll find it if you head to the western end of the Hofstallgasse to find Herbert-von-Karajan-Platz (named after Salzburg's second-greatest musical son, maestro Herbert von Karajan, the legendary conductor and music director of the Salzburg Festival for many decades and also founder of its Easter Festival in 1967, whose 100th birthday will be celebrated in 2008). On the Mönchsberg side of the square is the Pferdeschwemme—a royal trough where prize horses used to be cleaned and watered, constructed in 1695; as they underwent this ordeal they could delight in the frescoes of their pin-up fillies on the rear wall. The Baroque monument in the middle represents the antique legend of the taming of a horse, Bellerophon and his mount, Pegasus. ✉ *Herbert-von-Karajan-Platz.*

Rathaus (Town Hall). Where Sigmund-Haffner-Gasse meets the Getreidegasse you will find the Rathaus, a remarkably insignificant building in the Salzburg skyline—no doubt reflecting the historical weakness of the burghers vis-à-vis the Church, whose opulent monuments and churches are evident throughout the city. On the other hand, this structure is a prime example of the Italian influence in Salzburg's architecture, an influence that extends back to the city's merchant class. From their Salzburg perch, they sometimes handled a goodly portion of the Italian goods flowing from Venice to Germany. Originally this was a family tower (and the only one still remaining here), but it was then sold to the city in 1407. Its clock chimes every quarter hour. ⊠ *Getreidegasse and Sigmund-Haffner-Gasse.*

9 **Rupertinum.** If you are interested in 20th-century art, don't miss the chance to see changing exhibitions of paintings and graphic art on display in this gallery, now part and parcel of Salzburg's new **Museum der Moderne** (which you can spot, shining in white marble atop the Mönchsberg hill, from the Rupertinum's main entrance). ⊠ *Wiener-Philharmoniker-Gasse 9* ☎ *0662/8042–2336* ⊕ *www.rupertinum.at* ⊠ *€9* ⊗ *Sept.–mid-July, Tues. and Thurs.–Sun. 10–5, Wed. 10–9; mid-July–Aug., Thurs.–Tues. 10–6, Wed. 10–9.*

6 **St. Peter's Cemetery.** The eerie but intimate Petersfriedhof, or St. Peter's Cemetery, is the oldest Christian graveyard in Salzburg, in the present condition dating back to 1627. Enclosed on three sides by elegant wrought-iron grilles, Baroque arcades contain chapels belonging to Salzburg's old patrician families. The graveyard is far from mournful: the individual graves are tended with loving care, decorated with candles, fir branches, and flowers—especially pansies (because their name means "thoughts"). In Crypt XXXI is the grave of Santino Solari, architect of the cathedral; in XXXIX that of Sigmund Haffner, a patron for whom Mozart composed a symphony and named a serenade. The final communal crypt LIV (by the so-called "catacombs") contains the body of Mozart's sister Nannerl and the torso of Joseph Haydn's younger brother Michael (his head is now in his museum in St. Peter's). The cemetery is in the shadow of the Monchsberg mount; note the early Christian tombs carved in the rockface. ⊠ *St. Peter Bezirk* ☎ *0662/ 844578–0* ⊗ *Open daily dawn–dusk.*

14 **Spielzeugmuseum** (Toy Museum). On a rainy day this is a delightful diversion for both young and old, with a collection of dolls, teddy bears, model trains, and wooden sailing ships. At 3 on Tuesday, Wednesday, and the first Friday of the month, special Punch and Judy–style puppet shows are presented. Performance days change in the summer, so call ahead. The museum also has a collection of ancient instruments, including Michael Haydn's own fortepiano. ⊠ *Bürgerspitalplatz 2* ☎ *0662/ 620808–300* ⊕ *www.smca.at* ⊠ *€2.70* ⊗ *Daily 9–5.*

10 **Toscaninihof** (Arturo Toscanini Courtyard). The famous Italian maestro Arturo Toscanini conducted some of the Salzburg Festival's most legendary performances during the 1930s. Throughout the summer months the courtyard of his former festival residence is a hive of activity, with sets for the stage of the "House for Mozart" being brought in through the massive iron folding gates.

Wiener Philharmoniker-Gasse. Leading into Max-Reinhardt-Platz at the head of the grand Hofstallgasse, this street (once known as Marktgasse, or Market Street) was renamed after the world-famous Vienna Philharmonic Orchestra in recognition of the unique contribution it has made annually to the Salzburg Festival, playing for most opera productions and for the majority of orchestral concerts. ■ TIP→ **The street blooms with an open-air food market every Saturday morning; note that there is a fruit and vegetable market on Universitätsplatz every day except Sunday and holidays.**

Across the River Salzach: From the Fortress to the New Town

According to a popular saying in Salzburg, "If you can see the fortress, it's just about to rain; if you can't see it, it's already raining." Fortunately there are plenty of days when spectacular views can be had of Salzburg and the surrounding countryside from the top of this castle. Looking across the River Salzach to the Neustadt (New Town) area of historic Salzburg, you can pick out the Mirabell Palace and Gardens, the Landestheater, the Mozart Residence and the Mozarteum, the Church of the Holy Trinity, and the Kapuzinerkloster perched atop the Kapuzinerberg. Ranging from the "acropolis" of the city—the medieval Fortress Hohensalzburg—to the celebrated Salzburg Marionette Theater, this part of Salzburg encapsulates the city's charm. If you want to see the most delightful Mozart landmark in this section of town, the Zauberflötenhäuschen—the mouthful used to describe the little summerhouse where he finished composing *The Magic Flute*—it can be viewed when concerts are scheduled in the adjacent Mozarteum.

▶ A GOOD WALK

Start with Salzburg's number-one sight—especially at night, when it is spectacularly spotlit—the famed **Fortress Hohensalzburg** ⑲ ▶, the 11th-century castle that dominates the town. Take the Mönchsberg elevator or the Festungsbahn cable car on Festungsgasse, located behind the cathedral near St. Peter's Cemetery. If it's not running, you can walk up the zigzag path that begins a little farther up Festungsgasse; it's steep in parts but gives a better impression of the fortress's majestic nature. Once you've explored this, the largest medieval fortress in Central Europe, head back to the footpath, but instead of taking the steps back into town, turn right toward the **Nonnberg Convent** ⑳. Explore the church—the real Maria von Trapp almost found her calling here—then return along the path to the first set of steps, take them down into Kaigasse, and continue on to Mozartplatz. From here you can cross the Salzach River over the oldest extant footbridge in the city, Mozartsteg. Cross the road and walk west a minute or two along Imbergstrasse until you see a bookstore on the corner. Here a little street runs into **Steingasse** ㉑—a picturesque medieval street, and the old Roman street coming into town from the south. After exploring this "time machine," walk through the Steintor gate, past the chapel of St. Johann am Imberg to the Hettwer Bastion on the **Kapuzinerberg Hill** ㉒ for another great vista of the city.

Continue up the path to the Kapuziner-Kloster. From here, follow the winding road down past the stations of the cross. Turn right at the bottom of the road into Linzergasse, the New Town's answer to the Getreidegasse. Continue up this street to St. Sebastian's Church on the left. An archway will lead you into the tranquil **St. Sebastian's Cemetery** ㉓— if it looks somewhat familiar, that's because it inspired the scene at the end of *The Sound of Music,* where the von Trapps are nearly captured. When you leave the cemetery, walk north through a passageway until you reach Paris-Lodron-Strasse. To the left as you walk west down this street is the Loreto Church. At Mirabellplatz, cross the road to the **Mirabell Gardens** ㉔—the Pegasus Fountain (remember "Do-Re-Mi"?) and the Dwarfs' Garden are highlights here.

3

Take in Prince-Archbishop Wolf-Dietrich's private Xanadu, the adjacent **Mirabell Palace** ㉕ and its noted 18th-century Angel Staircase. Turn left out of the garden park onto busy Schwarzstrasse. Along this road you will find the famous center of Mozart studies, the **Mozarteum** ㉖, whose Great Hall is often the setting for chamber concerts (during which you can view the "Magic Flute" House in the nearby Bastionsgarten). Next door is the **Marionettentheater** ㉗—home to those marionettes known around the world. Turn left at the corner, around the Landestheater, and continue onto Makartplatz, dominated at the far end by Fischer von Erlach's **Dreifaltigkeitskirche** ㉘. Across from the Hotel Bristol is the second most-famous Mozart residence in the city, the **Mozart Wohnhaus** ㉙, where you can complete your homage to the city's hometown deity. Just to its right is the house where another famous Salzburger, the physicist Christian Doppler (remember the Doppler-effect), was born in 1803.

TIMING Allow half a day for the fortress, to explore it fully both inside and out. If you don't plan an intermission at one of the restaurants on the Mönchsberg, you can stock up on provisions at Fasties (Pfeifergasse 3, near Kajetanerplatz). Call the Mozarteum to see if there will be evening recitals in their two concert halls; hearing the *Haffner* or another of Mozart's symphonies could be a wonderfully fitting conclusion to your day.

Main Attractions

★ ☺ ⓲ **Fortress Hohensalzburg.** Founded in 1077, the Hohensalzburg is Salzburg's acropolis and the largest preserved medieval fortress in Central Europe. Brooding over the city from atop the Festungsberg, it was originally founded by Salzburg's Archbishop Gebhard, who had supported the pope in the investiture controversy against the Holy Roman Emperor. Over the centuries the archbishops gradually enlarged the castle, using it originally only sometimes as a residence, then as a siege-proof haven against invaders and their own rebellious subjects. The exterior may look grim, but inside there are lavish state rooms, such as the glittering **Golden Room,** the **Burgmuseum**—a collection of medieval art—and the **Rainer's Museum,** with its brutish arms and armor. Politics and Church are in full force here: there's a torture chamber not far from the exquisite late-Gothic **St. George's Chapel** (although, in fact, the implements on view came from another castle and were not used here). The 200-pipe organ from the beginning of the 16th century, played during the warmer months daily after the carillon in the Neugebäude, is best heard from a respectful distance, as it is not called "the Bull" without reason. ■ TIP→ **Climb up the 100 tiny steps to the Reckturm, a grand lookout post with a sweeping view of Salzburg and the mountains.** Children will love coming here, especially as some rooms of the castle are now given over to a special exhibitions, the **Welt der Marionetten,** which offers a fascinating view into the world of marionettes—a great preview of the treats in store at the nearby Marionettentheater.

To reach the fortress, walk up the zigzag path that begins just beyond the Stieglkeller on Festungsgasse. Note that you don't need a ticket to walk the footpath. The more-than-110-year-old **Festungsbahn** (funicular railway) (✉ Festungsgasse 4 ☎ 0662/842682 ⊕ www.festungsbahn. at ⊙ Every 10 min Oct.–Mar., daily 9–5; May–Sept., daily 9–9) is the easy way up (advisable with young children). It is behind St. Peter's Cemetery. A round-trip pass including the entrance fee to all the museums in the fortress is €9.50, and a one-way ticket down is €2.10.

Remember that visitor lines to the fortress can be long, so try to come early. ✉ *Fortress Hohensalzburg, Mönchsberg 34* ☎ *0662/842430–11* ⊕ *www.salzburg-burgen.at* ✆ *Fortress including all museums €6.90* ⊙ *Mid-Mar.–mid-June, daily 9–6; mid-June–mid-Sept., daily 8:30–8; mid-Sept.–mid-Mar., daily 9–5.*

㉒ **Kapuzinerberg Hill.** Directly opposite the Mönchsberg on the other side of the river, Kapuzinerberg Hill is crowned by several interesting sights. By ascending a stone staircase near Steingasse 9 you can start your climb up the peak. At the top of the first flight of steps is a tiny chapel, **St. Johann am Imberg,** built in 1681. Farther on are a signpost and gate to the **Hettwer Bastion,** part of the old city walls. ■ TIP→ **Hettwer Bastion is one of the most spectacular viewpoints in Salzburg.** At the summit is the gold-beige **Kapuzinerkloster** (Capuchin Monastery), originally a fortification built to protect the one bridge crossing the river, which dates from the time of Prince-Archbishop Wolf-Dietrich. It is still an active monastery and thus cannot be visited (except for the church). The road downward—note the Stations of the Cross along the path—is called Stefan Zweig Weg, after the great Austrian writer who rented the **Paschingerschlössl** house (on the Kapuzinerberg to the left of the monastery) until 1934, when he left Austria after the Nazis had murdered chancellor Dollfuss. As he was one of Austria's leading critics and esthetes, his residence became one of the cultural centers of Europe.

★ ⟳ ㉗ **Marionettentheater** (Marionette Theater). The Salzburger Marionettentheater is both the world's greatest marionette theater and—surprise!—a sublime theatrical experience. Many critics have noted that viewers quickly forget the strings controlling the puppets, which assume lifelike dimensions and provide a very real dramatic experience. The Marionettentheater is identified above all with Mozart's operas, which seem particularly suited to the skilled puppetry; a delightful production of *Così fan tutte* captures the humor of the work better than most stage versions. The theater itself is a Rococo concoction. The company is famous for its world tours, but is usually in Salzburg around Christmas, during the late-January Mozart Week, at Easter, and from M ber (schedule subject to change). ⊠ *Schwarzstrasse 24* ☎ *0(🖨 0662/882141* ⊕ *www.marionetten.at* 🎫 *€18–€35 Mon.–Sat. 9–1 and 2 hrs before performance; Salzburg sea Christmas, Mozart Week (Jan.), Easter.*

🐾 **24** **Mirabellgarten** (Mirabell Gardens). While there are at least four entrances to the Mirabell Gardens—from the Makartplatz (framed by the statues of Roman gods), the Schwarzstrasse, and the Rainerstrasse—you'll want to enter from the Rainerstrasse and head for the Rosenhügel (Rosebush Hill): you'll arrive at the top of the steps where Julie Andrews and her seven charges showed off their singing ability in *The Sound of Music*. This is also an ideal vantage point from which to admire the formal gardens and one of the best views of Salzburg, as it shows how harmoniously architects of the Baroque period laid out the city. The center of the gardens—one of Europe's most beautiful parks, partly designed by Fischer von Erlach as the grand frame for the Mirabell Palace—is dominated by four large groups of statues representing the elements water, fire, air, and earth, and designed by Ottavio Mosto, who came to live in Salzburg from Padua. A bronze version of the horse Pegasus stands in front of the south facade of the palace in the center of a circular water basin. The most famous part of the Mirabell Gardens is the **Zwerglgarten** (Dwarfs' Garden), which can be found opposite the Pegasus fountain. Here you'll find 12 statues of "Danubian" dwarves sculpted in marble—the real-life models for which were presented to the bishop by the landgrave of Göttweig. Prince-Archbishop Franz Anton von Harrach had the stone figures made for a kind of stone theater below. The **Heckentheater** (Hedge Theater) is an enchanting natural stage setting that dates from 1700. The Mirabell Gardens are open daily 7 AM–8 PM. Art lovers will make a beeline for the **Barockmuseum** (⊠ Orangeriegarten ☎ 0662/877432), beside the Orangery of the Mirabell Gardens. It houses a collection of late-17th- and 18th-century paintings, sketches, and models illustrating the extravagant vision of life of the Baroque era— the signature style of Salzburg. Works by Giordano, Bernini, and Rottmayr are the collection's highlights. The museum is open Tuesday to Saturday, 9 to noon and 2 to 5, and Sunday and holidays 10 to 1; admission is €3.

25 **Mirabell Palace.** The "Taj Mahal of Salzburg," Schloss Mirabell was built in 1606 by the immensely wealthy and powerful Prince-Archbishop Wolf-Dietrich for his mistress, Salomé Alt, and their 15 children. It was originally called Altenau in her honor. Such was the palace's beauty that it was taken over by succeeding prince-archbishops, including Markus Sittikus (who renamed the estate), Paris Lodron, and finally, Franz Anton von Harrach, who brought in Lukas von Hildebrandt to give the place a Baroque facelift in 1727. A disastrous fire hit in 1818, but happily, three of the most spectacular set-pieces of the palace—the Chapel, the Marble Hall, and the Angel Staircase—survived. The Marble Hall is now used for civil wedding ceremonies, and is regarded as the most beautiful registry office in the world. Its marble floor in strongly contrasting colors and its walls of stucco and marble ornamented with elegant gilt scrollwork are splendid. The young Mozart and his sister gave concerts here, and he also composed *Tafelmusik* (Table Music) to accompany the prince's meals. ■ TIP➔ **Candlelight chamber music concerts in the Marble Hall provide an ideal combination of performance and atmosphere.** Beside the chapel in the north-east-corner, the only other part of the palace to survive the fire was the magnificent marble Angel Staircase, laid out by von Hildebrandt, with sculptures by Georg Rafael Donner. The staircase is romantically draped with white marble putti, whose faces and gestures reflect a multitude of emotions, from questioning innocence to jeering mockery. The very first putto genuflects in an old Turkish greeting (a reminder of the Siege of Vienna in 1683). Outdoor concerts are held at the palace and gardens May though August, Sunday mornings at 10:30 and Wednesday evenings at 8:30. ✉ *Off Makartplatz* ☎ *0662/889–87-330* ✆ *Free* ☉ *Weekdays 8–6.*

★ ☾ ㉙ **Mozart Wohnhaus** (Mozart Residence). The Mozart family moved from their cramped quarters in Getreidegasse to this house on the Hannibal Platz, as it was then known, in 1773. Wolfgang Amadeus Mozart lived here until 1780, his sister Nannerl stayed here until she married in 1784, and their father Leopold lived here until his death in 1787. The house is accordingly referred to as the Mozart Residence, signifying that it was not only Wolfgang who lived here. During the first Allied bomb attack on Salzburg in October 1944, the house was partially destroyed, but was reconstructed in 1996. Mozart composed the "Salzburg Symphonies" here, as well as all five violin concertos, church music and some sonatas, and parts of his early operatic masterpieces, including *Idomeneo*. Besides an interesting collection of musical instruments (for example, his own pianoforte), among the exhibits on display are books from Leopold Mozart's library. Autograph manuscripts and letters can be viewed, by prior arrangement only, in the cellar vaults. One room offers a multimedia show and wall-size map with more personal details about Mozart, like his numerous travels across Europe. Another salon has been decorated in the domestic decor of Mozart's day. ✉ *Makartplatz 8* ☎ *0662/874227–40* 🖷 *0662/872924* ⊕ *www.mozarteum.at* ✆ *Mozart residence €6, combined ticket for Mozart residence and birthplace €9.50* ☉ *Sept.–June, daily 9–5:30; July and Aug., daily 9–6:30.*

❷⓿ **Nonnberg Convent.** Just below the south side of the Fortress Hohensalzburg—and best visited in tandem with it—the Stift Nonnberg was founded right after 700 by St. Rupert, and his niece St. Erentrudis was the first abbess (in the archway a late-Gothic statue of Erentrudis welcomes the visitor). ■ TIP➔ **Spend the extra €.50 to illuminate the frescos just below the steeple. They are some of the oldest in Austria, painted in the Byzantine style during the 10th century.** The church is more famous these days as "Maria's convent"—both the one in *The Sound of Music* and that of the real Maria. She returned to marry her Captain von Trapp here in the Gothic church (as it turns out, no filming was done here— "Nonnberg" was re-created in the film studios of Salzburg-Parsch). Each evening in May at 7 the nuns sing a 15-minute service called Maiandacht in the old Gregorian chant. Their beautiful voices can be heard also at the 11 PM mass on December 24. Parts of the private quarters for the nuns, which include some lovely, intricate woodcarving, can be seen by prior arrangement. ⊠ *Nonnberggasse 2* ☎ *0662/841607–0* ✆ *Fall–spring, daily 7–5; summer, daily 7–7.*

★ ㉓ **St. Sebastian's Cemetery.** Memorably recreated for the escape scene in *The Sound of Music* on a Hollywood soundstage, final resting place for many members of the Mozart family, and situated in the shadows of St. Sebastian's Church, the Friedhof St. Sebastian is one of the most peaceful spots in Salzburg. Prince-Archbishop Wolf-Dietrich commissioned the cemetery in 1600 to replace the old cathedral graveyard, which he planned to demolish. It was built in the style of an Italian *campo santo,* (sacred field) with arcades on four sides, and in the center of the square he had the Gabriel Chapel, an unusual, brightly tiled Mannerist mausoleum, built for himself, in which he was interred in 1617 (now closed for visitors). Several famous people are buried in this cemetery, including the medical doctor and philosopher Theophrastus Paracelsus, who settled in Salzburg in the early 16th century (his grave is by the church door). Around the chapel is the grave of Mozart's widow, Constanze, her second husband, Georg Nikolaus Nissen, and probably also the one of Genoveva Weber, the aunt of Constanze and the mother of Carl Maria von Weber (by the central path leading to the mausoleum). According to the latest research, Mozart's father Leopold came to rest in the unmarked community grave here, too. If the gate is closed, enter through the back entrance around the corner in the courtyard. ⊠ *Linzergasse* ✆ *Daily 9 ᴀᴍ–6 ᴘᴍ.*

㉑ **Steingasse.** This narrow medieval street, walled in on one side by the bare cliffs of the Kapuzinerberg, was originally the ancient Roman entrance into the city from the south. The houses stood along the riverfront before the Salzach was regulated. Nowadays it's a fascinating mixture of artists' workshops, antiques shops, and trendy nightclubs, but with its tall houses the street still manages to convey an idea of how life used to be in the Middle Ages. The **Steintor** marks the entrance to the oldest section of the street; here on summer afternoons the light can be particularly striking. House No. 23 on the right still has deep, slanted peep-windows for guarding the gate. House No. 31 is the birthplace of Josef Mohr, the poet of "Silent Night, Holy Night" fame (not No. 9, as is incorrectly noted on the wall).

Also Worth Seeing

㉘ **Dreifaltigkeitskirche** (Church of the Holy Trinity). The Makartplatz—named after Hans Makart, the most famous Austrian painter of the mid-19th-century—is dominated at the top (east) end by Fischer von Erlach's first architectural work in Salzburg, built 1694–1702. It was modeled on a church by Borromini in Rome and prefigures von Erlach's Karlskirche in Vienna. Dominated by a lofty, oval-shape dome—which showcases a painting by Michael Rottmayr—this church was the result of the archbishop's concern that Salzburg's new town was developing in an overly haphazard manner. The church interior is small but perfectly proportioned, surmounted by its dome, whose trompe-l'oeil fresco seems to open up the church to the sky above. ⊠ *Dreifaltigkeitsgasse 14* ☎ *0662/877495* ✆ *Mon.–Sat. 6:30–6:30, Sun. 8–6:30.*

"Oh, the Hills Are Alive . . ."

FEW SALZBURGERS WOULD PUBLICLY ADMIT IT, but *The Sound of Music*, Hollywood's interpretation of the trials and joys of the local Trapp family, has become their city's most eminent emissary when it comes to international promotion. The year after the movie's release, international tourism to Salzburg jumped 20%, and soon *The Sound of Music* was a Salzburg attraction.

Perhaps the most important *Sound* spin-offs are the **tours** offered by several companies (for a number of them, *see* Tour Options *in* Salzburg Essentials, *below*). Besides showing you some of the film's locations (usually very briefly), these four-hour rides have the advantage of giving a very concise tour of the city. The buses generally leave from Mirabellplatz; lumber by the "Do-Re-Mi" staircase at the edge of the beautifully manicured Mirabell Gardens; pass by the hardly visible Aigen train station, where in reality the Trapps caught the escape train; and then head south to Schloss Anif. This 16th-century water castle, which had a cameo appearance in the opening scenes of the film, is now in private hands and not open to the public.

First official stop for a leg-stretcher is at the gazebo in the manicured park of Schloss Hellbrunn at the southern end of the city. Originally built in the gardens of Leopoldskron Palace, it was brought out here to give the chance for taking pictures. This is where Liesl von Trapp sings "I Am Sixteen Going on Seventeen" and where Maria and the Baron woo and coo "Something

Good." The simple little structure is the most coveted prize of photographers. The bus then drives by other private palaces with limited visiting rights, Schloss Frohnburg and Schloss Leopoldskron, with its magical watergate terrace, adorned with rearing horse sculptures and "site" of so many memorable scenes in the movie. The bus continues on to Nonnberg Convent at the foot of the daunting Hohensalzburg fortress, then leaves the city limits for the luscious landscape of the Salzkammergut. You get a chance for a meditative walk along the shore of the Wolfgangsee in St. Gilgen before the bus heads for the pretty town of Mondsee, where, in the movie, Maria and Georg von Trapp were married at the twin-turreted Michaelerkirche.

Tour guides are well trained and often have a sense of humor, with which they gently debunk myths about the movie. Did you know, for example, that Switzerland was "moved" 160 km (100 mi) eastward so the family could hike over the mountains to freedom (while singing "Climb Every Mountain")? It all goes to show that in Hollywood, as in Salzburg and its magical environs, almost anything is possible.

For something different, try the **Sternbräu Dinner Theater** (✉ Griesgasse 23 ☎ 0662/826617). Their dinner show features those unforgettable songs from the movie, as well as traditional folksongs from Salzburg and a medley of Austrian operettas. The cost of the dinner show is €43; without dinner it's €31.

Mozart Audio and Video Museum. In the same building as the Mozart Wohnhaus (Residence) is the Mozart Audio and Video Museum, an archive of thousands of Mozart recordings as well as films and video productions, all of which can be listened to or viewed on request. ✉ *Makartplatz 8* ☎ *0662/883454* ⊕ *www.mozarteum.at* ▧ *Free* ⊘ *Mon., Tues., and Fri. 9–1, Wed. and Thurs. 1–5.*

㉖ Mozarteum. Two institutions share the address in this building finished just before World War I—the International Foundation Mozarteum, set up in 1870, and the University of Music and Performing Arts, founded in 1880. Scholars come here to research in the **Bibliotheca Mozartiana,** the world's largest Mozart library (for research only and therefore not open to public). The Mozarteum also organizes the annual Mozart Week festival in January. Many important concerts are offered from October to June in its two recital halls, the Grosser Saal (Great Hall) and the Wiener Saal (Vienna Hall).

Behind the Mozarteum, sheltered by the trees of the Bastiongarten, is the famous **Zauberflötenhäuschen**—the little summerhouse where Mozart finished composing *The Magic Flute* in Vienna, with the encouragement of his frantic librettist, Emanuel Schikaneder, who finally wound up locking the composer inside to force him to complete his work. The house was donated to the Mozarteum by Prince Starhemberg. It is much restored: back in the 19th century, the faithful used to visit it and snatch shingles off its roof. The house can generally be viewed only when concerts are offered in the adjacent Grosser Saal. ✉ *Schwarzstrasse 26* ☎ *0662/88940–21* ⊕ *www.mozarteum.at* ⊘ *Summerhouse: only during Grosser Saal concerts.*

Short Side Trips from Salzburg

Gaisberg and Untersberg. Salzburg's "house mountains" are so-called because of their proximity to the city settlements. You can take the bus to the summit of the Gaisberg, where you'll be rewarded with a spectacular panoramic view of the Alps and the Alpine foreland. In summer Dr. Richard/Albus bus (☎ 0662/424–000–0) leaves from Mirabellplatz at 10, noon, 2, and 5:15, and the journey takes about a half hour. The Untersberg is the mountain Captain von Trapp and Maria climbed as they escaped the Nazis in *The Sound of Music.* In the film they were supposedly fleeing to Switzerland; in reality, the climb up the Untersberg would have brought them almost to the doorstep of Hitler's retreat at the Eagle's Nest above Berchtesgaden. A cable car from St. Leonhard (about 13 km [8 mi] south of Salzburg) takes you up 6,020 feet right to the top of the Untersberg, giving you a breathtaking view. In winter you can ski down (you arrive in the village of Fürstenbrunn and taxis or buses take you back to St. Leonhard); in summer there are a number of hiking routes from the summit. ✉ *Untersbergbahn* ☎ *06246/72477.0* ⊕ *www.untersberg.net* ▧ *Round-trip €18* ⊘ *Mid-Dec.–Feb., daily 10–4; Mar.–June and Oct., daily 9–5; July–Sept., daily 8:30–5:30.*

Hallein. The second-largest town of the region, 15 km (10 mi) south of Salzburg, Hallein was once famed for its caves of "white gold"—salt.

Centuries ago, salt was often used as payment; Roman soldiers received a certain quantity: that's where the word "salary" comes from. Salt was converted into hard cash to finance the construction of Salzburg's Baroque monuments by the prince-archbishops. It was especially prized because it was used to smoke (or salt) meat and preserve it long before the days of refrigerators. "Hall" is the old Celtic word for salt, and this treasure was mined in the neighboring Dürrnberg mountain. To learn all about Hallein, head to the **Keltenmuseum** (Museum of the Celts; ✉ Pflegerplatz 5 ☎ 06245/80783 🖙 €4), where more than 30 rooms explore the history of the region's Celtic settlements (before the birth of Christ). In the three staterooms more than 70 oil paintings show the working conditions of the salt mines and the salina. You can get to Hallein by regular bus system, by car along the B159 Salzachtal-Bundesstrasse, or by bicycle along the River Salzach. Once in Hallein, you can pay your respects to Franz Gruber, the composer of "Silent Night, Holy Night," who lies in the only grave still extant next to the town's parish church.

> ### BICYCLING
>
> As most Salzburgers know, one of the best and most pleasurable ways of getting around the city and the surrounding countryside is by bicycle. Bikes can be rented, and local bookstores have maps of the extensive network of cycle paths. The most delightful ride in Salzburg? The **Hellbrunner Allee** from Freisaal to Hellbrunn Palace is a pleasurable run, taking you past Frohnburg Palace and a number of elegant mansions on either side of the tree-lined avenue. The more adventurous can go farther afield, taking the **Salzach cycle path** north to the village of Oberndorf, or south to Golling and Hallein. For rental places, *see* Salzburg Essentials, *below*.

Oberndorf. This little village 21 km (13 mi) north of Salzburg has just one claim to fame: it was here on Christmas Eve, 1818, that the world-famous Christmas carol "Silent Night, Holy Night," composed by the organist and schoolteacher Franz Gruber to a lyric by the local priest, Josef Mohr, was sung for the first time. The church was demolished and replaced in 1937 by a tiny commemorative chapel containing a copy of the original composition (the original is in the Museum Salzburg), stained-glass windows depicting Gruber and Mohr, and a Nativity scene. ■ TIP→ **Every December 24 at 5 PM, a traditional performance of the carol—two male voices plus guitar and choir—in front of the chapel is the introduction to Christmas.** About a 10-minute walk from the village center along the riverbank, the local **Heimatmuseum** (✉ Stille-Nacht-Platz 7 ☎ 06272/4422–0), opposite the chapel, documents the history of the carol. The museum is open daily 9–noon and 1–5; admission is €2.50. You can get to Oberndorf by the local train (opposite the main train station), by car along the B156 Lamprechtshausener Bundesstrasse, or by bicycle along the River Salzach.

⏱ **Schloss Hellbrunn** (Hellbrunn Palace). Just 6½ km (4 mi) south of Salzburg,
Fodor'sChoice the Lustschloss Hellbrunn was the prince-archbishops' pleasure palace.
★ It was built early in the 17th century by Santino Solari for Markus Sittikus, after the latter had imprisoned his uncle, Wolf-Dietrich, in the fortress. The castle has some fascinating rooms, including an octagonal music room and a banquet hall with a trompe-l'oeil ceiling. From the magnificent gardens and tree-lined avenues to the silent ponds, Hellbrunn Park is often described as a jewel of landscape architecture. It became famous far and wide because of its **Wasserspiele,** or trick fountains: in the formal gardens, a beautiful example of the Mannerist style including a later-added outstanding mechanical theater, some of the exotic and humorous fountains spurt water from strange places at unexpected times—you will probably get doused (bring a raincoat). A visit to the gardens is highly recommended: nowhere else can you experience so completely the realm of fantasy that the grand Salzburg archbishops indulged in. The **Monatsschlösschen,** the old hunting lodge (built in one month), contains an excellent folklore museum. Following the path over the hill you find the **Steintheater** (Stone Theater), an old quarry made into the earliest open-air opera stage north of the Alps. The former palace deer park has become a **zoo** featuring free-flying vultures and Alpine animals that largely roam unhindered. You can get to Hellbrunn by Bus 20, by car on Route 159, or by bike or on foot along the beautiful Hellbrunner Allee past several 17th-century mansions. On the estate grounds is the little gazebo filmed in *The Sound of Music* ("I am 16 . . . ")—the doors are now locked because a person once tried to repeat the movie's dance steps, leaping from bench to bench, and managed to fall and break a hip. ⊠ *Fürstenweg 37, Hellbrunn* ☎*0662/820372* ⊕*www.hellbrunn.at* 🖅*Tour of palace and water gardens €8.50* ☉ *Apr. and Oct., daily 9–4:30; May–Sept., daily 9–5:30; evening tours July and Aug., daily on the hr 6–10.*

Schloss Frohnburg (Frohnburg Palace). Only walkers and bikers can pass by this charming little yellow building from the 17th century along the Hellbrunner Allee, the old road that leads out to Schloss Hellbrunn at the southern end of the city. Producer Robert Wise chose this palace as the front and also the back of Baron van Trapp's house in *The Sound of Music*—from here they set out on their first attempt to escape. The house belongs to the University of Music and Performing Arts "Mozarteum" (closed to public) and contains the **Orff Institute,** named after the great Bavarian composer Carl Orff. He developed the "Orff Schoolwork," a special musical training method for children, which has its central headquarters here.

WHERE TO EAT

Salzburg has some of the best—and most expensive—restaurants in Austria, so if you happen to walk into one of the Altstadt posheries without a reservation, you may get a sneer worthy of Captain von Trapp. Happily, the city is plentifully supplied with pleasant eateries, offering not only good, solid Austrian food (not for anyone on a diet), but also exceptional Italian dishes and newer-than-now *neue Küche* (nouvelle cui-

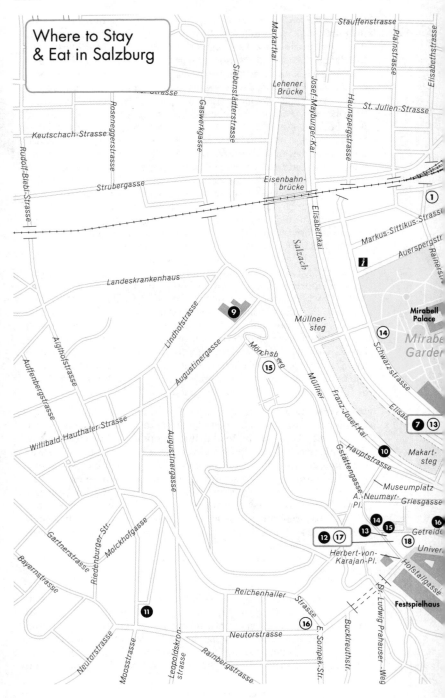

Where to Stay
& Eat in Salzburg

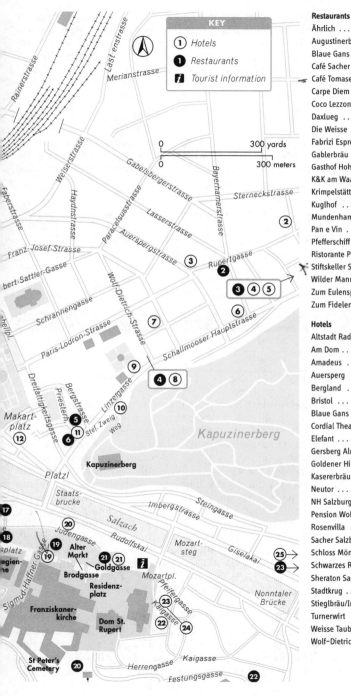

sine) delights. There are certain dining experiences that are quintessentially Salzburgian, including restaurants perched on the town's peaks that offer "food with a view"—in some cases, it's too bad the food isn't up to the view—or rustic inns that offer "Alpine evenings" with entertainment. Some of the most distinctive places in town are the fabled hotel restaurants, such as those of the Goldener Hirsch or the "Ratsherrenkeller" of the Hotel Elefant (⇨ Where to Stay).

For fast food, Salzburgers love their broiled-sausages street-stands. Some say the most delicious are to be found at the Balkan Grill at Getreidegasse 33 (its recipe for spicy Bosna sausage has always been a secret). ■ TIP➔ **For a quick lunch on weekdays, visit the market in front of the Kollegienkirche—a lot of stands offer a large variety of boiled sausages for any taste, ranging from mild to spiced.**

In the more expensive restaurants the set menus give you an opportunity to sample the chef's best; in less expensive ones they help keep costs down. Note, however, that some restaurants limit the hours during which the set menu is available. Many restaurants are open all day; otherwise, lunch is served from approximately 11 to 2 and dinner from 6 to 10. In more expensive restaurants it's always best to make a reservation. At festival time most restaurants are open seven days a week, and have generally more flexible late dining hours.

WHAT IT COSTS In euros				
$$$$	**$$$**	**$$**	**$**	**¢**
AT DINNER over €22	€18–€22	€13–€17	€7–€12	under €7

Prices are per person for a main course at dinner.

★ **$$$$** ✕ **Gasthof Hohlwegwirt.** It's worth a detour on the way to Hallein along the B159 Salzachtal-Bundesstrasse about 10 km (6 mi) south of Salzburg to dine at this inviting inn, run by the same family for more than 130 years. Visitors to the summer music festival may find a hard time landing a table, since there are so many local regulars, all here to enjoy the suburban cooking, the wine cellar filled with more than 100 different vintages, and the unmistakable atmosphere of this *stile Salzburg* house with its four nicely decorated salons. Chef Ernst Kronreif uses recipes from his legendary mother, Ida: spring for the delicious *Butternockerlsuppe* (soup-broth with buttered dumplings), the *Kalbsbries* (calf's sweetbreads), or the *Salzburger Bierfleisch* (beef boiled in beer)—all Salzburgian classics and yet always so up-to-date. Upstairs are some delightfully gemütlich guest rooms. ⊠ *Salzachtal-Bundesstrasse Nord 62, A-5400 Hallein-Taxach* ☎ *06245/82415-0* 🖷 *06245/8241572* ⟐ *Reservations essential* ⊗ *Closed Mon., except during summer festival* ▭ *MC, V.*

★ **$$$$** ✕ **Pfefferschiff.** The "Pepper Ship" is one of the most acclaimed restaurants in Salzburg—or, actually, 3 km (2 mi) northeast of the center. It's in a pretty, renovated rectory, dated 1640, adjacent to a pink-and-cream chapel. Klaus Fleishhaker, an award-winning chef, and his German wife Petra make your table feel pampered in the country-chic atmosphere, nicely adorned with polished wooden floors, antique hutches, and table-tops laden with fine bone china and Paloma Picasso silverware. The menu changes seasonally. A taxi is the least stressful way of getting here, but if you have your own car, drive along the north edge of the Kapuziner-berg toward Hallwang and then Söllheim. ⊠ *Söllheim 3, A-5300 Hallwang* ☎ *0662/661242* ⌦ *Reservations essential* ▭ *AE.*

$$$–$$$$ ✕ **Pan e Vin.** This tiny trattoria has only a handful of tables, and they're hard to obtain, since the Italian specialties on tap are top-flight. Burnt sienna walls are lined with wine bottles, colorful ceramic plates, and Italian dry stuffs, and the chef cooks in full view. The upstairs restaurant of the same name has a more extensive menu, but it's also much more expensive. ⊠ *Gstättengasse 1* ☎ *0662/844666* 📠 *0662/844666–15* ▭ *AE, DC, MC, V* ⌦ *Reservations essential* ⊗ *Closed Sun. and Mon.*

$$–$$$$ ✕ **Stiftskeller St. Peter.** Legends swirl about the famous "St. Peter's Beer
Fodor's Choice Cellar." Locals claim that Mephistopheles met Faust here, others say
★ Charlemagne dined here, and some believe Columbus enjoyed a glass of its famous Salzburg Stiegl beer just before he set sail for America in 1492. But there is no debating the fact that this place—first mentioned in a document dating back to 803—is Austria's oldest restaurant, part of the famous abbey whose Benedictine monks were Christianity's first ambassadors in these formerly pagan parts. If this is Europe's oldest Gasthaus, it still remains one of the most dazzling dining experiences in Salzburg. Choose between the fairly elegant, dark-wood-panel Prälaten-zimmer (Prelates' Room) or one of several less-formal banqueting rooms. On hot summer days the dramatic gray-stone courtyard is a favorite for drinking a glass of wine or a glass of that noted beer, accompanied by finger-licking-good morsels of fried Wiener Schnitzel. Along with other Austrian standards, you can dine on fish caught in local rivers and lakes, and, of course, Salzburger Nockerl. For the full St. Peter splendor, attend a candlelight Mozart Dinner Concert (€45, plus drinks) in the abbey's beautiful Baroque Hall—a dazzling white-and-blue chandeliered wonder. Almost every evening at 8 PM, 18th-century delectables are served while musicians in historic costume play tunes by the Wolfgang. Dessert is "Mozart's Secret Sweet." ⊠ *St. Peter Bezirk 4* ☎ *0662/841268–0, 0662/828695–0 Mozart dinner* ⊕ *www.stiftskellerstpeter.at* ▭ *AE, DC, MC, V.*

★ **$–$$$$** ✕ **Carpe Diem.** Did you ever really consider the possibilities of "finger food"? Dietrich Mateschitz (who also invented the Red Bull energy drink) together with Jörg Wörther did, and they came up with something truly unique: small dishes–both savory and sweet–served in "cones." Pickled perch with artichokes and asparagus tips arrives in a polenta cone, while a potato cone bursts with prime beef with creamed spinach and horseradish. Mix and match to create a delicious meal and an outstanding experience. For dessert, try the cold-warm dark chocolate with re-fried apricot. You can either sit inside in the barlike atmosphere or, in summer, have your cones outside on the open terrace at the northern end of this shopping street. ⊠ *Getreidegasse 50* ☎ *0662/848800* ▭ *AE, DC, MC, V* ⌦ *Reservations essential.*

★ **$$–$$$** ✕ **Blaue Gans.** In a 500-year-old building with vaulted ceilings and windows looking out onto the bustling Getreidegasse, this formerly old-style restaurant in the Blaue Gans hotel has been revamped to showcase a more innovative style of Austrian cooking. There are always vegetarian choices, too. Service is top-notch, the *Wolfsbarsch* (perch) comes with a cilantro-chili cream sauce, and you can peer through a glass floor to study an old cellar—this, as it turns out, was the site of the oldest inn in Salzburg. ⊠ *Getreidegasse 41–43* ☎ *0662/842491–0* ▤ *AE, DC, MC, V* ⊙ *Closed Tues.*

$$–$$$ ✕ **Mundenhamer.** Set next to Mirabell Palace, this old-fashioned restaurant is masterminded by chef Ernst Breitschopf. He knows the repertoire of good old Upper Austrian dishes inside out. So just come here and feast: an Innviertler (raw ham with horseradish, dark bread, and butter); a garlic soup with bread croutons; a roast pork chop served in a pan with bread dumplings and warm bacon-cabbage salad; homemade spaetzle with braised white cabbage and bacon; a Salzburger Schnitzel (scallop of veal filled with minced mushrooms and ham) with buttered finger dumplings. Dessert? Who can resist the Mohr im Hemd (Moor-in-a-shirt), the warm chocolate cake garnished with fruits, chocolate sauce, vanilla ice cream, and whipped cream? Only problem? You may not be able to move after your last bite. ⊠ *Rainerstrasse 2* ☎ *0662/875693* ▤ *AE, DC, MC, V* ⊙ *Closed Sun.*

★ **$$–$$$** ✕ **Zum Eulenspiegel.** What has Till Eulenspiegel, the 14th-century jester from Germany's Braunschweig, to do with Salzburg? Not much, but when Hans Grassl opened this restaurant in 1950 (just across the way from Mozart's birthplace), he saw the surrounding medieval townscape—the old town wall, the "little gate," and its historic 1414 'Griess rooms—and decided to go for it. This inn actually was first mentioned In 1713 and, today, spiffily restored, it allures with rustic wooden furniture, old folio volumes, antique weapons, and open fireplaces. Tables gleaming with white linen are set in wonderful nooks and crannies reached by odd staircases and charming salons, like the tiny "women's apartment," offer delightful views over the city and river. The unique setting is matched by the delicious food. Try the potato goulash with chunks of sausage and beef in a creamy paprika sauce, or the house specialty, fish stew Provençal. These are served at lunch, or all day in the bar downstairs. A final plus: the staff speaks English. ⊠ *Hagenauerplatz 2* ☎ *0662/843180–0* ⊯ *Reservations essential* ▤ *AE, DC, MC, V* ⊙ *Closed Sun., except during festival, and Jan.–mid-Mar.*

$–$$$ ✕ **Café Sacher.** Red-velvet banquettes, sparkling chandeliers, and lots of gilt mark this famous gathering place, a favorite of well-heeled Salzburgers and an outpost of the celebrated Vienna landmark. It's a perfect choice for a leisurely afternoon pastry (especially the famous chocolate Sachertorte) and coffee—and of course the coffee is second to none. Full meals are also served and they offer a no-smoking room, too. (Pastries and coffee are in the $ category.) ⊠ *Schwarzstrasse 5–7* ☎ *0662/889770* ▤ *AE, DC, MC, V.*

$$ ✕ **Ährlich.** Just because this restaurant is all-organic doesn't mean it isn't fun. The dining room has a country casual ambience with cozy booths. It's a good historic-district choice for vegetarians. ⊠ *Wolf-Dietrich-Strasse 7* ☎ *0662/871275* ▤ *AE, DC, MC, V* ⊙ *Closed Sun. and Mon. No lunch.*

$$ ✕**Coco Lezzone.** You'll always find a lively crowd at this popular spot on the quay on the Altstadt side of the river. Spacious with a contemporary, informal dining room, it can be a bit noisy at night. The menu changes with the seasons. ⊠ *Franz-Josef-Kai 7* ☎ *0662/846735* ⊟ *AE, MC, V* ⊘ *Closed Sun. No lunch Sat.*

★ $$ ✕**Daxlueg.** If you really want to enjoy "food-with-a-view," drive 3 km (2 mi) north along the B1 Linzer Bundesstrasse to Mayrwies and turn right up through the woods. Here you can take in a Cineramic view of Salzburg from the mountainside perch of this former Rupertialm (St. Rupert's Pasture), a famous scenic lookout even in Mozart's time. Owned by St. Peter's Monastery and now nicely renovated, this restaurant allures with the romantic charm of an Alpine chalet. Seasonal specialties of the region top the bill: not only venison and fried trout but heavenly garnishes—cress, elder blossoms, herbs from the meadows, raspberries, blueberries, *Schwammerl* (mushrooms) fresh out of the forest, cheese from goat and sheep. ⊠ *Daxluegstrasse 5, A-5300 Hallwang* ☎ *0662/665800* ⊟ *MC, V.*

★ $$ ✕**Die Weisse.** This *Weissbierbrauerei* occupies one of Salzburg's most historic breweries, and many locals consider it to be their ultimate private retreat (so much so that from Wednesday through Saturday it's best to make a reservation). The beer garden really hits the spot on a hot summer day, but all year long you can delight in traditional Bavarian goodies (veal sausages with sweet mustard) as well as the usual array of tempting Salzburg delights. ⊠ *Rupertgasse 10* ☎ *0662/8722460* ⊟ *MC, V* ⊘ *Closed Sun.*

$$ ✕**Gablerbräu.** Many like to stop here for a fast bite, but you should ponder the historic vibes, too. In this old inn Richard Mayr—a famous star of Vienna's State Opera House (he was the first to record Baron Ochs in Strauss's *Der Rosenkavalier*)—was born. He later became one of the organizers of the famous Salzburg music festival. After studying the parlor of Mayr's parents—a dark, wood-carved, neo-Gothic interior from the end of the 19th century—head for a table and settle down to "hot breads and cold beer": a selection of beers from different provinces along with a large variety of sandwiches for any taste. There is also a self-service salad buffet. Other treats on the menu are northern Italian (in former days, of course, Austrian), including the polenta croquets with ratatouille and Gorgonzola cream sauce or the homemade linguine with courgettes in tomato sauce—best paired with a glass of white or red wine from Guttmann's cellars. ⊠ *Linzergasse 9* ☎ *0662/88965* ⊟ *AE, DC, MC, V.*

$$ ✕**K&K am Waagplatz.** This old house was once the domicile of the Freysauff family, who counted among their close friends Leopold Mozart, the composer's father. Its cellar, the downstairs section of the restaurant, is still called the Freysauff (but don't be misled—this translates into "free drinks"). The restaurant is particularly pleasant, with white-linen tablecloths, candles, and flowers, and windows opening onto the street. Menu selections consist of locally caught fish, delicious chicken-breast medallions, lentil salad with strips of goose breast, and traditional Austrian dishes and game in season. Service is friendly. ⊠ *Waagplatz 2* ☎ *0662/842156* ⊟ *AE, DC, MC, V.*

★ **$$** ✕ **Kuglhof.** In Maxglan, a famous Austrian "farmer's village," now part of the city tucked behind the Mönchsberg and next to the Stiegl Brewery (best, therefore, reached by taxi), Alexander Hawranek perfects Old Austrian specialties by giving them a nouvelle touch. The setting is your archetypal black-shuttered, yellow-hue, begonia-bedecked Salzburgian farmhouse, oh-so-cozily set with a tile oven, mounted antlers, embroidered curtains, and tons of *gemütlichkeit*. The menu is seasonal, so you might not be able to enjoy the signature *Beuschl* (calf's lights) with dumplings. Best bet for dessert is the *Apfelschmarrn*, sliced pancake with apples. In summer opt for a table out in the shady garden. ✉ *Kuglhofstrasse 13* ☎ *0662/832626* ⊕ *www.kuglhof.at* ▤ *AE, DC, MC, V* ☉ *Closed Mon. and Tues.*

> **ON THE MENU**
>
> Many restaurants favor the *neue Küche*—a lighter version of the somewhat heavier traditional specialties of Austrian cooking, but with more substance than nouvelle cuisine. Salzburgers also have a wonderful way with fish—often a fresh catch from the nearby lakes of the Salzkammergut. Favorite fish dishes are usually *gebraten* (fried). The only truly indigenous Salzburg dish is *Salzburger Nockerln*, a snowy meringue of sweetened whisked egg whites with a little bit of flour and sugar.

$-$$ ✕ **Café Tomaselli.** Not many years after the attacking Turks fled Vienna, leaving behind tons of coffee beans, this inn opened its doors in 1705 as an example of that new-fangled thing, a "Wiener Kaffeehaus" (Vienna coffeehouse). It was an immediate hit. Enjoying its more than 14 types of coffee was none other than Mozart's beloved, Constanze, who often dropped in, as her house was just next door. The Tomasellis set up shop here in 1753, became noted as "chocolatmachers," and are still running the place. Feast on the famous "Tomaselliums Café" (mocca, Mozart liqueur, and whipped cream) and the large selection of excellent homemade cakes, tarts, and strudels. Inside, the decor is marble, wood, and walls of 18th-century portraits. In the summer, however, the best seats are on the terrace and at the pretty "Tomaselli-Kiosk" on the square. ✉ *Alter Markt 9* ☎ *0662/844488–0* ⊕ *www.tomaselli.at* ▤ *No credit cards.*

FodorsChoice
★

$-$$ ✕ **Fabrizi Espresso.** Named after the former Italian owner of this historic house (note the beautiful small archway passage), this is a top spot for tasting Marzemino, the red wine Don Giovanni drinks in Mozart's opera. But there are plenty of other goodies here: some of the best Italian coffees in the city; outstanding Austrian *Apfel-oder Topfenstrudel* (apple or cheese pie—worth any money, but not expensive) and the best Salzburger Nockerl; excellent prosecco Italian sparkling wine; various salads; and a fine wiener schnitzel. ✉ *Getreidegasse 21* ☎ *0662/845914* ▤ *No credit cards.*

★ **$** ✕ **Krimpelstätter.** About a 15-minute walk downriver from the Altstadt in the Müllner neighborhood, this is one of the top spots where the artists of the summer festival like to celebrate after their premieres. Everyone enjoys the traditional Salzburg cooking: seasonal and delicious *Bärlauch* (wild wood garlic) soup, or the potato goulash with chunks of country ham, or the homemade pork sausage with dumplings, or the *Zander-filet* (pike perch). Happily, all this is served up in a delicious, centuries-old building with fetching accents provided by vaulted ceilings, leaded-glass windows, and homespun tablecloths. Augustiner beer (from the monastery next door) is fresh on tap, and there's a big shady garden for dining in summer. ⊠ *Müllner Hauptstrasse 31* ☎ *0662/432274* ⚐ *Reservations essential* ⊟ *No credit cards* ⊙ *Closed Sun. and Mon., Sept.–Apr.; Mon., May–Aug.*

$ ✕ **Wilder Mann.** "After a certain time all men become wild." So goes a famous Salzburg saying, perhaps coined after someone drank too much of the local "liquid bread"—Stiegl beer. In fact, when this inn opened its doors in 1884 it became one of the most important burgher houses in the Altstadt. Today it offers a true time-stained ambience of an old Salzburg *Gasthaus*, right down to the wooden chairs that generations of locals have sat on and the enormous plates of *Bauernschmaus* (farmer's dish) overflowing with veal, pork, sausage, sour cabbage, and dumplings. ⊠ *Getreidegasse 20* ☎ *0662/841787* ⊟ *No credit cards* ⊙ *Closed Sun.*

★ $ ✕ **Zum Fidelen Affen.** The name means "At the Faithful Ape," which explains the ape motifs in this popular Gasthaus dominated by a round copper-plated bar and stone pillars under a vaulted ceiling. Besides the beer on tap, the kitchen offers tasty Austrian dishes, such as *Schlutzkrapfen,* cheese ravioli with a light topping of chopped fresh tomatoes, or a big salad with strips of fried chicken. It's always crowded, so be sure to arrive early or book ahead. ⊠ *Priesterhausgasse 8* ☎ *0662/877361* ⚐ *Reservations essential* ⊟ *DC, MC, V* ⊙ *Closed Sun. No lunch.*

★ ¢–$ ✕ **Augustinerbräu.** One of the largest beer cellars in Europe and Salzburg's homegrown version of a Munich beer house, the celebrated Augustinerbräu is at the north end of the Mönchsberg next to St. Augustine's church. You can even bring your own food—a relic of the old tradition that forbade breweries from serving meals in order to protect the status of restaurants. Pick up a stone jug of strong, frothy Augustiner beer and sit in the gardens or at a dark-wood table in one of the large refectory halls. Shops in the huge monastery complex sell a vast array of salads, breads, and pastries, as well as sausage and spit-roasted chicken. If you don't feel up to cold beer, there's an old copper beer warmer in the main hall. During Advent and Lent a special beer is offered, with the blessing of past popes, one of whom commented, "drinking does not interrupt fasting." ⊠ *Augustinergasse 4* ☎ *0662/431246* ⊟ *No credit cards* ⊙ *Weekdays 3–11, weekends 2:30–11.*

¢–$ ✕ **Ristorante Pizzeria al Sole.** Next to the Mönchsberg elevator you sit in this Italian restaurant upstairs in a pretty room lined with Venetian prints or in the more casual downstairs area. Choose from an impressive menu of scrumptious thin-crust pizzas. Pasta dishes are numerous and delicious, and may include tagliatelle with grilled shrimp or penne with tuna and capers. ⊠ *Gstättengasse 15* ☎ *0662/843284* ⊟ *AE, DC, MC, V* ⊙ *Closed Tues. in spring and fall.*

WHERE TO STAY

It is difficult for a Salzburg hotel not to have a good location—you can find a room with a stunning view over the Kapuzinerberg or Gaisberg or one that simply overlooks a lovely Old City street—but it is possible. Salzburg is not a tiny town, and location is important. It is best to be near the historic city center; it's about a mile from the railway station to historic Zentrum (center), right around the main bridge of the Staatsbrücke. The Old City has a wide assortment of hotels and pensions, but there are few bargains. Also note that many hotels in this area have to be accessed on foot, as cars are not permitted on many streets. If you have a car, you may opt for a hotel or converted castle on the outskirts of the city. Many hostelries are charmingly decorated in *Bauernstil*—the rustic look of Old Austria; the ultimate in peasant-luxe is found at the world-famous Hotel Goldener Hirsch.

If you're looking for something really cheap (less than €50 for a double), clean, and comfortable, stay in a private home, though the good ones are all a little way from downtown. The tourist information offices don't list private rooms; try calling Eveline Truhlar of **Bob's Special Tours** (☎ 0662/849511–0), who runs a private-accommodations service.

If you're planning to come at festival time (July and August), you must book as early as possible; try to reserve at least two months in advance. Prices soar over their already high levels. So much so that, during the high season a hotel may edge into the next-higher price category.

Room rates include taxes and service charges. Many hotels include a breakfast in the room rate—check when booking—but the more expensive hostelries often do not. A property that provides breakfast and dinner daily is known as *halb pension*, and one that serves three meals a day is *voll pension*. If you don't have a reservation, go to one of the tourist information offices or the accommodations service (*Zimmernachweis*) on the main platform of the railway station.

WHAT IT COSTS In euros					
	$$$$	$$$	$$	$	¢
FOR 2 PEOPLE	over €270	€170–€270	€120–€170	€80–€120	under €80

Prices are for a standard double room in high season, including taxes and service.

★ **$$$$** 🖼 **Altstadt Radisson SAS.** Venerable is the word to describe this current outpost of the Radisson group: after its founding in 1372 it was a brewery for centuries, then became one of the city's first inns, and has been a luxury hotel since 1992. The exterior is an Old City charmer, done up in buff pink, white trim, sash windows, and iron lanterns. Inside, much has been renovated to within a inch of its life, but historic stone arches and a supertasteful assortment of antiques adorns many rooms, so the ambience allures. On one side, rooms overlook the river and the picturesque Capuchin cloister atop the hill opposite; on the other, upper rooms sneak a peek at the fortress. Despite smaller windows and original beamed ceilings, rooms are light and spacious, and most are furnished with reproduction antiques and traditional accents. The Symphonie Restaurant is elegance personified, with royal-blue and gold hues ashimmer under Rococo chandeliers. Added bonuses are the central yet quiet location and generous buffet breakfast. ⊠ *Judengasse 15/Rudolfskai 28, A-5020* ☎ *0662/848571–0* 🖷 *0662/ 848–5716* ⊕ *www.austria-trend.at/ass* 🛏 *42 rooms, 20 suites* � *Restaurant, bar* ▭ *AE, DC, MC, V* ⋈ *BP.*

$$$$

Fodor'sChoice

★

🏨 **Goldener Hirsch.** Picasso and Pavarotti, Rothschilds and Gettys, Taylor and Burton, Sayn-Wittgensteins and Queen Elizabeth—all have made the "Golden Stag" their Salzburg home away from home. Experience its unique champagne *Gemütlichkeit,* patrician pampering, and adorable decor, if not with a stay, then with a meal. The location is tops— just down the street from Mozart's Birthplace and steps from the Festspielhaus. This means crowds, but double-paned windows ensure you won't hear a thing once you enter this special, private world. Inside it's delightfully rustic, with woodwork, peasant-luxe furniture, medieval statues, and some of the lowest ceilings in town; the stag motif is even on lamp shades, which were hand-painted by an Austrian countess. The hotel actually comprises four separate town houses, all connected in a welter of staircases and elevators. As it's a historic treasure, expect some rooms to have snug (yet cozy) dimensions (in fact, some readers have written in alarm about some far-flung rooms tucked under the eaves—still, other "distant" chambers, such as those in the Kupferschmied Haus annex across the street, are prized for their privacy). There are two restaurants: the regal dining room and its smaller bistro-brother, "s'Herzl." The latter is set on the pretty Sigmundsplatz, next to the hotel, and big stars and locals love its cozy, timbered look and the house specialty, *Nürnberger Bratwürstl* (half a dozen little roasted Nürnberg sausages served with sauerkraut and served on pewter heart-shaped plates). During festival time, tables for aprés-performance dinners in the main restaurant are impossible to come by, having been booked eight months in advance, so why not try to rub elbows with *le tout Salzburg* in the hotel bar, probably the world's most beautifully decorated *Bauernstil* room. Long run by Count Johannes Walderdorff, the hotel has now been taken over by the Starwood hotel chain, so some high-rollers are complaining that the hotel is not what it used to be (but what is?). The expensive breakfast is not included in the room price. ⊠ *Getreidegasse 37, A-5020* ☎ *0662/8084–0* 🖷 *0662/848511–845* ⊕ *www. goldenerhirsch.com* 🛏 *64 rooms, 5 suites* � *2 restaurants, minibars, bar, Internet, parking (fee)* ▭ *AE, DC, MC, V.*

★ $$$$

🏨 **Sacher Salzburg.** Formerly famous as the Österreichischer Hof, this mammoth hotel on the bank of the Salzach River has attracted guests from the Beatles and the Rolling Stones to Hillary and Chelsea Clinton. A great fave of the Salzburg Festival crowd, it's owned by the Gürtler family, who also own the famous Hotel Sacher in Vienna. The staff has recently taken the monocle out of its eye, so even if you don't have a Vuitton steamer trunk, you'll probably feel welcome here. The main atrium is a symphony in marble, while the grand staircase still looks like the Empress Sisi could make a dazzling entrance amidst its ferns. Upstairs,

3

guest rooms are so lovely there is a danger you won't want to leave to explore the city (especially if you get one with picture-perfect views of the Old City). Each is different, but all are exquisitely decorated. Room prices include a delicious buffet breakfast, including *Sekt* (Austrian sparkling wine). In nice weather tables are set outside on the terrace, where you can enjoy a salad or hamburger (called a "Salzburger") for lunch while gazing across at the fortress. Restaurants include haute, tavern, and the Salzburg outpost of Vienna's fabled Café Sacher—enjoy your slice of Sachertorte at the latter. ✉ *Schwarzstrasse 5–7, A-5020* ☎ *0662/88977* 📠 *0662/88977–14* 🌐 *www.sacher.com* *118 rooms* *5 restaurants, minibars, in-room broadband, gym, massage, sauna, steam room, bar, Internet, meeting rooms, parking (fee), no-smoking rooms* 💳 *AE, DC, MC, V* 🍽 *BP.*

★ **$$$$** **Schloss Mönchstein.** With gardens and hiking trails, yet just minutes from the city center, it's little wonder the 19th-century naturalist Alexander von Humboldt called this palatial mountain retreat a "small piece of paradise." Catherine of Russia and the Duchess of Liechtenstein are just two of the notables who have stayed in the gable-roofed, tower-studded mansion. Inside, a series of lovely, luxurious rooms are hung with tapestries and adorned with painted chests and Old Master daubs; some salons have views of the woods and Salzburg in the distance. The castle has its own wedding chapel, which is particularly popular with American and Japanese couples. Getting in and out of town calls for a car or taxi, unless you are willing to negotiate steps or take the nearby Mönchsberg elevator, which is about an eight-minute walk away. ✉ *Mönchsberg 26, A-5020* ☎ *0662/848555–0* 📠 *0662/848559* 🌐 *www.monchstein.com* *23 rooms* *Minibars, tennis court, bar, free parking* 💳 *AE, DC, MC, V.*

$$$$ **Sheraton Salzburg.** With the lovely Mirabell park and gardens virtually at its back door, this beige, modern hotel tastefully blends in with the Belle Époque buildings that surround it. Rooms are spacious and soothing in tone with contemporary furniture, and contain all the little extras and then some. Try to get a room facing the gardens. The buffet breakfast is outstanding—enough to keep you going all day. The house café, with attractive garden seating, bakes all its tempting pastries and strudels on the premises. It's about a 10-minute walk from the Altstadt across the river. ✉ *Auerspergstrasse 4, A-5020* ☎ *0662/889990* 📠 *0662/881776* 🌐 *www.sheraton.at* *163 rooms* *2 restaurants, café, minibars, gym, sauna, bar, Internet, parking (fee), no-smoking floor* 💳 *AE, DC, MC, V* 🍽 *BP.*

★ **$$$–$$$$** **Bristol.** Just across the river from the Altstadt, next to the Mirabell Gardens, this grand, pale-yellow palace-hotel dating from 1890 has hosted, in turn, Franz Josef I, Freud, and the cast of *The Sound of Music*. The sunny lobby showcases a huge ancient tapestry along one wall and works by the Salzburg-born painter Hans von Makart, and the piano bar contains framed black-and-white photos of prominent guests (including Max, the Captain, and Liesl from the film cast). No two rooms are alike, but all have impressive fabrics, chandeliers, and marble baths (some have inner doors with their original etched glass). A few rooms are done in a whimsical Napoleonic-style with tented ceilings. The

3

classy rooftop suite, known simply as "The View," has arguably the most stupendous views in the entire city. ✉ *Makartplatz 4, A-5020* ☎ *0662/ 873557* 📠 *0662/873557–6* 🌐 *www.bristol-salzburg.at* ⟆ *60 rooms* ♨ *Restaurant, minibars, bar, Internet, parking (fee)* ▤ *AE, DC, MC, V* ☾ *Closed Feb. and Mar.* ⊺◉⟊ *BP.*

$$$ 🏨 **Blaue Gans.** "The Blue Goose" has always been a popular option—its location on the main shopping drag of Getreidegasse, within sight of the Festival theaters, Mozart's Birthplace, and the Pferdeschwemme fountain, is tops. It has a 400-year-old pedigree and still retains its ancient wood beams, winding corridors, and low archways. But today this is an "art hotel," the first in Salzburg. The avant-garde works of local artists Erich Shobesberger, Christian Ecker, and Waldemar Kufner adorn the walls. Upstairs, the guest rooms are spacious and have contemporary furnishings, whitewashed walls with cheeky framed posters and cheerful curtains; a few have skylights. The popular restaurant has lively contemporary art on the walls and nouvelle Austrian delights on the dishes. Now that Salzburg's profile in the modern art world has expanded considerably with its new Museum der Moderne, artists and curators are touching down here, so be sure to make reservations well in advance. ✉ *Getreidegasse 43, A-5020* ☎☎ *0662/842491–0* 🌐 *www.blauegans. at* ⟆ *40 rooms* ♨ *Restaurant, minibars, bar, Internet, parking (fee); no a/c in some rooms* ▤ *AE, DC, MC, V* ⊺◉⟊ *BP.*

$$$ 🏨 **Stieglbräu/Imlauer.** Named after a noted Salzburg brewery, this hotel has some leafy gardens and serves up the old-fashioned treats the beer coachmen of yore liked, such as *Liptauer* (hot spiced cheese served with radish, bacon, cold pork, sausages, butter, and bread, along with a mug of the fresh beer on tap). Stieglbräu/Imlauer, which is affiliated with Best Western, has comfortably equipped rooms that come with individually adjustable air-conditioners and sound-proof windows. The hotel is midway between the train station and the Mirabell Gardens; the No. 1 bus takes you to the city center. ✉ *Rainerstrasse 12–14, A-5020* ☎ *0662/ 88992* 📠 *0662/8899271* 🌐 *www.imlauer.com* ⟆ *99 rooms* ♨ *Restaurant, free parking* ▤ *AE, DC, MC, V* ⊺◉⟊ *BP.*

$$–$$$ 🏨 **Auersperg.** Would you like to start your mornings with a stroll by a pool flowered with water lilies? You'll find this green oasis between the two buildings that comprise the Auersperg—the hotel, built in 1892 by the noted Italian architect Ceconi and its neighboring "villa." The lobby welcomes you with Biedermeier antiques, while upstairs, the soigné guest rooms contain mostly modern pieces accented with classic ornaments. A rich breakfast buffet and the use of the roof sauna and a steam bath are included. Outside the door, and you are but five minutes from the historic section. A big plus: just around the corner is that Salzburg treasure of a restaurant/beer garden, Die Weisse. ✉ *Auerspergstrasse 61, A-5020* ☎ *0662/88944* 📠 *0662/889–4455* 🌐 *www.auersperg.at* ⟆ *51 rooms* ♨ *Sauna, steam room, Internet, free parking; no a/c* ▤ *AE, DC, MC, V* ⊺◉⟊ *BP.*

$$–$$$ 🏨 **Elefant.** An old-time favorite, this hotel was once graced by the real Maria von Trapp (her personal check, written when she stayed here in 1981, is set under glass on the second floor). But we mean really old: this 700-year-old house began life as an inn run by Salzburg citizen Hans

Goldeisen, provisioner to Duke Ernst, and host to the likes of Maximilian II, who on his way from Spain via Italy to Vienna was accompanied by his new pet, an Indian elephant named Soliman. That's also the reason why guests are welcomed by the sight of an elephant sculpture in the lobby. Most of the decor is decidedly less exotic in fact, much of the local color has disappeared since the Elephant was rounded up by Best Western. Some rooms are alluring, with pale yellow striped wallpaper, blue accents, and antique-style furniture, but others are much more generic. For real history, repair to the hotel's "Ratsherrenkeller," one of Salzburg's most famous wine cellars in the 17th century. Today it's the restaurant Bruno, and serves alluring candlelight dinners. Cars can be parked in the Altstadt Garage. ⊠ *Sigmund-Haffner-Gasse 4, A-5020* ☎ *0662/843397* ⊠ *0662/840109–28* ⊕ *www.elefant.at* ⤳ *31 rooms* ⌂ *Restaurant, minibars, Internet, parking (fee)* ☰ *AE, DC, MC, V* ⦿❘ *BP.*

$$–$$$ ⊡ **Rosenvilla.** A haven of peace and tranquillity, this upscale bed-and-breakfast is across the Salzach River from the Altstadt. You enter the pretty suburban villa through an arbored garden gate. Guest rooms, all designed with taste, are a seductive mixture of contemporary, French Empire, and Biedermeier accents, with pretty fabrics and lots of light. Some have balconies overlooking the soothing garden with its expanse of velvet green lawn, tiled pathways, and a little pond with ducks. A special three-day offer includes dinner at the owners' top-ranked restaurant, the important Pfefferschiff (⇨ Where to Eat), which is a great value. The Rosenvilla is a 15-minute walk from the center, or you can take Bus 7, which normally runs every 10 minutes. ⊠ *Höfelgasse 4, A-5020* ☎ *0662/621765* ⊠ *0662/6252308* ⊕ *www.rosenvilla.sbg.at* ⤳ *14 rooms* ⌂ *Free parking; no a/c* ☰ *AE, DC, MC, V* ⦿❘ *BP.*

$$ ⊡ **Amadeus.** There isn't much here to clue you into why the hotel has adopted Mozart's second name, but dig a bit. You'll learn that this 500-year-old, rather ramshackle yet charming house is not far from the St. Sebastian church and cemetery where many members of his family are booked for an eternal stay. The hotel site was once home to one of Salzburg's communal baths. Back in Wolfgang's time there was no running water in houses, so travelers—especially those arriving through the nearby Linz Gate—would immediately repair to this official bath after their long trip along dusty roads. Today travelers still make a beeline here. The guest rooms are each decorated differently, with several featuring charming wood armoires and beds, others in a calm and modern fashion. Downstairs, greet the day in one of the cutest breakfast nooks in Salzburg, festively done up in Alpine red, white, and green (the large breakfast buffet is included in the room rate, as well as afternoon coffee and tea). But if you have a problem with Salzburg's incessantly ringing church bells, beware—there is a church next door and its bell goes off every quarter hour. It stops at 11 PM but will prove a rather loud alarm clock at 5 AM. ⊠ *Linzergasse 43–45, A-5020* ☎ *0662/871401* ⊠ *0662/876163–7* ⊕ *www.hotelamadeus.at* ⤳ *23 rooms* ⌂ *No a/c* ☰ *AE, DC, MC, V* ⦿❘ *BP.*

★ **$$** ⊡ **Gersberg Alm.** A picture-perfect Alpine chalet on the lofty perch of the Gersberg high above Salzburg, this Romantic Hotel is less than 15 minutes by car from the center of the city. Inside, it has all the warmth and rustic coziness you would expect in a country house; indeed, it was originally a 19th-century farmhouse. Guest rooms are pleasantly decorated with contemporary furniture and have wooden balconies overlooking the mountain scenery. The house restaurant is excellent—top choices include ravioli stuffed with spinach in a tomato-butter sauce, or lightly fried pike perch in a tomato-olive crust with pesto spaghetti. Be sure to try the warm apricot fritters for dessert. The wine list has an outstanding selection of Austrian wines. ⊠ *Gersberg 37, A-5020* ☎ *0662/ 641257* 🖷 *0662/644248* ⊕ *www.gersbergalm.at* ⤳ *43 rooms* ⚮ *Restaurant, minibars, pool, sauna, free parking; no a/c* ⊟ *AE, DC, MC, V* ⦿*BP.*

$$ 🏨 **Kasererbräu.** Standing on the site of an ancient Roman temple and just a few blocks from Salzburg's grand cathedral, this hotel offers a compatible mixture of folkloric kitsch and sleek elegance. The public rooms are decorated with antiques and Oriental carpets; some of the guest rooms have sleigh beds or pretty carved and handpainted headboards, although others are more plainly decorated. Apart from the friendly staff, the hotel has two big advantages: in the Old City, it's close to everything, and it has pleasant sauna and steam-bath facilities included in the price. ⊠ *Kaigasse 33, A-5020* ☎ *0662/842445-0* 🖷 *0662/84244551* ⊕ *www.kasererbraeu.at* ⤳ *43 rooms* ⚮ *Sauna, Internet, parking (fee); no a/c* ⊟ *AE, DC, MC, V* ⊘ *Closed early Feb.–mid-Mar.* ⦿ *BP.*

$$ 🏨 **Neutor.** A two-minute walk from the Old City and next to the historic tunnel that plows through the Mönchsberg, this modern but classy option, run by the Schwärzler hotel group, is divided between two buildings on opposite sides of the street. The decor is bright and shiny—a real blessing on a gray, rainy day—and all rooms are equipped with modern technology. Children ages six and under are free; ages 7–12 they get a 50% reduction for the third bed in the parent's room. There are a few parking spaces behind the hotel, but if they are occupied you will have to pay to park either along the street or in a garage. ⊠ *Neutorstrasse 8, A-5020* ☎ *0662/844154-0* 🖷 *0662/84415416* ⊕ *www. schwaerzler-hotels.com* ⤳ *89 rooms* ⚮ *Restaurant, bar, parking; no a/c* ⊟ *AE, DC, MC, V* ⦿ *BP.*

$$ 🏨 **NH Salzburg.** Run by a Spanish hotel chain, this modern construction is a pretty building, with Art Nouveau awnings, Secession-style sash windows, and white stone trim. Inside all is sleek and comfy. The location is nice—you're around the corner from the shopping street leading to the Salzach river or five minutes away from the beautiful Mirabell Gardens. There is a rich buffet-style breakfast and the restaurant has a garden terrace. ⊠ *Franz-Josef-Strasse 26, A-5020* ☎ *0662/8820410* 🖷 *0662/874240* ⊕ *www.nh-hotels.com* ⤳ *140 rooms* ⚮ *Restaurant, bar, Wi Fi, parking (fee); no a/c* ⊟ *AE, DC, MC, V* ⦿ *BP.*

$$ 🏨 **Pension Wolf.** The embodiment of Austrian *gemütlichkeit,* just off Mozartplatz, the small, family-owned, in-the-center-of-everything Wolf offers spotlessly clean and cozy rooms in a rustic 1429 building. Rooms are idiosyncratically arranged on several upper floors, connected by narrow, winding stairs, and are decorated with a pleasing Salzburg mix of rag rugs and rural furniture. This is popular, so be sure to book far in advance. ⊠ *Kaigasse 7, A-5020* ☎ *0662/843453–0* 🖷 *0662/842423–4* ⊕ *www.hotelwolf.com* ⤳ *12 rooms* ⚮ *Sauna, parking (fee); no a/c* ⊟ *AE* ⊘ *Closed early Feb.–early Mar.* ⦿ *BP.*

$$ ⊞ **Stadtkrug.** Snuggled under the monument-studded Kapuzinerberg and a two-minute walk from the bridge leading to the center of the Altstadt, the Stadtkrug (dated 1353) hits an idyllic, romantic, and quiet vibe, thanks to its mountainside setting. A traditional wrought-iron sign greets you, the lobby tinkles with chandeliers, and the main-floor restaurant is your archetypal, white, classic, vaulted Salzburg sanctorum. Upstairs you find a charming atmosphere, even if some of the rustically furnished rooms are tiny. Head up to the roof to enjoy a restaurant that is terraced into the mountainside and set with statues, potted begonias, echoes of Italy, and lovely views. ⊠ *Linzergasse 20, A-5020* ☎ *0662/873545–0* 🖷 *0662/87353454* ⊕ *www.stadtkrug.at* ⇨ *34 rooms* ⚒ *2 restaurants; no a/c* ⊟ *AE, DC, MC, V* ⓘⓄⓘ *BP.*

$$ ⊞ **Weisse Taube.** In the heart of the pedestrian area of the Altstadt, the centuries-old "White Dove" is around the corner from Mozartplatz, the Residenz, and a block from the cathedral. Comfortably renovated into a hotel—now family-run for four generations—this 14th-century burgher's house has been traditionally restored, but some time-burnished touches remain: uneven floors, ancient stone archways, and wood-beam ceilings. Guest rooms are simply furnished, with dark-wood accents. Several no-smoking rooms are available, and the main section of the breakfast room is also no-smoking. The staff is most friendly. ⊠ *Kaigasse 9, A-5020* ☎ *0662/842404* 🖷 *0662/841783* ⊕ *www.weissetaube.at* ⇨ *33 rooms* ⚒ *Bar, Internet, parking (fee), no-smoking rooms; no a/c* ⊟ *AE, DC, MC, V* ⊗ *Closed 2 wks in Jan.* ⓘⓄⓘ *BP.*

★ **$$** ⊞ **Wolf-Dietrich.** Two houses opposite each other: the Altstadt and the Residenz. Guest rooms in this small, family-owned hotel across the river from the Altstadt are elegantly decorated (some with Laura Ashley fabrics—two "romantic" apartments are designed like stage settings for Mozart's *The Magic Flute*) and have extra amenities, such as attractive sitting areas. Those in the back look out over the looming Gaisberg and the cemetery of St. Sebastian. The staff is warm and helpful. ⊠ *Wolf-Dietrich-Strasse 7, A-5020* ☎ *0662/871275* 🖷 *0662/882320* ⊕ *www.salzburg-hotel.at* ⇨ *32 rooms* ⚒ *Restaurant, indoor pool, sauna, steam, room, in-room data ports, parking (fee); no a/c, no smoking* ⊟ *AE, DC, MC, V* ⓘⓄⓘ *BP.*

$ ⊞ **Bergland.** A 10-minute walk from the train station, this cheerful, pleasant, family-owned pension offers modern, comfortable rooms with breakfast included in the price. The sitting room includes an English library. ⊠ *Rupertgasse 15, A-5020* ☎ *0662/872318* 🖷 *0662/872318–8* ⊕ *www.berglandhotel.at* ⇨ *17 rooms* ⚒ *Sauna, free parking; no a/c, no smoking* ⊟ *AE, DC, MC, V* ⊗ *Closed Nov.–Christmas* ⓘⓄⓘ *BP.*

$ ⊞ **Cordial Theaterhotel.** Music lovers will enjoy studying the myriad production posters and photographs of famous artists that festoon the lobby here. Part of a classy chain, this is a modern option, with comfy guest rooms. The location is about a 10-minute walk from the city center, as are the auditoriums on both sides of the Salzach River. ⊠ *Schallmooser Hauptstrasse 13, A-5020* ☎ *0662/881681–0* 🖷 *0662/88168692* ⊕ *www.cordial.at* ⇨ *58 rooms, 10 apartments* ⚒ *Café, sauna, bar; no a/c* ⊟ *AE, DC, MC, V* ⓘⓄⓘ *BP.*

$ ⊞ **Turnerwirt.** In the former farmer's village of Gnigl, part of Salzburg's outskirts, this is a quaint complex of buildings. The most charming is the small "Villa," an adorable mansion fitted out with begonia-hung windows, red storybook roof, and fairy-tale turret. Out front is the massive Gasthaus—an Alpine roof and its name picked out in Gothic lettering on the front makes the building look on sabbatical from an Albrecht Dürer engraving. Both offer a friendly family-owned atmosphere, and guest rooms are decorated in a traditional and pleasing style. The largest suites have three and four bedrooms. To get to Salzburg's center city, hop on the No. 4 bus for a 10-minute ride. By car, the Turnerwirt can be reached from Salzburg by taking the motorway and exiting after 2 mi (1 km) at Salzburg Nord or Wallersee. ⊠ *Linzer Bundesstrasse 54, A-5020* ☎ *0662/640630* 🖷 *0662/6406–3077* ⊕ *www.turnerwirt.at* 🛏 *62 rooms* ♿ *Parking; no a/c* ▭ *AE, DC, MC, V* ⊠ *BP.*

¢–$ ▥ **Am Dom.** Tucked away on a tiny street near Residenzplatz, this small pension in a 14th-century building offers simply furnished, rustic-style rooms, some with oak-beam ceilings. Note the beautiful hand-carved Renaissance reception desk. The selling point here is the great location in the heart of the Altstadt. ⊠ *Goldgasse 17, A-5020* ☎ *0662/842765* 🖷 *0662/842765–55* ⊕ *www.amdom.at* 🛏 *15 rooms* ♿ *No a/c, no room TVs* ▭ *AE, DC, MC, V* ⊗ *Closed 2 wks in Feb.* ⊠ *BP.*

¢   ▥ **Schwarzes Rössl.** Once a favorite with Salzburg regulars, this traditional Gasthof now serves as student quarters for most of the year, but is well worth booking when available. Rooms are fresh and immaculate, if not charming, and the location is excellent—close to the nighttime action. ⊠ *Priesterhausgasse 6, A-5020* ☎ *0662/874426* 🖷 *01/401–76–20* 🛏 *51 rooms, 4 with bath* ♿ *No a/c* ▭ *AE, DC, MC, V* ⊗ *Closed Oct.–June* ⊠ *BP.*

NIGHTLIFE & THE ARTS

The Arts

Before you arrive in Salzburg, do some advance research to determine the city's music schedule for the time you will be there, and book reservations; if you'll be attending the summer Salzburg Festival, this is a must. After you arrive in the city, any office of the Salzburg Tourist Office and most hotel concierge desks can provide you with schedules for all the arts performances held year-round in Salzburg, and you can find listings in the daily newspaper, *Salzburger Nachrichten.*

The Salzburg Music Festival

The biggest event on the calendar—as it has been since it was first organized by composer Richard Strauss, producer Max Reinhardt, and playwright Hugo von Hofmannsthal in 1920—is the world-famous **Salzburger Festspiele** (⊠ Hofstallgasse 1, A-5020 Salzburg ☎ 0662/8045–500 for summer festival, 0662/8045–361 for Easter festival 🖷 0662/8045–555 for summer festival, 0662/8045–790 for Easter festival ⊕ www.salzburgfestival.at). The main summer festival is usually scheduled for the last week of July through the end of August. In addition, the festival presents two other major annual events: the Easter Festival (early April), and the Pentecost Baroque Festival (late May).

The most star-studded events—featuring the top opera stars and conductors such as Riccardo Muti and Nikolaus Harnoncourt—have tickets ranging from €22 to €340; for these glamorous events, first-nighters still pull out all the stops—summer furs, Dior dresses, and white ties stud the more expensive sections of the theaters. Other performances can run from €8 to €190, with still lesser prices for events outside the main festival halls, the **Grosses Festspielhaus** (Great Festival Hall) and the **Haus für Mozart** (House for Mozart), located shoulder to shoulder on the grand promenade of Hofstallgasse. This street, one of the most festive settings for a music festival, is especially dazzling at night, thanks to the floodlighted Fortress Hohensalzburg, which hovers on its hilltop above the theater promenade. Behind the court stables first constructed by Wolf-Dietrich in 1607, the Festspielhäser (festival halls) are modern constructions—the Grosses Haus was built in 1960 with 2,200 seats—but are actually "prehistoric," being dug out of the bedrock of the Mönchsberg mountain. Also hewn into the mountainside are vast parking lots that can be used by theatergoers. There are glittering concerts and operas performed at many other theaters in the city. You can catch Mozart concertos in the 18th-century splendor of two magnificent state rooms the composer himself once conducted in: the Rittersaal of the Residenz and the Marble Hall of the Mirabell Palace. Delightful Mozart productions are offered by the Salzburger Marionetten Theater. In addition, many important concerts are offered in the two auditoriums of the Mozarteum.

> **A LOT OF NIGHT MUSIC**
>
> Of course, Salzburg is most renowned for the Salzburger Festspiele. But much of Salzburg's special charm can be best discovered and enjoyed off-season. Music lovers face an embarrassment of riches, including chamber concerts held in Mirabell Palace, the Fortress, or at St. Blasius. Salzburg concerts by the Mozarteum Orchestra and the Camerata are now just as much in demand as the subscription series by the Vienna Philharmonic in the Musikverein in Vienna. The Landestheater season runs from September to June. And no one should miss the chance to be enchanted and amazed by the skill and artistry of the Salzburg Marionette Theater.

■ TIP→ Note that you *must* order your tickets as early as possible, therefore make your decisions as soon as the program comes out (usually in the middle of November, though sometimes earlier). Many major performances are sold out two or three months in advance, as hordes descend on the city to enjoy staged opera spectacles, symphony concerts by the Vienna Philharmonic and other great orchestras, recitals, church oratorios, and special evenings at the Mozarteum year after year. Tickets can be purchased directly at the box office, at your hotel, or, most conveniently, at the festival Web site listed above. Next to the main tourist office is a box office where you can get tickets for Great Festival Hall concerts Monday through Friday, 8 to 6: **Salzburger Kulturvereinigung** (⊠ Waagplatz 1A ☎ 0662/845346). The following agencies also sell tickets: **Salzburg**

Ticket Service (⊠ Mozartplatz 5 ☏ 0662/840310 🖷 0662/842476). **Polzer** (⊠ Residenzplatz 3 ☏ 0662/846500 🖷 0662/840150). **American Express** (⊠ Mozartplatz 5 ☏ 0662/8080–0 🖷 0662/8080–9).

Music

There is no shortage of concerts in this most musical of cities. Customarily, the Salzburg Festival headlines the Vienna Philharmonic, but other orchestras can be expected to take leading roles as well. Year-round there are also the Palace-Residenz Concerts and the Fortress Concerts, while in the summer there are Mozart Serenades in the Gothic Room at St. Blase's Church. In addition, there are the Easter Festival, the Pentecost Baroque Festival, Mozart Week (late January), and the Salzburg Cultural Days (October). Mozart Week is always special; in recent seasons Nikolaus Harnoncourt, Zubin Mehta, and Sir Charles Mackerras have conducted the Vienna Philharmonic, while Sir Neville Marriner, Daniel Harding, and Sir Roger Norrington were in charge with other orchestras.

Fodor'sChoice ★ The **Salzburger Schlosskonzerte** (⊠ Theatergasse 2 ☏ 0662/848586 ⊕ www.salzburger.schlosskonzerte.at 🎫 €29–€35) presents concerts in the legendary Marmorsaal (Marble Hall) at **Mirabell Palace,** where Mozart performed. The **Salzburger Festungskonzerte** (⊠ Fortress Hohensalzburg ☏ 0662/825858 ⊕ www.mozartfestival.at 🎫 €31–€38) are presented in the grand Prince's Chamber at Festung Hohensalzburg. Concerts often include works by Mozart. A special candlelight dinner and concert-ticket combo is often offered.

Organizer of the important Mozart Week held every January, the **Mozarteum** (⊠ Schwarzstrasse 26 ☏ 0662/88940–21 ⊕ www.mozarteum.at) center is open to scholars only. However, thousands flock here for its packed calendar of important concerts. The two main concert rooms are in the main facility on Schwarzstrasse. At this writing, the new building at Mirabellplatz 1 was scheduled to open in October 2006. It contains the Solitär (a chamber music hall), the large studio, and smaller performance rooms.

Opera

The great opera event of the year is, of course, the **Salzburger Festspiele** (⇨ above), which mount a full calendar of operas every year. These performances are held in the Grosses Festspielhaus (Great Festival Hall), the Haus für Mozart (House for Mozart), the Landestheater, the Felsenreitschule, the Mozarteum, and numerous other smaller venues, where lieder recitals and chamber works predominate. Prices range from €5 to €600.

The season at the **Landestheater** (⊠ Schwarzstrasse 22 ☏ 0662/871512–21 🖷 0662/871512–70 ⊕ www.theater.co.at) runs from September to June. New productions in 2007 will include Bizet's *Carmen* and Britten's *Albert Herring*. You may place ticket orders by telephone Monday and Saturday 10–2, Tuesday–Friday 10–5.

Fodor'sChoice ★ The delightful, acclaimed **Salzburger Marionettentheater** (⊠ Schwarzstrasse 24 ⊕ www.marionetten.at ☏ 0662/872406–0 🖷 0662/882141) is also devoted to opera, with a particularly renowned production of *Così fan* *tutte* to its credit. The Marionettentheater not only performs operas by Mozart, but also goodies by Rossini, the younger Strauss, Offenbach, Humperdinck, and Mendelssohn (who wrote the music for the troupe's delightful show devoted to William Shakespeare's *A Midsummer Night's Dream*). Performances are staged during the first week of January, during Mozart Week (late January), from May through September, and December 25 through January 7. Tickets usually range from €18 to €35. The box office is open Monday through Saturday 9–1 and two hours before the performance.

Theater

The morality play **Jedermann** (*Everyman*), by Hugo von Hofmannsthal, is famously performed annually (in German) in the forecourt of the **Cathedral** (✉ Salzburger Festspiele, Postfach 140 ☎ 0662/8045–500 🖷 0662/8045–555 ⊕ www.salzburgfestival.at). This is a spine-tingling presentation, and few of the thousands packing the plaza are unmoved when at the height of the banquet the voice of Death is heard calling "Jedermann—Jedermann—Jed-er-*mann*" from the Franziskanerkirche tower, and is then followed with echoes of voices from other steeples and from atop the Fortress Hohensalzburg. As the sun sets, the doors of the great cathedral hover open and the sounds of its organ announce the salvation of Everyman's soul.

Nightlife

Music in Salzburg is not just *Eine Kleine Nachtmusik*. The city's nightlife is livelier than it is reputed to be. The "in" areas include the "Bermuda Triangle" (Steingasse, Imbergstrasse, and Rudolfskai) and Kaigasse; young people tend to populate the bars and discos around Gstättengasse.

Salzburg loves beer, and has some of the most picturesque Bierkeller in Austria. The Augustinerbräu (⇨ Where to Eat) is a legendary Munich-style beer hall. A top beer paradise is the **Stieglkeller** (✉ Festungsgasse 10 ☎ 0662/842681 ⊕ www.imlauer.com ☾ May–Sept.), by the funicular station of the Hohensalzburg tram. The noted local architect Ceconi devised this sprawling place around 1901. The Keller is partly inside the Mönchsberg hill, so its cellars guarantee the quality and right temperature of the drinks. The gardens here have chestnut trees and offer a marvelous view above the roofs of the Old City—a lovely place to enjoy your *Bauernschmaus* (farmer's dish). The **Sternbräu** (✉ Griesegasse 23 ☎ 0662/842140) is a mammoth Bierkeller with eight rambling halls festooned with tile stoves, paintings, and wood beams. The chestnut-tree beer garden or the courtyard are divine on hot summer nights. Many travelers head here for the **Sound of Salzburg Dinner Show**, presented May through October, daily 7:30 to 10 PM, which includes some Mozart in addition to the best of *The Sound of Music*. A three-course meal and show costs €40, or you can arrive at 8:15 PM to see the show and just have Apfelstrudel and coffee for €25.

SHOPPING

For a small city, Salzburg has a wide spectrum of stores. The specialties are traditional clothing, like lederhosen and loden coats, jewelry, glassware, handicrafts, confectionary, dolls in native costume, Christmas decorations, sports equipment, and silk flowers. A *Gewürzsträussl* is a bundle of whole spices bunched and arranged to look like a bouquet of flowers (try the markets on Universitätsplatz). This old tradition goes back to the time when only a few rooms could be heated, and people and their farm animals would often cohabitate on the coldest days. You can imagine how lovely the aromas must have been—so this spicy room-freshener was invented.

At Christmas there is a special **Advent market** on the Domplatz, offering regional decorations, from the week before the first Advent Sunday until December 24, daily from 9 AM to 8 PM. Stores are generally open weekdays 10–6, and many on Saturday 10–5. Some supermarkets stay open until 7:30 on Thursday or Friday. Only shops in the railway station, the airport, and near the general hospital are open on Sunday.

Shopping Streets

The most fashionable specialty stores and gift shops are found along Getreidegasse and Judengasse and around Residenzplatz. Linzergasse, across the river, is less crowded and good for more practical items. There are also interesting antiques shops in the medieval buildings along Steingasse and on Goldgasse.

Specialty Stores

Antiques

Internationale Messe für Kunst und Antiquitäten (⊠ Residenzplatz 1 ☎ 0662/8042–2690) is the annual antiques fair that takes place from Palm Sunday to Easter Monday in the state rooms of Salzburg's Residenz.

Ilse Guggenberger (⊠ Brodgasse 11 ☎ 0662/843184) is the place to browse for original Austrian country antiques. **Marianne Reuter** (⊠ Gstättengasse 9 ☎ 0662/842136) offers a fine selection of porcelain and 18th-century furniture. **Schöppl** (⊠ Gstättengasse 5 ☎ 0662/842154) has old desks, hutches, and some jewelry. For an amazing assortment of secondhand curiosities, try **Trödlerstube** (⊠ Linzergasse 50 ☎ 0662/871453).

Confectionary

If you're looking for the kind of *Mozartkugeln* (chocolate marzipan confections) you can't buy at home, try the store that claims to have invented them in 1890: **Konditorei Fürst** (⊠ Brodgasse 13 ☎ 0662/843759–0). They still produce the candy by hand according to the original recipe that the family never gave away. Stock up at one of their four locations while you're in town—Konditorei Fürst does not offer overseas shipping. **Konditorei Schatz** (⊠ Getreidegasse 3, Schatz passageway ☎ 0662/842792) makes their own version of Mozartkugeln and other delectable goodies.

Crafts

Fritz Kreis (⊠ Sigmund-Haffner-Gasse 14 ☎ 0662/841768) sells ceramics, wood carvings, handmade glass objects, and so on. **Salzburger Heimatwerk** (⊠ Residenzplatz 9 ☎ 0662/844110–0) has clothing, fabrics, ceramics, and local handicrafts at good prices. **Christmas in Salzburg** (⊠ Judengasse 10 ☎ 0662/846784) has rooms of gorgeous Christmas-tree decorations, some hand-painted and hand-carved. **Gehmacher** (⊠ Alter Markt 2 ☎ 0662/845506–0) offers whimsical home decorations.

Traditional Clothing

Dschulnigg (⊠ Griesgasse 8/corner of Münzgasse ☎ 0662/842376–0) is a favorite among Salzburgers for lederhosen, dirndls, and *Trachten,* the typical Austrian costume with white blouse, print skirt, and apron. For a wide selection of leather goods, some made to order, try **Jahn-Markl** (⊠ Residenzplatz 3 ☎ 0662/842610). **Lanz** (⊠ Schwarzstrasse 4 ☎ 0662/874272) sells a good selection of long dirndls, silk costumes, and loden coats. **Madl am Grünmarkt** (⊠ Universitätsplatz 12 ☎ 0662/845457) has more flair and elegance in its traditional designs.

> **SOUVENIR SWEETS**
>
> *Mozartkugeln,* candy balls of pistachio-flavored marzipan rolled in nougat cream and dipped in dark chocolate, which bear a miniportrait of Mozart on the wrapper, are omnipresent in Salzburg. Taste-test and compare to find the best. Those handmade by Konditorei Fürst cost more but can be purchased individually. In hot summer months, ask for a thermos bag to prevent melting. Industrial products like those from Mirabell—500,000 pieces every day—or from the German competitor Reber you get almost everywhere. Special cheap offers are easy to find in supermarkets or in duty-free shops at the airport.

SALZBURG ESSENTIALS

Transportation

BY AIR

Salzburg Airport, 4 km (2½ mi) west of the city center, is Austria's second-largest international airport. There are direct flights from London and other European cities to Salzburg, but not from the United States. Americans can fly to Munich and take the 90-minute train ride to Salzburg.

🛫 **Flughafen München (MUC)** ☎ 08997500 ⊕ www.munich-airport.de **Salzburg Airport (SZG)** ⊠ Innsbrucker Bundesstrasse 96 ☎ 0662/8580 ⊕ www.salzburg-airport.com.

GROUND TRANSPORTATION If you fly to Munich, you can take the 90-minute train ride to Salzburg. Alternatively, you can take a transfer bus from or to the Munich airport: contact Salzburger Mietwagenservice for details. Taxis are the easiest way to get downtown from the Salzburg airport; the ride costs around €13–€14 and takes about 20 minutes. City Bus No. 2, which makes a stop by the airport every 15 minutes, runs down to Salzburg's train station (about 20 minutes), where you can change to Bus No. 3 or 5 for the city center.

🚖 Taxis & Shuttles **Salzburger Mietwagenservice** ✉ Ignaz-Harrer-Strasse 79a ☎ 0622/8161-0 🖷 0622/436324.

BY BIKE

Salzburg is fast developing a network of bike paths as part of its effort to reduce car traffic in the city. A detailed bicycle map with suggested tours will help you get around. You can rent a bike by the day or the week from Top Bike or VELO active. It's best to call and reserve in advance; you will need to leave your passport or a deposit.

🚲 Bike Rentals **Top Bike** ✉ Rainerstrasse/Café Intertreff and Griesgasse ☎ 06272/4656 or 0676/476-7259. **VELO active** ✉ Willibald-Hauthaler-Strasse 10 and Mozartplatz ☎ 0662/4355950 or 0676/4355950.

BY BUS

The Old City, composed of several interconnecting squares and narrow streets, is best seen on foot. An excellent bus service covers the rest of the city. A tourist map (available from tourist offices in Mozartplatz and the train station) shows all bus routes and stops; there's also a color-coded map of the public transport network, so you should have no problem getting around. Virtually all buses and trolleybuses (O-Bus) run via Mirabellplatz and/or Hanuschplatz.

Single tickets bought from the driver cost €1.80. Special multiple-use tickets, available at tobacconists (*Tabak-Trafik*), ticket offices, and tourist offices, are much cheaper. You can buy five single tickets for €1.60 each (not available at tourist offices), a single 24-hour ticket for €3.40.

🚌 Bus Information **Salzburger Verkehrsverbund (Main ticket office)** ✉ Schrannengasse 4 ☎ 0662/44801500.

BY CAR

The fastest routes into Salzburg are the autobahns. From Vienna (320 km [198 mi]), take A1; from Munich (150 km [93 mi]), A8 (in Germany it's also E11); from Italy, A10.

The only advantage to having a car in Salzburg itself is that you can get out of the city for short excursions or for cheaper accommodations. The Old City on both sides of the river is a pedestrian zone (except for taxis), and the rest of the city, with its narrow, one-way streets, is a driver's nightmare. A park-and-ride system covering the major freeway exits is being developed, and there are several underground garages throughout the city. Try the Altstadt-Garagen. The entrance is at the back of the Mönchsberg hill, to the right of the main tunnel through. It costs €14 for 24 hours; one hour is rather expensive at €2.40. However, many shops and restaurants in town offer a reduction of €3.00 for the 4 hour fee.

BY TAXI

There are taxi stands all over the city; for a radio cab, call the number listed below. Taxi fares start at €3. Sunday and holidays a special offer is the bus-taxi running between 11:30 and 1:30 at night, which has routes through the city and into the neighboring villages—the fare is €3.70. Limousines can be hired for €210 to €250 per hour (three-hour minimum) from Salzburg Panorama Tours. They also offer a private "Sound of Music" limousine tour for €280.

🖪 Taxi Information **Radio Cab** ☎ 0662/8111. **Salzburg Panorama Tours** ☎ 0662/883211–0 🖷 0662/871628 ⊕ www.panoramatours.com.

BY TRAIN

You can get to Salzburg by rail from most European cities. The ÖBB, the Austrian Federal Train Service, has a Web site in English. Train information is also available by phone through the Salzburg Hauptbahnhof; don't be put off by the recorded message in German—eventually, you will be put through to a real person who should be able to speak English. You can buy tickets at any travel agency or at the station.

Salzburg Hauptbahnhof is a 20-minute walk from the center of town in the direction of Mirabellplatz. The bus station and the suburban railroad station are at the square in front. A taxi to the center of town should take about 10 minutes and cost €9.

🖪 Train Information **ÖBB** ⊕ www.oebb.at **Salzburg Hauptbahnhof** ✉ Südtirolerplatz ☎ 05/1717.

Contacts & Resources

EMERGENCIES

For medical emergencies or an ambulance, dial 144.

If you need a doctor or dentist, call the Ärztekammer für Salzburg. For emergency service on weekends and holidays, call the Ärzte-Bereitschaftsdienst Salzburg-Stadt. The main hospital is the St. Johannsspital-Landeskrankenanstalten, just past the Augustinian monastery heading out of town.

In general, pharmacies are open weekdays 8–12:30 and 2:30–6, Saturday 8–noon. When they're closed, the name and location of a pharmacy that's open are posted on the door.

🖪 Doctors & Dentists **Ärztekammer für Salzburg** ✉ Bergstrasse 4 ☎ 0662/871327–0. **Ärzte-Bereitschaftsdienst Salzburg-Stadt** ✉ Dr.-Karl-Renner-Strasse 7 ☎ 0662/141. 🖪 Emergency Services **Ambulance** ☎ 144. **Fire** ☎ 122. **Police** ☎ 133. 🖪 Hospitals **St. Johannsspital-Landeskrankenanstalten** ✉ Müllner Hauptstrasse 48 ☎ 0662/44820.

TOUR OPTIONS

Because the Old City is largely a pedestrian zone, bus tours do little more than take you past the major sights. You would do better seeing the city on foot unless your time is really limited.

BICYCLE TOURS The Salzburg Land Tourist Office, together with some travel agents, created the Mozart *Radweg* (bicycle route). Cyclists and music lovers can follow his path around Salzburg and through the lake districts of Austria and Bavaria. All told, the itinerary can take 13 days and runs 410 km (255 mi), but shorter versions are custom-tailored by various outfitters in the region. Austria Radreisen arranges an eight-day tour heading west to Bavaria. Heading east for five days is a planned itinerary mapped out by Oberösterreich Touristik.

🚗 **Austria Radreisen** ✉ Joseph-Haydn-Strasse 8, A-4780 Schärding ☎ 07712/5511-0 ⊕ www.austria-radreisen.at. **Oberösterreich Touristik** ✉ Freistädter Strasse 49, A-4041 Linz ☎ 0732/663024-0 ⊕ www.touristik.at.

BOAT TOURS For a magically different vantage point, take a round-trip boat ride along the relentlessly scenic Salzach River, departing at the Markartsteg in the Altstadt from April until October. The boat journeys as far south as Hellbrunn Palace (depending on the water level). In June, July, and August you can also take the cruise as you enjoy a candlelight dinner—the real dessert is a floodlit view of Salzburg.

🚗 Fees & Schedules **Salzburger Festungskonzerte GmbH** ✉ Anton-Adlgasser-Wegasse 22 ☎ 0662/825769-12 🖶 0662/825859 ⊕ www.salzburgschifffahrt.at.

BUS TOURS American Express is one of several companies that offer day bus trips from Vienna to Salzburg. Vienna Sightseeing Tours runs one-day bus trips in winter on Tuesday and Saturday to Salzburg from Vienna, and in summer on Tuesday, Thursday, and weekends. The €100 fare includes a tour of the city, but not lunch. Cityrama Sightseeing offers a schedule similar to Vienna Sightseeing Tours.

Several local companies conduct 1½- to 2-hour city tours. The desk clerks at most hotels will book for you and arrange hotel pickup. The tour will be in a minibus, since large buses can't enter the Old City. Tours briefly cover the major sights in Salzburg, including Mozart's Birthplace, the festival halls, the major squares, the churches, and the palaces at Hellbrunn and Leopoldskron. Bob's Special Tours is well known to American visitors—the company offers a 10% discount to Fodor's readers who book directly with them without help from their hotel. Salzburg Panorama Tours and Salzburg Sightseeing Tours offer similar tours.

🚗 Bus Tours from Vienna **American Express** ✉ Kärntnerstrasse 21-23, A-1010 Vienna ☎ 01/515-400 🖶 01/515-4070. **Cityrama Sightseeing** ✉ Börsegasse 1, A-1010 Vienna ☎ 01/534-130 🖶 01/534-13-16. **Vienna Sightseeing Tours** ✉ Stelzhammergasse 4/11, A-1030 Vienna ☎ 01/712-4683-0 🖶 01/714-1141 ⊕ www.viennasightseeingtours.com.
🚗 Bus Tours Within Salzburg **Bob's Special Tours** ✉ Rudolfskai 38, Salzburg ☎ 0662/849511 🖶 0662/849512. **Salzburg Panorama Tours** ✉ Schrannengasse 2/2, Salzburg ☎ 0662/883211-0 🖶 0662/871618 ⊕ www.panoramatours.com. **Salzburg Sightseeing Tours** ✉ Am Mirabellplatz 2, Salzburg ☎ 0662/881616 🖶 0662/878776 ⊕ www.welcome-salzburg.at.

FIAKER/HORSE One of the most delightful ways to tour Salzburg is by horse-drawn carCAB TOURS riage. Most of Salzburg's Fiaker are stationed in Residenzplatz, and cost €33 (up to 4 people) for 20 minutes, €66 for 50 minutes. During the Christmas season, large, decorated horse-drawn carts take people around the Christmas markets.

🚗 **Fiaker** ☎ 0662/844772.

SOUND OF MUSIC The *Sound of Music* tour—for the complete scoop, *see* "Oh, the Hills
TOURS are Alive" *earlier in this chapter*—has been a staple of visits to Salzburg for the past 30 years, and is still a special experience. All tour operators conduct one. For a more personal approach, with smaller groups and private minivans, opt for Bob's Special Tours. The most popular

tours, however, are run by Salzburg Sightseeing Tours and Salzburg Panorama. Their large excursion buses usually offer four-hour tours departing daily, which include such sights as Anif Castle, Mondsee Church, and the little summerhouse in the gardens of Hellbrunn. Invariably, they are packed with fun-loving crowds just itching to burst out into choruses of "Do-re-mi."

WALKING TOURS Salzburg's official licensed guides offer a one-hour walking tour through the Old City every day at 12:15, which starts in front of the Information Mozartplatz (€8—owners of the Salzburg Card get a reduced fee).

VISITOR INFORMATION
The Salzburg City Tourist Office handles written and telephone requests for information. You can get maps, brochures, and information in person from Information Mozartplatz in the center of the Old City. The railway station also has a tourist office.

Don't forget to consider purchasing the Salzburg Card. SalzburgKarten are good for 24, 48, or 72 hours at €20–€34, respectively, and allow no-charge entry to most museums and sights, use of public transport, and special discount offers. Children under 15 pay half.

All the major highways into town have their own well-marked information centers. The Salzburg-Mitte center is open April–October, daily 9–7, and November–March, Monday–Saturday 11–5; the Salzburg-Süd, April–October, daily 9–7; and the Salzburg-Nord Kasern service facility is open June–mid-September, daily 9–7.

🚺 **Salzburg City Tourist Office** ✉ Auerspergstrasse 6, A-5024 Salzburg ☎ 0662/88987-0 🖷 0662/88987-435 ⊕ www.salzburginfo.at.

🚺 Tourist Information Centers **Information Mozartplatz** ✉ Mozartplatz 5. **Railway Station tourist office** ✉ Platform 2A ☎ 0662/88987-330. **Salzburg-Süd** ✉ Park & Ride-Parkplatz, Alpensiedlung-Süd, Alpenstrasse 67 ☎ 0662/88987-360.

UNDERSTANDING
AUSTRIA

AUSTRIA AT A GLANCE

Fast Facts

Capital: Vienna
National anthem: "Land der Berge, Land am Strome" ("Land of Mountains, Land on the River")
Type of government: Federal republic
Administrative divisions: Nine states
Independence: 1156 (from Bavaria)
Constitution: 1920; revised 1929, reinstated 1945
Legal system: Civil law system with Roman law origin; judicial review of legislative acts by the Constitutional Court; separate administrative and civil/penal supreme courts
Suffrage: 18 years of age; universal; compulsory for presidential elections
Legislature: Bicameral Federal Assembly consists of Federal Council (62 members; members represent each of the states on the basis of population, but with each state having at least three representatives; members serve a five- or six-year term) and the National Council (183 seats; members elected by direct popular vote to serve four-year terms)
Population: 8.2 million
Median age: Female 42, male 39.8
Life expectancy: Female 82, male 76
Infant mortality rate: 4.6 deaths per 1,000 live births
Literacy: 98%
Language: German (official nationwide), Slovene (official in Carinthia), Croatian (official in Burgenland), Hungarian (official in Burgenland)
Ethnic groups: Austrian 91%, former Yugoslavs 4% (includes Croatians, Slovenes, Serbs, and Bosniaks), Turks 1.6%, German 0.9%, other or unspecified 2.4%
Religion: Roman Catholic 74%; other 17%; Protestant 5%; Muslim 4%

Geography & Environment

Land area: 82,444 square km (31,832 square mi)
Terrain: Steep Alps in the west and south; mostly flat along the eastern and northern borders; at the crossroads of central Europe with many easily traversable Alpine passes and valleys
Natural resources: Antimony, coal, copper, graphite, hydropower, iron ore, lignite, magnesite, natural gas, oil, salt, timber, tungsten, uranium, zinc
Natural hazards: Avalanches, earthquakes, landslides
Environmental issues: Forest degradation caused by air and soil pollution; soil pollution results from the use of agricultural chemicals; air pollution results from emissions by coal- and oil-fired power stations and industrial plants and from trucks transiting Austria between northern and southern Europe

Economy

Currency: Euro
Exchange rate: 0.79 EUR
GDP: $293.4 billion (2005 est.)
Inflation: 2%
Unemployment: 5.2%
Work force: 4.3 million; services 67%; industry and crafts 29%; agriculture and forestry 4%
Major industries: Chemicals, communications equipment, construction, food, lumber and wood processing, machinery, paper and paperboard, vehicles and parts, tourism
Agricultural products: Cattle, dairy products, fruit, grains, lumber, pigs, potatoes, poultry, sugar beets, wine

Exports: $122.5 billion
Major export products: Chemicals, foodstuffs, iron and steel, machinery and equipment, metal goods, motor vehicles and parts, paper and paperboard, textiles
Export partners: Germany 31.5%; Italy 9.3%; Switzerland 5.4%; US 4.9%; UK 4.9%; France 4.7%; Hungary 4.3%
Imports: $118.8 billion
Major import products: Chemicals, foodstuffs, machinery and equipment, metal goods, motor vehicles, oil and oil products
Import partners: Germany 42.6%; Italy 6.6%; Hungary 5.1%; Switzerland 4.8%; Netherlands 4.4%

Who could deny that our Austria is richer than any other country? As the saying goes: "We have money like manure."

–Franz Grillparzer

Political Climate

Austria has been moving to the right in recent years. After three decades of social-democratic governments, political battles have centered on which parties belong in the ruling right-wing coalition, with reactionary politicians garnering enough support to create a stir. Austria has long been one of the most developed and self-sufficient nations, so its entry into the EU has been a prickly one. Inside its borders, pension and healthcare reform as well as lower taxes and unemployment form the boilerplate of the debate.

Did You Know?

• The Vienna Staatsoper, the venue of many of the world's most famous musical performances, is the site of the world's longest round of applause. For 90 minutes and 101 curtain calls, an Austrian crowd applauded Placido Domingo for his performance in Othello in 1991.

• Austria recycles around 80% of its glass products, second only to Switzerland with 91%.

• Austria has the most organically farmed land of any nation. An estimated 10% of the land is farmed without chemically formulated fertilizers, growth stimulants, antibiotics, or pesticides. It's also considered to be nearly self-sufficient in terms of food production.

• The Alps take up three-fourths of Austria.

• Though almost nine-tenths of Austria's people are of Germanic origin, the nation has received almost 2 million refugees since 1945. About 300,000 of Austria's workforce are now foreign laborers.

DO I HEAR A WALTZ?

AN OFT-TOLD STORY CONCERNS an airline pilot whose pre-landing announcement advised, "Ladies and gentlemen, we are on the final approach to Vienna Airport. Please make sure your seat belts are fastened, please refrain from smoking until you are outside the terminal, and please set your watches back one hundred years." Apocryphal or not, the pilot's observation suggests the allure of a country where visitors can sense something of what Europe was like before the pulse of the 21st century quickened to a beat that would have dizzied our great-grandmothers. Today's Austria—and in particular its capital, Vienna—reminds many of a formerly fat man who is now at least as gaunt as most people but still allows himself a lot of room and expects doors to open wide when he goes through them. After losing two world wars and surviving amputation, annexation, and occupation, a nation that once ruled Europe now endures as a somewhat balkanized republic but endures as one of the most popular tourist meccas in the world.

Julie Andrews may wish it wasn't so, but *The Sound of Music* hangs on as one of the most beloved films of all time and, in recent years, the annual New Year's Day Musikverein concerts televised from Vienna have attracted millions of equally devoted fans. The year of 2003 saw the 100th anniversary of Wiener Werkstätte, whose decorative arts masterworks by Adolf Loos, Otto Wagner, Josef Hoffman, and Koloman Moser enchant collectors and connoisseurs everywhere. And the 2006 Mozart Year touched everyone with the magic of the Mozart baton. These and other manifestations remind us of the large—and apparently growing—public still entranced by the champagne-splashed whirl of once-Imperial Austria. But despite the spell cast by Austria's never-never land, with its castles, turrets, swords, gold-braid, ravishing Secession School art, and clouds of whipped cream, the stop-press news is that this dowager of Old Europe is ready to once again lead the vanguard. Museums of contemporary art are opening across the country; Vienna's *beisl*-bistros are getting trumped by nouvelle novelties; and cities everywhere are rumbling with architectural activity, from Vienna's massively renovated MuseumsQuartier to Salzburg's Museum fur Moderner Kunst. In many ways, it appears that Austria is taking a Giant Step Forward, virtually leapfrogging from yesterday to tomorrow.

In some sense, we should not be surprised, for Austria has always been "modern." In the purely geographic sense, the country only dates from 1918, the year in which the great and polyglot Austro-Hungarian Monarchy of the Habsburgs came to an end. Before that date, many of its millions had no consciousness of belonging to a race of "Austrians." They were simply the German-speaking peoples of the many-tongued Austro-Hungarian empire, which once reached from the black pine woods of Eastern Poland to the blue shores of the Adriatic. Those were the great times and many Austrians today just can't forget their exalted past. So, is it any wonder that History has given the Austrians a strong feeling for tradition?

Indeed, the most important clue to the Austrians is their love of the Baroque—not, of course, just its 18th-century architectural technicalities, but its spirit. When you understand this, you will not longer be a stranger in Austria. The *Barock* was the style taken up in painting, sculpture, and decoration to celebrate the Austrians' emergence from a century of tribulation—the woeful 17th-century, when the Viennese had battled invading Turks and the plague. Conquering both, the people embraced this new, flamboyant, bejeweled, and emotional import from Italy and went to town creating gilded saints and cherubs, gilt columns, painted heavens on ceilings, joyous patinated domes. From this theater, from this dream, the spirit of Austria has never really departed.

You can enter this dream at certain moments, such as those Sunday mornings from September to June when—if you've reserved months in advance—you can hear (but not see) those "voices from heaven," the Vienna Boys' Choir, sing mass in the marble-and-velvet royal chapel of the Hofburg. Lads of 8 to 13 in sailor suits, they peal out angelic notes from the topmost gallery, and you might catch a glimpse of them after mass as you cut across the Renaissance courtyard for the 10:45 performance of the Lipizzaner stallions in the Spanish Riding School around the corner. Here, expert riders in brown uniforms with gold buttons and black hats with gold braid put these aristocrats of the equine world through their classic paces to the minuets of Mozart and the waltzes of Strauss.

Music, like wine, takes its flavor from the soil and the season in which it grows, and the roots of Mozart's and Strauss's melodies were nourished by moments in history in which an aging civilization had reached peaks of mellowness. Nowhere but in Austria could they have composed their melodious messages, for they are Austria—her quiet lakes, her laughing streams and rushing rivers, her verdant forests, her sumptuous Baroque palaces. Somehow in Austria, everything seems to come back to music, and at nearly every bend in the road, you can see where masterpieces were committed to paper, whether it be Mozart's "Magic Flute" Cottage in Salzburg, Beethoven's Pasqualati House (where he wrote much of *Fidelio*), or the apartment of Johann Strauss the Younger on the Praterstrasse, in whose salon he composed his greatest waltzes, including "The Beautiful Blue Danube."

It is thanks to the Strausses, father and son, that the Viennese traditionally live in two countries. One is on the map. The other is the imaginary region where wine flows, love triumphs, and everything is silk-lined.

This is the land of the waltz. This region of the Viennese mind is not just a shallow, sybaritic fantasy. Like Viennese music itself, it embodies a substantial premise. At its surprising best—in such creations as "Tales from the Vienna Woods" or the "Emperor's Waltz"—the waltz is perhaps the closest description of happiness ever attained in any art. Paradoxically, the music is not merry. A haze of wistfulness lies over the sunniest tunes, and their sweetness sometimes touches on melancholy. Though the dance is a swirling embrace, the music countermands sensual abandonment. It insists on grace; it remains pensive in the midst of pleasure.

Clearly, no other city has ever been so suffused by an art as Vienna was by music. What other nations say with words, the Austrians say with music. In Paris or London, music was regarded as entertainment. Not so in Vienna. Here it was a personal necessity, an indispensable part of everyday life, shared alike by countesses as well as shopkeepers and janitors. Is it any wonder that poets and musicians have always felt at home in Austria? The land pulses with the heartbeat of humanity. Mozart and Strauss were just two of the composers who felt that pulse and shaped it into special music that lifted Austria from its moorings on the map and fixed it to the souls of people everywhere.

CHRONOLOGY

ca. 800 BC   Celts move into Danube Valley.

ca. 100 BC   Earliest fortresses set up at Vindobona, now the inner city of Vienna. Roman legions, and Roman civilization, advance to Danube. Carnuntum (near Petronell, east of Vienna) is established about 30 years later as a provincial capital.

AD 180   Emperor Marcus Aurelius dies at Vindobona. Other Roman settlements include Juvavum (Salzburg) and Valdidena (Innsbruck).

ca. 400–700   The Danube Valley is the crossing ground for successive waves of barbarian invaders. Era of the events of the Nibelung saga, written down circa 1100.

ca. 700   Christian bishop established at Salzburg; conversion of pagan tribes begins.

791–99   Charlemagne, king of the Franks, conquers territory now known as Austria.

800   Pope Leo III crowns Charlemagne Emperor of the West.

ca. 800–900   Invasion of Magyars; they eventually settle along the Danube.

962   Pope John XII crowns Otto the Great, of Germany, emperor of the Holy Roman Empire, constituting the eastern portion of Charlemagne's realm. Neither holy, nor Roman, nor an empire, this confederation continued until 1806.

The House of Babenberg

976   Otto II confers the eastern province of the Reich—Österreich, or Austria—upon the margrave Leopold of Babenberg.

1095–1136   Reign of Leopold III, later canonized and declared patron saint of Austria.

1156   Austria becomes a duchy. Duke Heinrich II makes Vienna his capital, building a palace in Am Hof.

1192   Leopold V imprisons King Richard the Lion-Hearted of England, who is on his way back from a crusade. Parts of Vienna and several town walls, particularly Wiener Neustadt, south of Vienna, are later built with the ransom money.

The House of Habsburg

1273   Rudolf of Habsburg in Switzerland is chosen duke by the electors of the Rhine; his family rules for 640 years.

1282   Habsburgs absorb the land of Austria.

1365   University of Vienna founded.

1496   Maximilian's son, Philip, marries Juana of Castile and Aragon, daughter of Ferdinand and Isabella of Spain.

1519   Death of Maximilian; his grandson, Charles I of Spain, inherits Austria, Burgundy, and the Netherlands; he is elected Holy Roman Emperor as Charles V.

1521   Charles V divides his realm with his brother Ferdinand, who becomes archduke of Austria and the first Habsburg to live in the Hofburg in Vienna.

1529   Turks lay siege to Vienna.

1556   Charles V abdicates; Ferdinand becomes Holy Roman Emperor. A Catholic with many Protestant subjects, he negotiates the Peace of Augsburg, which preserves a truce between the Catholic and Protestant states of his realm until 1618.

1618–48   Thirty Years' War begins as a religious dispute but becomes a dynastic struggle between Habsburgs and Bourbons, fought on German soil by non-Germans. The Peace of Westphalia, 1648, gives Austria no new territory and reestablishes the religious deadlock of the Peace of Augsburg.

1683   Turks besiege Vienna; are routed by combined forces of Emperor Leopold I, the duke of Lorraine, and King Jan Sobieski of Poland. By 1699, armies led by Prince Eugene of Savoy drive the Turks east and south, doubling the area of Habsburg lands. The Turkish legacy: a gold crescent and a sack of coffee beans; Vienna's coffeehouses open for business.

1740   Last male Habsburg, Charles VI, dies; succession of his daughter Maria Theresa leads to attack on the Habsburg dominions; long-term rivalry between Austria and Prussia begins.

1740–80   Reign of Maria Theresa, a golden age, when young Mozart entertains at Schönbrunn Palace and Haydn and Gluck establish Vienna as a musical mecca. Fundamental reforms modernize the Austrian monarchy.

1780–90   Reign of Maria Theresa's son Joseph II, who continues her liberalizing tendencies by freeing the serfs and reforming the Church. Her daughter, Marie Antoinette, has other problems.

1806   Napoléon forces Emperor Franz II to abdicate, and the Holy Roman Empire is no more; Franz is retitled emperor of Austria and rules until 1835.

1814–15   The Congress of Vienna defines post-Napoleonic Europe; Austria's Prince Metternich (who had arranged the marriage between Napoléon and Franz II's daughter Marie Louise) gains territory and power.

1815–48   Rise of nationalism threatens Austrian Empire; as chief minister, Metternich represses liberal and national movements with censorship, secret police, and force.

1848   Revolutions throughout Europe, including Budapest, Prague, Vienna; Emperor Ferdinand I abdicates in favor of his 18-year-old nephew

Franz Josef. Under his personal rule (lasting until 1916), national and liberal movements are thwarted.

1856–90   Modern Vienna is created and much of the medieval city torn down; the Waltz Kings, Johann Strauss father and son, dominate popular music. Sigmund Freud (1856–1939) begins his research on the human psyche in Vienna. By 1900 artistic movements include the Secession and Expressionism.

1866   Bismarck's Prussia defeats Austria in a seven-week war, fatally weakening Austria's position among the German states.

1867   In response to Hungarian clamor for national recognition, the Ausgleich, or compromise, creates the dual monarchy of Austria-Hungary with two parliaments and one monarch.

1889   Franz Josef's only son, Rudolf, dies mysteriously in an apparent suicide pact with his young mistress, Baroness Marie Vetsera.

1898   Empress Elisabeth is murdered in Geneva by an anarchist.

1914   June 28: Archduke Franz Ferdinand, nephew and heir of Franz Josef, is assassinated by a Serbian terrorist at Sarajevo in Bosnia-Herzegovina. By August 4, Europe is at war: Germany and Austria-Hungary versus Russia, France, and Britain.

1916   Death of Franz Josef.

The Republic

1918   End of World War I; collapse of Austria-Hungary. Emperor Karl I resigns; Republic of Austria is carved out of Habsburg crown lands, while nation-states of the empire declare autonomy. Kept afloat by loans from the League of Nations, Austria adjusts to its new role with difficulty. Culturally it continues to flourish: Arnold Schoenberg's 12-tone scale recasts musical expression, while the Vienna Circle redefines philosophy.

1934   Dollfuss suppresses the Socialists and creates a one-party state; later in the year he is assassinated by Nazis. His successor, Kurt von Schuschnigg, attempts to accommodate Hitler.

1938   Anschluss: Hitler occupies Austria without resistance.

1945   Austria, postwar, is divided into four zones of occupation by the Allies; free elections are held.

1955   Signing of the Austrian State Treaty officially ends the occupation. Austria declares itself "perpetually" neutral.

1989   Austria becomes the first destination for waves of Eastern European emigrants as the borders are opened.

1990   Austria applies for membership in the European Union.

1999   Spearheaded by Jörg Haider, the anti-immigration and extremist Freedom Party is admitted to Austria's national cabinet, setting the government on a collision course with fellow members of the

European Union, who subsequently issue economic and political sanctions against Austria.

2002   The Austrian government is in full upheaval. The status of the ÖVP coalition as the leading party in power is in doubt, with the SPÖ party coming to the fore. The leaders of the Freedom Party resign because of differences with Jörg Haider, who in the September elections becomes head of this party again, only to back down from taking over the leadership. Happily, the launch of euro notes and coins continues to be a tremendous success in Austria.

2004   Elfriede Jelinek wins the Nobel Prize for Literature, confirming her status as one of Austria's most important and controversial cultural figures. Her novels deal with sexual violence and oppression and right-wing extremism. After years of friction with the government, her plays are once again performed in her homeland. The revered and respected president of Austria, Dr. Thomas Klestil, dies of heart failure just days before his second four-year term expires in July. He is replaced by Dr. Heinz Fischer, a prominent member of the Socialist Pary, who is elected in April. Pope John Paul II beatifies the last Austrian emperor, Karl I, who was against fighting in WWI. And Austria's most famous export since Mozart, Arnold Schwarzenegger, completes his first year as governor of California.

WORDS AND PHRASES

Austrian German is not entirely the same as the German spoken in Germany. Several food names are different, as well as a few basic phrases.

Umlauts have no similar sound in English. An ä is pronounced as "eh." An äu or eu is pronounced as "oy". An ö is pronounced by making your lips like an "O" while trying to say "E" and a ü is pronounced by making your lips like a "U" and trying to say "E".

Consonants are pronounced as follows:

CH is like a hard H, almost like a soft clearing of the throat.

J is pronounced as Y.

Rs are rolled.

ß, which is written "ss" in this book, is pronouced as double S.

S is pronounced as Z.

V is pronounced as F.

W is pronounced as V.

Z is pronounced as TS.

An asterisk (*) denotes common usage in Austria.

English	German	Pronunciation
Basics		
Yes/no	Ja/nein	yah/nine
Please	Bitte	**bit**-uh
May I?	Darf ich?	darf isch?
Thank you (very much)	Danke (vielen Dank)	**dahn**-kuh (**fee**-len dahnk)
You're welcome	Bitte, gern geschehen	**bit**-uh, gairn geshay-un
Excuse me	Entschuldigen Sie	ent-**shool**-di-gen zee
What? (What did you say?)	Wie, bitte?	vee, **bit**-uh?
Can you tell me?	Können Sie mir sagen?	kunnen zee meer **sah**-gen?
Do you know ____?	Wissen Sie ____?	**viss**-en zee
I'm sorry	Es tut mir leid.	es toot meer lite
Good day	Guten Tag	**goo**-ten tahk
Goodbye	Auf Wiedersehen	owf **vee**-der-zane
Good morning	Guten Morgen	**goo**-ten **mor**-gen
Good evening	Guten Abend	**goo**-ten **ah**-bend
Good night	Gute Nacht	**goo**-tuh nahkt
Mr./Mrs.	Herr/Frau	hair/frow

Miss	Fräulein	**froy**-line
Pleased to meet you	Sehr erfreut.	zair air-**froyt**
How are you?	Wie geht es Ihnen?	vee **gate** es **ee**-nen?
Very well, thanks.	Sehr gut, danke.	sair goot, **dahn**-kuh
And you?	Und Ihnen?	oont **ee**-nen?
Hi!	*Servus!	**sair**-voos

Days of the Week

Sunday	Sonntag	**zohn**-tahk
Monday	Montag	**moan**-tahk
Tuesday	Dienstag	**deens**-tahk
Wednesday	Mittwoch	**mitt**-voak
Thursday	Donnerstag	**doe**-ners-tahk
Friday	Freitag	**fry**-tahk
Saturday	Samstag	**zahm**-stahk

Useful Phrases

Do you speak English?	Sprechen Sie Englisch?	**shprek**-hun zee **eng**-glisch?
I don't speak German.	Ich spreche kein Deutsch.	isch **shprek**-uh kine doych
Please speak slowly.	Bitte sprechen Sie langsam.	**bit**-uh **shprek**-en zee **lahng**-zahm
I don't understand	Ich verstehe nicht	isch fair-**shtay**-uh nicht
I understand	Ich verstehe	isch fair-**shtay**-uh
I don't know	Ich weiss nicht	isch vice nicht
Excuse me/sorry	Entschuldigen Sie	ent-**shool**-di-gen zee
I am American/ British	Ich bin Amerikaner(in)/Engländer(in)	isch bin a-mer-i-**kahn**-er(in)/**eng**-len-der(in)
What is your name?	Wie heissen Sie?	vee **high**-sen zee
My name is . . .	ich heiße . . .	isch **high**-suh
What time is it?	Wieviel Uhr ist es? *Wie spät ist es?	**vee**-feel oor ist es **vee** shpate ist es
It is one, two, three . . . o'clock.	Es ist ein, zwei, drei . . . Uhr.	es ist ine, tsvy, dry . . . oor
Yes, please/	Ja, bitte/	yah **bi**-tuh/
No, thank you	Nein, danke	**nine** dahng-kuh
How?	Wie?	vee

When?	Wann? (as conjunction, als)	vahn (ahls)
This/next week	Diese/nächste Woche	**dee**-zuh/**nehks**-tuh **vo**-kuh
This/next year	Dieses/nächstes Jahr	**dee**-zuz/ **nehks**-tuhs yahr
Yesterday/today/ tomorrow	Gestern/heute/ morgen	**geh**-stern/ **hoy**-tuh/**mor**-gen
This morning/ afternoon	Heute morgen/ nachmittag	**hoy**-tuh **mor**-gen/ **nahk**-mit-tahk
Tonight	Heute Nacht	**hoy**-tuh nahkt
What is it?	Was ist es?	**vahss** ist es
Why?	Warum?	vah-**rum**
Who/whom?	Wer/wen?	vair/vehn
Who is it?	Wer ist da?	vair ist dah
I'd like to have . . .	Ich hätte gerne . . .	isch **het**-uh gairn
a room	ein Zimmer	ine **tsim**-er
the key	den Schlüssel	den **shluh**-sul
a newspaper	eine Zeitung	i-nuh **tsy**-toong
a stamp	eine Briefmarke	i-nuh **breef**-mark-uh
a map	eine Karte	i-nuh **cart**-uh
I'd like to buy . . .	ich möchte . . . kaufen	isch **merhk**-tuh **cow**-fen
cigarettes	Zigaretten	tzig-ah-**ret**-ten
How much is it?	Wieviel kostet das?	**vee**-feel **cost**-et dahss?
It's expensive/ cheap	Es ist teuer/billig	es ist **toy**-uh/**bill**-ig
A little/a lot	ein wenig/sehr	ine **vay**-nig/zair
More/less	mehr/weniger	mair/**vay**-nig-er
Enough/too much/ too little	genug/zuviel/ zu wenig	geh-**noog**/tsoo-**feel**/ tsoo **vay**-nig
I am ill/sick	Ich bin krank	isch bin krahnk
I need . . .	Ich brauche . . .	isch **brow**-khuh
a doctor	einen Arzt	I-nen artst
the police	die Polizei	dee po-lee-**tsai**
help	Hilfe	**hilf**-uh
Fire!	Feuer!	**foy**-er
Caution/Look out!	Achtung!/Vorsicht!	**ahk**-tung/**for**-zicht
Is this bus/train/ subway going to . . . ?	Fährt dieser Bus/ dieser Zug/ diese U-Bahn nach . . . ?	fayrt **deez**er buhs/ **deez**-er tsook/ **deez**-uh **oo**-bahn nahk . . .

Where is . . .	Wo ist . . .	**vo** ist
the train station?	der Bahnhof?	dare **bahn**-hof
the subway station?	die U-Bahn-Station?	dee **oo**-bahn-**staht**-sion
the bus stop?	die Bushaltestelle?	dee **booss**-hahlt-uh-**shtel**-uh
the airport?	der Flugplatz? *der Flughafen?	dare **floog**-plats dare **floog**-hafen
the hospital?	das Krankenhaus?	dahs **krahnk**-en-house
the elevator?	der Aufzug?	dare **owf**-tsoog
the telephone?	das Telefon?	dahs te-le-**fone**
the rest room?	die Toilette?	dee twah-**let**-uh

open/closed	offen/geschlossen	**off**-en/ge-**schloss**-en

left/right	links/rechts	links/recktz

straight ahead	geradeaus	geh-**rah**-day-owws

is it near/far?	ist es in der Nähe/ist es weit?	ist es in dare **nay**-uh? ist es vite?

MENU GUIDE

English	German
Entrées	Hauptspeisen
Homemade	Hausgemacht
Lunch	Mittagsessen
Dinner	Abendessen
Dessert	Nachspeisen
At your choice	Önach Wahl
Soup of the day	Tagessuppe
Appetizers	Vorspeisen

Breakfast

Bread	Brot
Butter	Butter
Eggs	Eier
Hot	Heiss
Cold	Kalt
Caffeine-free coffee	Café Hag
Jam	Marmelade
Milk	Milch
Juice	Saft
Bacon	Speck
Lemon	Zitrone
Sugar	Zucker

Soups

Stew	Eintopf
Goulash soup	Gulaschsuppe
Chicken soup	Hühnersuppe
Potato soup	Kartoffelsuppe
Liver dumpling soup	Leberknödelsuppe
Onion soup	Zwiebelsuppe

Fish and Seafood

Trout	Forelle
Prawns	Garnele
Halibut	Heilbutt
Lobster	Hummer
Crab	Krabbe
Salmon	Lachs
Squid	Tintenfisch
Tuna	Thunfisch
Turbot	Steinbutt

Meats

Veal	Kalb

Lamb	Lamm
Beef	Rindfleisch
Pork	Schwein

Game and Poultry

Duck	Ente
Pheasant	Fasan
Goose	Gans
Chicken	Hühner
Rabbit	Kaninchen
Venison	Reh
Turkey	Truthahn
Quail	Wachtel

Vegetables and Side Dishes

Red cabbage	Rotkraut
Cauliflower	Karfiol
Beans	Bohnen
Button mushrooms	Champignons
Peas	Erbsen
Cucumber	Gurke
Cabbage	Kohl
Lettuce	Blattsalat
Potatoes	Kartoffeln
Dumplings	Knödel
French fries	Pommes frites

Fruits

Apple	Apfel
Orange	Orangen
Apricot	Marillen
Blueberry	Heidelbeere
Strawberry	Erdbeere
Raspberry	Himbeere
Cherry	Kirsche
Cranberry	Preiselbeere
Grapes	Trauben
Pear	Birne
Peach	Pfirsich

Desserts

Cheese	Käse
Crepes	Palatschinken
Soufflé	Auflauf
Ice cream	Eis
Cake	Torte

Drinks

Tap water	Leitungswasser
With/without water	Mit/ohne wasser
Straight	Pur
Non-alcoholic	Alkoholfrei
A large/small dark beer	Ein Krügel/Seidel Dunkles
A large/small light beer	Ein Krügel/Seidel Helles
Draft beer	Vom Fass
Sparkling wine	Sekt
White wine	Weisswein
Red wine	Rotwein
Wine with mineral water	Gespritz

CONVERSIONS

DISTANCE

KILOMETERS/MILES

To change kilometers (km) to miles (mi), multiply km by .621. To change mi to km, multiply mi by 1.61.

km to mi	mi to km
1 = .62	1 = 1.6
2 = 1.2	2 = 3.2
3 = 1.9	3 = 4.8
4 = 2.5	4 = 6.4
5 = 3.1	5 = 8.1
6 = 3.7	6 = 9.7
7 = 4.3	7 = 11.3
8 = 5.0	8 = 12.9

METERS/FEET

To change meters (m) to feet (ft), multiply m by 3.28. To change ft to m, multiply ft by .305.

m to ft	ft to m
1 = 3.3	1 = .30
2 = 6.6	2 = .61
3 = 9.8	3 = .92
4 = 13.1	4 = 1.2
5 = 16.4	5 = 1.5
6 = 19.7	6 = 1.8
7 = 23.0	7 = 2.1
8 = 26.2	8 = 2.4

TEMPERATURE

METRIC CONVERSIONS

To change centigrade or Celsius (C) to Fahrenheit (F), multiply C by 1.8 and add 32. To change F to C, subtract 32 from F and multiply by .555.

°F	°C
0	-17.8
10	-12.2
20	-6.7
30	-1.1
32	0
40	+4.4
50	10.0
60	15.5
70	21.1
80	26.6
90	32.2
98.6	37.0
100	37.7

WEIGHT

KILOGRAMS/POUNDS

To change kilograms (kg) to pounds (lb), multiply kg by 2.20. To change lb to kg, multiply lb by .455.

kg to lb	lb to kg
1 = 2.2	1 = .45
2 = 4.4	2 = .91
3 = 6.6	3 = 1.4
4 = 8.8	4 = 1.8
5 = 11.0	5 = 2.3
6 = 13.2	6 = 2.7
7 = 15.4	7 = 3.2
8 = 17.6	8 = 3.6

GRAMS/OUNCES

To change grams (g) to ounces (oz), multiply g by .035. To change oz to g, multiply oz by 28.4.

g to oz	oz to g
1 = .04	1 = 28
2 = .07	2 = 57
3 = .11	3 = 85
4 = .14	4 = 114
5 = .18	5 = 142
6 = .21	6 = 170
7 = .25	7 = 199
8 = .28	8 = 227

LIQUID VOLUME

LITERS/U.S. GALLONS

To change liters (L) to U.S. gallons (gal), multiply L by .264. To change U.S. gal to L, multiply gal by 3.79.

L to gal	gal to L
1 = .26	1 = 3.8
2 = .53	2 = 7.6
3 = .79	3 = 11.4
4 = 1.1	4 = 15.2
5 = 1.3	5 = 19.0
6 = 1.6	6 = 22.7
7 = 1.8	7 = 26.5
8 = 2.1	8 = 30.3

CLOTHING SIZE

WOMEN'S CLOTHING

US	UK	EUR
4	6	34
6	8	36
8	10	38
10	12	40
12	14	42

WOMEN'S SHOES

US	UK	EUR
5	3	36
6	4	37
7	5	38
8	6	39
9	7	40

MEN'S SUITS

US	UK	EUR
34	34	44
36	36	46
38	38	48
40	40	50
42	42	52
44	44	54
46	46	56

MEN'S SHIRTS

US	UK	EUR
14½	14½	37
15	15	38
15½	15½	39
16	16	41
16½	16½	42
17	17	43
17½	17½	44

MEN'S SHOES

US	UK	EUR
7	6	39½
8	7	41
9	8	42
10	9	43
11	10	44½
12	11	46

Austria
Essentials

PLANNING TOOLS, EXPERT INSIGHT,
GREAT CONTACTS

There are planners, and there are those who fly by the seat of their pants. We happily place ourselves among the planners. Our writers and editors try to anticipate all the issues you may face before and during any journey, and then they do their research. This section is the product of their efforts. Use it to get excited about your trip to Austria, to inform your travel planning, or to guide you on the road should the seat of your pants start to feel threadbare.

www.fodors.com/forums

GETTING STARTED

We're really proud of our Web site: Fodors.com is a great place to begin any journey. Scan Travel Wire for suggested itineraries, travel deals, restaurant and hotel openings, and other up-to-the-minute info. Check out Booking to research prices and book plane tickets, hotel rooms, rental cars, and vacation packages. Head to Talk for on-the-ground pointers from travelers who frequent our message boards. You can also link to loads of other travel-related resources.

▌ RESOURCES

ONLINE TRAVEL TOOLS

All About Austria For Austria, here are some top Web sites: **train information** (select English from the drop-down menu) ⊕ www.oebb.at; and **Austria. At Last!** ⊕ www.austria.info."About Austria" is a nice general overview of facts and figures is www.aboutaustria.org.

All About Salzburg For basic information: **Salzburg** ⊕ www.salzburg.info.

All About Vienna For basic information: **Vienna** ⊕ www.wien.info. Here are some other top Web sites for Vienna: **Wien Online** ⊕ www.magwien.gv.at–the city government's official Web site; **Wienerzeitung** ⊕ www.wienerzeitung.at–a newspaper site with English translation; **Die Presse** ⊕ www.diepresse.at–German only, but the Web site of the city's leading serious newspaper; **Die Falter** ⊕ www.falter.at–unfortunately also mostly in German, but with excellent movie and restaurant reviews and comprehensive coverage of the city's "alternative" scene; **Time Out Vienna** ⊕ www.timeout.com/vienna/index.html; **Jirsa Tickets Wien** ⊕ www.viennaticket.at/english–for prebooking event tickets online; and **MuseumsQuartier** ⊕ www.mqw.at–for the scoop on what's happening in Vienna's trendy museum quarter.

Currency Conversion **Google** ⊕ www.google.com does currency conversion. Just type in the amount you want to convert and an explanation of how you want it converted (e.g., "14 Swiss francs in dollars"), and then voilà. **Oanda.com** ⊕ www.oanda.com also allows you to print out a handy table with the current day's conversion rates. **XE.com** ⊕ www.xe.com is a good currency conversion Web site.

Safety **Transportation Security Administration** (TSA) ⊕ www.tsa.gov

Time Zones **Timeanddate.com** ⊕ www.timeanddate.com/worldclock can help you figure out the correct time anywhere in the world.

Weather **Accuweather.com** ⊕ www.accuweather.com is an independent weather-forecasting service with especially good coverage of hurricanes. **Weather.com** ⊕ www.weather.com is the Web site for the Weather Channel.

Other Resources **CIA World Factbook** ⊕ www.odci.gov/cia/publications/factbook/index.html has profiles of every country in the world. It's a good source if you need some quick facts and figures.

VISITOR INFORMATION

Austrian National Tourist Office ☎ 212/944–6880 ⊕ www.austria.info.

▌ THINGS TO CONSIDER

GOVERNMENT ADVISORIES

The U.S. Department of State's Web site has more than just travel warnings and advisories. The consular information sheets issued for every country have general safety tips, entry requirements (though be sure to verify these with the country's embassy), and other useful details.

▪ TIP→ If you're a U.S. citizen traveling abroad, consider registering online with the State Department (https://travelregistration.state.gov/ibrs/), so the government will know to look for you should a crisis occur in the country you're visiting. If you travel frequently, look into the TSA's Registered Traveler pro-

ogram, which is still being tested
J.S. airports, is designed to cut
down... idlock at security checkpoints by allowing prescreened travelers to pass quickly through kiosks that scan an iris and/or a fingerprint. How sci-fi is that?

General Information & Warnings **U.S. Department of State** ⊕ www.travel.state.gov.

GEAR

Austrians, particularly the Viennese, are dapper dressers, and Vienna's tony First District is no place to lounge around in shorts, flip-flops, and a T-shirt. Packing "musts" include at least one nice shirt and sport coat for men and a casual but stylish shirt and skirt combination for women. These will see you through nearly any occasion, from a decent dinner out on the town to a night at the opera. Men should bring a nicer pair of dress shoes than might otherwise be on the packing list, since this is a wardrobe staple that the locals pay particular attention to. As a general rule of thumb, the more expensive the shoes, the more respect you're likely to get. High on the list, too, would be comfortable walking or hiking shoes. Austria is a walking country, in cities and mountains alike. And since an evening outside at a Heurige (wine garden) may be on your agenda, be sure to take a sweater or light wrap; evenings tend to get cool even in the summer. Music lovers might consider toting those rarely used opera glasses; the cheaper seats, understandably, are usually far from the action (and standby tickets will have you craning your neck at the back). Finally if you happen to be in possession of a fine, dark green loden mantle and an accompanying cap with a feather, bring them along. That style has never gone out of fashion here and isn't likely to anytime soon. But leave the *Lederhosen,* leather pants, at home—that's more a Bavarian thing anyway.

If you are heading into the mountains, bring sunscreen, even in winter. Sunglasses are a must as well—make sure that they prevent lateral rays. Boots that rise above the ankle and have sturdy soles are best for hiking. Consider packing a small folding umbrella for the odd deluge, or a waterproof windbreaker. Mosquitoes can become quite a bother in summer around the lakes and along the rivers, especially the Danube. Bring or buy some good insect repellent.

SHIPPING LUGGAGE AHEAD

Imagine globetrotting with only a carry-on in tow. Shipping your luggage in advance via an air-freight service is a great way to cut down on backaches, hassles, and stress—especially if your packing list includes strollers, car-seats, etc. There are some things to be aware of, though. First, research carry-on restrictions; if you absolutely need something that isn't practical to ship and isn't allowed in carry-ons, this strategy isn't for you. Second, plan to send your bags several days in advance to U.S. destinations and as much as two weeks in advance to some international destinations. Third, plan to spend some money: it will cost least $100 to send a small piece of luggage, a golf bag, or a pair of skis to a domestic destination, much more to places overseas. Some people use Federal Express to ship their bags, but this can cost even more than air-freight services. All these services insure your bag (for most, the limit is $1,000, but you should verify that amount); you can, however, purchase additional insurance for about $1 per $100 of value.

Luggage Concierge ☏ 800/288-9818 ⊕ www.luggageconcierge.com. **Luggage Express** ☏ 866/744-7224 ⊕ www. usxpluggageexpress.com. **Luggage Free** ☏ 800/361-6871 ⊕ www.luggagefree.com.

PACKING 101

Why do some people travel with a convoy of huge suitcases yet never have a thing to wear? How do others pack a duffle with a week's worth of outfits *and* supplies for every contingency? We realize that packing is a matter of style, but there's a lot to be said for traveling light. These tips help fight the battle of the bulging bag.

MAKE A LIST. In a recent Fodor's survey, 29% of respondents said they make lists (and often pack) a week before a trip. You can use your list to pack and to repack at the end of your trip. It can also serve as record of the contents of your suitcase—in case it disappears in transit.

THINK IT THROUGH. What's the weather like? Is this a business trip? A cruise? Going abroad? In some places dress may be more or less conservative than you're used to. As you create your itinerary, note outfits next to each activity (don't forget accessories).

EDIT YOUR WARDROBE. Plan to wear everything twice (better yet, thrice) and to do laundry along the way. Stick to one basic look—urban chic, sporty casual, etc. Build around one or two neutrals and an accent (e.g., black, white, and olive green). Women can freshen looks by changing scarves or jewelry. For a week's trip, you can look smashing with three bottoms, four or five tops, a sweater, and a jacket.

BE PRACTICAL. Put comfortable shoes atop your list. (Did we need to say this?) Pack lightweight, wrinkle-resistent, compact, washable items. (Or this?) Stack and roll clothes, so they'll wrinkle less. Unless you're on a guided tour or a cruise, select luggage you can readily carry. Porters, like good butlers, are hard to find these days.

CHECK WEIGHT & SIZE LIMITATIONS. In the United States you may be charged extra for checked bags weighing more than 50 pounds. Abroad some airlines don't allow you to check bags over 60 to 70 pounds, or they charge outrageous fees for every excess pound—or bag. Carry-on size limitations can be stringent, too.

CHECK CARRY-ON RESTRICTIONS. Research restrictions with the TSA. Rules vary abroad, so check them with your airline if you're traveling overseas on a foreign carrier. Consider packing all but essentials (travel documents, prescription meds, wallet) in checked luggage. This leads to a "pack only what you can afford to lose" approach that might help you streamline.

RETHINK VALUABLES. On U.S. flights, airlines are liable for only about $2,800 per person for bags. On international flights, the liability limit is around $635 per bag. But items like computers, cameras, and jewelry aren't covered, and as gadgetry can go on and of the list of carry-on no-no's, you can't count on keeping things safe by keeping them close. Although comprehensive travel policies may cover luggage, the liability limit is often a pittance. Your homeowner's policy may cover you sufficiently when you travel—or not.

LOCK IT UP. If you must pack valuables, use TSA-approved locks (about $10) that can be unlocked by all U.S. security personnel.

TAG IT. Always tag your luggage; use your business address if you don't want people to know your home address. Put the same information (and a copy of your itinerary) inside your luggage, too.

REPORT PROBLEMS IMMEDIATELY. If your bags—or things inside them—are damaged or go astray, file a written claim with your airline *before leaving the airport*. If the airline is at fault, it may give you money for essentials until your luggage arrives. Most lost bags are found within 48 hours, so alert the airline to your whereabouts for two or three days. If your bag was opened for security reasons in the United States and something is missing, file a claim with the TSA.

Sports Express ☎ 800/357-4174 ⊕ www. sportsexpress.com specializes in shipping golf clubs and other sports equipment. **Virtual Bellhop** ☎ 877/235-5467 ⊕ www. virtualbellhop.com.

PASSPORTS & VISAS

U.S. citizens need only a valid passport to enter Austria for stays of up to three months.

PASSPORTS

We're always surprised at how few Americans have passports—only 25% at this writing. This number is expected to grow in coming years, when it becomes impossible to reenter the United States from trips to neighboring Canada or Mexico without one. Remember this: a passport verifies both your identity and nationality—a great reason to have one.

U.S. passports are valid for 10 years. You must apply in person if you're getting a passport for the first time; if your previous passport was lost, stolen, or damaged; or if your previous passport has expired and was issued more than 15 years ago or when you were under 16. All children under 18 must appear in person to apply for or renew a passport. Both parents must accompany any child under 14 (or send a notarized statement with their permission) and provide proof of their relationship to the child.

There are 13 regional passport offices, as well as 7,000 passport acceptance facilities in post offices, public libraries, and other governmental offices. If you're renewing a passport, you can do so by mail. Forms are available at passport acceptance facilities and online.

The cost to apply for a new passport is $97 for adults, $82 for children under 16; renewals are $67. Allow six weeks for processing, both for first-time passports and renewals. For an expediting fee of $60 you can reduce this time to about two weeks. If your trip is less than two weeks away, you can get a passport even more rapidly by going to a passport office with the necessary documentation. Private expediters can get things done in as little as 48 hours, but charge hefty fees for their services.

■ TIP➜ Before your trip, make two copies of your passport's data page (one for someone at home and another for you to carry separately). Or scan the page and e-mail it to someone at home and/or yourself.

VISAS

A visa is essentially formal permission to enter a country. Visas allow countries to keep track of you and other visitors—and generate revenue (from application fees). You *always* need a visa to enter a foreign country; however, many countries routinely issue tourist visas on arrival, particularly to U.S. citizens. When your passport is stamped or scanned in the immigration line, you're actually being issued a visa. Sometimes you have to stand in a separate line and pay a small fee to get your stamp before going through immigration, but you can still do this at the airport on arrival. Getting a visa isn't always that easy. Some countries require that you arrange for one in advance of your trip. There's usually—but not always—a fee involved, and said fee may be nominal ($10 or less) or substantial ($100 or more).

If you must apply for a visa in advance, you can usually do it in person or by mail. When you apply by mail, you send your passport to a designated consulate, where your passport will be examined and the visa issued. Expediters—usually the same ones who handle expedited passport applications—can do all the work of obtaining your visa for you; however, there's always an additional cost (often more than $50 per visa).

Most visas limit you to a single trip—basically during the actual dates of your planned vacation. Other visas allow you to visit as many times as you wish for a specific period of time. Remember that requirements change, sometimes at the drop of a hat, and the burden is on you to make sure that you have the appropriate visas. Otherwise, you'll be turned away at the airport or, worse, deported after you arrive in the country. No company or travel insurer gives refunds if your travel plans are disrupted because you didn't have the correct visa.

U.S. Passport Information U.S. Department of State ☎ 877/487-2778 ⊕ http://travel. state.gov/passport.

U.S. Passport & Visa Expediters A. Briggs Passport & Visa Expeditors ☎ 800/806-0581 or 202/464-3000 ⊕ www.abriggs.com. **American Passport Express** ☎ 800/455-5166 or 603/559-9888 ⊕ www. americanpassport.com. **Passport Express** ☎ 800/362-8196 or 401/272-4612 ⊕ www. passportexpress.com. **Travel Document Systems** ☎ 800/874-5100 or 202/638-3800 ⊕ www.traveldocs.com. **Travel the World Visas** ☎ 866/886-8472 or 301/495-7700 ⊕ www.world-visa.com.

SHOTS & MEDICATIONS

No special shots are required before visiting Austria, but if you will be cycling or hiking through the eastern or southeastern parts of the country, get inoculated against encephalitis; it can be carried by ticks.

For more information, *see* Health *under* On the Ground in Austria, *below.*

■ TIP→ **If you travel a lot internationally—particularly to developing nations—refer to the CDC's** *Health Information for International Travel* **(aka Traveler's Health Yellow Book). Info from it is posted on the CDC Web site (www.cdc.gov/travel/yb), or you can buy a copy from your local bookstore for $24.95.**

Health Warnings National Centers for Disease Control & Prevention (CDC) ☎ 877/394-8747 international travelers' health line ⊕ www.cdc.gov/travel. **World Health Organization** (WHO) ⊕ www.who.int.

TRIP INSURANCE

What kind of coverage do you honestly need? Do you even need trip insurance at all? Take a deep breath and read on.

We believe that comprehensive trip insurance is especially valuable if you're booking a very expensive or complicated trip (particularly to an isolated region) or if you're booking far in advance. Who knows what could happen six months down the road? But whether or not you get insurance has more to do with how

Trip Insurance Resources

INSURANCE COMPARISON SITES		
Insure My Trip.com	800/487-4722	www.insuremytrip.com
Square Mouth.com	800/240-0369	www.quotetravelinsurance.com
COMPREHENSIVE TRAVEL INSURERS		
Access America	866/807-3982	www.accessamerica.com
CSA Travel Protection	800/873-9855	www.csatravelprotection.com
HTH Worldwide	610/254-8700 or 888/243-2358	www.hthworldwide.com
Travelex Insurance	888/457-4602	www.travelex-insurance.com
Travel Guard International	715/345-0505 or 800/826-4919	www.travelguard.com
Travel Insured International	800/243-3174	www.travelinsured.com
MEDICAL-ONLY INSURERS		
International Medical Group	800/628-4664	www.imglobal.com
International SOS	215/942-8000 or 713/521-7611	www.internationalsos.com
Wallach & Company	800/237-6615 or 504/687-3166	www.wallach.com

comfortable you are assuming all that risk yourself.

Comprehensive travel policies typically cover trip-cancellation and interruption, letting you cancel or cut your trip short because of a personal emergency, illness, or, in some cases, acts of terrorism in your destination. Such policies also cover evacuation and medical care. Some also cover you for trip delays because of bad weather or mechanical problems as well as for lost or delayed baggage. Another type of coverage to look for is financial default— that is, when your trip is disrupted because a tour operator, airline, or cruise line goes out of business. Generally you must buy this when you book your trip or shortly thereafter, and it's only available to you if your operator isn't on a list of excluded companies.

If you're going abroad, consider buying medical-only coverage at the very least. Neither Medicare nor some private insurers cover medical expenses anywhere outside of the United States besides Mexico and Canada (including time aboard a cruise ship, even if it leaves from a U.S. port). Medical-only policies typically re-

imburse you for medical care (excluding that related to preexisting conditions) and hospitalization abroad, and provide for evacuation. You still have to pay the bills and await reimbursement from the insurer, though. In Austria visitors must pay for all medical treatment, but rates tend to be much lower than comparable services in the United States.

Expect comprehensive travel insurance policies to cost about 4% to 7% of the total price of your trip (it's more like 12% if you're over age 70). A medical-only policy may or may not be cheaper than a comprehensive policy. Always read the fine print of your policy to make sure that you are covered for the risks that are of most concern to you. Compare several policies to make sure you're getting the best price and range of coverage available.

■ TIP→ **OK. You know you can save a bundle on trips to warm-weather destinations by traveling in rainy season. But there's also a chance that a severe storm will disrupt your plans. The solution? Look for hotels and resorts that offer storm/hurricane guarantees. Although they rarely allow refunds, most guarantees do let you rebook later if a storm strikes.**

BOOKING YOUR TRIP

Unless your cousin is a travel agent, you're probably among the millions of people who make most of their travel arrangements online. But have you ever wondered just what the differences are between an online travel agent (a Web site through which you make reservations instead of going directly to the airline, hotel, or car-rental company), a discounter (a firm that does a high volume of business with a hotel chain or airline and accordingly gets good prices), a wholesaler (one that makes cheap reservations in bulk and then resells them to people like you), and an aggregator (one that compares all the offerings so you don't have to)? Is it truly better to book directly on an airline or hotel Web site? And when does a real live travel agent come in handy?

ONLINE

You really have to shop around. A travel wholesaler such as Hotels.com or Hotel-Club.net can be a source of good rates, as can discounters such as Hotwire or Priceline, particularly if you can bid for your hotel room or airfare. Indeed, such sites sometimes have deals that are unavailable elsewhere. They do, however, tend to work only with hotel chains (which makes them just plain useless for getting hotel reservations outside of major cities) or big airlines (so that often leaves out upstarts like jetBlue and some foreign carriers like Air India). Also, with discounters and wholesalers you must generally prepay, and everything is nonrefundable. And before you fork over the dough, be sure to check the terms and conditions, so you know what a given company will do for you if there's a problem and what you'll have to deal with on your own.

■ TIP→ **To be absolutely sure everything was processed correctly, confirm reservations made through online travel agents, discounters, and wholesalers directly with your hotel before leaving home.**

Booking engines like Expedia, Travelocity, and Orbitz are actually travel agents, albeit high-volume, online ones. And airline travel packagers like American Airlines Vacations and Virgin Vacations—well, they're travel agents, too. But they may still not work with all the world's hotels.

An aggregator site will search many sites and pull the best prices for airfares, hotels, and rental cars from them. Most aggregators compare the major travel-booking sites such as Expedia, Travelocity, and Orbitz; some also look at airline Web sites, though rarely the sites of smaller budget airlines. Some aggregators also compare other travel products, including complex packages—a good thing, as you can sometimes get the best overall deal by booking an air-and-hotel package.

WITH A TRAVEL AGENT

If you use an agent—brick-and-mortar or virtual—you'll pay a fee for the service. And know that the service you get from some online agents isn't comprehensive. For example Expedia and Travelocity don't search for prices on budget airlines like jetBlue, Southwest, or small foreign carriers. That said, some agents (online or not) *do* have access to fares that are difficult to find otherwise, and the savings can more than make up for any surcharge.

A knowledgeable brick-and-mortar travel agent can be a godsend if you're booking a cruise, a package trip that's not available to you directly, an air pass, or a complicated itinerary including several overseas flights. What's more, travel agents that specialize in a destination may have exclusive access to certain deals and insider information on things such as charter flights. Agents who specialize in types of travelers (senior citizens, gays and lesbians, naturists) or types of trips (cruises, luxury travel, safaris) can also be invaluable.

Online Booking Resources

AGGREGATORS		
Kayak	www.kayak.com	also looks at cruises and vacation packages.
Mobissimo	www.mobissimo.com	
Qixo	www.qixo.com	also compares cruises, vacation packages, and even travel insurance.
Sidestep	www.sidestep.com	also compares vacation packages and lists travel deals.
Travelgrove	www.travelgrove.com	also compares cruises and packages.
BOOKING ENGINES		
Cheap Tickets	www.cheaptickets.com	a discounter.
Expedia	www.expedia.com	a large online agency that charges a booking fee for airline tickets.
Hotwire	www.hotwire.com	a discounter.
lastminute.com	www.lastminute.com	specializes in last-minute travel; the main site is for the U.K., but it has a link to a U.S. site.
Luxury Link	www.luxurylink.com	has auctions (surprisingly good deals) as well as offers on the high-end side of travel.
Onetravel.com	www.onetravel.com	a discounter for hotels, car rentals, airfares, and packages.
Orbitz	www.orbitz.com	charges a booking fee for airline tickets, but gives a clear breakdown of fees and taxes before you book.
Priceline.com	www.priceline.com	a discounter that also allows bidding.
Travel.com	www.travel.com	allows you to compare its rates with those of other booking engines.
Travelocity	www.travelocity.com	charges a booking fee for airline tickets, but promises good problem resolution.
ONLINE ACCOMMODATIONS		
Hotelbook.com	www.hotelbook.com	focuses on independent hotels worldwide.
Hotel Club	www.hotelclub.net	good for major cities worldwide.
Hotels.com	www.hotels.com	a big Expedia-owned wholesaler that offers rooms in hotels all over the world.
Quikbook	www.quikbook.com	offers "pay when you stay" reservations that let you settle your bill at check out, not when you book.
OTHER RESOURCES		
Bidding For Travel	www.biddingfortravel.com	a good place to figure out what you can get and for how much before you start bidding on, say, Priceline.

A top-notch agent planning your trip to Russia will make sure you get the correct visa application and complete it on time; the one booking your cruise may get you a cabin upgrade or arrange to have bottle of champagne chilling in your cabin when you embark. And complain about the surcharges all you like, but when things don't work out the way you'd hoped, it's nice to have an agent to put things right.

■ TIP➔ Remember that Expedia, Travelocity, and Orbitz are travel agents, not just booking engines. To resolve any problems with a reservation made through these companies, contact them first.

General travel agencies serving Austria include American Express, Kuoni Cosmos, and Österreichisches Verkehrsbüro. American Express, Kuoni Cosmos, and Vienna Ticket Service/Cityrama are agencies that offer tickets to various sights and events in Vienna.

Agent Resources **American Society of Travel Agents** ☎ 703/739–2782 ⊕ www.travelsense. org.

Austria Travel Agents **American Express** ☎ 01/512-4004 ⊕ www.americanexpress. com. **Kuoni Cosmos** ☎ 01/515-33-0 ⊕ www. kuoni.at. **Österreichisches Verkehrsbüro** ☎ 01/588-628 ⊕ www.verkehrsbuero.at. **Vienna Ticket Service/Cityrama** ☎ 01/534-130 ⊕ www.cityrama.at.

ACCOMMODATIONS

You can live like a king in a real castle in Austria or get by on a modest budget. Starting at the lower end, you can find a room in a private house or on a farm, or dormitory space in a youth hostel. Next up the line come the simpler pensions, many of them identified as a *Frühstückspensionen* (bed-and-breakfasts). Then come *Gasthäuser,* the simpler country inns. Fancier pensions in cities can often cost as much as hotels; the difference lies in the services they offer. Most pensions, for example, do not staff the front desk around the clock. Among the hotels, you can find accommodations ranging from the most modest, with a shower and toilet down the hall, to the most elegant, with every possible amenity. Increasingly, more and more hotels in the lower to middle price range are including breakfast with the basic room charge, but check when booking. Room rates for hotels in the rural countryside can often include breakfast and one other meal (in rare cases, all three meals are included).

Lodgings in Austria are generally rated from one to five stars, depending mainly on the facilities offered and the price of accommodation rather than on more subjective attributes like charm and location. In general, five-star properties are top of the line, with every conceivable amenity and priced accordingly. The distinctions get blurrier the further down the rating chain you go. There may little difference between a two- and three-star property except perhaps the price. In practice, don't rely heavily on the star system, and always try to see the hotel and room before you book. That's said, lodging standards are generally very good, and even in one- and two-star properties you can usually be guaranteed a clean room and a private bath.

Here is a list of German words that can come in handy when booking a room: air-conditioning (*Klimaanlage*); private bath (*privat Bad*); bathtub (*Badewanne*); shower (*Dusche*); double bed (*Doppelbett*); twin beds (*Einzelbetten*).

All hotels listed in this guide have private bath unless otherwise noted. Lodging price categories from ¢ to $$$$ are defined in the Where to Stay sections of the Vienna and Salzburg chapters and in the opening pages of each regional chapter.

Most hotels and other lodgings require you to give your credit-card details before they will confirm your reservation. If you don't feel comfortable e-mailing this information, ask if you can fax it (some places even prefer faxes). However you book, get confirmation in writing and have a copy of it handy when you check in.

10 WAYS TO SAVE

1. Join "frequent guest" programs. You may get preferential treatment in room choice and/or upgrades in your favorite chains.

2. Call direct. You can sometimes get a better price if you call a hotel's local toll-free number (if available) rather than a central reservations number.

3. Check online. Check hotel Web sites, as not all chains are represented on all travel sites.

4. Look for specials. Always inquire about packages and corporate rates.

5. Look for price guarantees. For overseas trips, look for guaranteed rates. With your rate locked in you won't pay more, even if the price goes up in the local currency.

6. Look for weekend deals at business hotels. High-end chains catering to business travelers are often busy only on weekdays; to fill rooms they often drop rates dramatically on weekends.

7. Ask about taxes. Verify whether local hotel taxes are included in quoted rates. In some places taxes can add 20% or more to your bill.

8. Read the fine print. Watch for add-ons, including resort fees, energy surcharges, and "convenience" fees for such things as unlimited local phone service you won't use or a free newspaper in a language you can't read.

9. Know when to go. If your destination's high season is December through April and you're trying to book, say, in late April, you might save money by changing your dates by a week or two. Ask when rates go down, though: if your dates straddle peak and non-peak seasons, a property may still charge peak-season rates for the entire stay.

10. Weigh your options (we can't say this enough). Weigh transportation times and costs against the savings of staying in a hotel that's cheaper because it's out of the way.

Be sure you understand the hotel's cancellation policy. Some places allow you to cancel without any kind of penalty—even if you prepaid to secure a discounted rate—if you cancel at least 24 hours in advance. Others require you to cancel a week in advance or penalize you the cost of one night. Small inns and B&Bs are most likely to require you to cancel far in advance. Most hotels allow children under a certain age to stay in their parents' room at no extra charge, but others charge for them as extra adults; find out the cutoff age for discounts.

■ TIP➔ Assume that hotels operate on the European Plan (EP, no meals) unless we specify that they use the Breakfast Plan (BP, with full breakfast), Continental Plan (CP, Continental breakfast), Full American Plan (FAP, all meals), or Modified American Plan (MAP, breakfast and dinner), or are all-inclusive (AI, all meals and most activities).

Information-Zimmernachweis ☎ 01/892–3392 in Westbahnhof. **Vienna Tourist Board's hotel assistance service** ☎ 01/24–555 ⊕ www.wien.info.

APARTMENT & HOUSE RENTALS

Rentals are an important part of the accommodations mix in Austria, with one-, two- or four-week rentals becoming increasing popular. Most of the rental properties are owned privately by individuals, and often the main rental organizers are simply the local tourist offices.

CASTLES

Schlosshotels und Herrenhäuser in Österreich, or "Castle Hotels and Mansions in Austria," is an association of castles and palaces that have been converted into hotels. The quality of the accommodation varies with the property, but many have been beautifully restored and can be a memorable alternative to standard hotels. The Web site is in English and has plenty of photos. The association also links a scattering of castles in the Czech Republic, Hungary, Slovenia, Croatia, and Italy. **Schlosshotels und Herrenhäuser in Österreich** ☎ 0662/8306–8141 ⊟ 0662/8306–8161 ⊕ www.schlosshotels.co.at.

FARM VACATIONS

See Eco Tours *in* Guided Tours *below.*

HOME EXCHANGES

With a direct home exchange you stay in someone else's home while they stay in yours. Some outfits also deal with vacation homes, so you're not actually staying in someone's full-time residence, just their vacant weekend place.

Exchange Clubs Home Exchange.com ☎ 800/877-8723 ⊕ www.homeexchange. com; $59.95 for a 1-year online listing. **HomeLink International** ☎ 800/638-3841 ⊕ www.homelink.org; $80 yearly for Web-only membership; $125 includes Web access and two catalogs. **Intervac U.S.** ☎ 800/756-4663 ⊕ www.intervacus.com; $78.88 for Web-only membership; $126 includes Web access and a catalog.

HOSTELS

Hostels offer bare-bones lodging at low, low prices—often in shared dorm rooms with shared baths—to people of all ages, though the primary market is young travelers, especially students. Most hostels serve breakfast; dinner and/or shared cooking facilities may also be available. In some hostels you aren't allowed to be in your room during the day, and there may be a curfew at night. Nevertheless, hostels provide a sense of community, with public rooms where travelers often gather to share stories. Many hostels are affiliated with Hostelling International (HI), an umbrella group of hostel associations with some 4,500 member properties in more than 70 countries. Other hostels are completely independent and may be nothing more than a really cheap hotel.

WORD OF MOUTH

Did the resort look as good in real life as it did in the photos? Did you sleep like a baby, or were the walls paper-thin? Did you get your money's worth? Rate hotels and write your own reviews in Travel Ratings or start a discussion about your favorite places in Travel Talk on www.fodors. com. Your comments might even appear in our books. Yes, you, too, can be a correspondent!

Membership in any HI association, open to travelers of all ages, allows you to stay in HI-affiliated hostels at member rates. One-year membership is about $28 for adults; hostels charge about $10–$30 per night. Members have priority if the hostel is full; they're also eligible for discounts around the world, even on rail and bus travel in some countries.

Austria has more than 100 government-sponsored youth hostels, for which you need an HI membership card. Inexpensively priced, these hostels are run by the Österreichischer Jugendherbergsverband and are popular with the back-pack crowd, so be sure to reserve in advance.

Hostelling International–USA ☎ 301/495-1240 ⊕ www.hiusa.org. **Österreichischer Jugendherbergsverband** ☎ 01/533-53-53 🖷 01/535-0861.

▮ AIRLINE TICKETS

Most domestic airline tickets are electronic; international tickets may be either electronic or paper. With an e-ticket the

---

Online Booking Resources

Barclay International Group	516/364-0064 or 800/845-6636	www.barclayweb.com
Drawbridge to Europe	541/482-7778 or 888/268-1148	www.drawbridgetoeurope.com
Interhome	954/791-8282 or 800/882-6864	www.interhome.us
Villas & Apartments Abroad	212/213-6435 or 800/433-3020	www.vaanyc.com
Villas International	415/499-9490 or 800/221-2260	www.villasintl.com

10 WAYS TO SAVE ✈

1. Nonrefundable is best. If saving money is more important than flexibility, then non-refundable tickets work. Just remember that you'll pay dearly (as much as $100) if you change your plans.

2. Comparison shop. Web sites and travel agents can have different arrangements with the airlines and offer different prices for exactly the same flights.

3. Beware those prices. Many airline Web sites—and most ads—show prices *without* taxes and surcharges. Don't buy until you know the full price.

4. Stay loyal. Stick with one or two frequent-flier programs. You'll rack up free trips faster and you'll accumulate more quickly the perks that make trips easier. On some airlines these include a special reservations number, early boarding, access to upgrades, and roomier economy-class seating.

5. Watch those ticketing fees. Surcharges are usually added when you buy your ticket anywhere but on an airline Web site. (That includes by phone—even if you call the airline directly—and paper tickets regardless of how you book).

6. Check early and often. Start looking for cheap fares up to a year in advance, and keep looking until you see something you can live with.

7. Don't work alone. Some Web sites have tracking features that will e-mail you immediately when good deals are posted.

8. Jump on the good deals. Waiting even a few minutes might mean paying more.

9. Fly mid-week. Look for departures on Tuesday, Wednesday, and Thursday, typically the cheapest days to travel.

10. Be flexible. Check on prices for departures at different times and to and from alternative airports.

only thing you receive is an e-mailed receipt citing your itinerary and reservation and ticket numbers. The greatest advantage of an e-ticket is that if you lose your receipt you can simply print out another copy or ask the airline to do it for you at check-in. You usually pay a surcharge (up to $50) to get a paper ticket, if you can get one at all. The sole advantage of a paper ticket is that it may be easier to endorse over to another airline if your flight is canceled and the airline with which you booked can't accommodate you on another flight.

■ TIP➔ Discount air passes that let you travel economically in a country or region must often be purchased before you leave home. In some cases you can only get them through a travel agent.

■ RENTAL CARS

When you reserve a car, ask about cancellation penalties, taxes, drop-off charges (if you're planning to pick up the car in one city and leave it in another), and surcharges (for being under or over a certain age, for additional drivers, or for driving across state or country borders or beyond a specific distance from your point of rental). All these things can add substantially to your costs. Request car seats and extras such as GPS when you book.

Rates are sometimes—but not always—better if you book in advance or reserve through a rental agency's Web site. There are other reasons to book ahead, though: for popular destinations, during busy times of the year, or to ensure that you get certain types of cars (vans, SUVs, exotic sports cars).

■ TIP➔ Make sure that a confirmed reservation guarantees you a car. Agencies sometimes overbook, particularly for busy weekends and holiday periods.

Rates in Vienna begin at about €50 a day and €132 a weekend for an economy car with manual transmission and unlimited mileage. This includes a 21% tax on car rentals. Rates are more expensive in winter months, when a surcharge for winter tires may be added. Renting a car may be cheaper in Germany, but make sure the rental agency knows you are driving into Austria and that the car is equipped with the *Autobahnvignette,* an autobahn sticker for Austria. Get your sticker, also known as a Pickerl, before driving to Austria (*see* Car Travel, *below*). When renting an RV be sure to compare prices and reserve early. It's cheaper to arrange your rental car from the U.S., but be sure to get a confirmation of your quoted rate in writing.

The age requirement for renting a car in Austria is generally 19, and you must have had a valid driver's license for one year. For some of the more expensive car models, drivers must be at least 25 years of age.

There is no extra charge to drive over the border into Italy, Switzerland, or Germany, but there may be some restrictions for taking a rental into Slovakia, Slovenia, Hungary, the Czech Republic, or Poland. If you're planning on traveling east, it's best to let the agency know beforehand.

In Austria your own driver's license is acceptable. An International Driver's Permit (IDP), while not strictly necessary, is a good idea; these international permits are universally recognized, and having one in your wallet may save you a problem with the local authorities. An International Driving Permit (IDP) can be used only in conjunction with a valid driver's license, and translates your license into 10 languages. Check the AAA Web site for more info as well as for IDPs ($10) themselves.

Car Rental Resources

AUTOMOBILE ASSOCIATIONS		
American Automobile Association	315/797–5000	www.aaa.com; most contact with the organization is through state and regional members.
National Automobile Club	650/294–7000	www.thenac.com; membership open to CA residents only.
Austrian Automobile Club/ÖAMTC	01/71199–0	www.oemtc.at
LOCAL AGENCIES		
Denzel Drive	Erdberg Center/U-Bahn (U3), A-1110, Vienna; 01/740–200	
Autovermietung Buchbinder	Schlachthausgasse 38, A-1030, Vienna; 01/717–5050, with offices throughout Austria.	
MAJOR AGENCIES		
Alamo	800/462–5266	www.alamo.com
Avis	800/230–4898	www.avis.com
Budget	800/527–0700	www.budget.com
Hertz	800/654–3131	www.hertz.com
National Car Rental	800/227–7368	www.nationalcar.com
WHOLESALERS		
Auto Europe	888/223–5555	www.autoeurope.com
Europe by Car	212/581–3040 in New York, 800/223–1516	www.europebycar.com
Eurovacations	877/471–3876	www.eurovacations.com
Kemwel	877/820–0668	www.kemwel.com

10 WAYS TO SAVE

1. **Beware of cheap rates.** Those great rates aren't so great when you add in taxes, surcharges, and insurance. Such extras can double or triple the initial quote.

2. **Rent weekly.** Weekly rates are usually better than daily ones. Even if you only want to rent for five or six days, ask for the weekly rate; it may very well be cheaper than the daily rate for that period of time.

3. **Don't forget the locals.** Price local companies as well as the majors.

4. **Airport rentals can cost more.** Airports often add surcharges, which you can sometimes avoid by renting from an agency whose office is just off airport property.

5. **Wholesalers can help.** Investigate wholesalers, which don't own fleets but rent in bulk from firms that do, and which frequently offer better rates (note that you must usually pay for such rentals before leaving home).

6. **Look for rate guarantees.** With your rate locked in, you won't pay more, even if the price goes up in the local currency.

7. **Fill up farther away.** Avoid hefty refueling fees by filling the tank at a station well away from where you plan to turn in the car.

8. **Pump it yourself.** Don't buy the tank of gas that's in the car when you rent it unless you plan to do a lot of driving.

9. **Get all your discounts.** Find out whether a credit card you carry or organization or frequent-renter program to which you belong has a discount program. And confirm that such discounts really are a deal. You can often do better with special weekend or weekly rates offered by a rental agency.

10. **Check out package rates.** Adding a car rental onto your air/hotel vacation package may be cheaper than renting a car separately on your own.

CAR-RENTAL INSURANCE

Everyone who rents a car wonders whether the insurance that the rental companies offer is worth the expense. No one—including us—has a simple answer. It all depends on how much regular insurance you have, how comfortable you are with risk, and whether or not money is an issue.

If you own a car, your personal auto insurance may cover a rental to some degree, though not all policies protect you abroad; always read your policy's fine print. If you don't have auto insurance, then seriously consider buying the collision- or loss-damage waiver (CDW or LDW) from the car-rental company, which eliminates your liability for damage to the car. Some credit cards offer CDW coverage, but it's usually supplemental to your own insurance and rarely covers SUVs, minivans, luxury models, and the like. If your coverage is secondary, you may still be liable for loss-of-use costs from the car-rental company. But no credit-card insurance is valid unless you use that card for *all* transactions, from reserving to paying the final bill. All companies exclude car rental in some countries, so be sure to find out about the destination to which you are traveling.

■ TIP→ **Diners Club offers primary CDW coverage on all rentals reserved and paid for with the card. This means that Diners Club's company—not your own car insurance—pays in case of an accident. It *doesn't* mean your car-insurance company won't raise your rates once it discovers you had an accident.**

Some countries require you to purchase CDW coverage or require car-rental companies to include it in quoted rates. Ask your rental company about issues like these in your destination. In most cases it's cheaper to add a supplemental CDW plan to your comprehensive travel-insurance policy (⇨ Trip Insurance *under* Things to Consider *in* Getting Started, *above*) than to purchase it from a rental company. That said, you don't want to pay for a supplement if you're required to buy insurance from the rental company.

GETTING STARTED / **BOOKING YOUR TRIP** / TRANSPORTATION / ON THE GROUND

■ TIP→ You can decline the insurance from the rental company and purchase it through a third-party provider such as Travel Guard (www.travelguard.com)—$9 per day for $35,000 of coverage. That's sometimes just under half the price of the CDW offered by some car-rental companies.

■ TRAIN PASSES

Austria is one of 18 countries in which you can use Eurailpasses, which provide unlimited first-class rail travel, in all of the participating countries, for the duration of the pass. If you plan to rack up the miles, get a standard pass. These are available for 15 days ($605), 21 days ($785), one month ($975), two months ($1,378), and three months ($1,703).

In addition to standard Eurailpasses, ask about special rail-pass plans. Among these are the Eurail Youthpass (for those under age 26), the Eurail Saverpass (which gives a discount for two or more people traveling together), a Eurail Flexipass (which allows a certain number of travel days within a set period), and the Euraildrive Pass (which combines travel by train and rental car). Whichever pass you choose, remember that you must purchase your pass before you leave for Europe.

Another option that gives you discount travel through various countries is the European East Pass, offered by Rail Europe, good for travel within Austria, the Czech Republic, Hungary, Poland, and Slovakia: the cost is $244 (first class) or $172 (second class) for any 5 days of unlimited travel within a one-month period.

The ÖBB, the Austrian Austrian Federal Train Service has a Web site, but it is not particularly user-friendly. As it is often impossible to get through to them on the phone, it is best to get to the train station early for questions. The ÖBB offers a large number of discounts for various travel constellations. If you are traveling with a group of people, even small, there are percentages taken off for each member. Fam-

ilies can also get discounts. School children and students also get good deals. The Vorteilscard is valid for a year and costs about €100, allowing 45% fare reduction on all rail travel. If you are planning lots of travel in Austria, it could be a good deal. Ask for other special deals, and check travel agencies. Children between 6 and 15 travel at half price, under 6 years of age for free.

You can buy an Austrian Rail Pass in the United States for travel within Austria for 15 days ($181 first class, $124 second class). It's available for purchase in Austria also, but only at travel agencies, such as SNS Tours.

For about €30 and a passport photo, women over 60 and men over 65 can obtain a Seniorenpass, which carries a 45% discount on rail tickets. The pass also has a host of other benefits, including reduced-price entry into museums. Most rail stations can give you information.

Travelers under 26 should inquire about discount fares under the Billet International Jeune (BIJ). The special one-trip tickets are sold by Eurotrain International, travel agents, and youth-travel specialists, and at rail stations.

Many travelers assume that rail passes guarantee them seats on the trains they wish to ride. Not so. You need to book seats ahead even if you are using a rail pass; seat reservations are required on some European trains, particularly high-speed trains, and are a good idea on trains that may be crowded—particularly in summer on popular routes. You will also need a reservation if you purchase sleeping accommodations.

Train Passes **CIT Tours Corp** ☎ 212/730-2400, 800/248-7245 in U.S. ⊕ www.cit-tours. com. **DER Travel Services** ☎ 800/782-2424 ⊕ www.dertravel.com. **ÖBB (Österreichische Bundesbahnen)** ⊕ www.oebb.at. **Rail Europe** ☎ 914/682-5172 or 800/438-7245 ⊕ www.raileurope.com. **SNS Tours** ⊕ www. snstours.com/ausrail.htm.

▮ VACATION PACKAGES

Packages *are not* guided excursions. Packages combine airfare, accommodations, and perhaps a rental car or other extras (theater tickets, guided excursions, boat trips, reserved entry to popular museums, transit passes, but they let you do your own thing. During busy periods packages may be your only option, as flights and rooms may be sold out otherwise. Packages will definitely save you time. They can also save you money, particularly in peak seasons, but—and this is a really big "but"—you should price each part of the package separately to be sure. And be aware that prices advertised on Web sites and in newspapers rarely include service charges or taxes, which can up your costs by hundreds of dollars.

▮ TIP→ Some packages and cruises are sold only through travel agents. Don't always assume that you can get the best deal by booking everything yourself.

Each year consumers are stranded or lose their money when packagers—even large ones with excellent reputations—go out of business. How can you protect yourself? First, always pay with a credit card; if you have a problem, your credit-card company may help you resolve it. Second, buy trip insurance that covers default. Third, choose a company that belongs to the United States Tour Operators Association, whose members must set aside funds to cover defaults. Finally, choose a company that also participates in the Tour Operator Program of the American Society of Travel Agents (ASTA), which will act as mediator in any disputes. You can also check on the tour operator's reputation among travelers by posting an inquiry on one of the Fodors.com forums.

Organizations **American Society of Travel Agents** (ASTA) ☎ 703/739-2782 or 800/965-2782 ⊕ www.astanet.com. **United States Tour Operators Association** (USTOA) ☎ 212/599-6599 ⊕ www.ustoa.com.

▮ TIP→ Local tourism boards can provide information about lesser-known and small-niche operators that sell packages to only a few destinations.

▮ GUIDED TOURS

Guided tours are a good option when you don't want to do it all yourself. You travel along with a group (sometimes large, sometimes small), stay in prebooked hotels, eat with your fellow travelers (the cost of meals sometimes included in the price of your tour, sometimes not), and follow a schedule. But not all guided tours are an if-it's-Tuesday-this-must-be-Belgium experience. A knowledgeable guide can take you places that you might never discover on your own, and you may be pushed to see more than you would have otherwise. Tours aren't for everyone, but they can be just the thing for trips to places where making travel arrangements is difficult or time-consuming (particularly when you don't speak the language). Whenever you book a guided tour, find out what's included and what isn't. A "land-only" tour includes all your travel (by bus, in most cases) in the destination, but not necessarily your flights to and from or even within it. Also, in most cases prices in tour brochures don't include fees and taxes. And remember that you'll be expected to tip your guide (in cash) at the end of the tour.

Among companies that sell tours to Austria, the following are nationally known, have a proven reputation, and offer plenty of options. The classifications used below represent different price categories, and you'll probably encounter these terms when talking to a travel agent or tour operator. The key difference is usually in accommodations. Note that each company doesn't schedule tours to Austria every year; check by calling.

Super-Deluxe **Abercrombie & Kent** ☎ 800/554-7016 ⊕ www.abercrombiekent.com. **Travcoa** ☎ 866/591-0070 ⊕ www.travcoa.com.

Deluxe **Globus** ☎ 866/755-8581 ⊕ www.globusjourneys.com. **Maupintour** ✉ 1515 St. Andrews Dr., Lawrence, KS 66047 ☎ 785/843-

1211 or 800/255-4266 🖷 785/843-8351. **Tauck Tours** ☎ 800/788-7885 ⊕ www.tauck.com. **First-Class Brendan Tours** ☎ 800/421-8446 ⊕ www.brendanvacations.com. **Collette Tours** ☎ 800/340-5158 ⊕ www. collettevacations.com. **DER Travel Services** ✉ 9501 W. Devon Ave., Rosemont, IL 60018 ☎ 800/937-1235 🖷 847/692-4141, 800/282-7474, 800/860-9944 for brochures. **Gadabout Tours** ☎ 760/325-5556 or 800/952-5068 ⊕ www.gadabouttours.com. **Trafalgar Tours** ✉ 11 E. 26th St., New York, NY 10010 ☎ 212/689-8977 or 800/854-0103 🖷 800/457-6644. **Budget Cosmos** (see Globus, above). **Trafalgar Tours** (see above).

SPECIAL-INTEREST TOURS

BIKING

The Austrian national tourist information Web site ⊕ www.austria.info includes excellent sections on hotels that welcome cyclists, as well as some of the better-known tours and routes. You can no longer rent a bike at train stations in Austria. The cost of renting a bike (21-gear) from a local agency is around €27 a day. Tourist offices have details (in German), including maps and hints for trip planning and mealtime and overnight stops that cater especially to cyclists. Ask for the booklet "Radtouren in Österreich." There's also a brochure in English: "Biking Austria—On the Trail of Mozart" that provides details in English on the cycle route through the High Tauern mountains in Salzburg Province.

■ TIP→ **Most airlines accommodate bikes as luggage, provided they're dismantled and boxed.**
Austria Radreisen ☎ 07712/5511-0 🖷 07712/4811 ⊕ www.austria-radreisen.at. **Backroads** ✉ 801 Cedar St., Berkeley, CA 94710-1800 ☎ 510/527-1555 or 800/462-2848 🖷 510/527-1444. **Butterfield & Robinson** ☎ 416/864-1354 or 800/678-1147 🖷 416/864-0541 ⊕ www.butterfield.com. **Euro-Bike Tours** ✉ Box 990, De Kalb, IL 60115 ☎ 800/321-6060 🖷 815/758-8851. **Mountain Bike Hotels** ☎ 0810/101818 🖷 0810/101819 ⊕ www.austria.info. **Pedal Power** ☎ 01/729-7234

🖷 01/729-7235 ⊕ www.pedalpower.at. **VBT (Vermont Biking Tours)** ☎ 800/245-3868 ⊕ www.vbt.com offers a spectacular Salzburg Sojourn tour.

CHRISTMAS/NEW YEAR'S

Annemarie Victory Organization ☎ 212/486-0353 🖷 212/751-3149 ⊕ www.annemarievictory.com is known for its spectacular "New Year's Eve Ball in Vienna" excursion. Annemarie Victory also organizes a "Christmas in Salzburg" trip, with rooms at the Goldener Hirsch and a side trip to the Silent Night Chapel in Oberndorf. **Smolka Tours** (see Barge/River Cruises, above) has also conducted festive holiday-season tours that included concerts, gala balls, and the famous Christmas Markets of Vienna and Salzburg.

ECO TOURS

Austria is a popular vacation spot for those who want to experience nature—many rural hotels offer idyllic bases for hiking in the mountains or lake areas. The concept of the *Urlaub am Bauernhof* (farm vacation), where families can stay on a working farm and children can help take care of farm animals, is increasingly popular throughout Austria. There are numerous outfitters that can provide information on basic as well as specialty farms, such as organic farms or farms for children, for the disabled, or for horseback riders.
Landidyll-Hotels in Österreich ⊕ www.landidyll.at—unfortunately the Web site is in German only, but there are plenty of photos to show what the accommodations look like. **Austrian Tourist Board** ⊕ www.austria.info. **Information on Farm Vacations Farmhouse Holidays in Austria** ⊕ www.farmholidays.com—based in Salzburg, with an English language Web site and online booking. **Kärnten/Landesverband Urlaub auf dem Bauernhof** ⊕ www.urlaubambauernhof.com.—based in Carinthia and with English language Web site booking. **Oberösterreich/Das Land vor den Alpen** Upper Austria ☎ 050/69-02-1248 ⊕ www.upperaustria.farmholidays.com—German-only Web site, but filled with

photos. **Salzburg/Das Land der Tradition**
☎ 0662/870-571-248 ⊕ www.salzburg.
farmholidays.com. **Tirol/Das Land der Berge**
☎ 05/9292-1172 ⊕ www.bauernhof.cc.

HIKING & MOUNTAIN CLIMBING

With more than 50,000 km (about 35,000 mi) of well-maintained mountain paths through Europe's largest reserve of unspoiled landscape, the country is a hiker's paradise. Three long-distance routes traverse Austria, including the E-6 from the Baltic, cutting across mid-Austria via the Wachau valley region of the Danube and on to the Adriatic. Wherever you are in Austria, you will find shorter hiking trails requiring varying degrees of ability. Routes are well marked, and maps are readily available from bookstores, the Österreichische Alpenverein/ÖAV, and the automobile clubs.

If you're a newcomer to mountain climbing or want to improve your skill, schools in Salzburg province will take you on. Ask the ÖAV for addresses. All organize courses and guided tours for beginners as well as for more advanced climbers.

Tourist offices have details on hiking holidays; serious climbers can write directly to **Österreichischer Alpenverein/ÖAV** (Austrian Alpine Club) for more information. Membership in the club (€48.50, about $60) will give you a 30%–50% reduction from the regular fees for overnights in the 275 mountain refuges it operates. Senior citizen memberships have a reduced price.
Alpine Adventure Trails Tours ⊠ 322 Pio Nono Ave., Macon, GA 31204 ☎ 912/478-4007. **Mountain Travel-Sobek** ⊠ 6420 Fairmount Ave., El Cerrito, CA 94530 ☎ 510/527-8100 or 800/227-2384 🖷 510/525-7710. **Österreichischer Alpenverein** ☎ 0512/59547 🖷 0512/575528 ⊕ www.alpenverein.at.

▌ CRUISES

For leisurely travel between Vienna and Linz or eastward across the border into Slovakia or Hungary, consider taking a Danube boat. **Blue Danube Schifffahrt** offers a diverse selection of pleasant cruises, including trips to Melk Abbey and Dürnstein in the Wachau, a grand tour of Vienna's architectural sights from the river, and a dinner cruise, featuring Johann Strauss waltzes as background music. **Brandner Schifffart** offers the same kind of cruises between Krems and Melk, in the heart of the Danube Valley.

Most of the immaculate white-painted craft carry about 1,000 passengers each on their three decks. As soon as you get on board, give the steward a good tip for a deck chair and ask him to place it where you will get the best views. Be sure to book cabins in advance. Day trips are also possible on the Danube. You can use boats to move from one riverside community to the next, and along some sections, notably the Wachau, the only way to cross the river is to use the little shuttles (in the Wachau, these are special motorless boats that use the current to cross).

For the cruises up and down the Danube, the DDSG/Blue Danube Steamship Company departs and arrives at Praterlände near Vienna's Mexikoplatz. The Praterlände stop is a two-block taxi ride or hike from the Vorgartenstrasse subway station on the U1 route of Vienna's U-Bahn. There is no pier number, but you board at Handelskai 265. Boat trips from Vienna to the Wachau are on Sunday only from May to September. The price is about €20 one-way and €30 round-trip. There are other daily cruises within the Wachau, such as from Melk to Krems. Other cruises, to Budapest for instance, operate from April to early November. The Web site has dozens of options and timetables in English. For cruises from Krems to Melk, contact Brandner Schifffahrt. For more information, *see the* "Danube River Cruises" *box in* Chapter 4.
Cruise Lines Brandner Schifffahrt ☎ 07433/2590-21 ⊕ www.brandner.at. **DDSG/Blue Danube Schifffahrt** ☎ 01/588-80 🖷 01/588-8044-0 ⊕ www.ddsg-blue-danube.at.

TRANSPORTATION

▌BY AIR

Flying time is 8 hours to Vienna from New York, 9 hours from Washington, D.C., and 2 hours from London.

Airlines & Airports Airline and Airport Links.com ⊕ www.airlineandairportlinks.com has links to many of the world's airlines and airports.

Airline Security Issues Transportation Security Administration ⊕ www.tsa.gov has answers for almost every question that might come up.

AIRPORTS

Austria's major air gateway is Vienna's **Schwechat Airport,** about 12 mi southeast of the city. **Salzburg Airport** is Austria's second-largest airport, about 2½ mi west of the center. Just south of Graz, in Thalerhof, is the **Graz Airport.** Two other airports you might consider, depending on where in Austria you intend to travel, are Bratislava's M. R. Stefanik international airport in neighboring Slovakia, and Munich's airport, not far from Salzburg. Bratislava is about 60 kms (36 mi east of Vienna) and is the hub for SkyEurope, a relatively new budget carrier with low-cost connections to several European cities. Frequent buses can take you from Bratislava airport to central Vienna in about an hour. Consider Munich if your primary destination is western Austria, Salzburg, or Innsbruck.

Note that airport taxes can be steep, and comprise a significant portion of the overall ticket price. Some quotes will include airport tax, others won't. The best bet is to ask specifically whether the tax is included.

Airport Information Graz Airport (GRZ) ☎ 0316/2902-0. **M. R. Stefanik Airport (Bratislava, BTS)** ☎ 00421-2-4857-3353 from outside of Slovakia. **Munich Airport International (MUC)** ☎ 0049-89-97500 from outside Germany. **Salzburg Airport (SZG)** ☎ 0662/8580. **Schwechat Airport (Vienna, VIE)** ☎ 01/7007-0.

FLIGHTS

Austria is easy to reach from the United States. Austrian Airlines, Austria's national carrier, flies nonstop to Vienna from the U.S., departing from New York's JFK airport and Washington Dulles. From Canada, Austrian flies direct from Toronto. Austrian Airlines is a member of the Star Alliance, and is partnered with United in the U.S., meaning usually good connections from cities serviced by United. Once in Vienna, Austrian Airlines has an excellent network of internal flights linking the capital with major regional cities like Salzburg and Graz. It's also possible to travel from North America with major U.S. carriers—such as American, Northwest, and United—but you'll be routed to a major European hub, such as London, Amsterdam, or Frankfurt, to change planes for Vienna. Be sure to leave plenty of time between connections (two hours is ideal), as these hubs tend to be enormous and getting from your arrival gate to your new departure point will inevitably take some time.

Travelers from North America should note too that many international carriers offer service to Vienna after stopovers at major European airports. For instance, Lufthansa flies from the U.S. to Frankfurt and other cities in Germany and then can offer connections to Vienna. British Airways (which has several gateways from the U.S.) offers direct flights to Vienna from its London hub. Note, too, that the western sector of Austria—including Tirol and Vorarlberg—is actually closer to Munich than to Vienna, so you might consider using an international carrier to Munich, then traveling by train to Salzburg or Innsbruck. The airport at nearby Bratislava in Slovakia is an easy hour-long bus ride away from Vienna and offers the same advantages for travel to eastern Austria.

GETTING STARTED / BOOKING YOUR TRIP / **TRANSPORTATION** / ON THE GROUND

FLYING 101

Flying may not be as carefree as it once was, but there are some things you can do to make your trip smoother.

MINIMIZE THE TIME SPENT STANDING IN LINE. Buy an e-ticket, check in at an electronic kiosk, or—even better—check in on your airline's Web site before leaving home. Pack light and limit carry-on items to only the essentials.

ARRIVE WHEN YOU NEED TO. Research your airline's policy. It's usually at least an hour before domestic flights and two to three hours before international flights. But airlines at some busy airports have more stringent requirements. Check the TSA Web site for estimated security waiting times at major airports.

GET TO THE GATE. If you aren't at the gate at least 10 minutes before your flight is scheduled to take off (sometimes earlier), you won't be allowed to board.

DOUBLE-CHECK YOUR FLIGHT TIMES. Do this especially if you reserved far in advance. Schedules change, and alerts may not reach you.

DON'T GO HUNGRY. Ask whether your airline offers anything to eat; even when it does, be prepared to pay.

GET THE SEAT YOU WANT. Often you can pick a seat when you buy your ticket on an airline Web site. But it's not guaranteed; the airline could change the plane after you book, so double-check. You can also select a seat if you check in electronically. Avoid seats on the aisle directly across from the lavatories. Frequent fliers say those are even worse than back-row seats that don't recline.

GOT KIDS? GET INFO. Ask the airline about its children's menus, activities, and fares. Sometimes infants and toddlers fly free if they sit on a parent's lap, and older children fly for half price in their own seats. Also inquire about policies involving car seats; having one may limit seating options. Also ask about seat-belt extenders for car

seats. And note that you can't count on a flight attendant to produce an extender; you may have to ask for one when you board.

CHECK YOUR SCHEDULING. Don't buy a ticket if there's less than an hour between connecting flights. Although schedules are padded, if anything goes wrong you might miss your connection. If you're traveling to an important function, consider departing a day early.

BRING PAPER. Even when using an e-ticket, always carry a hard copy of your receipt; you may need it to get your boarding pass, which most airports require to get past security.

COMPLAIN AT THE AIRPORT. If your baggage goes astray or your flight goes awry, complain before leaving the airport. Most carriers require that you file a claim immediately.

BEWARE OF OVERBOOKED FLIGHTS. If a flight is oversold, the gate agent will usually ask for volunteers and offer some sort of compensation for taking a different flight. If you're bumped from a flight *involuntarily*, the airline must give you some kind of compensation if an alternate flight can't be found within one hour.

KNOW YOUR RIGHTS. If your flight is delayed because of something within the airline's control (bad weather doesn't count), the airline must get you to your destination on the same day, even if they have to book you on another airline and in an upgraded class. Read the Contract of Carriage, which is usually buried on the airline's Web site.

BE PREPARED. The Boy Scout motto is especially important if you're traveling during a stormy season. To quickly adjust your plans, program a few numbers into your cell: your airline, an airport hotel or two, your destination hotel, your car service, and/or your travel agent.

In addition to the major international carriers, a new breed of European budget airlines, including Ryanair, German Wings, and SkyEurope, has expanded greatly in recent years, offering low-cost flights from major cities around the Continent. These airlines save money by using smaller, more out-of-the-way airports like London's Stansted. Although these airlines are not normally ideal for connecting with transatlantic flights because of the hassle of changing airports, they provide an extremely low-cost way of getting around for travel within Europe.

Within Austria, Austrian Airlines and its subsidiary **Austrian Arrows** offer service from Vienna to Linz and Innsbruck; they also provide routes to and from points outside Austria. In addition, **Welcome** is now providing some air links between Innsbruck, Graz, and other European cities. Winter schedules on all domestic lines depend on snow conditions.

Airline Contacts **Air France** ☎ 01/5022-2440 within Austria ⊕ www.airfrance.fr. **American Airlines** ☎ 800/433-7300 ⊕ www.aa.com. **Austrian Airlines** ☎ 800/843-0002, 01/051-789 within Austria ⊕ www.aua.com. **British Airways** ☎ 800/247-9297, 020/8897-4000 London, 0345/222-111 outside London, 01/7956-7567 within Austria. **Continental Airlines** ☎ 800/523-3273 for U.S. and Mexico reservations, 800/231-0856 for international reservations ⊕ www.continental.com. **Delta Airlines** ☎ 800/221-1212 for U.S. reservations, 800/241-4141 for international reservations ⊕ www.delta.com. **KLM** ☎ 0900/359-556 within Austria ⊕ www.klm.at. **Lufthansa** ☎ 800/645-3880, 0810/1025-8080 within Austria ⊕ www.lufthansa.com. **Northwest Airlines** ☎ 800/225-2525 ⊕ www.nwa.com. **Swiss** ☎ 0810/810-840 within Austria ⊕ www.swiss.com. **United Airlines** ☎ 800/864-8331 for U.S. reservations, 800/538-2929 for international reservations ⊕ www.united.com.

Smaller Airlines **Air Berlin** ☎ 0870/738-8880 in London and international inquiries ⊕ www.airberlin.com. **German Wings** ☎ 0870/252-1250 in London and for international inquiries ⊕ www.germanwings.com. **Ryanair** ⊕ www.ryanair.com. **SkyEurope** ⊕ www.skyeurope.com.

Within Austria **Welcome** ☎ 0512/295-296 in Innsbruck ⊕ www.welcomeair.at.

▌ BY BUS

Austria features extensive national networks of buses run by post offices and railroads. Where Austrian trains don't go, buses do, and you'll find the railroad and post-office buses (bright yellow for easy recognition) in even remote regions carrying passengers as well as mail. You can get tickets on the bus, and in the off-season there is no problem getting a seat, but on routes to favored ski areas during holiday periods reservations are essential. Bookings can be handled at the ticket office (there's one in most towns with bus service) or by travel agents. In most communities bus routes begin and end at or near the railroad station, making transfers easy. Increasingly, coordination of bus service with railroads means that many of the discounts and special tickets available for trains apply to buses as well. There are private bus companies in Austria, too. Buses in Austria run like clockwork, typically departing and arriving on time.

Bus Information **Columbus** ☎ 01/534-110. **Blaguss Reisen** ☎ 01/5018-0150. **Post und Bahn** ☎ 01/71101. **Dr. Richard** ☎ 01/33100-0.

▌ BY CAR

Carefully weigh the pros and cons of car travel before choosing to rent. If your plans are to see Vienna and one or two other urban destinations, you're much better off saving yourself the hassles and added expense and taking the train. Bear in mind that in addition to the not inconsiderable cost of renting, you'll have to pay for gasoline (which remains stubbornly high at more than twice the cost as in the U.S.) and frequent tolls. In addition you'll find yourself having to deal with bumper-to-bumper traffic on most of the trunk roads connecting the major cities. Added to that is the constant headache of finding a place to park. Central Vienna is completely restricted and the situation is not much better in the smaller cities.

On the other hand, if you have the time and your plan is a more leisurely tour of the country, including back roads and off-the-beaten-track destinations, then car rental is certainly an option. You'll have more freedom and be able to reach places where public transportation is scarce.

Vienna is 300 km (187 mi) east of Salzburg, 200 km (125 mi) north of Graz. Main routes leading into the city are the A1 Westautobahn from Germany, Salzburg, and Linz and the A2 Südautobahn from Graz and points south.

GASOLINE

Gasoline and diesel are readily available, but on Sunday stations in the more out-of-the-way areas may be closed. Stations carry only unleaded (*bleifrei*) gas, both regular and premium (super), and diesel. If you're in the mountains in winter with a diesel, and there is a cold snap (with temperatures threatening to drop below -4°F [-20°C]), add a few liters of gasoline to your diesel, about 1:4 parts, to prevent it from freezing. Gasoline prices are the same throughout the country, slightly lower at discount and self-service stations. Expect to pay about €1 per liter for regular gasoline and slightly less for diesel. If you are driving to Italy, fill up before crossing the border, because gas in Italy is even more expensive. Oil in Austria is expensive, retailing at €9 upward per liter. If need be, purchase oil, windshield wipers, and other paraphernalia at big hardware stores. The German for receipt is *Quittung* or *Rechnung*.

ROAD CONDITIONS

Roads in Austria are excellent and well maintained—perhaps a bit too well maintained, judging by the frequently encountered construction zones on the autobahns. Secondary roads may be narrow and wind-ing. Remember that in winter you will need snow tires and often chains, even on well-traveled roads. It's wise to check with the automobile clubs for weather conditions, since mountain roads are often blocked, and ice and fog are hazards.

ROADSIDE EMERGENCIES

Austria has two automobile clubs, ÖAMTC and ARBÖ, both of which operate motorist service patrols. You'll find emergency (orange-color) phones along all highways. If you break down along the autobahn, a small arrow on the guardrail will direct you to the nearest phone. Otherwise, if you have problems, call ARBÖ or ÖAMTC from anywhere in the country. Both clubs charge nonmembers for emergency service.

Emergency Services ARBÖ ☎ 123 **ÖAMTC** ☎ 120. No area or other code is needed for either number.

RULES OF THE ROAD

Tourists from EU countries may bring their own cars into Austria with no documentation other than the normal registration papers and their regular driver's license. A Green Card, the international certificate of insurance, is recommended for EU drivers and compulsory for others. All cars must carry a first-aid kit (including rubber gloves) and a red warning triangle to use in case of accident or breakdown. These are available at gas stations along the road, or at any automotive supply store or large hardware store.

The minimum driving age in Austria is 18, and children under 12 must ride in the back seat; smaller children require a restraining seat. Note that all passengers must use seat belts.

Drive on the right side of the road in Austria. Unmarked crossings, particularly in residential areas, are common, so exercise caution at intersections. In general at unmarked intersections, vehicles coming from the right have the right of way; the only obvious exception is for trams, which always have the right of way. No turns are allowed on red.

Drinking and driving: the maximum blood-alcohol content allowed is 0.5 parts per thousand, which in real terms means very little to drink. Remember when driving in Europe that the police can stop you anywhere at any time for no particular reason.

Unless otherwise marked, the speed limit on autobahns is 130 kph (80 mph), although this is not always strictly enforced. But if you're pulled over for speeding, fines are payable on the spot, and can be heavy. On other highways and roads the limit is 100 kph (62 mph), 80 kph (49 mph) for RVs or cars pulling a trailer weighing more than 750 kilos (about 1,650 lbs). In built-up areas a 50-kph (31-mph) limit applies and is likely to be taken seriously. In some towns special 30-kph (20-mph) limits apply. More and more towns have radar cameras to catch speeders. Remember that insurance does not necessarily pay if it can be proved you were going above the limit when involved in an accident.

■ TIP➔ **If you're going to travel Austria's highways, make absolutely sure your car is equipped with the *Autobahnvignette*, a little sticker with a highway icon and the Austrian eagle, or with a calendar marked with an M or a W.** This sticker, sometimes also called a *Pickerl,* allows use of the autobahn. It costs €72.60 for a year and is available at gas stations, tobacconists, and automobile-club outlets in neighboring countries or near the border. Rental cars should already have them. You can also purchase a two-month vignette for €21.80, or a 10-day one for €7.60. Prices are for vehicles up to 3.5 tons and RVs. For motorcycles it is €29.00 for one year, €10.90 for two months, and €4.30 for 10 days. If you are caught without a sticker you may be subjected to extremely high fines. Get your Pickerl before driving to Austria from another country.

Besides the Pickerl, if you are planning to drive around a lot, budget in a great deal of toll money: for example, the tunnels on the A10 autobahn cost around €10, the Grossglockner Pass road will cost about €30 per car—less after 6 PM. Driving up some especially beautiful valleys, such as the Kaunertal in Tirol, or up to the Tauplitzalm in Styria, also costs money—around €20 per car for the Kaunertal.

■ BY TRAIN

Austrian train service is excellent: it's fast and, for Western Europe, relatively inexpensive, particularly if you take advantage of discount fares. Trains on the mountainous routes are slow, but no slower than driving, and the scenery is gorgeous. Many of the remote rail routes will give you a look at traditional Austria, complete with Alpine cabins tacked onto mountainsides and a backdrop of snowcapped peaks.

Austrian Federal Railways trains are identifiable by the letters that precede the train number on the timetables and posters. The IC (InterCity) or EC (EuroCity) trains are fastest, and a supplement of about €5 is included in the price of the ticket. EN trains have sleeping facilities. The EC trains usually have a dining car with fairly good food. The trains originating in Budapest have good Hungarian cooking. Otherwise there is usually a fellow with a cart serving snacks and hot and cold drinks. Most trains are equipped with a card telephone in or near the restaurant car.

The difference between *erste Klasse* (first class), and *zweite Klasse* (second class) on Austrian trains is mainly a matter of space. First- and second-class sleepers and couchettes (six to a compartment) are available on international runs, as well as on long trips within Austria. Women traveling alone may book special compartments on night trains or long-distance rides (ask for a *Damenabteilung*). If you're driving and would rather watch the scenery than the traffic, you can put your car on a train in Vienna and accompany it to Salzburg, Innsbruck, Feldkirch, or Villach. You relax in a compartment or sleeper for the trip, and the car is unloaded when you arrive.

Allow yourself plenty of time to purchase your ticket before boarding the train. If you purchase your ticket on board the train, you must pay a surcharge, which is around €7 or more, depending on how far you're going. All tickets are valid without supplement on D (express), E (*Eilzug;* semi-fast), and local trains. Make certain that you inquire about possible supplements payable on board trains traveling to destinations outside Austria when you are purchasing your ticket. Austrians are not generally forthcoming with information, and you might be required to pay a supplement in cash to the conductor while you are on the train. For information, call 05/1717 from anywhere in Austria. Unless you speak German fairly well, it's a good idea to have your hotel call for you.

You can reserve a seat for €3.40 up until a few hours before departure. Be sure to do this on the main-line trains (Vienna–Innsbruck, Salzburg–Klagenfurt, Vienna–Graz, for example) at peak holiday times. For information on buying Eurail and other rail passes, *see* Train Passes *in* Booking Your Trip *above.* Some passes must be booked before you arrive in Austria, but there are some that can be purchased within Austria as well.

For train schedules from the Austrian rail service, the ÖBB, ask at your hotel, stop in at the train station and look for large posters labeled ABFAHRT (departures) and ANKUNFT (arrivals), or log on to their Web site. In the Abfahrt listing you'll find the departure time in the main left-hand block of the listing and, under the train name, details of where it stops en route and the time of each arrival. There is also information about connecting trains and buses, with departure details. Workdays are symbolized by two crossed hammers, which means that the same schedule might not apply on weekends or holidays. A little rocking horse means that a special playpen has been set up for children in the train.

There's a wide choice of rail routes to Austria, but check services first; long-distance passenger service across the Continent is undergoing considerable reduction. There is regular service from London's Waterloo station to Vienna via Brussels and points south and east. An alternative is to travel via Paris, where you can change to board an overnight train to Salzburg and Vienna. Be sure to leave plenty of time between connections to change stations. First- and second-class sleepers and second-class couchettes are available as far as Innsbruck.

ÖBB (Österreichische Bundesbahnen)
⊕ www.oebb.at.

ON THE GROUND

▌ COMMUNICATIONS

INTERNET

Austria generally lags behind much of Europe in its use and availability of the Internet. Nevertheless, the better hotels have worked hard to upgrade their Internet offerings and most of them will offer some form of Internet access for jacking in your laptop, either via a LAN line or, often spotty, Wi-Fi. Occasionally these services are offered free of charge; usually you have to pay a surcharge. Once connected, you can use your browser to surf the Net. Alternatively, you can use the telephone jack in your room to phone one of the major Internet service providers, like AOL, though these connections are slower and telephone charges can add up. Before you leave home, contact your Internet service provider to get the local access number in Austria. Hotels that don't offer Internet access in the rooms will usually have a computer standing by somewhere in the business center or the lobby available for guests to check e-mail. Outside of hotels it's usually not hard to find an Internet café somewhere nearby (ask at your hotel). The standard rate is about €2 an hour. Occasionally, especially in large cities, you'll find cafés that offer Wi-Fi to customers. The charge for this is usually around €2 an hour.
Cybercafés ⊕ www.cybercafes.com lists more than 4,000 Internet cafés worldwide.

PHONES

The good news is that you can now make a direct-dial telephone call from virtually any point on earth. The bad news? You can't always do so cheaply. Calling from a hotel is almost always the most expensive option; hotels usually add huge surcharges to all calls, particularly international ones. In some countries you can phone from call centers or even the post office. Calling cards usually keep costs to a minimum, but only if you purchase them locally. And then there are mobile phones, which are sometimes more prevalent—particularly in the developing world—than land lines; as expensive as mobile phone calls can be, they are still usually a much cheaper option than calling from your hotel.

When calling Austria, the country code is 43. When dialing an Austrian number from abroad, drop the initial 0 from the local Austrian area code. For instance, the full number to dial for the Hotel Palais Schwarzenberg in Vienna from America is 011 (international dial code)—43 (Austria's country code)—1 (Vienna's full city code is 01, but drop the 0)—and 798–4515 (the hotel number). All numbers given in this guide include the city or town area code.

CALLING WITHIN AUSTRIA

As the number of cell phones has risen in Austria, the number of coin-operated pay telephones has dwindled. If you're lucky enough to find one, it may be out of order or available only for emergency calls. But if you find one that works, a local call costs €0.20 for the first minute and €0.20 for every three minutes thereafter. Most pay phones have instructions in English.

When placing a long-distance call to a destination within Austria, dial the local area codes with the initial zero (for instance, 0662 for Salzburg). Note that calls within Austria are one-third cheaper between 6 PM and 8 AM on weekdays and from 1 PM on Saturday to 8 AM on Monday.

For information concerning numbers within the EU and neighboring countries, 01/118–877; for information outside Europe, dial 0900/118–877. Most operators speak some English; if yours doesn't, you'll most likely be passed along to one who does.

CALLING OUTSIDE AUSTRIA

It costs more to telephone from Austria than it does to telephone to Austria. Calls

LOCAL DO'S & TABOOS

CUSTOMS OF THE COUNTRY

Austrians are keen observers of social niceties, and there are strongly embedded cultural norms for guiding behavior in all sorts of public interactions, ranging from buying a piece of meat at the butcher's (be extremely polite) to offering your seat on the metro to an elderly or disabled person. In general, always err of the side of extreme politeness and deference (particularly to age).

GREETINGS

Greetings are an important part of day-to-day interaction with strangers. On entering a shop, for example, it's customary to say *Grüss Gott* or *Guten Tag,* "good day," to the shopkeeper as if he or she were an old friend. Don't forget to say a hearty *Auf Wiedersehen,* good-bye, on leaving. And watch out for titles. The appellation *Doktor,* or more commonly *Herr Doktor,* literally "Mr. Doctor," is widely conveyed on any man of a certain age as a sign of respect, regardless of whether or not he has academically earned it.

OUT ON THE TOWN

In restaurants it's not uncommon to have share a table with strangers—particularly in crowded places at meal times. You're not expected to make conversation across the table, but you should at least offer a tip-of-the-hat *Grüss Gott* when sitting down and a farewell *Auf Wiedersehen* on leaving. When your neighbor's food arrives, turn and wish him or her *Mahlzeit,* literally "meal time," the Austrian-German equivalent of "Bon Appetit." When it comes to table manners, there are a few departures from standard American practice (beyond how one holds a knife and fork). Toothpicks are sometimes found on restaurant tables, and it is normal to see people clean their teeth after a meal, discreetly covering their mouth with their free hand. Austria is a dog-loving society, and you will often find dogs accompanying their masters to restaurants.

Austrians tend to smoke more than Americans, and no-smoking rules are not as well developed here as in the U.S. Most restaurants will try to oblige a request to be seated away from smokers, but in pubs and smaller places you may not have an option.

If you have the pleasure of being invited to someone's home for a meal, it's customary to bring a small gift, like a bouquet of flowers or a nice bottle of wine. Note that if you bring wine, it's considered a gift and probably won't be served (unless of course you go through every other bottle in the house!).

Austrians tend to be far more comfortable with public nudity than Americans. Women routinely remove their tops on public beaches (and you're naturally invited to do the same if you wish). At hotels and resorts with saunas, the facilities are usually used by both sexes and the towel is optional.

LANGUAGE

One of the best ways to avoid being an Ugly American is to learn a little of the local language. You need not strive for fluency; even just mastering a few basic words and terms is bound to make chatting with the locals more rewarding. German is the official language in Austria. In larger cities and most resort areas you will usually have no problem finding people who speak English; hotel employees in particular speak it reasonably well, and many young Austrians speak it at least passably. However, travelers do report that they often find themselves in stores, restaurants, and railway and bus stations where it's hard to find someone who speaks English—so it's best to have some native phrases up your sleeve. Note that all public announcements on trams, subways, and buses are in German. Train announcements are usually given in English as well, but if you have any questions, try to get answers before boarding.

from post offices are usually the least expensive way to go, and you can get helpful assistance in placing a long-distance call; in large cities these centers at main post offices are open around the clock. To use a post office phone you first go to the counter to be directed to a certain telephone cabin; after your call you return to the counter and pay your bill. Faxes can be sent from post offices and received as well, but neither service is very cheap.

To make a collect call—you can't do this from pay phones—dial the operator and ask for an *R-Gespräch* (pronounced airga-*shprayk*). Most operators speak English; if yours doesn't, you'll be passed to one who does.

The country code for the United States is 1.

Access Codes AT&T Direct ☎ 01/0800-200-288, 800/435-0812 for other areas. **MCI WorldPhone** ☎ 0800-200-235, 800/444-4141 for other areas.

CALLING CARDS

If you plan to make calls from pay phones, a *Telephon Wertkarte* is a convenience. You can buy this electronic phone card at any post office for about €7, which allows you to use the card at any SOS or credit-card phone booth. You simply insert the card and dial; the cost of the call is automatically deducted from the card, and a digital window on the phone tells you how many units you have left (these are not minutes). A few public phones in the cities also take American Express, Diners Club, MasterCard, and Visa credit cards.

MOBILE PHONES

In Austria a cell phone is called a *Handy*. If you have a multiband phone (some countries use different frequencies from what's used in the United States) and your service provider uses the world-standard GSM network (as do T-Mobile, Cingular, and Verizon), you can probably use your phone abroad. Roaming fees can be steep, however: 99¢ a minute is considered reasonable. And overseas you normally pay the toll charges for incoming calls. It's al-

CON OR CONCIERGE?

Good hotel concierges are invaluable—for arranging transportation, getting reservations at the hottest restaurant, and scoring tickets for a sold-out show or entree to an exclusive nightclub. They're in the know and well connected. That said, sometimes you have to take their advice with a grain of salt.

It's not uncommon for restaurants to ply concierges with free food and drink in exchange for steering diners their way. Indeed, European concierges often receive referral *fees*. Hotel chains usually have guidelines about what their concierges can accept. The best concierges, however, are above reproach. This is particularly true of those who belong to the prestigious international society of Les Clefs d'Or.

What can you expect of a concierge? At a typical tourist-class hotel you can expect him or her to give you the basics: to show you something on a map, make a standard restaurant reservation (particularly if you don't speak the language), or help you book a tour or airport transportation.

Savvy concierges at the finest hotels and resorts, can arrange for just about any goods or services imaginable—and do so quickly. You should compensate them appropriately. A $10 tip is enough to show appreciation for a table at a hot restaurant. But the reward should really be much greater for tickets to that U2 concert that's been sold out for months or for those last-minute sixth-row-center seats for *The Lion King*.

most always cheaper to send a text message than to make a call, since text messages have a very low set fee (often less than 5¢).

If you just want to make local calls, consider buying a new SIM card (note that your provider may have to unlock your phone for you to use a different SIM card) and a prepaid service plan in the destination. You'll then have a local number and can make local calls at local rates. If your trip is extensive, you could also simply buy a new cell phone in your destination, as the initial cost will be offset over time.

■ TIP→ **If you travel internationally frequently, save one of your old mobile phones or buy a cheap one on the Internet; ask your cell phone company to unlock it for you, and take it with you as a travel phone, buying a new SIM card with pay-as-you-go service in each destination.**

If you want to use your own mobile phone in Austria, first find out if it's compatible with the European 1800 GSM standard (usually this is the case with a "tri-band" telephone, but be sure to ask specifically). Once in Austria, stop by a mobile phone store, usually identifiable by the word "Handy" in the name, and purchase a prepaid SIM card (make sure your existing SIM card is unlocked). Prepaid cards start at around €20–€30. Local mobile calls are then billed at about €0.15 to €0.20 a minute. If you don't have a phone, but want to use one here, look into buying a used phone. Rates are reasonable. Buy the prepaid card in the same way you would as if you were bringing in your own phone.

When dialing an Austrian "Handy" from abroad (generally 0676, 0699, or 0664), dial 00–43, then the number without the 0. **Cellular Abroad** ☎ 800/287-5072 ⊕ www.cellularabroad.com rents and sells GMS phones and sells SIM cards that work in many countries. **Mobal** ☎ 888/888-9162 ⊕ www.mobalrental.com rents and sells GSM phones (starting at $49) that will operate in 140 countries. Per-call rates vary throughout the world. **Planet Fone** ☎ 888/988-4777

⊕ www.planetfone.com rents cell phones, but the per-minute rates are expensive.

▌CUSTOMS & DUTIES

You're always allowed to bring goods of a certain value back home without having to pay any duty or import tax. But there's a limit on the amount of tobacco and liquor you can bring back duty-free, and some countries have separate limits for perfumes; for exact figures, check with your customs department. The values of so-called "duty-free" goods are included in these amounts. When you shop abroad, save all your receipts, as customs inspectors may ask to see them as well as the items you purchased. If the total value of your goods is more than the duty-free limit, you'll have to pay a tax (most often a flat percentage) on the value of everything beyond that limit.

Travelers over 17 who are residents of European countries—regardless of citizenship—may bring in, duty free, 200 cigarettes or 50 cigars or 250 grams of tobacco, 2 liters of wine and 2 liters of 22% spirits or 1 liter of over 22% spirits, and 50 milliliters of perfume. Travelers from all other countries (such as those coming directly from the United States or Canada) may bring in twice these amounts. All visitors may bring gifts or other purchases valued at up to €175 (about $210), although in practice you'll seldom be asked.

U.S. Information **U.S. Customs and Border Protection** ⊕ www.cbp.gov.

▌EATING OUT

When dining out, you'll get the best value at simpler restaurants. Most post menus with prices outside. If you begin with the *Würstelstand* (sausage vendor) on the street, the next category would be the *Imbiss-Stube*, for simple, quick snacks. Many meat stores serve soups and a daily special at noon; a blackboard menu will be posted outside. A number of cafés also offer lunch, but watch the prices; some can turn out to be more expensive than restaurants. *Gasthäuser* are simple restaurants or country inns. Austrian hotels have some of the best restaurants in the country, often with outstanding chefs. In the past few years the restaurants along the autobahns have developed into very good places to eat (besides being, in many cases, architecturally interesting). Some Austrian chain restaurants offer excellent value for the money, such as Wienerwald, which specializes in chicken dishes, and Nordsee, which has a wide selection of fish.

■ TIP➜ **In all restaurants be aware that the basket of bread put on your table isn't free.** Most of the older-style Viennese restaurants charge €0.70–€1.25 for each roll that is eaten, but more and more establishments are beginning to charge a per-person cover charge—anywhere from €1.50 to €4—which includes all the bread you want, plus usually an herb spread and butter. Tap water (*Leitungswasser*) in Austria comes straight from the Alps and is some of the purest in the world. Be aware, however, that a few restaurants in touristy areas are beginning to charge for tap water.

Austrians are manic about food quality and using agricultural techniques that are in harmony with the environment. The country has the largest number of organic farms in Europe, as well as some of the most stringent food-quality standards. An increasing number of restaurants use food and produce from local farmers, ensuring the freshest ingredients for their guests.

MEALS & MEALTIMES

Besides the normal three meals—*Frühstück* (breakfast), *Mittagessen* (lunch), and *Abendessen* (dinner)—Austrians sometimes throw in a few snacks in between, or forego one meal for a snack. The day begins with an early continental breakfast of rolls and coffee. *Gabelfrühstück,* normally served a little later in the morning, is a slightly more substantial breakfast with eggs or cold meat. A main meal is usually served between noon and 2, and an afternoon *Jause* (coffee with cake) is taken at teatime. Unless you are

dining out, a light supper ends the day, usually between 6 and 9, but tending toward the later hour. Many restaurant kitchens close in the afternoon, but some post a notice saying *durchgehend warme Küche,* meaning that hot food is available even between regular mealtimes. In Vienna some restaurants go on serving until 1 and 2 AM, a tiny number also through the night. The rest of Austria is more conservative. Unless otherwise noted, the restaurants listed in this guide are open daily for lunch and dinner.

PAYING

Restaurant price categories from ¢ to $$$$ are defined in the Where to Eat sections of the Vienna and Salzburg chapters and in the opening pages of each regional chapter.

For guidelines on tipping *see* Tipping *below.*

RESERVATIONS & DRESS

Regardless of where you are, it's a good idea to make a reservation if you can. In some places (Hong Kong, for example), it's expected. We only mention them specifically when reservations are essential (there's no other way you'll ever get a table) or when they are not accepted. For popular restaurants, book as far ahead as you can (often 30 days), and reconfirm as soon as you arrive. (Large parties should always call ahead to check the reservations policy.) We mention dress only when men are required to wear a jacket or a jacket and tie.

WINES, BEER & SPIRITS

Austrian wines range from unpretentious *Heurigen* whites to world-class varietals. Look for the light, fruity white grüner veltliner, intensely fragrant golden traminer, full-bodied red blaufränkisch, and the lighter red zweigelt. Sparkling wine is called Sekt, some of the best coming from the Kamptal region northwest of Vienna. Some of the best sweet dessert wines in the world (Spätlesen) come from Burgenland. Austrian beer rivals that of Germany for quality. Each area has its own brewery and local beer that people are loyal to. A specialty unique to Austria is the dark, sweet Dunkles beer. Look for Kaiser Doppelmalz in Vienna. Schnapps is an after-dinner tradition in Austria; many restaurants offer several varieties to choose from.

■ ELECTRICITY

The electrical current in Austria is 220 volts, 50 cycles alternating current (AC); wall outlets take Continental-type plugs, with two round prongs.

Consider making a small investment in a universal adapter, which has several types of plugs in one lightweight, compact unit. Most laptops and mobile phone chargers are dual voltage (i.e., they operate equally well on 110 and 220 volts), so require only an adapter. These days the same is true of small appliances such as hair dryers. Always check labels and manufacturer instructions to be sure. Don't use 110-volt outlets marked FOR SHAVERS ONLY for high-wattage appliances such as hair-dryers. **Steve Kropla's Help for World Traveler's** ⊕ www.kropla.com has information on electrical and telephone plugs around the world. **Walkabout Travel Gear** ⊕ www.walkabouttravelgear.com has a good coverage of electricity under "adapters."

■ EMERGENCIES

On the street, some German phrases that may be needed in an emergency are: *Hilfe!* (Help!), *Notfall* (emergency), *Ret-tungswagen* (ambulance), *Feuerwehr* (fire department), *Polizei* (police), *Arzt* (doctor), and *Krankenhaus* (hospital).

Foreign Embassies Embassy of the United States ✉ Boltzmanngasse 16, A-1090, 9th District, Vienna ☎ 31339-0. **Consulate of the U.S./Passport Division** ✉ Gartenbauprome-nade 2-4, A-1010, 1st District, Vienna ☎ 31339-7580.

General Emergency Contacts Ambulance ☎ 144. **Fire** ☎ 122. **Police** ☎ 133.

■ HEALTH

Travel in Austria poses no specific or unusual health risks. The tap water is generally safe to drink. If in doubt, buy bottled water—available everywhere. The only potential risk worth mentioning is tick-bite encephalitis, which is only a danger if you're planning to do extensive cycling or hiking in the back country.

OVER-THE-COUNTER REMEDIES

You must buy over-the-counter remedies in an *Apotheke,* and most personnel speak enough English to understand what you need. Try using the generic name for a drug, rather than its brand name. You may find over-the-counter remedies for headaches and colds less effective than those sold in the U.S. Austrians are firm believers in natural remedies, such as homeopathic medicines and herbal teas.

■ HOURS OF OPERATION

In most cities banks are open weekdays 8–3, Thursday until 5:30 PM. Lunch hour is from 12:30 to 1:30. All banks are closed on Saturday, but you can change money at various locations (such as American Express offices on Saturday morning and major railroad stations around the clock), and changing machines are also found here and there in the larger cities.

Gas stations on the major autobahns are open 24 hours a day, but in smaller towns and villages you can expect them to close early in the evening and on Sunday. You can usually count on at least one station to stay open on Sunday and holidays in most medium-size towns, and buying gas in larger cities is usually not a problem.

Pharmacies (called *Apotheken* in German) are usually open from 9 to 6, with a mid-day break between noon and 2. In each area of the city one pharmacy stays open 24 hours; if a pharmacy is closed, a sign on the door will tell you the address of the nearest one that is open. Call 01/1550 for names and addresses (in German) of the pharmacies open that night.

HOLIDAYS

All banks and shops are closed on national holidays: New Year's Day; Jan. 6, Epiphany; Easter Sunday and Monday; May 1, May Day; Ascension Day (6th Thursday after Easter); Pentecost Sunday and Monday; Corpus Christi; Aug. 15, Assumption; Oct. 26, National Holiday; Nov. 1, All Saints' Day; Dec. 8, Immaculate Conception; Dec. 25–26, Christmas. Museums are open on most holidays, but are closed on Good Friday, on Dec. 24 and 25, and New Year's Day. Banks and offices are closed on Dec. 8, but most shops are open.

▌MAIL

All mail goes by air, so there's no supplement on letters or postcards. Within Europe a letter or postcard of up to 20 grams (about ¾ ounce) costs €0.55. To the United States or Canada, a letter of up to 20 grams takes postage of €1.25. If in doubt, mail your letters from a post office and have the weight checked. The Austrian post office also adheres strictly to a size standard; if your letter or card is outside the norm, you'll have to pay a surcharge. Postcards via airmail to the United States or Canada need €1.25. Always place an airmail sticker on your overseas letters or cards. Shipping packages from Austria to destinations outside the country can get expensive.

You can also have mail held at any Austrian post office; letters should be marked *Poste Restante* or *Postlagernd*. You will be asked for identification when you collect mail.

SHIPPING PACKAGES

For overnight services, Federal Express, DHL, and UPS service Austria; check with your hotel concierge for the nearest address and telephone number.

▌MONEY

ATMS & BANKS

Your own bank will probably charge a fee for using ATMs abroad; the foreign bank you use may also charge a fee. Nevertheless, you'll usually get a better rate of exchange at an ATM than you will at a currency-exchange office or even when changing money in a bank. And extracting funds as you need them is a safer option than carrying around a large amount of cash.

▌ TIP➔ **PIN numbers with more than four digits are not recognized at ATMs in many countries. If yours has five or more, remember to change it before you leave.**

Called *Bankomats* and fairly common throughout Austria, ATMs are one of the easiest ways to get euros. Cirrus and Plus locations are easily found throughout large city centers, and even in small towns. Look for branches of one of the larger banks, including Bank Austria/Creditanstalt, Raiffeisen, BAWAG, or Die Erste. These are all likely to have a bank machine attached somewhere nearby. If you have trouble finding one, ask your hotel concierge. Note, too, that you may have better luck with ATMs if you're using a credit card or debit card that is also a Visa or MasterCard rather than just your bank card. **ATM Locations Cirrus** ☎ 800/424-7787. **Plus** ☎ 800/843-7587.

CREDIT CARDS

Throughout this guide, the following abbreviations are used: **AE**, American Express; **DC**, Diners Club; **MC**, MasterCard; and **V**, Visa.

It's a good idea to inform your credit-card company before you travel, especially if you're going abroad and don't travel internationally very often. Otherwise, the credit-card company might put a hold on your card owing to unusual activity—not a good thing halfway through your trip. Record all your credit-card numbers—as well as the phone numbers to call if your cards are lost or stolen—in a safe place, so you're prepared should something go wrong. Both MasterCard and Visa have general numbers you can call (collect if you're abroad) if your card is lost, but you're better off calling the number of your issuing bank, since MasterCard and Visa usually just transfer you to your bank; your bank's number is usually printed on your card.

If you plan to use your credit card for cash advances, you'll need to apply for a PIN at least two weeks before your trip. Although it's usually cheaper (and safer) to use a credit card abroad for large purchases (so you can cancel payments or be reimbursed if there's a problem), note that some credit-card companies *and* the banks that issue them add substantial percentages to all foreign transactions, whether they're in a foreign currency or not. Check on these fees before leaving home, so there won't be any surprises when you get the bill.

■ TIP➔ Before you charge something, ask the merchant whether or not he or she plans to do a dynamic currency conversion (DCC). In such a transaction the credit-card *processor* (shop, restaurant, or hotel, not Visa or MasterCard) converts the currency and charges you in dollars. In most cases you'll pay the merchant a 3% fee for this service in addition to any credit-card company and issuing-bank foreign-transaction surcharges.

Dynamic currency conversion programs are becoming increasingly widespread. Merchants who participate in them are supposed to ask whether you want to be charged in dollars or the local currency, but they don't always do so. And even if they do offer you a choice, they may well avoid mentioning the surcharges. The good news is that you *do* have a choice. And if this practice really gets your goat, you can avoid it entirely thanks to Amer-

ican Express; with its cards DCC simply isn't an option.

Reporting Lost Cards **American Express** ☎ 800/992-3404 in U.S., 336/393-1111 collect from abroad ⊕ www.americanexpress.com. **Diners Club** ☎ 800/234-6377 in U.S., 303/799-1504 collect from abroad ⊕ www.dinersclub.com. **Discover** ☎ 800/347-2683 in U.S., 801/902-3100 collect from abroad ⊕ www.discovercard.com. **MasterCard** ☎ 800/622-7747 in U.S., 636/722-7111 collect from abroad ⊕ www.mastercard.com. **Visa** ☎ 800/847-2911 in U.S., 410/581-9994 collect from abroad ⊕ www.visa.com.

CURRENCY & EXCHANGE

As it is a member of the European Union (EU), Austria's unit of currency is the euro. Under the euro system there are eight coins: 1 and 2 euros, plus 1, 2, 5, 10, 20, and 50 euro cent, or cents of the euro. All coins have one side that has the value of the euro on it and the other side with a country's own national symbol. There are seven banknotes: 5, 10, 20, 50, 100, 200, and 500 euros. Banknotes are the same for all EU countries. At this writing (fall 2006), the euro had strengthened against the U.S. dollar, and one euro was worth about 1.28 U.S. dollars. With respect to other major currencies, the euro was worth 0.70 British pounds, 1.45 Canadian dollars, and 1.70 Australian dollars.

Although fees charged for ATM transactions may be higher abroad than at home, Cirrus and Plus exchange rates are excellent, because they are based on wholesale rates offered only by major banks. Otherwise, the most favorable rates are through a bank. You won't do as well at exchange booths in airports or rail and bus stations, in hotels, in restaurants, or in stores, although you may find their hours more convenient than at a bank.

■ TIP➔ Even if a currency-exchange booth has a sign promising no commission, rest assured that there's some kind of huge, hidden fee. (Oh . . . that's right. The sign didn't say no *fee*.). And as for rates, you're almost always better off getting foreign currency at an ATM or exchanging money at a bank.

TRAVELER'S CHECKS & CARDS

Some consider this the currency of the cave man, and it's true that fewer establishments accept traveler's checks these days. Nevertheless, they're a cheap and secure way to carry extra money, particularly on trips to urban areas. Both Citibank (under the Visa brand) and American Express issue traveler's checks in the United States, but Amex is better known and more widely accepted; you can also avoid hefty surcharges by cashing Amex checks at Amex offices. Whatever you do, keep track of all the serial numbers in case the checks are lost or stolen.

American Express ☎ 888/412-6945 in U.S., 801/945-9450 collect outside of the U.S. to add value or speak to customer service ⊕ www.americanexpress.com.

▌ RESTROOMS

Vienna has a scattering of public toilets that are suitably clean and cost about €0.50 to use. Metro stations invariably have decent public facilities. Public toilets are less common outside the big cities, but you can usually use the facilities of hotels and restaurants without too much fuss. It's courteous to purchase something in a bar or restaurant beforehand, but this is rarely a problem and nothing that can't usually be resolved with a smile and a *Danke*. Gas stations along highways usually have restrooms attached, and these are generally open to the public whether you purchase gas or not. Cleanliness standards vary, but are usually on the acceptable side.

Find a Loo The Bathroom Diaries ⊕ www. thebathroomdiaries.com is flush with unsanitized info on restrooms the world over—each one located, reviewed, and rated.

▌ SAFETY

Austrians are remarkably honest in their everyday dealings, and Vienna, given its

---

WORST-CASE SCENARIO

All your money and credit cards have just been stolen. In these days of real-time transactions, this isn't a predicament that should destroy your vacation. First, report the theft of the credit cards. Then get any traveler's checks you were carrying replaced. This can usually be done almost immediately, provided that you kept a record of the serial numbers separate from the checks themselves. If you bank at a large international bank like Citibank or HSBC, go to the closest branch; if you know your account number, chances are you can get a new ATM card and withdraw money right away. **Western Union** (☎ 800/325-6000 ⊕ www.westernunion. com) sends money almost anywhere. Have someone back home order a transfer online, over the phone, or at one of the company's offices, which is the cheapest option. The U.S. State Department's **Overseas Citizens Services** (☎ 202/647-5225) can wire money to any U.S. consulate or embassy abroad for a fee of $30. Just have someone back home wire money or send a money order or cashier's check to the State Department, which will then disburse the funds as soon as the next working day after it receives them.

---

size, is a refreshingly safe and secure city. It's one of the world's few big cities where lost wallets routinely turn up found (and sometimes even with the money and credit cards still intact). That said, be sure to watch your purses and wallets in crowded spaces like subways and trams, and to take the standard precautions when walking at night along empty streets. Be particularly careful if you're traveling with a bicycle. Here, as everywhere else, bikes routinely go missing. Always lock your bike firmly and never leave it outside unattended for more than a few minutes.

■ TIP→ **Distribute your cash, credit cards, IDs, and other valuables between a deep front pocket, an inside jacket or vest pocket, and a hidden money pouch. Don't reach for the money pouch once you're in public.**

▌TAXES

The Value Added Tax (V.A.T.) in Austria is 20% generally, but this is reduced to 10% on food and clothing. If you are planning to take your purchases with you when you leave Austria (export them), you can get a refund. Wine and spirits are heavily taxed—nearly half of the sale price goes to taxes. For every contract signed in Austria (for example, car-rental agreements), you pay an extra 1% tax to the government, so tax on a rental car is 21%.

When making a purchase, ask for a V.A.T. refund form and find out whether the merchant gives refunds—not all stores do, nor are they required to. Have the form stamped like any customs form by customs officials when you leave the country or, if you're visiting several European Union countries, when you leave the EU. After you're through passport control, take the form to a refund-service counter for an on-the-spot refund (which is usually the quickest and easiest option), or mail it to the address on the form (or the envelope with it) after you arrive home. You receive the total refund stated on the form, but the processing time can be long, especially if you request a credit-card adjustment.

Global Refund is a Europe-wide service with 225,000 affiliated stores and more than 700 refund counters at major airports and border crossings. Its refund form, called a Tax Free Check, is the most common across the European continent. The service issues refunds in the form of cash, check, or credit-card adjustment.

V.A.T. Refunds Global Refund ☎ 800/566–9828 ⊕ www.globalrefund.com.

▌TIME

The time difference between New York and Austria is 6 hours (so when it's 1 PM in New York, it's 7 PM in Vienna). The time difference between London and Vienna is 1 hour; between Sydney and Vienna, 14 hours; and between Auckland and Vienna, 13 hours.

▌TIPPING

Although virtually all hotels and restaurants include service charges in their rates, tipping is still customary, but at a level lower than in the United States. In very small country inns such tips are not expected but are appreciated. In family-run establishments, tips are generally not given to immediate family members, only to employees. Tip the hotel concierge only for special services or in response to special requests. Maids normally get no tip unless your stay is a week or more or service has been special. Big tips are not usual in Austrian restaurants, since 10% has already been included in the prices.

INDEX

PHOTO CREDITS

Cover Photo *(Mozart Boys' Choir): Wiesenhofer/Austrian Views.* 8, *Vienna Philharmonic.* 9 (left), *Austrian Tourist Office.* 9 (right), *online/Alamy.* 10-11, *Javier Larrea/age fotostock.* 12, *Photodisc.* 13 (left), *Photodisc.* 13 (right), *Florian Monheim/age fotostock.* 14, *Austrian Tourist Office.* 15 (left), *ImageState/Alamy.* 15 (right), *Austrian Tourist Office.*

NOTES

NOTES

NOTES

NOTES

NOTES

NOTES

ABOUT OUR WRITERS

Mark Baker is a freelance journalist and travel writer residing in Prague, though he spent five years living and working in Vienna as an editor for *Economist Intelligence Unit*. He's a frequent visitor to Austria and still considers Vienna his "hometown." Mark handled Austria Essentials.

"Life in Vienna is just wonderful" says Yorkshire born **Diane Naar-Elphee.** After living in the capital city for 30 years, Diane has become an authority on its art, history, and nightlife. She has worked for many years as a guide-lecturer, and she has traveled the whole country. She warns "Austria can become addictive."

Horst E. Reischenböck is an authority not only for his hometown of Salzburg but also for Austria in general. The author of two books on Salzburg's music history, he has worked for four decades as a journalist and as a personal guide for English-speaking visitors.

Matt Savage, a native of New Orleans, has lived in Austria since 1997. When not enjoying the many pleasures afforded by Austria's wine region, you can find him teaching and writing on art history at the University of Vienna.